Encyclopedia of
Vampire Mythology

Encyclopedia of Vampire Mythology

THERESA BANE

McFarland & Company, Inc., Publishers
Jefferson, North Carolina

The present work is a reprint of the illustrated case bound edition of Encyclopedia of Vampire Mythology, *first published in 2010 by McFarland.*

LIBRARY OF CONGRESS CATALOGUING-IN-PUBLICATION DATA

Bane, Theresa, 1969–
Encyclopedia of vampire mythology / Theresa Bane.
p.   cm.
Includes bibliographical references and index.

ISBN 978-1-4766-8177-1
softcover : acid free paper ∞

1. Vampires—Encyclopedias.   I. Title.
GR830.V3B34   2020   398.21'003—dc22   2010015576

British Library cataloguing data are available

Front cover illustration by Joseph Maclise, from his *Surgical Anatomy,* 1859

Printed in the United States of America

McFarland & Company, Inc., Publishers
Box 611, Jefferson, North Carolina 28640
www.mcfarlandpub.com

To my father,
Amedeo C. Falcone,
Noli nothi permittere te terere.

Table of Contents

Preface

I am a vampirologist—a mythologist who specializes in cross-cultural vampire studies. There are many people who claim to be experts on vampire lore and legend who will say that they know all about Vlad Tepes and Count Dracula or that they can name several different types of vampiric species. I can do that, too, but that is not how I came to be a known vampirologist. Knowing the "who, what and where" is one thing, but knowing and more importantly understanding the "why" is another.

Throughout history, every culture of man has had an incarnation of the vampire, a being responsible for causing plagues and death. A hobbyist or enthusiast may know that the hili is a vampiric creature who hunts the Xhosa people of Lesotho, South Africa, and to be certain it is a rather obscure bit of trivia. But knowing the "why" of the hili is what a vampirologist does. *Why* did the Xhosa people of that region of South Africa develop their vampire the way they did? *Why* does the hili look the way it does? *Why* is it an indiscriminate killer, attacking anyone at any time of the day or night? *Why* are the vampires that live due west completely different in every way? *Why* do they not cross into each other's territories? I know the answers to all these questions because I have delved into the history, anthropology, psychology, sociology, and religious studies of just about every culture I could get my hands on.

One of the questions I am frequently asked is how I ever came to be interested in vampires. I am always hesitant to answer because as simple a question as it may seem, the answer, like the vampire itself, is complex. For me, there was no single event that sparked a sudden interest, no chance meeting with someone who inspired me. As best as I can trace it back, my parents were people who encouraged learning and valued education in their children. At least once a week we would go to the library, returning home with a hodgepodge of books on various subjects. Each night around the dinner table we discussed what we learned that day and it seems to me that nothing brought my parents greater joy than when the whole family became deeply involved in a conversation where all of our cumulative knowledge was pooled, compared, and debated.

Obviously at some point in my youth I discovered the mythology of the vampire went beyond Bram Stoker's *Dracula*, although I cannot honestly say when it happened. I had always wanted to be an author, and some years ago I set out to write a trilogy of vampire novels. I knew then that I did not want my vampires to be just like all the fictional vampires that were already out there; I wanted my vampires to be less like Ann Rice's vampires and more like the original mythology.

What started out as what was going to be just a little bit of looking into the subject matter quickly became a full-time endeavor lasting five years. At the end of my research what I had written was not a trilogy of books about a fictional vampire but rather a compendium of vampire lore.

Through self-examination, I can say that I love the vampire because there is always something new to discover, that its mystery still exists. Every time an ancient piece of parchment is found or newly translated there is the potential for an undiscovered species of vampire to be named or for a new story to be told about a type we already know to exist. In the past there have been books both rare and expensive that have been kept out of the reach of most researchers either because the researchers lacked the clout to have access to them or because the books were locked up tight in a distant library. However, with today's technology these books are being transcribed and scanned into electronic documents so that everyone, no matter his reason, income level, or academic credentials, can have access to them. What was once forbidden or lost knowledge is now posted in PDF format on the Internet. I love the idea that there will always be one more book to read and a new discovery to be made. As a researcher this excites me—this is why I love the vampire.

To take on the task of writing an encyclopedia, on any subject, is tremendously exciting and daunting. My very first order of business had to be how I intended to establish what specific information it was going to contain as well as how inclusive it was going to be. My intent was to make a reference book that pulled together the disseminated knowledge from all over the world, from all cultures of people, from our ancient ancestors to our modern kinsmen.

Additionally, I wanted my book to not only be useful to the serious-minded academics that would need my book for their own varied research but also something that could appeal to fans. To achieve this goal I committed myself to not exclude any culture, religion, or people from any historical time period and to report the facts for each entry without any personalization, dramatization, emphasis, or hyperbole. In doing so, I could ensure that each entry would be treated equally with a measured level of professional dégagé.

My next task was perhaps more difficult, for to write an encyclopedia about vampires one has to have a clear definition of what a vampire is. Most interesting, there is not a pre-existing or commonly accepted idea, let alone a singular, all-encompassing definition that clearly says what a vampire is, specifically. That being the case, I would have to create one and apply it even-handedly against all potential entries for the book. This was more difficult than it sounds as what is considered a vampire in modern-day Brazil would not in side-by-side comparison be considered a vampire by the ancient Celts of Ireland—and yet, each of these mythical beings are by their people's standards every bit a vampire.

For starters, not all vampires are undead, that is, the animated corpse of a human being, such as the *brykolakas* of Greece. There are mythologies where a living person is a vampire, such as with the *bruja* of Spain. Not all vampires are considered evil; the *talamaur* of Australian lore is not only a living person but may choose to be a force of "good." Not all vampires survive on human blood; the *grobnik* of Bulgarian lore feeds strictly on cattle and animal carcasses. Not even blood is a requirement; the *algul* of Arabic lore consumes rice while the *gaki* from Japan can feed off either samurai topknots or the thoughts generated while one meditates. It is a popular misconception that vampires can only come out at night as the light of day is said to be most deadly; however, this is hardly the case for the sixty-some species of vampire that are said to originate on the Greek isles. There it seems that many of their vampires are particularly deadly at noon, when the sun is at its apex. The Aztecs of ancient Meso-America had vampiric gods as well as vampiric demons in their pantheon, and so do the Hindus, whose religion is just as old but still practiced today throughout the world. Nor is the vampire a stagnant creature, as the *pishtaco* of Peru has been evolving in appearance and hunting tactics throughout the written history of the Andean people.

What, then, do all these different species of vampires, from all around the world, have in common? The answer is simple: basic human fear. No matter when or where, how it hunts or what it hunts, the vampire attacks that which man considers most precious. The reason that there is no single definition of a vampire is because each culture of people, from their various time periods and from their various locations, has feared different things. The vampire has become man's fear manifest; as man has evolved, so too has the vampire. What is culturally important to one people is not necessarily so to another. Because of this, I used the definition that each unique and diverse culture throughout history used; I let the people who lived with their fears dictate to me what a vampire is.

With my definition of a vampire as fixed as it ever could ever be, I had to determine if fictional vampires were to be included. A "fictional" vampire is, for the sake of classification, a vampire that is the creation of an author or group of creative-minded individuals. These fictional characters were deliberately not included. As fond as I am of Joss Whedon and his vampires, they will not be represented here. It would be impossible to publish a book containing those creations considered the most popular fictional vampires, let alone all of them. Only time will tell what, if any, vampire characters from various forms of entertainment will one day be considered "historically relevant." I do not believe that the time has come to make that call.

Also not included in this encyclopedia are those homicidal individuals, mass murderers, cannibals, sadists and serial killers who have displayed vampiric tendencies. These types of people are not only irrelevant to the vampire as a mythological being but are themselves not vampires. The tag "vampire" is often applied to individuals who consume human blood, like Fritz Haarman, the "Vampire of Hanover," most often by the media in an attempt to sensationalize a story. People who have a blood fetish and kill to fulfill it, like Elizabeth Bathory, the "Blood Countess," for instance, are not considered vampires. She did not consider herself a vampire. Her peers did not consider her a vampire. She had nothing in common with how a vampire is created, lives, or hunts. She had no powers or special physical abilities that one would consider vampire-like. She was a living, breathing, historical person and clearly not a vampire.

I also did not include cryptozoological creatures, such as the Vampire Beast of Greensboro which is alleged to be an A.B.C. (alien big cat) that attacks livestock, draining them of their blood. Pumas, or mountain lions as some people call them, were once native to North Carolina. The state's Department of Wildlife Management stands firm on the fact that there are no big cats living there in the wild. Isaac Harrold, a section manager for the North Carolina Wildlife Resources Commission, has assured me that although the NCWRC continues to investigate numerous reported cougar "sightings" every year, "there is no documented physical evidence to suggest that a population of wild eastern cougars continues to exist in North Carolina. In the absence of any physical evidence to the contrary, it is our position that wild cougars do not exist in the state." Regardless of the NCDW's stance, scores of hunters and eyewitnesses report seeing these cats every year; often these claims are accompanied by blurry photos of the beast itself or of its tracks. On the one hand, it would seem ridiculous to argue that there are panthers in the mountains and piedmont of North Carolina. On the other hand, eyewitness reports and blurry photographs do make one wonder if they are indeed real. The standard, as it were, must be maintained. Furthermore, the Vampire Beast of Greensboro has only been sighted and reported since the early 1950s, and although it is most certainly a part of local history, it is neither culturally significant nor mythologically relevant. (The complete story of this vampiric creature can be found my book *Haunted Historic Greensboro*.) I did, however, include those vampiric creatures, such as the *chupacabra* of Mexico, that are culturally noteworthy and historically pertinent. This species of vampire has been sighted since the 1500s and has long been part of the history and mythology of its people.

Whenever possible, at the end of each individual entry I have included the source material I used so that it may be referenced by others. I went back to the oldest source I could find to confirm what was written and tried to consult the most authoritative works available. Much of the information I discovered about vampires was taken from a wide array of sources on different subjects that appeared in scholarly studies and folklore journals, not the New Age or the occult section of the bookstore. It took me five years of intensive research to gather the information I would need to sit down and write this book. Sometimes a single piece of information came from one book and another tidbit from another. No one entry came from any single book. A complete bibliography is provided at the back for the reader who wants to learn more or start his or her own research.

For ease of readability, I have used SMALL CAPS for cross-references. I find that cross-referencing is important, particularly when it comes to the reader's desire to learn more. Cross-references let them know that additional information is available and that it is right there at their fingertips. To complement this, there is a thoroughly exhaustive index that can be found at the very back of the book. Compiled here, in this one place, is a list of terms any researcher would ever need to look up in this encyclopedia.

There are an untold number of nonfiction books about the vampire, and although I cannot personally vouch for even the smallest percentage of them, there are several books that I consider to be relevant and worth reading. All are nonfiction and the information that they contain is fairly timeless. For example, the history of ancient Rome has been written and is well established. Although new bits of information may come along or a new understanding of situations may be brought to light, Edward Gibbon's book *The History of the Decline and Fall of the Roman Empire*, first published in 1781, is still a valid historical reference book.

Matthew Bunson's *The Vampire Encyclopedia* offers readers a good mixture of mythological and fictional vampires as does J. Gordon Melton's *The Vampire Book: The Encyclopedia of the Undead*. Rosemary Ellen Guiley's *The Complete Vampire Companion: Legend and Lore of the Living Dead* covers mythological and fictional vampires as well as the real or living vampires, those who live the "vampire lifestyle." As mentioned, these books present varying amounts of information about fictional vampires from books, movies and television. While it is interesting and entertaining, this material is irrelevant to the mythology and history of the vampire and not appropriate for this encyclopedia. Naturally, Montague Summers' books *The Vampire, His Kith and Kin*, *The Vampire in Lore and Legend* and *The Vampire in Europe* are "must-reads" for anyone who takes their vampire lore seriously. Be advised, however, that Summers was a very religious individual and oftentimes conveyed his feelings when not adding outright his own Christian opinion. I am personally fond of Orenlla Volta's *The Vampire*, although it does not go into great depth on the various species of vampires; what it does offer, however, is wonderful insight into the human psyche as it relates to the vampire. A similar comment can be made for the book written by Ernest Jones, *On the Nightmare*. Perhaps I am especially fond of these two books because they dwell less on the "who, what and where" and focus more directly on the "why."

I am frequently asked the age-old question "Do you believe that vampires are real?" and time and again my answer is an unhesitating and unwavering "No, I do not." My rational and scientific self cannot accept their existence. I do not believe that there are animated corpses wandering the countryside and dark alleys looking for suitable prey to lure into a quiet shadow so that they may sustain their life by consuming a human's blood. That is not to say that I do not experience the same cultural fears as my fellow man; I just do not lay the blame for the manifestations of those fears on the vampire.

All the same, just in case I am wrong, don't take candy from any strangers.

On that note, I would like to express my appreciation to those in the field who went before me, a list too long to present in its entirety but is comprised of those editors, artists, and historical experts who work in occult research, paranormal investigation, psychology, para-psychology, and translation. Also I would like to thank Gina Farago, my beta-reader extraordinaire; June Williams, who was instrumental in my pronunciation guides; and especially my husband, Glenn, who makes my writing and being an author possible. To you all I extend my heartfelt thanks. I couldn't have done it without you.

Introduction

Vampire.

To those people who believe that there are such creatures in the supernatural, blood-sucking predators who stalk mankind in the night, just hearing this word aloud in a crowded room instantly draws their attention to the speaker. All eyes turn to face him as their bodies tense up, becoming like a herd of deer in the communal process of deciding whether or not to bolt.

Perhaps there is still some primitive part of our brain that is hardwired yet into fearing this life-taking entity of the night. Modern man, for all his achievements and developments in the fields of science and technology, knows that there is no such thing as a vampire, and yet ... there is that little voice in the back of our heads or in the twitch we get in the bottom of our stomachs at night that whispers, *"But what if..."*

Then, there are those people who hold a deep-rooted fascination with the vampire; to them the vampire is not a monster seeking lives to claim in sadistic acts of terror and violence night after eternal night. Rather, the image they fancy is that of a poor Byronic figure in need of understanding, compassion, and love. To the fans of paranormal romance, the vampire with his hundreds of years of sexual experience to draw from is a near perfect lover: passionate, dominant and seductive—it loves only her, wants only her, needs only her, the one person who can save him from an isolated, dismal and droning eternity of loneliness.

I would think that the fewest number of people think "parasitic life form" when they heard the word "vampire"; perhaps this one word is the rogue exception of Occam's Razor, the principle that the simplest and most logical answer is most likely the correct one. Seeing a bat flying at night, who among us truly thinks, "There is a creature that eats 8,000 mosquitoes a night, and without it we'd all have died of malaria by now." It may be safe to say that the opposite is true, that we see a bat and think illness and death, all words akin to the vampire because it has always been blamed as the carrier for such horrors.

Since the dawn of man, there has been the belief in supernatural vampires. Just like flood myths, every society has had vampire myths as well. In fact, one of the earliest pieces of writing that archeologists have discovered was not a love poem, recipe, or a religious text but rather a magical spell written around 4000 B.C. It is alleged to have been written by a mother in an attempt to keep her child safe from the attack of the EKIMMOU, a type of vampiric spirit that even then was considered to be an ancient evil. A February 13, 1892, article in the *New York Times* discusses ad nauseam some ancient letters transcribed between the Assyrian monarch, Dusratta, king of Mitain, to Amenophis III, king of Egypt. Dating from around 1500 B.C., these letters discuss the arrival of envoys and ambassadors. What makes the letters so valuable is that they contain 500 lines of Acadian and Babylonian ideas regarding the belief of witches and maligned spirits that haunt mankind. The article even translates into English for its readers' pleasure most of an incantation used to exorcize a demon as well as a complete translation for a brief magical formula for use against ten different types of devils, including LILITH and the EKIMMOU:

> *I hold aloft the torch, set fire to the images*
> *Of Utukku, Schedu, Rabisu, Ekimmou,*

Lamastu, Labasn, Achahaza,
Lila, Lilitu of the maid Lilu,
Of all that is hostile, that attacks me.
May their smoke mount heaven,
May their sparks cover the sun,
May the priest, the son of the god Ea, break their spell.

Often reality and the perception of reality are two very different things. It seems highly unlikely that there ever were such beings, or that the ancient Babylonians, Egyptians and Inuits all could develop and fear this very same vampire at about the same time, and yet they did.

To be certain, this is not proof that vampires such as the EKIMMOU once existed, only that ancient man believed they did. In fact, man need not be all that ancient to have a profound belief in vampires.

In 1576 the plague was ravaging the Italian city of Venice; it was believed by some to be spread by vampires. In an attempt to gain the upper hand on the undead and help bring the widespread disease under control it is speculated that the gravediggers who buried plague victims took matters into their own hands. Matteo Borrini of the University of Florence in Italy found the skeletal remains of a woman who had a brick wedged into her mouth, a telltale sign that it was assumed that she was a vampire. Borrini believes that the gravediggers would have returned to the mass grave with more bodies for burial after a two- or three-day absence.

It would have been at that time that they would have noticed that one of the corpses, a woman, had apparently chewed through her burial shroud. He also suspects that the men would have noticed what would have appeared to look like fresh blood on her lips and teeth as well as on the remains of her shroud. Five hundred years ago it was commonly believed and widely accepted that vampires spread the plague by chewing their own burial shrouds while they lay in their graves, that this act somehow mystically spread the plague to their surviving family members. The gravediggers thought that placing the brick in the mouth of the vampire prevented the creature from continuing to chew on its shroud and thereby saved the lives of an untold number of people. The "blood" that the gravediggers must have seen was in fact not blood but rather bodily fluids loaded with enzymes escaping the corpse, some of which apparently bubbled up from the mouth and, being mildly acidic, dissolved part of the shroud.

By the time the brick would have been placed in the jaws of the corpse, that stage of decomposition would have already passed, so if the gravediggers ever did check on their vampire, they would have been very pleased with themselves to have seen that the remedy worked. Hardly an isolated incident, this folkloric custom was also practiced in Poland and through the Greek isles. Shards of pottery know as POTSHERD would have been inscribed with the words INNK ("Jesus Christ conquers") by a priest before being placed in the mouth of the deceased.

Vampires are without a doubt the single most adaptable monster that mankind has ever dreamt up. Unicorns and griffons have come and gone within the dreams of man, yet the vampire has remained.

At every stage of our social development, the vampire was there. When man was a hunter-gatherer, the vampire lurked in the dark jungles and ambushed, an invisible entity that left nothing behind but the mangled and unwanted remains of its kill. Only in the light of day or in the glow of the nightly campfires was a person safe from the WURWOLAKA of Albanian lore, for example. And just to be fair, just because a vampire attacked its prey at night did not mean that it was automatically susceptible to sunlight; it very well could mean that it for the most part is nocturnal and by use of cunning takes advantage of mankind's natural fear of the night.

The MRART of Australia is one such ambush predator. Its supernatural powers are at their peak at night, but that does not mean that one is automatically safe from its attack during the light of day. As cultures continued to become more socially dynamic, so did the most insidious and notorious stalker.

When man stopped following the animal herds and decided to make permanent settlements, cultivate crops and develop societies, the vampire settled down with him. It had the power to cause droughts and destroy precious grains. It made rivers run dry and sent the plague.

All throughout eastern Europe, a vampiric REVENANT known as a TAXIM, fueled by a lust for vengeance, spread the plague wherever it wandered. In societies where herds of cattle were considered invaluable, vampires attacked them; the NUCKELAVEE, a vampiric fay of the Orkney Islands, Scotland, was known to drive herds off the steep cliffs and into the ocean. If a tribe of people considered their children to be most precious, their children were the only food their vampire would feed on, as is the case with the UPOR of Russia. High in the mountains and in the near–Arctic regions where keeping warm was the most important priority, the vampires in those places, like the KHARISIRI, LIK'ICHIRI, ÑAKAQ and the PISHTACO, survived on body fat and heat.

Furthermore, no matter where in the world man settled or how his societies were established and run, the vampires of that particular region always appeared as that which man found to be the most terrifying aspect of his society imaginable. Be it an invisible and intangible spirit, a corpse risen up and animated by a demonic force, or one's very own next door neighbor, the vampire was always near and ready to strike.

It is no wonder that such a far-reaching fear, namely the vampire, would have an equally far-reaching resource to confront it: GARLIC. Not only did this vegetable grow in abundance in the wild in most parts of the world in a wide range of soil conditions, it was very easy to cultivate, a delicious and healthy food to eat, and just so happened to be a natural vampire repellant. From the ASEMA of the Republic of Suriname to the ZBURATOR of Romanian lore, a simple clove of garlic is used to stave off mankind's worst and most dangerous supernatural enemy.

In truth garlic is not a universal deterrent; other common foods that can be used to thwart a vampire attack are poppy seeds, grains of rice, sesame seeds, iron shavings and peppercorns. Each of these items when thrown or left for a vampire to discover will compel it to stop and count each one. Ideally, this obsessive counting will take the monster all night, stalling it long enough for the sun to rise and destroy it; this is believed to be true of the SUCOYAN of the West Indies.

Additionally, as it so happened, in just about every spot in the world where early man settled, *fraxinus excelsior*, more commonly known as the ash tree, was revealed to be the most perfect wood for making stakes to drive into vampires' hearts. According to Pliny the Elder, "All things evil fear ash." The vampiric REVENANTS know as STRIGON of Istrian lore can be destroyed only with such a weapon. Even when organized religions began to gain power and influence, their gods and faith alone could not quench the innate and deep-rooted fear and belief that people had always had in the vampire. Rather than trying to dispel the creature, they accepted it, gave validity to the fear and then applied their own beliefs onto the existing vampire lore, further legitimizing it themselves. No better example of this process can be given than the transformation of the TOMTIN. Once they were feared as the vampiric fay that served the fertility gods of the ancient Germanic tribes, whipping travelers to death with chains and then lapping up the blood from the corpses. Christianity and the church's desire to have new converts absorbed the regional TOMTIN lore. Rather than serving their pagan gods the TOMTIN became Christian converts themselves and freely chose to serve Saint Nicholas. In true vampiric fashion the TOMTIN, many years later, evolved once again, but this time into something we are all very familiar with—Santa Claus's toy-making elves.

Once the CRUCIFIX and rice paper prayer sheets were easily accessible to the common man, it was small wonder that these easy to get religious items could protect a person from the attack of the TLACIQUES and the HULI JING. No matter how vicious or violent or bloodthirsty the vampire, there is always a simple, inexpensive and common means by which it can be defeated, that is, providing one is able to stand up, confront and face the fear.

Even today, in the twenty-first century, people all over the world still believe in vampires. Why is that? There has never been a shred of archeological evidence to prove that one of the more than 600 different species included in this encyclopedia ever existed. We have discovered the fossilized remains of flora and fauna that lived millions and millions of years ago. We are cloning animals with such frequency in laboratories around the world now that it hardly even makes the news. Regularly, rocket ships and satellites penetrate our atmosphere and send humans into outer space, so often in fact that their debris is becoming a serious travel hazard, turning our sky into a landfill, and no one even thinks this to be exciting or newsworthy. We have found life thriving on the deepest parts of our oceans' floors. We have even found what in all likelihood is significant scientific proof that life once existed on Mars— a planet some 36 million miles from Earth. We are clever and smart and learned people, and yet the belief of the vampire remains. Why is that? How can it be? Why does the belief in this mythical being linger in spite of the lack of any supporting facts or corroborating evidence, especially in our modern day and age? Could it possibly be that somewhere we, as a species, need to believe that vampires are real? That such horrors exist just beyond our sight, just out of our reach, that are far worse than the ones we know to be real and accept and live with? Will we ever grow beyond this fear we seem to have as a species that causes us to need to believe in the existence of the vampire, or at the very least, need the fear it causes within ourselves? Thus far we have been unable to shake it off. We overcame our fear of fire, why not the vampire?

The shark, perhaps the natural world's most perfect killer, has changed very little over the eons, whereas the vampire has been in a constant state of flux. A Darwinian delight, the undead beings that we are apparently forever to be in fear of are always adapting to new environments. Today, the vampire is seen by many as an object of sexual desire, a Byronic and wounded soul that needs and seeks out a living human companion to inspire him to continue on.

Books, comics, movies, music, television shows, theater—there is no form of media that the vampire has not conquered. And as our world grows smaller, due to the ease and accessibility of communication devices such as the Internet and due to the ever-increasing world population, the vampire is right there in the mix. As cultures collide, their mythologies mingle and the vampire once again is morphed into something modern and newly fearsome to a wider audience.

It is difficult to remain stoic and objective about a supernatural predatory being such as the vampire because even if one is not inclined to believe that they are real and walk among us, the crimes that they are believed to have committed are absolutely the most horrific that our society can imagine. Simply trying to imagine what its victims experience as they are consumed alive is enough to turn one's hair white and inspire one to sleep with his lights on.

It is because of the horrific nature of the crimes they commit, the methodology that they employ, the feelings of trust and safety that they so easily shatter, that we would be hard pressed to find someone who had no opinion on the matter at all. That is exactly the reason why encyclopedias, regardless of the subject matter, are so important to researchers. These books are meant to be a comprehensive resource on a subject, pulling together all related bits of reliable data from all branches of knowledge in one place—and this is the most important part—in an impartial and unbiased voice. Admittedly this sort of book is seldom the sort seen on best selling lists, as they opt for the credible rather than the sensational, but long after the title du jour is forgotten the encyclopedia remains, its factual content and integrity intact.

The Encyclopedia

For foreign terms where the pronunciation is known, a key is given.

Abchanchu

This vampire from Bolivia hunts its human prey by appearing to them as a kindly old man who is lost and in need of assistance. Anyone who helps this creature will soon meet with a tragic end. If the victim does not contract a fatal disease soon after the ill-fated meeting, his body will be discovered drained of its blood.

Source: Maberry, *Vampire Universe*, 2

Abhartach (Ah-BART-tig)

Variations: Murbhheo

The oldest known recorded vampire story in Western Europe comes from ancient Celtic lore and took place in the rural parish of Glenullin, in the town of Slaughtaverty, Ireland (see ALNWICK CASTLE). It is the tale of the merciless tyrant and powerful sorcerer, Abhartach. Traditionally, he is described as being a short man, a dwarf in many tellings, and having a physical deformity.

The story goes that one night Abhartach, a jealous and suspicious man, convinced himself that his wife was being unfaithful to him. Unwilling to confront her directly and wanting to catch her in the act of adultery, he climbed out of a window and crept along the ledge toward his wife's bedroom. Before he could clear the distance and have a peek into his wife's room, he slipped and fell to his death. Abhartach's body was discovered in the morning and the people of the town buried him as if he were a king, standing upright in his grave.

The day after his funeral, Abhartach returned to Slaughtaverty demanding that each person cut their wrist and bleed into his bowl daily in order to sustain his life. His people complied—they were too terrified of Abhartach to oppose his will while he was alive, so they certainly did not want to do anything that would further upset him now that he was dead. However, it did not take them long to decide that they were unwilling to live under the tyranny of such an obvious REVENANT, so the citizenry hired an assassin to kill him. Although the attempt was initially successful, Abhartach returned, demanding his daily allotment of blood. Undeterred, another assassin was hired, but with the same results. After several more failed assassination attempts, a druid came forward and promised that he could free them from the creature, Abhartach, once and for all. The druid explained that because of the nature of the magic that was used to return the tyrant combined with the type of creature that he became, a *murbhheo* (ancient Gaelic for vampire), their evil ruler could not be permanently destroyed, only trapped. The druid, using a sword made of yew wood, ran Abhartach through and while he was in a weakened state, he was buried upside down in a grave that was then covered with ash branches, thorns, and a large boulder.

In the town of Slaughtaverty (the name means "Abhartach's Grave") to this day Abhartach will attack anyone who comes too near his gravesite, as he is unable to fully escape it. Next to the boulder that helps imprison him, a large thorn tree now grows out of the burial site, pinning him to the earth.

Source: Borlase, *The Dolmens of Ireland*, 825; Cork Historical Society, *Journal of the Cork Historical*, 350; Harris, *Folklore and the Fantastic*, 135; Hayward, *In Praise of Ulster*, 263; MacKillop, *Dictionary of Celtic Mythology*, 1; Russo, *Vampire Nation*, 38

Abruzzi (Ah-BRUTS-ee)

Variations: Abruzzo

Each November 1, the citizens of the town of Abruzzi, located in central Italy, hold a ceremony for their dead. Both the ceremony and the type of vampiric spirit they call are named after the town.

An offering of bread and water is placed on the kitchen table and beckoning candles are lit and placed in the windows of the home. Similar candles are placed on the graves of loved ones, allowing their spirits to rise up. Slowly the spirits gather together and form a line as they march back into town and to the homes they once lived in. Leading the procession are those that in life would have been considered "good" people, followed by "evil" people, then those who had been murdered, and finally, those who are condemned. Once they return to their old homes, they consume the essence of the food offering left for them.

There is a very complex magical ritual that can be performed at a crossroads that would allow the practitioner to see this procession of the dead. However, this is a very dangerous undertaking, as to see the dead walk will cause insanity, followed by death.

The celebration of Abruzzi is all that is left of the ancient Roman religious tradition that pertains to the Feast of Lemuria, which is similar to the ancient Greek festival, Anthesteria.

Source: Canziani, *Through the Apennines*, 326; Frazer, *The Golden Bough*, 77; Summers, *Vampire in Europe*, 15; Summers, *Vampire in Lore and Legend*, 77

Adze (ADS)

The Ewe people of southeastern Ghana and southern Togo, Africa, believe that this vampiric spirit looks like a CORPSE CANDLE, the constant light of a firefly, or like a shining beetle when not possessing the tribe's sorcerer (see AFRICAN VAMPIRE WITCH). The adze, whose name means "an axelike tool," is attracted to, hunts, and takes the blood from only the tribe's most beautiful children. Although the creature would normally drink blood, it can be staved off with offerings of kokosmilch (coconut milk) and palmoel (palm oil). If captured while in its ball of light or insect form, the adze will immediately shape-shift into the form of a human. While it is in this form, any means that would normally kill a human will destroy the vampire.

Source: Arens, *The Man-Eating Myth*, 153; Bunson, *Vampire Encyclopedia*, 2; Hollinge, *Blood Read*, 87; Spauldin, *Re-forming the Past*, 104

African Vampire Witch

Variations: Nthum, Owang, Saf In Deam, Sefaf In Dem

Generally speaking, African vampire mythology is not based on the wholly undead or animated corpses like that of so many other cultures (see UNDEATH). However, what it does have are vampiric creatures and witches with vampiric tendencies that practice forms of cannibalism and necrophilia, as well as committing acts of vampirism. The ability to become a witch is not always an inheritable trait and is not necessarily something that can be taught to someone who desires to learn.

There is no reliable test that can be performed to determine who may become a witch, although women who are naturally barren or are postmenopausal are most commonly suspect. But anyone has the potential to become a witch. A person suspected of being a witch will find herself blamed for any unfortunate event that happens in the community, more so if the mishap happens to involve a child.

If a witch is discovered, she may be lucky enough to be banished and driven out of her community. Since there are several tribes who blame all of their misfortunes on witches, there have been pocket societies that have developed that consist of nothing but people who were labeled as witches. These small communities are very close-knit and quick to take in new arrivals.

However, if the witch has been directly connected to a specific crime, she will literally become a scapegoat and be ritualistically slain. When the witch is killed, the evil she wrought will die as well.

Once discovered, the witch's tongue will be immediately cut out and pinned to her chin with a thorn so that she cannot speak and cast a spell on her captors. She is then beheaded, her body impaled upon a stake, and cremated. Her head is thrown away so that predatory and scavenging animals may consume it.

Even a deceased person can be accused of being a witch. The suspect's grave will first be examined, as the grave of a true witch will have a small tunnel dug into it so that at night she may leave in the guise of a small animal. If a hole is found, the grave will be exhumed and the body examined for signs of decay. If the body is not considered properly decomposed, it will be destroyed, rendering the witch's spirit impotent.

African witches have an array of talents and abilities, such as astral projection, causing ulcers, flight, removing organs, and necromancy (speaking to the spirits of the dead). They can also capture a spirit and use it to harm crops, livestock, and people.

Source: Allman, *Tongnaab*, 120; Broster, *Amagqirha*, 60; Guiley, *Complete Vampire Companion*, 7; Hodgson, *God of the Xhosa*, 32, 35, 49; Laubscher, *Pagan Soul*, 128–31; White, *Speaking with Vampires*, 19n

Afrit (AFF-reet)

Variations: Afreet, Afreeti, Afrite, Efreet, Efreeti, Efrit, Ifreet, Ifrit

African and Muslim folklore alike speak of a vampiric spirit called the afrit, or afriti when found in numbers. Its name means "blood-drinking nomad." When a person is murdered, his spirit returns to the place of death. At the very spot where the last drop of his lifeblood fell, the newly created afrit rises up. Some sources say it looks like a larger version of the jinni, but others claim it appears as a desert dervish, a ghost-like form, a tall column of smoke, or a being resembling the Christian devil complete with cloven hooves, horns, and a tail. Just to see the creature will cause a person to be overcome with fear. To prevent this vampiric being from entering into existence, a nail must be driven into the exact spot where the last drop of lifeblood fell. This will force the spirit to remain in the earth.

In all, there are five types of jinni, and although the afrit is the second most powerful, it is the most ruthless and cruel toward its victims.

Source: Hoiberg, *Students' Britannica India*, 5–6; Jacobs, *Folklore*, vol. 11, 389–94; Philp, *Jung and the Problem of Evil*, 56–57; Rose, *Giants, Monsters, and Dragons*, 6

Agriogourouno (Ah-ghree-oh-GHOO-roo-no)

In Macedonia it is believed that Turkish people who have led very wicked lives and have never eaten pork will become agriogourounos ("wild boars") upon death. As much a were-creature as a vampire, this shape-shifting being is well known for its gluttonous appetite for human blood.

Source: Jackson, *Compleat Vampyre*, 56

Agta

Variations: Agre

In the Philippines there is a species of ENERGY VAMPIRE called an agta. A reputed cigar smoker, the agta can always be found wherever the fishing is good, as this vampire lives solely off the life energy of fish. As the fish are caught and killed, the agta absorbs the life energy as it escapes. The agta is normally invisible and can only be seen if a person bends over backward far enough so that they can see between their own legs.

Source: Maberry, *Vampire Universe*, 11; Ramos, *Creatures of Philippine*, 28

Aipalookvik

Variations: Aipaloovik

This vampiric spirit is part of the folklore of the arctic regions, including Alaska, Greenland, and Northern Canada. Sailors and those who live near the water have described it as a severely rotting corpse leaving the water and seeking out human prey to drain—not of blood, but rather of body heat. The spirit that inhabits the corpse can access the memory and adopt the personality of the deceased. It is considered the epitome of destruction.

Source: Bilby, *Among Unknown Eskimo*, 266; Guirand, *Larousse Encyclopedia*, 436; Rose, *Spirits, Fairies, Gnomes*, 7

Aisha Qandisha (A-sha CON-da-sha)

Most likely, this vampiric goddess originated in the ancient city-state of Carthage. Her name, Aisha Qandisha. translates to "loving to be wa-tered," as in, covered with semen. Her name has been connected to Qadesha, the sexually free temple women of Canaan who served Astarte.

She, like the SUCCUBUS she is associated with, is described as being beautiful, but along the northern coast of present-day Morocco she is also said to have the feet of a goat. Then as now, she is found near wells and waterways, dancing wildly, bare-chested, lustfully enchanting anyone who will let her. Soon these unfortunate souls will find themselves her sexual slaves. Men whom she has seduced will be rendered impotent and lose interest in all other women. She has a constant consort companion, a jinni named Hammu Qaiyu.

As a goddess, she cannot be destroyed, only driven away by plunging an iron knife as hard as one can deep into the ground before becoming entranced by her beauty. For a man to break the enchantment he must endure ritual sacrifice and enter into a trance where he must see for himself her cloven goat feet. Once he has, he must then stab an iron knife into the ground, breaking her hold over him.

Source: Crapanzano, *The Hamadsha*; Gregg, *Culture and Identity*, 262; Gulick, *The Middle East*, 181; Westermarck, *Pagan Survivals*, 21–23

Aitvar (ATE-var)

This vampire from Lithuania is essentially an ALP but is described as having very large hands and feet.

Source: Meyer, *Mythologie der Germanen*

Akakharu (Oak-a-CAH-roo)

Variations: Akakarm, Akakhura, AKHKHARU, Rapganmekhab

An ancient Chaldean epic written in the third millennium B.C. tells the tale of this vampiric REVENANT. When the goddess Ishtar journeyed into the underworld to rescue her son and lover Tammuz, she said aloud, "I will cause the dead to arise and devour the living." And so it came to be that these vampiric lesser demons or semisolid ghosts came into being, seeking human flesh. Interestingly, the word *devour* originally translated to mean "waste away," as in from an illness.

Source: Cramer, *Devil Within*, 104; Jones, *On the Nightmare*, 121; Masters, *Eros and Evil*, 187

Akhkharu (Ack-CAH-roo)

Variations: AKAKHARU, Rapganmekhab

In the language of the ancient Sumerians, this is the word that is used when referring to a vampiric spirit during magical ceremonies or practices. This creature, which feeds exclusively on human blood, is summoned into this plane of existence through a rather simplistic magical ceremony. As soon as the akhkharu arrives in our dimension, the creature immediately begins seeking out prey. If it can consume enough human blood, it will become human itself.

Source: Conway, *Demonology and Devil-lore*, 49, 55; Fradenburg, *Fire from Strange Altars*, 75; Jennings, *Black Magic, White Magic*, 122

Ala (Ah-la)

Variations: Eclipse Vampire, VARACOLACI, Vudolak

In Turkey, this vampire may appear as either an average-looking person or as a giant eagle. In its human form it is known to drink boiled milk, wine, and vodka in addition to blood. As it approaches in its eagle form, the sky begins to grow dark and soon a full-blown thunderstorm complete with lightning and hail soon follows. During the storm the ala will swoop down and eat all of the grapes off the vine from vineyards. In either of its forms, the ala causes violent storms that ruin crops. Fortunately for the farmers, an ala can be slain by shooting it with shotguns that have been loaded with rounds filled with equal parts of gold, lead, silver, and steel.

According to Greek and Serbian lore, an ala is a creature that eats the sun and moon (see GREEK VAMPIRES).

Source: Royal Anthropological Institute, *Indian Antiquary*, 86

Alfemoe (ALF-a-moe)

Variations: ALP

This type of parasitic vampire from Iceland is essentially a species of vampire known as an ALP. Interestingly enough, there is a belief amongst the people of Iceland that if an elderly person and a child fall asleep in the same room, the older person will unintentionally drain the life from the child. Also it is common there for the vampire to be used satirically as a metaphor of the rich draining the lifeblood from the overworked and abused poor.

Source: Meyer, *Mythologie der Germanen*, 77

Algul (AL-GIL)

Variations: Aigul, ALQUL

Coming from Arabic lore, this vampiric demon whose name translates as "horse leech" or "blood-sucking jinni" was immortalized as Amine in the tale *One Thousand and One Nights*, also known as *Arabian Nights*. There are other tales where an

algul tricks travelers into accompanying it and then, upon reaching an isolated place, turns and attacks. Although its preferred prey is infants, an algul can survive from eating only a few grains of rice every day. Normally this demon lives in cemeteries, but since it can pass for human, it occasionally marries and has children. An algul cannot die due to the effects of age or disease and is notoriously difficult to slay since it is impervious to the attack of bladed weapons. Since the creature is such a fierce combatant, magic is often employed to turn it into a less dangerous monster that can easily be captured and burned down to ashes, the only way to destroy it.

Source: Bunson, *Vampire Encyclopedia*, 3; Needham, *Science and Civilisation China*, 273; Rafinesqu, *Genius and Spirit*, 101; Wright, *Vampires and Vampirism*, 189

Alitos (AL-LEE-toes)

This vampire comes specifically from the Kithnos region of Greece (see GREEK VAMPIRES). Other than that its name translates to mean "rascal" or "vagabond" and it is elusive; nothing else is known about it.

Source: Summers, *Vampire: His Kith and Kin*

Allu (AH-loo)

According to Akkadian mythology, this creature is in fact not entirely a vampire but rather is considered to be a CAMBION, a being that is half human and half demon. Described as being faceless, it is conceived when a SUCCUBUS has intercourse with a man. Assuming that the man survives his encounter with the succubus, as the time of his natural death draws near, his demonic son will return and linger at his bedside. Just as the father expires, the cambion snatches up the soul and enslaves it. Allu are particularly vicious and seek to destroy everything.

Source: Curran, *Vampires*, 29–33; Robinson, *Myths and Legends of All Nations*, 266; Thompson, *Devils and Evil Spirits of Babylonia*, 132

Alnwick Castle (ANN-ick CAS-el)

In the year 1096 a baron by the name of Yves de Vescy first built Alnwick Castle. It has been sieged upon, occupied, invaded, abandoned, restored, and added on to over the years by the nobility that have laid claim to it. Today the castle stands as the second largest occupied castle in England. Alnwick Castle is open to the public and has been utilized in numerous films, but few tourists who visit it are aware that one of its past lords was a vampire.

The story, which originates in the twelfth century, claims that an unnamed ruling lord of Alnwick Castle was an evil and paranoid man (see ABHARTACH). One night he climbed out of his chamber window with the intent of creeping along the ledge to his wife's bedroom window to see if he could catch her in an adulterous act. Before he could reach her window, however, he slipped and fell, hitting the ground with a fatal impact but not dying right away. He lay there helpless until dawn, when he finally expired shortly after his discovery. He was given a proper Christian burial; however, the lord of the castle returned from his grave that very night as a vampiric REVENANT and began to attack the local populace, spreading a plague as he went. It was decided to return to the lord's grave and exhume the body. His corpse was discovered to be bloated and completely filled with blood. The body was stabbed and it exploded with such force it destroyed the corpse.

Source: Bunson, *The Vampire Encyclopedia*, 4; Hartshorne, *Guide to Alnwick Castle*, 16; Lawson, *Modern Greek Folklore*, 362; Stuart, *Stage Blood*, 15; Summers, *Vampire in Europe*, 85

Aloubi (EL-bee)

Variations: Alobuy, Alouby

There is little known about this vampire from the Aquitaine region of France. Other than that, its name translates to mean "twelve" and it is described as being notably thin with a ghostlike glide to its gait.

Source: Tondriau, *Dictionary of Devils and Demons*

Alouqâ (AH-low-ka)

Variations: ALOUQUE, ALQUL

A vampiric demon from ancient Hebrew lore, the alouqâ exhausts men to death with its lovemaking (see SUCCUBUS). Eventually, it drives its lovers insane, causing them to commit suicide.

Source: Langton, *La Démonologie*, 59; Masson, *Le Diable et la Possession Démoniaque*

Alouque (AH-low-kwa)

Alouque is an alternate word used in the ancient Hebrew language to mean "vampire."

Source: Bouquet, *Alouqa ou la Comédie des Morts*

Alp (ALP)

Variations: Alb, Alf, ALFEMOE, Alpdaemon, Alpen, Alpes, Alpmann, APSARAS, BOCKSHEXE, BOCKSMARTE, Cauquemare, Chauche Vieille, Dochje, DOCKELE, Dockeli, Doggi, Druckerl, DRUDE, Drut, Drutt, ELBE, Fraueli, Inuus, LEETON, Lork, Maar, MAHR, Mahrt, Mahrte, Mar, MARA, Mare, MÄRT, Moor, Mora, Morous, Mura, Murawa, Nachtmaennli, Nachtmahr, Nachtmanndli, Nachtmännlein, Nachtmerrie, Nachtschwalbe, Nachttoter, Nielop, Nightmare, Night Terror, Old Hag, Quauquemaire, Racking One, Rätzel, Schrätlein, Schrättel, Schrättele, Schrätteli, Schrattl, Schrettele, Schrötle, Schrötlein, Schrsttel, Stampare, Stampen, Stampfen, Stempe, Sukkubus, Toggeli, Trampling, Trempe, Trud, Trude, Trutte, Tryd, Tudd, Vampyr, Walrider, Walriderske, Wichtel, and numerous others through history and geographic region

Originating from Germany, this vampiric demon does not have a single true form. Throughout the ages the only consistency in its description is that it wears a white hat. Generally the alp is male, and although there are a scant few reports of it being female, it should be noted that this creature has exceptional shape-shifting abilities. An alp can assume the form of any animal it pleases, but it prefers that of birds, cats, demon dogs, dogs, pigs, and snakes. It is very strong, can become invisible, can fly, and has the unique ability to spit butterflies and moths from its mouth. Because of its shape-shifting ability, the alp has been linked to werewolf lore in the Cologne, Germany, region (see GERMAN VAMPIRES).

Typically a demon is an infernal, immortal being that was never human, but this is not the case for the lecherous and ravenous alp. In fact, it became what it is through one of a few fairly mundane acts, such as when a newborn male child dies, when a child whose mother went through a particularly long and painful childbirth dies, or when a family member dies and his spirit simply just returns with no further explanation added.

At night the alp seeks out its most common prey, a sleeping woman, although it has been known to occasionally attack men and young boys, as well as cattle, geese, horses, and rabbits. Once the prey is selected, the alp shape-shifts into mist and slips into the person's home completely undetected. Next, it sits upon the victim's chest and compresses the air out of their lungs so that they cannot scream. Then the alp will drink blood (and milk if the victim is a woman who is lactating), which will cause her to have both horrible nightmares and erotic dreams. The next day the victim will have vivid memories of the attack and be left feeling drained of energy and miserable. The attack event in its entirety is called an alpdrücke. It is interesting to note that if a woman calls an alp to her, then the creature will be a gentle lover with her.

The alp, when it attacks a horse, is usually referred to as a mare. It will mount up and ride the animal to death. The alp, however, may also choose to crush the animal instead, as it is known to do when it crushes geese and rabbits to death in their pens. When an alp crushes cattle to death, it is called a schrattl attack.

Fortunately, as powerful as the alp is, its attacks can be fairly easily thwarted. To protect horses and cattle from being ridden and/or crushed to death, simply hang a pair of crossed measuring sticks in the barn or place a broom in the animal's stall.

There are numerous ways to prevent oneself or others from being attacked by an alp. According to lore, the alp's power is linked to its hat. If a person can steal the hat off its head, it will lose its superhuman strength and the ability to become invisible. Desperate to have its hat back, the alp will greatly reward anyone who returns it, although with what or how this will happen specifically is not known.

Another way to keep an alp at bay is during the Festival of the Three Kings (January 6); a person can draw a magical hexagram on the bedroom door with chalk and imbue it with the names of the three magi who visited the Christ child after his birth: Balthasar, Caspar, and Melchior. Variations of this preventative method say that the head of the household must make a pentagram on the bedroom door and empower it with names of the patriarchic prophets, Elias and Enoch.

Burying a stillborn child under the front door of one's home will protect all the occupants who sleep there not only from alp attacks, but also from attacks by other species of vampires as well.

A less invasive defensive method is to keep one's shoes at the side of the bed at night when falling asleep. If the toes are pointed toward the bedroom door, it will keep the alp from entering. Also, sleeping with a mirror upon one's chest will scare it off should it somehow manage to enter into the room.

At one time there was the practice of singing a specific song at the hearth before the last person in the house went to bed for the night. Sadly, this method is no longer with us, as the words, melody, and even the name of the song have been lost to history; only the memory of once doing so remains.

If despite the best attempts, all preventative measures have been taken and alp attacks continue to persist, there is hope to fend it off yet. If a person should awaken during the attack and find herself being pressed down upon by an alp, she can put her thumb in her hand and it will flee.

Occasionally a witch binds an alp to her in order to inflict harm upon others. Witches who have an alp in their possession have the telltale sign of letting their eyebrows grow together. They allow this to happen because the alp, in this instance, lives inside the witch's body when not in use. When it leaves her through an opening in her eyebrow, it takes on the guise of a moth or white butterfly. If it ever happens that a person awakens in the night and sees such an insect upon her chest, she should say to it, "Trud, come back tomorrow and I will lend you something." The insect should immediately fly away and the next day the alp, appearing as a human, will come to the home looking to borrow something. When that happens, the person should give it nothing but say to it, "Come back tomorrow and drink with me." The alp will leave and the following day the witch who sent the alp to attack will come to the home, seeking a drink. The person should give it to her and the attacks should stop.

Sometimes an alp will return night after night to assault the same person. Fortunately, there is a powerful, if bizarre, way to prevent this from continuing to happen. The victim needs to urinate into a clean, new bottle, which is then hung in a place where the sun can shine upon it for three days. Then, without saying a single word, the person carries the bottle to a running stream and throws it over his head into the water.

For all the trouble an alp can prove to be, it is as easy to kill as most every other form of vampire. Once it is captured, place a lemon in its mouth and set the creature ablaze.

Source: Grimm, *Teutonic Mythology*, 423, 442, 463; Jones, *On the Nightmare*, 126; Nuzum, *Dead Travel Fast*, 234, Riccardo, *Liquid Dreams*, 139

Alqul (AL-QUIL)

Alqul is an Arabic word used to describe a type of vampiric GHOUL from Arabic lore.

Source: Brewer, *Character Sketches*, 34; Meyes, *Mythologie der Germanen*

Alû (Oll-LOO)

An invisible, demonic vampire from ancient Babylon, the alû attacks its victims (men) at night while they sleep. Its victims awake the next day ill and feeling drained of energy (see ENERGY VAMPIRE).

Source: Curran, *Vampires*, 25; Jastrow, *Religion of Babylonia and Assyria*, 262; Turner, *Dictionary of Ancient Deities*, 28, 38, 146, 291; van der Toorn, *Dictionary of Deities and Demons*, 24

Aluga (Ah-lou-GA, A-LUGA)

The aluga takes its name from the Hebrew word that is synonymous with vampirism and translates to mean "leach." This vampiric creature that originates from Mediterranean lore is considered by some sources to be nothing more than a blood-drinking demon, while others claim it to be the demonic king of vampires. A handful of references say that it is nothing more than a flesh-eating GHOUL.

The aluga is mentioned in the Bible, Proverbs 30:15: "The horseleech hath two daughters, crying Give, give. There are three things that are never satisfied, yea, four things say not, It is enough: (16) The grave; and the barren womb; the earth that is not filled with water; and the fire that saith not, It is enough."

Source: Bunson, *Vampire Encyclopedia*, 5; Preece, *New Encyclopaedia Britannica*, 461

Aluka (Ah-LOU-ka)

This vampiric GHOUL lives off carrion, human flesh, and blood. It is described as being able to cling, or stick, to the corpse as it feeds. It can only be removed from the body once it is slain. Since this vampire takes its name from one of the many Hebrew words that means "leach," it is often cited as being the father of the two daughters who cry "Give" in the biblical book of Proverbs.

Source: Briggs, *International Critical Commentary*, 528; Delitzsch, *Biblical Commentary*, 287–89, 291–93; Pashley, *Travels in Crete*, 209

'Alukah A (Ah-LOU-ca A)

Originally, 'Alukah A was a specific demon from ancient Babylonian lore that was absorbed into Hasidic lore. (See ANCIENT BABYLONIAN AND ASSYRIAN VAMPIRES.) There, she became a SUCCUBUS and the mother of two demon daughters—Deber (pestilence) and Keeb (smiter), the siblings who cry "Give" in the Book of Proverbs. Her name, 'Alukah A, closely resembles the Arabic word for horseleech, AULAK. She is accredited as being the demon that tormented Saul.

The only way to protect oneself from her attack is through God's intervention, which can be evoked through the psalm "*Shir shel Pega'im*." In fact, the only way for 'Alukah A to be destroyed should she appear in our realm is by God smiting her through a supernatural means of His choosing.

Source: Graves, *White Goddess*, 448; Masters, *Eros and Evil*, 181; Phillips, *Exploring Proverbs*, 557, 559

Aluqa

An ancient vampiric demon from Hasidic lore, the aluqa looks like a beautiful woman with a face suggesting nothing but pure innocence. However, despite this demon's beauty, a snake lives coiled around its heart. Typically it attacks men as if it were a SUCCUBUS, but it can also cause madness in its prey. Its victims oftentimes are made to feel the full weight of their shame for having been seduced by such a creature and they will commit suicide. The aluqa is indestructible but can easily be driven off with prayers. Sleeping with an iron nail under one's pillow will offer protection from its attacks while sleeping.

Source: Maberry, *Vampire Universe*

Alvantin (AL-von-tin)

Variations: CHUREL, Jakhai, Jakhin, MUKAI, Nagulai

This vampire from India is created when a woman dies unnaturally, such as in childbirth.

Source: Hastings, *Encyclopedia of Religion*, 481; Melton, *Vampire Book*, 323; Verm, *Social, Economic, and Cultural*, 199–200

Alytos (Al-ly-TOSS)

This particular word was used to refer to a vampire from ancient Greece, because the word *alytos* translates to mean "undissolved," aptly describing the amazingly well-preserved state of the vampire's body (see GREEK VAMPIRES).

Source: Bunson, *Vampire Encyclopedia*, 5; Hartnup, *On the Beliefs of the Greeks*, 174; Smith, *The Great Island*, 149–50

Am Fear Liath Mor

In the mountains of Scotland there is a vampiric ghost of a giant called Am Fear Liath Mor, Gaelic for "the Big Gray Man."

Source: Ashley, *Complete Book of Vampires*

Anaïkatoumenos

Variations: Anakathoumenos

Specifically from the Tenos region of Greece, this vampire is like many other GREEK VAMPIRES in that blood drinking is not required to sustain its unlife and neither is it susceptible to sunlight (see GREEK VAMPIRES).

Its name, anaïkatoumenos, translates to mean "one who has sat back up" and may have originally meant that the position of the corpse had changed. Movement from a corpse is not only possible but probable after rigor mortis has occurred in the body.

Another possible explanation as to how the anaïkatoumenos received its name may have to do with an ancient hatred that the Greeks had at one time for the Turks. Many GREEK VAMPIRE stories begin with a person being cursed to UN-DEATH because he had a heretical religious belief or had converted to Islam. According to Islamic beliefs, after death two angels, Munkar and Nakeer, come to question the departed who must sit upright in their presence. There is a Romanian story of how a man happened upon an undead being while it was still in its grave "sitting upright like a Turk."

Source: Summers, *Vampire: His Kith and Kin*

Anarracho (Ann-rha-CO)

Anarracho is a word that is used regionally in Cythera, Greece, to describe a vampire (see GREEK VAMPIRES).

Source: Summers, *Vampire: His Kith and Kin*

Ancient Babylonian and Assyrian Vampires

Variations: LAMIA, Lilatou, Lilats, Lîlît, LILITH

As far back as the 24th century B.C., the people of Babylon and then later Assyria supposed that vampires were demonic beings who were not of this plane of existence. Therefore, in order for them to interact and assault humans, the demons had to possess corpses. As an even greater insult to humanity, and as an example of how evil these beings were, the demons specifically chose to inhabit the bodies of women. To these ancient people, women were considered to be the living symbol of life, and this concept was a near-sacred thing—their menstrual cycles, which were in rhythm with the cycles of the moon, were linked to the planting and harvesting of crops. Nothing in their eyes could have been seen as being more perverse than the very symbols of life and life-giving beings turning into violent monstrosities that sought to consume the flesh and blood of children. These vampires were further described as being very fast and shameless in their pursuit of destruction. They needed to feed in order to maintain the capability of the corpse they utilized.

Source: Budge, *Babylonian Life and History*, 142–43; Campbell, *Masks of Gods;* Hayes, *Five Quarts*, 187; Summers, *Vampire: His Kith and Kin;* Summers, *Vampire in Lore and Legend*, 267; Thompson, *Devils and Evil Spirits of Babylonia;* Varner, *Creatures in the Mist*, 93

Anemia (Ah-NEE-me-ah)

Derived from the Greek word meaning "without blood," anemia is a disease of the blood that causes the red-cell count to be uncommonly low. There are numerous variations to the illness, but it is contracted by one of three ways: a disease, such as cancer; a hereditary condition; or severe blood loss. People who are suffering from this disease present symptoms that are indicative of vampiric assault: chest pain, fatigue, feeling tired and weak, high heart rate, pale complexion, shortness of breath, and unusual bleeding (see PORPHYRIA).

Source: Day, *Vampire Legends*, 64; Melton, *Vampire Book*, 15; Ramsland, *Science of Vampires*, 71

Angiak

Variations: Anghiak

Centuries ago, the Inuit people of Alaska would, in desperate times, be forced to take children that could not be cared for and abandon them out on the frozen plains. After a child died, its vengeful spirit would sometimes return and animate the body, creating a vampiric REVENANT known as an angiak. At night it would steal back into its family's home and nurse from its mother's breast. When it grew strong enough, the angiak would develop the ability to shape-shift into various wild animals, which it would use to kill off its family members onc by one.

Source: Allardice, *Myths, Gods*, 20; Nansen, *Eskimo Life*, 293–95; Rink, *Tales and Traditions*, 45

Animalitos (ON-ah-ma-lee-toes)

Animalitos is a Spanish word meaning "little animals." This vampiric creature has been described as having the head of a lizard and the mouth of a dog. Standing only about four inches tall, it hunts in natural water sources and pools that bathers and swimmers frequent. This is one of the few vampiric creatures that have proven to be helpful to mankind. Centuries ago animalitos were captured by healers and tamed enough to be used in treatments that would have otherwise required the use of leeches. Only the most skilled healers would utilize an animalitos in their practice, for if the creature drank up too much blood and killed the patient, the person's soul would immediately descend straight into Hell.

Source: Dominicis, *Repase y escriba*, 206; Espinosa, *Spanish Folk-Tales*, 66, 179; Maberry, *Vampire Universe*, 18

Anito

Variations: Anitu, Mamangkiks

From the Philippines comes a vampiric spirit

known as an anito. It rises from its grave, a burial mound, as a gaseous vapor. Although the anito seldom ventures too far from its grave, it will assault anyone who enters into its domain. It clings to the victim and allows itself to be inhaled. Although not consumed, the anito will infect the person with an illness that presents as an outbreak of boils. Eventually the disease spreads through the blood and enters into the lungs. Many people who fall victim to the attack of an anito die, especially children. Highly territorial, the anito can be abated with offerings of fruit left on top of its burial mound. There is a chant that offers protection for those who need to walk through an area that an anito is known to defend: "Honored spirit, please step aside, I am just passing through."

Although the anito does not seem to gain any apparent means of nourishment or sustenance from these aggressive assaults, that does not disqualify it as a vampiric being. Many species of vampires are plague carriers and gain no benefits from the death that they cause from the illnesses they spread.

Source: Benedict, *Study of Bagobo*, 115–16, 123–29; Blair, *Philippine Islands*, 170–73; Kroeber, *People of the Philippines*, 175–82

Aniuka (ON-ee-you-ka)

The Buryat people of Mongolia have a particular cultural fear of death. When one of their own dies, great care and attention to detail is given to the preparation of the body for the grave so that it may lie eternally in peace. Buryat shamans have the power to raise the dead and therefore when they die, the shamans can raise themselves. To prevent this from happening, the bodies of shamans are staked and cremated. Despite the fear that a shaman regenerates in death, he is very important to his people in life. Among his duties and responsibilities he must protect his people from the aniuka. Although no one has ever claimed to have seen one, perhaps because it is invisible or extremely stealthy, it is known that this vampiric being is small. It feeds exclusively on infants and small children, taking enough blood from them to make them sick and weak but not enough to kill them in one sitting. Only the magic that a shaman can offer will banish the creature.

Source: Lopatin, *Cult of the Dead*, 60

Aniukha (AH-nee-oo-k-ha)

In Mongolia, the shaman is a respected and feared member of his community. Part of the process of his becoming a shaman is to take part in a ritual death ceremony that will allow him to walk between the worlds of life and death. The shaman is expected to be able to use his powers responsibly and for working only good, but if he is selfish and uses his powers to pursue his own goals, he does so with dire consequences. Should he use his powers to return from the dead, he will come back as a type of vampire called an aniukha. In order to sustain its UNDEATH, the vampire will feed upon the blood of infants. Only staking it and burning the body to ash will destroy it.

Source: Hastings, *Encyclopædia of Religion*, 8; Keith, *Sanskrit Drama*, 328, 340; Lopatin, *Cult of the Dead*, 60

Aniukha (On-you-KHAH)

This vampiric creature has more in common with the CHUPACABRA of Mexico than the undead shaman of Mongolia, who shares its name with (see UNDEATH). This vampiric animal was first sighted in Siberia immediately after World War II. Numerous members of the Jewish community claimed to have seen a small woodland animal ranging in size from a large grasshopper to a small rabbit. Although it ran on all four legs, it would also stand erect and was able to leap with the skill and grace of a cat. Its body had plated skin and intermittent patches of thick, brown fur; huge, black eyes; pointed ears; and a short snout housing a mouth full of short, jagged, little teeth. As odd as this creature is described as being, it it has no extraordinary physical capabilities; rather, it had to use its cleverness and acts of trickery to snare its prey—small children and the elderly. Luckily for us, the aniukha is one of a dozen historical vampires that are reported to be repelled by GARLIC. By smearing some on one's chest or even along the doorways of one's home, garlic's presence will keep the aniukha at bay. The only way to completely destroy this creature is to cremate it, rendering it to nothing but ashes.

Source: Hastings, *Encyclopædia of Religion*, 8; Lopatin, *Cult of the Dead*, 60; Maberry, *Vampire Universe*, 19

Annis (AN-eez)

Variations: Agnes, Ana, Annan, Annowre, Ano, Anoniredi, Anu, Befind, Benie, Bheur, Black Annis, Blue Hag, Bric, Cailleach, Caillech, Cethlann, Cethlionn, Danu, Don, Donu, Gray Hag, Gry, Gyre Carlin, Hag of Beare, St. Anna

A singular being, this vampiric sorceress (whose name is said to mean "pure, as in virginal") has legends dating back to the founding of not only Ireland but also Scotland as well, a country that had been named in her honor. The name *Scota* from where Scotland originates, was originally called *Caledonia*, which means "lands given by Caillech," as she was then called. Annis is known in Arthurian lore as Annowre. Indeed, so ingrained is she in the minds of her people that she has even been preserved and converted into Christendom as St. Anna, the daughter of St. Joseph of Arimathea. In fact, Annis has had so many names throughout history and in different regions that it would be impossible to list them all.

Annis is reported to have shape-shifting abilities, most notably an owl. There are also stories in which she has the ability to control the weather, heal the wounded, conduct initiation ceremonies, and dispense wisdom to those who seek her out. She has in the past been worshipped as a goddess, revered as a saint, and cursed as a demon. Hills, rivers, and even countries have been named in her honor, but despite her long and varied history, she has always had one common thread—she regularly consumed the blood of children.

Source: Barber, *Dictionary of Fabulous Beasts*, 33; Briggs, *Nine Lives*, 57; Spence, *Minor Traditions*, 29, 93–94, 133, 173; Spence, *Mysteries of Celtic Britain*, 174; Turner, *Dictionary of Ancient Deities*, 55

Aoroi, Fay (Ow-roy)

In the British Isles the aoroi is a species of vampiric fay. They are created whenever a man dies in battle before his proper time or when a woman dies in childbirth. The babies who are born to dead mothers are immediately turned into this type of fay, as well as those babies who die before they can be named. Historically, these children were seen as bad omens and their bodies were usually taken outside of the town's limits and left to the elements as soon as the events of the birth were duly noted and recorded. Lore has it that these children cannot be intentionally slain or buried once deceased or else they will return to haunt the living as vengeful and angry aoroi. However, this vampiric fay can be captured and its magical properties tapped into and used in the casting of spells. The magic that it possesses will last until the day that its natural death would have occurred, had it lived.

Source: Collins, *Magic in the Ancient Greek World*, 70–72; Johnston, *Restless Dead*, 71; Meyer, *Mythologie der Germanen*, 94

Aoroi, Ghost (Ow-roy)

In ancient Greece, the aoroi is a vampiric ghost, as the word translates to mean "untimely dead," created when a person dies prematurely. Like the aoroi of the British Isles, it can be captured and its magical abilities tapped into and used in the casting of spells. Also, like its fairy cousin to the north, the magic that the ghost possesses will last only until the day that its natural death would have occurred, had it lived.

Source: Johnston, *Restless Dead*, 10, 61, 71, 73; Meyer, *Mythologie der Germanen*, 94

Apsaras (APS-sa-rahs)

Similar to the ALP of German folklore, the apsaras of India are female vampiric celestial creatures. They were created when Vishnu used Mount Mandara as a churning rod in the "Churning of the Ocean of Milk" legend. As he did so, aside from the other fabulous treasures and creatures he created, 35 million apsaras came forth, making it no surprise that their name should translate to mean "from the water."

They are known for their goddesslike beauty and charms, artistic talents, and excessive love of wine and dice, as well as their love of dance. Apsaras are sent to earth to defile virtuous men, particularly those seeking to become even more virtuous. The creature will seduce him off his path, thereby causing him to use up all the merit he had previously accumulated.

Apsaras have a wide array of talents and abilities to assist it in carrying out its tasks, such as the ability to cause insanity, having complete control over the animals of the forest, inspiring a warlike fury in a man, making frighteningly accurate predictions, shape-shifting into various forms, and sending inspiration to lovers. Although apsaras can also perform minor miracles, they do not have the power to grant a boon like the Devas or the gods.

Occasionally, an apsaras will enjoy the task it has been sent on. Should it succeed in breaking the man's will and finds him to be a pleasurable lover, it may offer him the reward of immortality. However, if despite its best efforts the apsaras cannot make the man succumb, it will either cause him to go insane or have his body torn apart by the wild animals of the forest.

Collectively, they are mated to the Gandharvas, who can play music as beautifully as the apsaras can dance; however, there have been times when an apsaras has fallen in love with the man it was sent to seduce. Rather than cause his ruin, she would marry him. Stories say they make for an excellent wife and mother.

When not seeking to undo righteous men, the apsaras fly about the heads of those who will be great warriors on the battlefield. If one of these warriors dies with his weapon still in hand, the apsaras will carry his soul up and into Paradise.

Source: Bolle, *Freedom of Man*, 69, 74–75; Dowson, *Classical Dictionary*, 19; Hopkins, *Epic Mythology*, 28, 45, 164; Meyer, *Mythologie der Germanen*, 138, 142, 148; Turner, *Dictionary of Ancient Deities*, 63

Aptrgongumenn (Apt-tra-go-GIM-in)

There is little known about the aptrgongumenn ("walking dead"), a REVENANT vampire from Norse mythology, except for the very specific way it must be slain. First, its grave must be found and the body exhumed. Then, it must be beheaded. Next, one of its feet must be severed. The two parts are then put in each other's place and the body reburied. Like many vampires from this region, the aptrgongumenn rises up from the grave due to the powerful magic of a sorcerer to do his bidding.

Source: Belanger, *Sacred Hunger*, 110; Flowers, *Runes and Magic*, 131

Arakh (AH-rack)

Variations: Preay ("vampire")

A demonic vampire from the mythology of Cambodia, the arakh takes possession of a person and causes them to kill themselves. Only by performing a successful exorcism can the possessed person be saved.

Source: Bitard, *Le Monde du Sorcier*, 309–10, 321; Smith, *Assyria from the Earliest Times*, 8; Southern Illinois University, *Southeast Asia*, vol. 1, 338

Ardat-Lile (AR-daht LIH-lee)

Variations: Ardat Lilî, Ardat Lili, Irdu, Lili

The ardat-lile is a demonic vampire that preys on men. It is mentioned in Hebrew lore and that of ancient Babylon and Sumeria. The literal translation of its ancient Sumerian name is "young females of marrying age now evil wanton spirits." What is most curious about this creature's name is that there is no singular form of the word.

When it can, an ardat-lile will marry a man with the intent of wreaking havoc in his life. It is known for its ravenous sexual appetite and for the absolute delight it takes in doing harm to others. It also causes men to have nocturnal emissions. It does this in the hopes of being able to harvest some of the semen in order to give birth to demonic children.

The ardat-lile is no doubt an early predecessor of the LILITH myth—part SUCCUBUS and part storm goddess.

Source: Gettings, *Dictionary of Demons*, 37; Landman, *Universal Jewish Encyclopedia*, 63; Morgenstern, *The Doctrine of Sin*, 15–18; Spence, *Encyclopædia of Occultism*, 35

Aripa Satanai (AH-ray-pa SAY-ta-ni-eye)

Variations: Avestita, BABA COAJA ("Mother Bark"), Mama Padurii, Samca

This vampiric spirit from Romania is described as being half bear and half old woman and has been given the title "queen of the forest." Particularly bloodthirsty, it has total control over the evil within the woods.

Source: Ankarloo, *Witchcraft and Magic*, 83; Cremene, *Mythologie du Vampire*; Dundes, *Vampire Casebook*, 12

Armenki (Armen-KEY)

Variations: Opiri, Opyri, Oupir

An invisible, intangible, vampiric spirit from Bulgarian mythology, the armenki drains young mothers and their infants dry of their blood.

Source: Dermott, *Bulgarian Folk Customs*, 81; Georgieva, *Bulgarian Mythology*, 102–3

Arpad (Ahr-PAWD)

Variations: Arpadim ("vampire")

Arpad is a word from the ancient Hebrew language that is used when describing a vampire. The arpad is mentioned throughout Hebrew lore from Hungary and means "exiled voyager."

Source: Ankori, *Palestinian Art*, 192; Gerrits, *Vampires Unstaked*, 87

Asanbonsam (Ah-SAN-bon-some)

Variation: Asambosam, Asanbosan, Asasabonsam, SASABONSAM

Similar to the YARA-MA-YHA-WHO of Australia, the asanbonsam terrorizes mankind from southern Ghana in Togo and along the Ivory Coast of Africa. Although it is rarely encountered, it looks like a human with hooks of iron for its hands and feet. Its preferred method of hunting is to patiently sit in a tree and wait for some luckless individual to pass directly underneath it. When this happens, the asanbonsam will use its hooks to snatch up its prey and drain it dry of blood. When times are lean, it will venture into a village at night and sip blood from a sleeping person's thumb. Fortunately, the regular sacrifice of a goat and the spilling of its blood on the ground will keep it satisfied enough to not hunt within the village.

Source: Bryant, *Handbook of Death*, 99; Bunson, *Vampire Encyclopedia*, 11; Masters, *Natural History of the Vampire*, 47; Volta, *The Vampire*, 152

Asema (AH-say-ma)

Variations: Aseman, ASIMAN, AZÉMAN, Aziman, LOOGAROO, OBAYIFO, SUCOYAN, SUKUYAN, WUME

From the Republic of Suriname, this VAMPIRIC WITCH looks like an old man or woman with red eyes and toes pointed downward.

At night, before it can go out hunting, the asema will remove its skin, fold it up neatly, and hide it. With its skin safely hidden away, the asema shape-shifts into a ball of blue light, much like a CORPSE CANDLE. Flying through the air, it slips in and out of people's homes through even the smallest of openings. Finicky blood drinkers, the asema will avoid those people whose blood has a bitter taste to it. Once they find someone whose blood they find palatable, they return to the victim again and again, night after night, until the person eventually dies. Telltale signs of attack are large red and blue spots at the site of the bite.

The simplest way to prevent being attacked by the asema is to regularly consume some herb, like GARLIC, that will make one's blood taste bitter. Another method is to keep a handful of tossed sesame seeds or rice mixed with some pieces of owl talon behind the bedroom door. The asema is one of the species of vampires that is mystically compelled to pick up or count seeds before it can attack its victim. Every time the asema picks up one of the owl talon pieces, it will become annoyed it is not a seed, drop all of the seeds it had already accumulated, and start the process all over again. Hopefully there will be enough seeds and talon pieces to distract it until daybreak, as the asema is vulnerable to sunlight when its skin is removed. If it does not flee before dawn, it will die.

One need not confront an asema to destroy it. If one can find where it has hidden its skin, all one needs to do is cover it with SALT so that the skin will shrivel and dry up. When the asema returns, it will find that its skin no longer fits. The light of day will then destroy it.

Source: American Folklore Society, *Journal of American Folklore*, vol. 58–59, 242; Brautigam, *Asema*, 16–17; Bryant, *Handbook of Death*, 99; Gallop, *Portugal*, 216

Asemann (Ah-SAY-min)

From the Republic of Suriname, this living VAMPIRIC WITCH, very similar to the ASEMA, has the ability to shape-shift into animals at night (see LIVING VAMPIRE). In her animal form, she goes hunting for humans to drain of their blood. Her name is a play on the word *azen*, which means "carrion" or "cadaver."

To prevent it from entering into a home uninvited, people should place a broom crosswise on the door. Should they find themselves outdoors at night and under threat of her attack, throw a handful of pepper seeds on the ground. The asemann is one of the vampire species that is mystically compelled to count. Should she still be counting come morning, she will automatically revert to her human form. Now exposed for what she is, the witch can be slain in any manner that would otherwise normally kill a person.

Source: American Folklore Society, *Journal of American Folklore*, vol. 58–59, 242; Melton, *Vampire Book*, 576

Asiman (Ass-AH-min)

From the folklore of the Dahomey people of Africa comes the asiman, a living VAMPIRIC WITCH. She gained her evil powers originally by casting a specific magical spell and is now forever changed; she can remove her skin and transform herself into a CORPSE CANDLE, a form that gives the ability to fly through the sky (see LIVING VAMPIRE). From the air she hunts for suitable prey, and after feeding, she is able to shapeshift into an animal. Only when it is in its animal form can the asiman be destroyed (see AFRICAN VAMPIRE WITCH).

Vampires that are similar to the asiman are the ASEMA, AZÉMAN, LOOGAROO, OBAYIFO and the SOUCAYANT.

Source: Davison, *Sucking Through the Century*, 358; Farrar, *Life of Christ*, 467; *Melbourne Review*, vol. 10, 225; Publications, *Folklore Society*, vol. 61, 71; Stefoff, *Vampires, Zombies, and Shape-Shifters*, 17

Asrapa (As-rap-ah)

Variations: Asurkpa

The creation of this VAMPIRIC WITCH or demonic vampiric being from India is uncertain. Some lore says that it was born the offspring of Kasyapa the sage and his wife Muni, daughter of Daksha, while other stories say that the asrapa, whose name translates to mean "blood drinker," was a thought form that came into being when the Brahma was angry. No matter how it came to be, the asrapa is usually depicted as a naked woman. It is a shape-shifter who can raise the dead through a boon given to it by the goddess KALI. It can usually be found wandering in a cemetery. It prefers to consume human flesh: man, woman, or child, living or deceased—it does not matter.

Source: Gandhi, *Penguin Book of Hindu Names*, 40; Klostermaier, *A Concise Encyclopedia*, 53; Saletore, *Indian Witchcraft*, 120; Turner, *Dictionary of Ancient Deities*, 74, 140

Asrapas (As-rap-ahs)

Variations: Asra Pa, DAKIN

The female attendants of the goddess KALI are collectively known as asrapas.

Source: Blavatsky, *Theosophical Glossary*, 95; Dowson, *Classical Dictionary of Hindu Mythology*, 255; Shastri, *Ancient Indian Tradition*, 143

Astral Vampire

An astral vampire is a vampiric spirit or a vampiric thought form. Through a magical ceremony, a sorcerer may create an astral vampire from a newly deceased corpse. Another way to create an astral vampire is to practice a specific type of psychic vampirism during life so that as death nears, the spirit may slip from the body and enter into the astral plane. There it continues to exist, moving nightly between planes in order consume human blood. Signs of attack are that the victim feels weak and overly tired.

Source: Belanger, *Psychic Vampire Codex*, 270; Denning, *Practical Guide to Psychic Self-Defense*, 235; Slate, *Psychic Vampires*, 3, 20, 22, 50–53, 55–57

Aswang (Az-wang)

Aswang, the Tagalog word for "dog," is applied to anything and everything that is considered a vampire.

There are six different types of aswang vampires, the ASWANG MANDURUGO, ASWANG MANNANANGGAL, ASWANG SHAPE-SHIFTER, ASWANG TIK-TIK, ASWANG TIYANAK, ASWANG WITCH, and the TANGGAL.

Source: Cannell, *Power and Intimacy*, 144–45, 277; Hufford, *Terror That Comes*, 236–37; Ramos, *Aswang Syncrasy*, 39

Aswang Festival

In the Philippines, Roxas City in the Capiz province was the location of Dugo Capiznon Inc.'s annual Aswang Festival. A citywide event attracting tourists with its local seafood, parades, dancing, and fancy dress ball, the primary purpose of the event was to dispel the myth of the aswang. Roxas City has long been a haven for aswangs, as well as witches and warlocks. The two-day pre–Halloween celebration was not appreciated or encouraged by the local Catholic churches.

Source: Guerrero, *Stun of Islands*, 67; Lopez, *Handbook of Philippine Festivals*, 146, 227

Aswang Mandurugo (Az-wang Man-door-roo-go)

Variations: DANAG, Mandragore

In the Philippines, the Capiz province is known as a haven for witches and for a species of elusive demonic vampires known as the aswang mandurugo. It appears as a beautiful woman by day, but at night its true form, that of a monstrous winged being, is revealed. When it can, it will marry a man to ensure it has a constant supply of blood. It will "kiss" the sustenance it needs nightly from its husband prey by inserting its barbed tongue into the victim's mouth and draining off the blood it needs. The only symptom that the husband may present is a gradual and unexplainable weight loss. There is no test or discernable way to ascertain beforehand if a bride-to-be is an aswang mandurugo, but a preventative measure may be taken. If you sleep with a knife under your pillow at night, you may awake in time to witness your attacker. If you are fast enough to draw the knife and stab the vampire in the heart, it will be destroyed.

Source: Curran, *Vampires*, 35–44; Lopez, *Handbook of Philippine Folklore*, 227; Ramos, *Aswang Syncrasy*, 3; University of San Carlos, *Philippine Quarterly*, vol. 10–11, 213

Aswang Mannananggal (Az-wang Man-ah-non-gil)

Variations: Manananggal, Mannannagel

This VAMPIRIC WITCH gets its name from a derivative of the Tagalog word TANGGAL, which means "to separate." Rather unique for a vampire, this creature creates more of its own kind by tricking a woman into drinking the cooked blood of another person. Once the victim has been converted and transformed, the creature will look like a typical woman with long HAIR, but on nights of the full moon it will transform into its true form. Sprouting large, leathery, batlike wings with long clawed hands and a maw full of fanged teeth, the aswang mannananggal rips its upper body away from its lower and takes flight to hunt out its prey—unborn children from their mother's womb. Should it not be able to find a suitable meal, it will temporarily sate its appetite by dining on human entrails.

Like the ASEMA and the ASIMAN who can remove the skin from their bodies, and the PENANGGLAN who can also separate its body, the aswang mannananggal is also only vulnerable when it is separated. The only way to destroy this vampire is to find where its lower body is hidden and rub it with GARLIC or SALT, which will destroy it. When the upper and otherwise invulnerable half returns at dawn to rejoin itself, it will be unable to. When the sun rises, the upper half will revert to its human form and die.

Source: Alip, *Political and Cultural History*, 77–78; Garcia, *Philippine Gay Culture*, 176–77, 179; McAndrew, *People of Power*, 92; Ramos, *Creatures of Philippine*, 15, 130

Aswang Shape-Shifter

Variations: Ungo

This species of ASWANG is found throughout the Philippines. It can look either male or female but typically appears as an old woman with bloodshot eyes, long black HAIR, and a long black tongue. A sorcerer can decide to become this vampiric creature by performing a magical ceremony, but should he ever decide to convert someone against his will, all the vampire would have to do is simply blow down the person's back. Fortunately, there is a type of healer called a mananambal who knows how to brew a potion that will restore an ASWANG that was an unwilling convert. Naturally the vampire will resist, so the potion will have to be forcibly poured down its throat. The ASWANG will immediately begin to vomit up all sorts of weird things, like an egg or a live bird. When the purging has stopped, the victim is cured. Sadly, the willing sorcerer cannot be saved.

This species of ASWANG is particularly cruel, not because it preys on women, children, and those who are ill, but because of its hunting methods. Once the aswang shape-shifter has selected its prey, it may decide to attack while the victim is asleep. If so, it will emit a strong odor that will paralyze the person, in case he wakes up. Otherwise, the aswang will stalk and physically overpower him. In either case, once it has its prey, it will create a replica of its victim out of banana leaves, grass, and sticks. Then, using its magic, the vampire animates the facsimile. Over the course of the next few days, the replacement will become sick and die. The only way to tell if the sick person is in fact a person is to look closely into their eyes. If one can see one's reflection there, it is the actual person. However, if the reflection is upside-down, it is the animated replacement. In the meantime, the aswang has returned to its lair with its captive. Taking its time, the vampire slowly and torturously consumes its food. It is particularly fond of the liver.

The aswang shape-shifter is so named because of its amazing transformation abilities. It can change to look not only like any animal or person, but also like inanimate objects as well. It is possible to detect if this aswang is near, but it requires brewing a very complex oil that can only be made on Good Friday. When the vampire is near, the oil will begin to boil.

As if this vampire did not have enough predatory advantages, it can also fly due to an oily substance that is secreted through glands in its armpits.

Source: Buenconsejo, *Songs and Gifts*, 92; Woods, *Philippines*, 28–29

Aswang Tik-Tik (Az-wang TICK TICK)

This species of aswang from the Philippines gets its name from the small owl that accompanies it. The owl will make a cry of alarm that sounds like "tik-tik," alerting a potential sleeping victim.

This aswang only hunts at night when it shape-shifts from its human guise into that of a bird. It flies to the house of its intended victim, usually a child, and perches on the roof directly over the spot where its prey lies sleeping. Then it sends its long, thin, tubelike tongue into the house. Using a barb on the end of its tongue, it pierces a small hole in the flesh and sips up its meal. When the vampire has finished eating, the breasts of its bird form will be large and swollen with blood. It then flies back to its home where it will breastfeed its own children. In some tellings of the myth, rather than shape-shifting into a bird, the aswang tik-tik maintains its human appearance while hunting and feeding. Rather than looking like a bird with plump breasts, it looks like a pregnant woman.

If this species of aswang licks the shadow of a person, he will die.

Source: Curran, *Vampires*, 37; Ramo, *Creatures of Philippine*, 28, 66, 118; Roces, *Culture Shock*, 214; Serag, *Remnants of the Great Ilonggo*, 60

Aswang Tiyanak (Az-wang TEA-ya-nak)

Variations: Anak Ni Janice, Tyanak

This vampiric demon from the Philippines is the offspring between a woman and a demon, but it can also come into being when a child dies without having been baptized. Another way an aswang tiyanak can be created happens when a mother aborts a fetus. In this instance, it springs into life and brings nothing but hardship and misery to the woman who should have been its mother.

The aswang tiyanak is described as having red skin, no HAIR, and glowing red eyes. It hunts women by shape-shifting into an adorable baby and placing itself somewhere it will be found. When it is discovered, the aswang tiyanak waits until it has been taken home. Then when its would-be rescuer is asleep, the vampire will assume its true form and attack, draining the victim dry of blood.

Source: Demetrio, *Encyclopedia of Philippine Folk Beliefs*, 398; Jocano, *Folk Medicine*, 109, 169; Lopez, *Handbook of Philippine Folklore*, 146, 221, 227; University of the Philippines, *Asian Studies*, 297

Aswang Witch (AZ-wang Witch)

A living VAMPIRIC WITCH from the Philippines, the aswang witch is born a human female who is then trained in the art of magic and witchcraft (see LIVING VAMPIRE). As she ages, the witch learns to make a magical ointment that when applied makes her look young and beautiful. In her youthful guise she then finds suitable prey and lures him to a secluded place. Once alone, the aswang witch tears him apart, drinking the blood and consuming the heart and liver. Although her means of utilizing the seduction-lure works well, the witch prefers her food to come from children.

Apart from her magical ointment, the aswang witch is a mortal woman and can be slain in any method that would kill a human.

Source: Anima, *Witchcraft, Filipino-Style*, 53–54; Demetrio, *Myths and Symbols Philippines*, 170; Ramos, *Aswang Syncrasy*, 8, 38, 69

Aswid and Asmund (AH-swayed and AZ-mon)

Variations: Assueit and Asmund

This is a Scandinavian legend of two blood brothers, Aswid and Asmund. Each of these men was a great warrior, a general, and a constant companion to the other. They swore an oath to one another that whoever died first, the other would follow him to the grave. As it happened, Aswid grew ill and eventually died. True to his word, Asmund had himself entombed with his friend's body within his crypt along with all the honors they deserved and the treasures they had accumulated over the years, including their dogs, horses, and favorite weapons.

Before Asmund could decide how best to commit suicide, Aswid became alive with UNDEATH and awoke as a vampire. Ravenous from his re-birth, Aswid immediately attacked and killed the dogs and then moved on to the horses. When they were all dead and drained of their blood, Aswid sought out the only other living being in the crypt—his brother-in-arms, Asmund.

Three hundred years later, a group of friends had set out to find the now legendary tomb and resting place of the warriors, even though there had been stories that the barrow was haunted. Undaunted, the friends ventured on, eventually finding the site. Despite the religious implications for doing so, they opened the tomb.

From within, they heard the sounds of battle. One of the friends volunteered to be lowered into the tomb to scout ahead and see what was causing the noise. A few moments later the friends felt a mighty tug on the rope and together they quickly began to pull it back up. Hanging onto the other end, they found a man wearing old-style armor.

The man they had rescued was none other than Asmund. He struggled to catch his breath and explained as best he could the story of how he had been fighting for his life these last three hundred years. It was only when the young thrill-seeker was lowered into the tomb and caused a distraction that he, Asmund, was finally able to defeat his poor friend. Having told his tale, Asmund then died. The group of friends found the body of Aswid and beheaded it, then burned the remains and scattered the ashes in the wind. Then they reburied Asmund in the tomb with full honors.

Source: Cox, *An Introducion to Folk-lore*, 52, 58, 151; Elton, *The First Nine Books of the Danish History*, 331–34; Grammaticus, *The Danish History*, 210–11, 237–38; Masters, *Natural History of the Vampire*, 23–24

Aufhocker (OFF-hocker), plural: Aufhöcker

From Germany comes the tale of a huge and black vampiric dog (see GERMAN VAMPIRES). It singles out those who travel alone at night, typically attacking them at a crossroads. Standing on its hind legs, it rips out the throat of its victim.

Source: Grimm, *German Legends*, 342, 359; Petzoldt, *Demons*, 23; Rose, *Giants, Monsters, and Dragons*, 30; Wurmser, *Jealousy and Envy*, 94

Aulak

Variations: ALGUL

This vampire takes its name from the Arabic word meaning "leech." It prefers to drink the blood of women and children.

Source: Baskin, *Dictionary of Satanism*, 43; Langton, *Essentials of Demonology*, 50; Masters, *Eros and Evil*, 181; Oesterley, *Immortality*, 45

Axeman (AX-amen)

A VAMPIRIC WITCH from Suriname (see AFRICAN VAMPIRE WITCH), the axeman is traditionally a female and fairly common in the lore of vampiric witches throughout Africa. She is a woman by day, a LIVING VAMPIRE, but at night shape-shifts into a bat and flies over the village seeking out prey—someone asleep whose foot is exposed. Very carefully she cuts a small hole in the victim's big toe and drinks up the blood that spills forth from the wound. The axeman drinks until she is gorged with blood and then flies back to her home. The only sign of attack that the victim will experience is feeling drained and very weak the following day.

Source: Herskovits, *Suriname Folk-lore*, 744; Leach, *Funk and Wagnalls*, 99

Azéman (OZ-amen)

This is the name that is given to both the vampire and the werewolf in Suriname folklore. If a woman becomes infected with azéman blood, she will discover that she is now an azéman herself. By day she is a normal-looking person, but at night she transforms into a bat, a ghostly apparition, or she shape-shifts into a nocturnal predatory animal.

To prevent attack from an azéman, sprinkling seeds on the ground will cause it to stop whatever it is doing to count them, as it is inexplicably compelled to do so. To stop it from entering into one's home, a person can simply prop a broom across the doorway, as it will create a mystical barrier that the azéman cannot cross.

Source: American Folklore Society, *Journal of American Folklore*, vol. 30, 242; Benjamins, *Encyclopaedie van Nederlandsch West-Indië*, 63, 140; Rose, *Giants, Monsters, and Dragons*, 32; Shepard, *Encyclopedia of Occultism*, 116

Azeto (Ah-ZET-toe)

This is an evil vampiric ioa from Haitian mythology. *Ioa* is an African word that means "spirit of the dead."

Source: Herskovits, *Life in a Haitian Valley*, 241; Holloway, *Africanisms in American Culture*, 117; Núñez, *Dictionary of Afro-Latin American Civilization*, 44; Perusse, *Historical Dictionary of Haiti*, 5

Baba Coaja (BABA-CO-ya)

Variations: Samca

A vampiric forest spirit and nursery bogey from Romania, Baba Coaja ("The old woman of the tree bark") is a bloodthirsty monster described as being half bear and half woman. She is a singular entity who snatches up children who have wandered into the woods alone or away from the watchful eyes of their parents. Particularly evil, she will consume their physical bodies but locks their souls up in elderberry trees where they will rot away.

Source: Cremene, *Mythology of the Vampires of Romania;* Indian Psychoanalytical Society, *Samīkṣā*, 73; Róheim, *Fire in the Dragon*, 65, 76; Sylva, *Legends from River and Mountain*, 104–8

Baisea (Baa-SEE-ya)

This is the cooking pot or cauldron that some of the VAMPIRIC WITCHES of Africa use in their magical ceremonies to capture and hold the blood and life-giving essence of their victims (see AFRICAN VAMPIRE WITCH). The pot is created by the witch through the use of magic. To a non-witch, the baisea looks like a normal cooking pot that is full of water. However, a true VAMPIRIC WITCH can see what it truly contains. Witches will gather together and sit around the baisea, preparing a magical brew that is made with the vitality captured from their victims. Victims will not have any sign of physical abuse on their bodies, and if cut they will bleed freely as none of their blood has actually been removed, just the essence of their vitality. However, the victims will act as if they have been drained of their energy and desires (see ENERGY VAMPIRE). The only way to restore the stolen energy to the victim is to find out who the witch is. When confronted and convinced, forcibly or otherwise, to reform from their evil ways, they vomit up all of the blood that they have stolen from their victims over the years. Only once this is done will the victim be able to recover.

Source: Field, *Religion and Medicine of the Gā People*, 142; Guiley, *Complete Vampire Companion*, 7; International African Institute, *Ethnographic Survey of Africa*, 103; Manoukian, *Akan and Ga-Adangme*, 103

Baital (Bay-TILL)

Variations: Baitala, Baitel, Baitol, Bay Valley, Katakhanoso, Vetal, VETALA

A divine vampiric race first mentioned in *The Tibetan Book of the Dead*, the baital is described as being half man and half bat. It has a short, stubby tail and stands anywhere between four and seven feet tall. In ancient artwork the baital has been depicted as holding drinking cups to its mouth that are filled with human blood and made of human skulls. These beings are so horrific that to even look fully upon one will cause someone to lock up in fear, growing weak and dizzy; some people even faint. When not consuming the human flesh that is offered up to it in sacrifice, the baital can be found at rest, hanging upside down from trees in the jungle, usually near cemeteries. Despite their horrific appearance and taste for human flesh, the baital are not mindless monsters.

Capable of possession, they are known to animate corpses so that they can involve themselves in human affairs. The vampire from the Indian story *Vikram and the Vampire* is a baital. In the story, the vampire decided to help the hero, Rajah

Vikram, by giving him a reminder that the giant's advice should be taken seriously and that the sorcerer should be slain. Vikram was frightened by the baital's attempt to help, as the vampire had possessed the body of a murder victim, causing the hero to think it to be a devil.

Source: Burton, *Vikram and the Vampire*, 11; Icon Group, *Hanging: Webster's Quotations*, 400; Making of America Project, *The Atlantic Monthly*, vol. 49, 69–72

Baital Pachisi (Bay-TILL PAC-easy)

Also known as the *Vetala Panchvimshati (Twenty-Five Tales of a Baital)*, this is a collection of stories from ancient India, originally written in Sanskrit, that center around a BAITAL. The framework of the story is that King Vikram sets out to bring a baital to a sorcerer, but each time he attempts to do so, the baital tells him a story about someone being unfair. At the end of each story, the vampire then asks the king a theoretical ethical question. If the king knows the answer, he must give it lest his head will rupture. If he does not know the answer, he may sit there quietly. If the king answers the question, the baital flies away. Unfortunately, the king, who is very wise and knowledgeable, correctly answers the baital's question twenty-four times. It was only with the last tale told that the king was unable to answer.

Returning home with the vampire finally captured, the baital informs the king that the sorcerer knows that the king has 32 virtues and plans to sacrificially slay him to honor a goddess. By doing so, the baital will then be under the control of the sorcerer unless the sorcerer is slain first. The king kills the sorcerer and is granted a boon by Lord Indra. The king asks that the sorcerer be restored to life and that the baital will help him whenever he is needed.

Source: Arbuthnot, *Early Ideas*, 102; Forbes, *Baital Pachchise*; Masters, *Natural History of the Vampire*, 66; Summers, *The Vampire*, 220; *Vikram and the Vampire*

Bâjang (Bha-JANG)

Witches and sorcerers in Malaysia can bring forth a vampiric demon through a magical ceremony that involves the body of a stillborn child or the corpse of a family member. If the demon is male, it is called a bâjang; the female of the species is called a LANGSUIR. If the caster is strong enough, he can bind the demon to him as a familiar that can be passed down through the generations. The witch will then keep their bâjang familiar in a specially constructed container called a tabong. It is made of bamboo that is sealed with leaves and locked with a magical charm.

The person who possesses the bâjang must personally feed it a diet of milk and eggs or else it will turn on its owner and then start eating its favorite food—children.

The bâjang can shape-shift into three different forms: a cat, a weasel, or a large lizard. In its cat form, if its mews at a baby, the child will die.

The witch will oftentimes send its familiar out to do its bidding. When it is sent out to harm a person, the bâjang will inflict upon its intended victim a mysterious disease for which there is no cure. The person will grow weak, suffering from convulsions and fainting spells until he eventually dies.

There is no known way to destroy a bâjang, but there are charms that can be made or purchased to keep it at bay. Probably the best way to deal with it would be to deal with the witch who commands it.

Source: Clifford, *Dictionary of the Malay Language*, 121; Gimlette, *Malay Poisons and Charm*, 47; Hobart, *People of Bali*, 116–17; Winstedt, *Malay Magician*, 25

Baka

Variations: Benin

The baka is a vampiric spirit created when a bokor (a Vodun priest) who has led a life of evil dies. The baka has the ability to shape-shift into any animal it desires and by doing so will have a physical body. Once a form has been assumed, the baka can then hunt down humans to consume their flesh and drink their blood. The baka is especially dangerous because no matter what animal form it takes, it will retain its natural strength, which is powerful enough to kill a healthy adult man. In addition to sating its hunger for blood, the baka oftentimes is a vengeful being, especially if the bokor it was in life was murdered. To ensure that it has its revenge against those responsible for its death, the baka may decide to spread a fatal disease throughout a community.

Source: Davis, *Passage of Darkness*, 51; Owusu, *Voodoo Rituals*, 54, 79; Malbrough, *Hoodoo Mysteries*, 3–4, 131, 180

Balbal (BAWL-bawl)

A vampiric, GHOUL-like creature from Tagbanua, Philippines, the balbal can be found in or near Muslim villages. Its name, which literally translates to mean "one who licks up," is an apt description of its hunting technique. The balbal glides through the air and alights upon a home with a thatched roof. Then, using its long, curved nails, it rips open the roof and snatches up its sleeping prey with its very long, thick tongue.

After it kills and feeds, the balbal returns with a facsimile of its prey made of banana leaves and places it in the home.

Source: Dumont, *Visayan Vignettes*, 13, 121; Parais, *Balete Book*, 40; Ramos, *Creatures of Midnight*, 47; Ramos, *Creatures of Philippine*, 69, 72

Bali Djaka (BALI Jock-AH)

The Dayak people from the Isle of Borneo believe that people who are morally tainted are most susceptible to demonic possession by the bali djaka. Once this demon has entered into the person's body, it forces them to commit suicide, which is why the Dayak people associate this vampiric spirit with accidental, sudden, and suicidal deaths.

Source: De Leeuw, *Crossroads of the Caribbean*, 74

Bampira (Bam-PEER-ah)

Bampira is a Tagalog word, the language used in the Philippines, that means "vampire."

Source: Espiritu, *Intermediate Ilokano*, 367; Reyes, *Tellers of Tales, Singers of Songs*, 169; Tramp, *Waray-English Dictionary*, 36

Bampu (Bomb-POOH)

Variations: Kykketsuki, Kyuketsuki

Bampu is the word used in the Japanese language that means "bloodsucker." It is used in place of the word *kyuketsuki*.

Source: Bush, *Asian Horror Encyclopedia*, 20; Melton, *Vampire Book*, 337; Takenobu, *Kenkyusha's New Japanese-English Dictionary*, 80

Banshee (BAN-she)

Variations: Bean Chaointe, Bean-Nighe, Bean Sidhe, Beansidhe, Caoineag, Cointeach, Cyhiraeth, Cyoerraeth, Eur-Cunnere Noe, GWRACH Y RHIBYN, Kannerez-Noz, Washer at the Banks, Washer at the Ford, Washer of the Shrouds

Currently, the banshee is considered to be a type of fay with vampiric tendencies. However, originally the banshee was a singular entity, an ancestral spirit that wailed to announce an upcoming death for one of the five major families: the Kavanaghs, the O'Briens, the O'Connors, the O'Gradys, and the O'Neills.

The banshee's mourning wail is said to be heard every now and again, and its wailing cry is still considered to be a death omen. Those who hear it fear that someone will die the following night.

Although seldom seen, the banshee is typically naked when washing shrouds at the riverbank, its long, pendulous breasts getting in its way. When not at the river, it hunts in the hills near lakes and running water for young men, wearing a gray cloak over a GREEN gown; its long white HAIR is worn loose and let to blow in the wind. If it can, it will lure its victim away to a secluded place and drink his blood.

If by chance a person should catch a glimpse of a banshee as it is washing shrouds, it is best advised not to run from it. Rather, he should wait quietly until it slings its breast over its shoulder and carefully sneak up behind it. Then, he should place one of its nipples in his mouth and pretend that he is nursing from it. He can declare to the banshee that it is his foster mother, and should it accept him as a foster child, it will answer any question that he has. A far less intimate way of gaining information from a banshee is to capture it and threaten it at sword point.

Should a person happen upon a banshee while it is washing a shirt at the river and it sees him before he can act, it may speak, saying that it is washing the shirt of an enemy. He must name an enemy of his aloud and then not try to stop it from finishing its task or else the person he named will most certainly die. If he does not name an enemy for it, the banshee will attack and kill him, draining him of his blood.

Vampires that are similar to the banseee are LA DIABLESSE, LANGSUIR, LEANHAUM-SHEE, MATI-ANAK, PONTIANAK, SKOGSFRU, VELES and the WHITE LADIES.

Source: Davidson, *Roles of the Northern Goddess*, 137, 179–80; Folklore Society of Great Britain, *The Folk-lore Record*, vol. 4, 121–22; Lysaght, *The Banshee*; Yeats, *Fairy and Folk Tales*, 108

Bantu (Ban-TOO)

In Africa and India, *bantu* is a word used to describe a vampiric-type creature. However, in many African languages, the word *bantu* is also used to mean "people."

Source: Inter-university Committee, *Bantu-Speaking Peoples of Southern Africa*, 241; Summers, *Vampire: His Kith and Kin*, 10, 15–16; Werner, *Myths and Legends of the Bantu*; White, *Speaking with Vampires*, 9–12, 18–22, 51–54

Bantu, Africa (Ban-TOO Af-ri-ka)

The people of the Republic of Zambia in South Africa fear a vampiric REVENANT known as a bantu. It is created when the spirit of an evil person or a person who feels that he did not receive proper respect during his funeral returns and occupies their corpse.

The bantu is mystically drawn to blood, even a single drop, and drinks it out of both a compulsion and necessity, for without the blood, its corpse will begin the natural process of decomposition. Many victims of the bantu survive the experience, waking up with a fresh wound on their body and no memory of the attack.

The Zambian people are largely hemophobic, as even a single drop of blood on the ground will alert the vampire, who will now come when night falls. The only way to stave off the arrival of the vampire is to dig up the area where the blood fell and bury it in a secret location. The person from whom the blood came must go through an elaborate ritual purification process.

Source: Melland, *In Witch-Bound Africa*, 188; Peek, *African Folklore*, 105, 153; Summers, *Vampire: His Kith and Kin*, 10, 15–16; White, *Speaking with Vampires*, 9–12, 18–22, 51–54

Bantu Dodong (Ban-TOO Doe-DONG)

The bantu dodong is a vampiric REVENANT from India. It lives in caves and survives off animal blood.

Source: Konstantinos, *Vampire*, 25; Summers, *Vampire: His Kith and Kin*, 15–16

Bantu Parl (Ban-TOO PARL)

Variation: Han Parl, Hántu Parl

The bantu parl is a vampiric REVENANT from India that preys on people who are too weak to defend themselves, consuming their blood. Typically its victims include infants, the elderly, and those who are very ill.

Source: Konstantinos, *Vampire*, 25; Summers, *Vampire: His Kith and Kin*, 15–16; Wright, *The Book of Vampires*, 64

Bantu Saburo (Ban-TOO Sa-BAH-roo)

Variation: Hanh Saburi, Hanh Saburo, Hántu Saburo

The bantu saburo is a vampiric REVENANT from India that has command over dogs. It lures humans into the jungle and then has its dogs attack and kill its prey. The bantu saburo then drinks up the blood from the corpses.

Source: Bunson, *Vampire Encyclopedia*, 133; Konstantinos, *Vampire*, 25; Wright, *The Book of Vampires*, 64

Baobham Sith (BAA-van SITH or
   BO-vun SITH)

Variation: Baobhan Sith, Bean-Fionn, Bean Si, Oinopôlê ("She with an ass' leg"), ONOSCÉLES, Sybils, WHITE LADIES

When a woman dies in childbirth, in Scottish folklore, the woman may return as a type of REVENANT vampiric fay called a baobham sith.

According to the original and ancient myth, the baobham sith mingled with humans regularly, even becoming attached to a particular family. It was considered a sign of high status to have one in the family. It was not until after the introduction of Christendom that the baobham sith became an evil being.

Similar to the BANSHEE, the baobham sith is more often heard than seen, and will wail in sorrow, predicting the death of someone who heard its call. However, if many baobham siths gather together and wail as one, they are foretelling the death of a great person.

It is normally a solitary creature, described as being a tall, pale, beautiful young woman wearing a GREEN dress. In its human guise, it has deer hooves rather than feet that it keeps hidden under its dress. This is especially important as it will often lure young men, particularly shepherds who are up in the highlands, to a secluded place and offer to dance with them. Often it will do this in the guise of someone the man knows, trusts, or lusts after. It will dance wildly until the man is exhausted, then it will attack, draining him of his blood.

In addition to being able to shape-shift into women that their victims know, a baobham sith can also change into a crow and has the ability to create a thick fog.

Like all fay, the baobham sith can be warded off by iron, but this particular type of fay is also afraid of horses, possibly because horseshoes are made of iron. Carrying a pair of iron scissors in one's pocket while traveling through the highlands will also prevent it from attacking.

Source: Heldreth, *The Blood Is the Life*, 200; MacKillop, *Dictionary of Celtic Mythology*, 30; Masters, *Natural History of the Vampire*, 139; Senf, *Vampire in Nineteenth-Century English Literature*, 18; Turner, *Dictionary of Ancient Deities*, 92

Barabarlakos (BEAR-bur-lock-kose)

According to GREEK VAMPIRE lore, there are a number of ways that a person can have the misfortune of becoming the vampiric REVENANT known as a barabarlakos (see GREEK VAMPIRES). Like many vampire creation methods, the usual methods of coming into being apply, such as by being someone who was particularly evil in life, by having a cat jump over their corpse, by being a murder victim, or by having committed suicide. Furthermore, there is the additional rare creation method of having had the misfortune of having eaten, knowingly or not, meat from a sheep that had been slain by a wolf.

No matter how the barabarlakos came into

being, it will return with its skin drawn tight as a drum over the body but otherwise looking as it did in life with no other signs of decomposition.

Each night the vampire leaves its grave and goes from house to house knocking on doors or ringing the bell and calling the names of the people who live within. If no one quickly answers the door, it will waste no more time there and move on to the next house, never to return to the previous home again. Because this vampire does not have the patience to wait and knock a second time, it is customary in Greece not to open the door until there is a second round of knocking. It may be possible that through this custom the idea that a vampire cannot enter into one's home unless invited may have evolved. Nevertheless, if someone should answer the door before the second try, the vampire will immediately attack them, knocking them to the ground as quickly as possible. Then, it will mantle over its prey and pin them to the ground, crushing them to death. Once the person is deceased, the vampire will drain the blood from the corpse.

This vampire is not susceptible to sunlight and blood drinking is not a requirement for it to sustain its unlife. The barabarlakos also has a unique ability in that should a person see one, he may die on the spot, as its very presence can be deadly.

The only way to destroy this vampire is to find its grave, exhume the REVENANT, and burn it to ash.

Source: Borrmann, *Vampirismus*

Bas (BAS)

The folklore from the Chewong people of Malaysia tells of the bas, a psychic spirit vampire that lives off ruwai, a being's soul or life source (see ENERGY VAMPIRE). Typically the bas happily lives off wild pigs; it will only attack a human if it encounters one by accident or if driven to do so by hunger.

Source: Bunson, *Vampire Encyclopedia*, 30; Summers, *Vampire in Europe*, 30; Summers, *Vampire: His Kith and Kin*, 71; Summers, *Vampire in Lore and Legend*, 123

Bataks (Bah-TUCKS)

Variations: Battas

On the island nation of Sumatra there is a type of witch doctor known as a bataks who specializes in fighting the type of vampire called a NAGASJATINGARON that drains the soul from its human victims. The bataks works to reclaim the tendi, the soul, of the person who has fallen under vampiric attack. Using an herbal rub containing GARLIC, a culturally well-known, soul-compelling plant, he performs a magical ceremony that returns the soul to its rightful owner.

Source: Dana, *American Cyclopaedia*, 379; Ripley, *New American Cyclopædia*, 723; Santiago, *Solidaridad*, 161; Summers, *Vampire: His Kith and Kin*, 187, 209, 250

Bdemxhong

This word, *bdemxhong*, is used in Tibet when referring to a vampire.

Source: Vangh, *Tibetan Magic*

Bebarlangs (BEY-bar-lans)

In the Philippines there is a tribe of people, the Bebarlangs, who all claim to have been born with the ability to astral project and psychically attack people (see ASTRAL VAMPIRE). They claim that at night they leave their bodies using astral projection and seek out suitable human prey in order to steal their life-energy (see ENERGY VAMPIRE). Victims of these attacks often wake up the following morning feeling tired and weak. Any method that would harm or kill a human will do likewise to the Bebarlang people.

Source: Belanger, *Sacred Hunger*, 111; Bunson, *Vampire Encyclopedia*, 19

Begierig (Bur-GEAR-eg)

Variations: Nachttoter, Nachtzer, NACHZEHRER, Neuntöter

This is a GERMAN VAMPIRE and the literal translation of its name means "avid chewer." One of the earlier reports of this vampire came from Minister George Röhrer in a series of reports sent to the theologian Martin Luther.

The begierig can be created in one of three rather eclectic ways: by being born with a caul, by drowning, or by being buried in clothes that have one's name sewn into them.

Although this vampire is blamed for tying cows' tails together, it actually never leaves its grave. The begierig lies in its grave with its left eye open, chewing on its burial shroud. When its shroud is consumed, it begins to gnaw on its own body, all the while making piglike grunting noises. Every night the begierig uses its psychic powers to drain away the energy, both physical and emotional, from its family members (see ENERGY VAMPIRE). GARLIC, if heavily consumed by the family, is a known repellant but not a permanent fix to their problem.

The begierig is a known plague carrier and its body is covered with open sores, so one has to be especially careful when exhuming the body. Some object must be placed in its mouth to keep it from its incessant chewing, such as a stone or a coin.

Another method is to tie the mouth closed with clean white linen. As is the case with so many species of vampires, beheading it and burning the body down to ash will destroy it.

Source: Dundes, *Vampire Casebook*, 4; Hock, *Die Vampyrsagen*, 33–34; Perkowski, *Vampires of the Slavs*, 162

Begu Mentas (Bee-GOO Man-TIS)

Begu Mentas is a term used in Bataks, Indonesia, to describe a vampire. It is created when a person commits suicide.

Source: Rae, *Breath Becomes the Wind*, 22, 46

Belili (Bell-LEE-lee)

Variations: Baalat, Baalit, Belet-ili, Belit-Ill, Gesht-Inanna

Originally Belili was a minor goddess in the religion practiced in ancient Sumeria. Later she was adopted by the ancient Babylonians and was worshiped as a vampiric goddess. Associated with sacred prostitution, Belili accepted the offerings of children sacrificed to her by fire. Some sources describe her as having rather SUCCUBUS-like abilities and behaviors, thereby equating her as an early concept of LILITH (see ANCIENT BABYLONIAN AND ASSYRIAN VAMPIRES).

Source: Black, *Literature of Ancient Sumer*, 82, 361; Graves, *White Goddess*, 59, 239; Jastrow, *Religion of Babylonia and Assyria*, 417, 575, 588–89

Belu (BE-lou)

The *belu* ("wild-man") is described as a giant, vampiric, shape-shifting demon from Burma.

Source: Chit, *Colourful Burma*, 30; Enriquez, *Burmese Enchantment*, 233; Freedman, *Eerdmans Dictionary of the Bible*, 162; Golan, *Prehistoric Religion*, 491

Berwick Vampire (Bur-LICK Vam-pire or BER-ik Vam-pire)

Variations: Vampire of Berwick-Upon-Tweed

In 1196, in the village of Berwick (England or Scotland, sources conflict), a rich, corrupt, and overall sinful merchant died of the plague and was not buried in hallowed ground. The merchant returned to the village as a vampiric REVENANT—a smelling, rotting corpse that carried the plague. At night, the undead merchant would run through the streets screaming, "Until my body is burnt, you folk of Berwick shall have no peace!" Dogs would bark in alarm as he would near and nearly half of the village died of the plague. Eventually, the people of the town exhumed the body, severed the limbs and head, and burned the body down to ash.

Source: Aylesworth, *Story of Vampires*, 49–50; McNally, *A Clutch of Vampires*, 40–41; Summers, *Vampire in Europe*, 82; Twitchell, *The Living Dead*, 32

Betail (BAY-tail)

Variations: Betails

The betail is a vampiric spirit from India that possesses and then animates corpses to feed on human blood.

Source: Melton, *Vampire Book*, 322; Stefoff, *Vampires, Zombies, and Shape-Shifters*, 16

Bhayankara (Buy-ANN-car-ah)

The bhayankara is a vampire from Tibetan lore to which blood sacrifices are made. Its name, bhayankara, translates to mean "fear," "terror," or "terrifying." It is not uncommon for temples to make sacrifices and give blood offerings in order to appease these vampiric beings. A single-minded predator, it lives to consume the blood of animals and humans alike.

Source: Carter, *The Vampire in Literature*, 16; Somany, *Shiva and Shakti*, 14; Sundararajan, *Hindu Spirituality*, 470

Bhootums (BOO-pomes)

Variation: Bhut, BHUTA, Bhuts, Bhúts, Bhutu

A type of INCUBUS from India, the bhootums is a vampiric spirit that copulates with Hindu women. It can be driven off with a medium- or high-level MECARU CEREMONY, depending on the spirit's strength.

Source: Masters, *Eros and Evil*, 181; Rodrigues, *The Complete Hindoo Pantheon*, 27; Sugden, *The Gospel Among Our Hindu Neighbours*, 91

Bhuta (BOO-ta)

Variations: Brahmaparusha

A vampiric spirit from India, a bhuta ("bad nature spirit") is created when a person who has a physical deformity dies or when a person dies before their proper time, such as in suicide. It is described as looking like a shadow or a flickering light and has the supernatural ability to possess a corpse. Once it has a body, the bhuta spreads sickness and disease. It is also able to shape-shift into a bat or an owl.

Although the bhuta feeds primarily on human corpses, it gets the occasional craving for milk. When this happens, the vampire is known to attack infants who have recently been fed.

Typically, this species of vampire is found in cemeteries, but there are occasions of a bhuta being sighted in places that would have interested it back when it was a living person. For instance, if the body of the person that the bhuta possesses was an active alcoholic at the time of his death, the vampire may be spotted frequenting bars. No matter what area the bhuta haunts, its presence will permeate the area and people will experience an uncomfortable feeling there; it may even be strong enough to keep animals away. If a MECARU CEREMONY is celebrated every 15 days to honor and show respect to the bhuta, then it will not attack anyone and will find a way to be at peace with its environment.

Considered to be a companion of the Shiva, the bhuta casts no shadow, cannot stand on the ground, and is so susceptible to the smell of burning turmeric; if it is in its presence for too long, the vampire will dissipate.

Small shrines called bhandara can be found throughout India, especially in regions where the bhuta are revered. These shrines are places of worship and sacrifices are left there to placate the vampires. There is no specific design that the shrine must have, but there is always a cradle or some similar device that allows the bhuta to rest in it so that it does not touch the ground, as the earth is considered to be sacred.

Source: Crooke, *Popular Religion and Folk-lore*, 243; Encyclopedia Americana Corp, *Encyclopedia Americana*, 609; Folklore, *Folklore Society of Great Britain*, vol. 4, 217–18; Saletore, *Indian Witchcraft*, 99–105

Bibi (Bee-BEE)

One day a year the Gypsy tribes of the Balkans pay honor to a vampirelike being they call bibi ("aunt"). It is described as a tall, thin, and barefoot woman wearing a red dress and accompanied by two small girls. Some sources also include two white lambs to its entourage. An unforgiving being propelled by vengeance, the bibi visits homes at random. If invited inside, it will bless the home with good fortune; however, if it is turned away, the inhabitants of the house will fall ill with cholera. If there are children in the home, it will strangle them to death, but their bodies will show no signs of attack.

Source: Crowe, *History of the Gypsies of Eastern Europe and Russia*, 212, 214; Guile, *Complete Vampire Companion*, 8; Pearson, *National Minorities in Eastern Europe*, 204

Biloko

In the Democratic Republic of the Congo there is a vampiric creature called a biloko. A hairless humanoid, grass grows on its body and it uses leaves as clothing. This is possibly why its name translates to probably mean "food." It is described as having long, sharp claws, piercing eyes, and a snoutlike nose.

The biloko has a most unusual way of hunting—from a hiding place it rings a magical bell that can put a person to sleep and then it opens its mouth up wide enough to swallow its prey whole. With the use of its bell, the biloko is often appointed as a guardian of hidden treasure. It lives in the deepest parts of the rain forest in the hollows of trees. Fortunately, amulets and fetishes can be made that will protect the wearer.

Source: Chopra, *Dictionary of Mythology*, 53; Knappert, *Bantu Myths and Other Tales*, 142; Knappert, *Myths and Legends of the Congo*, 130

Bilu (BI-lou)

A vampiric demon from Burma, the bilu ("blue") is particularly difficult to detect because it looks exactly like a human, except on closer inspection it has blood-red eyes and casts no shadow. A highly skilled predator with enormous teeth, its very touch is corrosive.

Source: Balfour, *Cyclopædia of India and of Eastern and Southern Asia*, 362; DeCaroli, *Haunting the Buddha*, 171; Seekins, *Historical Dictionary of Burma*, 110; Spiro, *Burmese Supernaturalism*, 44

The Black Veil

Variations: The 13 Rules of the Community

The Black Veil is a sort of ethical code that can aid the moral compass of those who choose to live the vampiric lifestyle. It was originally written by Father Sebastian Todd for the Sanguinarian crowd and appeared in the 1998–99 edition of the *Vampyre Almanac*. It read as follows: "The central philosophy of the 'Black Veil' revolves around (1) hospitality (2) unity of the family (3) prevention of negative media exploitation and fundamentalist attacks (4) maintaining the mystique of the VAMPYRE aesthetic (5) inspiring chivalry and honor."

There are some people who feel that the Black Veil is a strict code that must be followed and there are those who feel that it is merely a set of guidelines. The number of the ideals and what they are have changed numerous times and vary by region.

Source: Belanger, *Sacred Hunger*, 10; Laderman, *Religion and American Cultures*, 281; Russo, *Vampire Nation*, 183; Varrin, *A Guide to New York's Fetish Underground*, 206–7

Blackthorn (Black-thorn)

Variations: Draighean, Mother of the Wood, *Prunus spinosa*, sloe, wild plum, wishing thorn

The blackthorn shrub, with its stiff black branches, has long been associated with the crown of thorns worn by Christ. Blackthorn grows in clusters, making thick, impenetrable thickets, with each individual shrub reaching a height of 15 feet. The short, lateral thorns that cover the branches are so strong and sharp that they can penetrate animal hide as well as virtually any man-made fabric. Blackthorn has long been considered a magical plant and offers protection against psychic and vampire attacks, as its branches make effective stakes. Folklore says that placing blackthorn branches over the grave of a vampire prevents it from rising from its grave.

Source: Gypsy Lore Society, *Journal of the Gypsy Lore Society*, 127; Hastings, *Encyclopaedia of Religion and Ethics*, 590; Perkowski, *Vampires of the Slavs*, 176

Bleiz-Garv (BLAZE-Gar-IF)

In the Breton region of France it is believed that when a werewolf dies, it will rise up as a vampire. Bleiz-garv means "cruel wolf."

Source: MacKillop, *Dictionary of Celtic Mythology*, 38; Ritson, *Ancient Engleish Metrical Romanceës*, 331; Rose, *Giants, Monsters, and Dragons*, 393; Summers, *Werewolf in Lore and Legend*, 11

Bloedzuiger (BLOWED-zweeg-er)

This is a word used in Holland to describe a vampire. From the Dutch language, it translates to mean "bloodsucker" or "leech."

Source: Jockin-La Bastide, *Cassell's English-Dutch, Dutch-English Dictionary*, 567; Maberry, *Vampire Universe*, 46

Blood Dogs

Variations: Scots Hound

In northern England blood dogs appear the day after a battle has occurred. They dig into the ground in order to drink up the blood that has pooled there. Described as being massive, gray hounds with red eyes, their panting breath is hot enough to scorch the earth. In some older versions, they are said to look like humans with the face of a dog. Both accounts agree that the blood dogs leave no mark upon the ground regardless of the terrain and in spite of their weight. In Scotland blood dogs are believed to be the ghosts of Bonnie Prince Charlie's (Prince Charles Edward Stewart, or Charles III) hunting hounds and feed exclusively off English blood.

Source: Hasluck, *Unwritten Law in Albania*, 256; Luther, *Works of Martin Luther*, 92; Maberry, *Vampire Universe*, 46

Bloodsucker

This is a word used in English-speaking countries to describe a vampire.

Source: Cassidy, *Dictionary of American Regional English*, 290; Jones, *On the Nightmare*, 98; Ogilvie, *Imperial Dictionary of the English Language*, 539

Bluatsauger (BLAUT-sauger)

Variations: BLUT AUSSAUGER, Blutsauger

Possibly originating in the Bosnia-Herzegovina region, the bluatsauger ("bloodsucker") is now one of the vampires that hunt throughout Southern Germany and Bavaria (see GERMAN VAMPIRES). It has no skeleton, but rather extremely large eyes and a body covered with HAIR. It has many of the typical vampiric traits in that it hunts for its human prey at night and is repelled by GARLIC. However, it has the most unique method of creating more of its own kind. The bluatsauger carries a handful of dirt from its tomb in a tightly clenched fist so that when it finds someone that it wishes to convert, it force-feeds them the dirt. Should the person actually consume it, they will be transformed into this species of vampire.

Source: Bryant, *Handbook of Death*, 99; Bunson, *Vampire Encyclopedia*, 30, 107

Blut Aussauger (BLOOT AUS-ah-gr)

Variations: Blutsauger, BLUATSAUGER, Blut-Sauger, Nachtzutzler, Totbeißer

A vampiric REVENANT, the blut aussauger ("drinker of blood") comes from the folklore in the countries of Bavaria, Bosnia, and Germany. Although similar to the BLUATSAUGER in some respects, this vampire differs in enough ways that it is clearly a separate species (although they may share a common ancestor).

Like the bluatsauger, the blut aussauger can transform a person into a vampire by force-feeding or tricking someone into eating dirt from its grave. However, a person could also become this type of vampire if he eats meat from an animal that a wolf killed, commits suicide, dies unbaptized, dies a witch, leads an immoral life, or if a nun walks over his grave.

With pale, waxy skin and large eyes, and being slightly hairier than the average person, the blut aussauger leaves its grave every night in search of human blood to consume (see HAIR). Combined with its supernatural strength and the fact it has no skeletal system to hinder the movements of its body, a blut aussauger can attack from nearly any location or angle. It can also shape-shift into a bat, dog, rat, snake, and wolf.

Repelled by GARLIC and sunlight alike, as one may expect, the blut aussauger has the curious fear of black dogs that have eyes drawn in white paint on the top of their heads. Smearing GAR-

LIC paste or hanging HAWTHORN on the windows will bar the vampire from entering, but planting hawthorn around the house will keep it off the property altogether.

GARLIC plays a heavy role in the destruction of this vampire. If someone can force-feed or trick it into eating GARLIC, the blut aussauger will be weakened enough to allow him to stake it through the heart. Then, GARLIC and holy water must be put in its grave while burning incense. Long-term exposure to direct sunlight will also destroy it, as long as GARLIC is placed in the mouth of the remains.

Source: Dundes, Vampire Casebook, 10–11; McNally, In Search of Dracula, 117; Petzoldt, Demons, 161; Summers, Vampire: His Kith and Kin, 315

Boboaña (Bo-BO-ana)

Boboaña is the Romanian word for "female vampire."

Source: Cremene, Mythology of the Vampires of Romania

Bobon (Bo-BON)

Bobon is the word used when referring to a male vampire in Romania.

Source: Cremene, Mythology of the Vampires of Romania

Bockshexe (BOX-hex)

The bockshexe is a male, vampiric demon from Germany (see GERMAN VAMPIRES). Essentially an ALP, it can shape-shift into a goat.

Source: Meyer, Mythologie der Germanen, 505

Bocksmarte (BOX-mert)

Variations: ALP

The bocksmarte is a male, vampiric demon from Germany (see GERMAN VAMPIRES). Essentially it is an ALP.

Source: Meyer, Mythologie der Germanen, 134

Boginki (Bow-GIN-key)

This is a vampiric demon from Poland. Found near riverbanks, the boginki ("little princess") is rather nymphlike in appearance. Created by the original deities of life that prey on the sky gods, the boginki attacks mothers with newborn babies, stealing the children to eat and replacing them with a type of evil changeling called an Odmience ("the changed one"). Making regular ritualistic sacrifices to it will prevent it from attacking.

Source: Georgieva, Bulgarian Mythology, 103; Icon Group International, Sacrificing, 232; Leary, Wisconsin Folklore, 445; Thomas, Polish Peasant in Europe and America, 238

Bori

Variations: Iskoki

In northwest Nigeria, Africa, the Hausa people tell tales of a type of vampiric nature spirit called bori. Described as looking like a human with hoofed feet or no head, the bori is not always an evil being. Occasionally it will bless a person with good luck but can as easily curse a person by sending them diseases.

Although the bori can shape-shift into a python, it oftentimes shape-shifts into a friend or family member of its intended prey in order to lure them into a trap. If ever people are unsure as to whether they have in fact coincidently met someone they know deep in the jungle, it is advised to look at his footprint. The tracks that a bori makes when it is in human guise are those of a rooster. Should a person be tricked or ambushed, his chances of survival are excellent, as it seldom kills those it feeds upon, choosing to drain away just enough life essence in order to survive. These victims often have a dreamy look upon their faces and behave in a trancelike fashion.

If someone can manage to learn a bori's true name, it will become bound to him and must do his bidding. However, should its owner ever accidently burn it, even with the stray embers from a cigarette, the bori will be set free from its magical enslavement. Immediately upon gaining its freedom, it will turn on its former master with a savage rage, killing him and his entire family if it can.

Bori can also possess a person, although to what ends, no one is sure. The Hausa believe that when a woman is possessed, anything she may do or say—even if she speaks out against her husband or the government—cannot be held against her.

Source: Hill, Rural Hausa, 212–13; Tremearne, Ban of the Bori, 382; Tremearne, The Tailed Head-Hunters of Nigeria, 254

Bottling (BOT-ul-ling)

Variations: Eikon Bottle

Bottling is a process by which some types of vampire hunters, like the DHAMPIRE of Bulgaria, capture and then destroy a vampire, such as the GROBNIK and the UBOR. The construction of the device is simple enough: a bottle filled with a small amount of blood, which will later be corked and sealed with wax and the image of a saint.

The bottle is left where the vampire will be able to smell the blood, and wanting to take advantage of such an easy meal, it shape-shifts into its invisible form and enters into the bottle. If the vampire is hesitant to enter, it can be driven into the bottle by the hunter who would use a series of holy relics to herd it. Once the vampire is in the bottle, the hunter corks it and, using wax, attaches a picture of a saint to it. As soon as the seal is made, the bottle, along with the vampire trapped within, is then thrown into a raging fire with enough force to break the glass and thereby destroy the vampire.

Naturally this method is only useable on certain types of vampires, specifically those who can become invisible or, at the very least, shape-shift into smoke. Otherwise, the hunter himself would have to be able to see an invisible vampire by some means.

Source: Summers, *Vampire: His Kith and Kin*, 186–87, 249; Tannahill, *Flesh and Blood*, 124; Wolf, *Dracula: Connoisseur's Guide*, 24

Bouda (Bow-DA)

A LIVING VAMPIRE found in Ethiopia, Morocco, and Tanzania, the bouda also uses its magical ability to shape-shift into a hyena. When it is transformed into its animal form, the bouda looks exactly like any other hyena save for the magical charm it wears. If, while in this animal form, the bouda loses its charm, it will be unable to return to human form and will eventually become a hyena.

Boudas are also highly skilled in the art of making magical amulets and charms. They are often at work at their forges, making magical amulets that will better focus or channel their powers and shape-shifting abilities.

Source: Folklore Society, *Folklore*, vol. 1, 273; Thompson, *Semitic Magic*, 103; Wood, *Natural History of Man*, 741; Wood, *Uncivilized Races of Men*, 666

Brahmaparush (BRAM-ah-pa-rosh)

Variation: Brahmaparus, Brahmaparusha, Brahmeparush, Bramaparush

A particularly cruel vampire from India, the brahmaparush has a very specific and highly ritualized means of killing its victims, usually travelers. It is described as a floating head with intestines hanging down from the neck and carrying a drinking cup made from a human skull in the tangle of its entrails. Once it has captured a person, the brahmaparush begins the killing ritual by first nibbling a small hole in the person's head to drink up their blood as it trickles out. Then it gnaws a section of skull away and begins to slurp up the brains, carefully keeping the person alive for as long as possible. Next, it does a bizarre dance, lashing at the corpse and eventually entangling itself in the corpse's intestines. Finally, the brahmaparush will play in the offal and has even been known to make a turban out of the viscera and wear it on its head.

Source: Belanger, *Sacred Hunger*, 113; Guiley, *Complete Vampire Companion*

Bram Stoker's *Dracula*

Bram Stoker's fictional Dracula, the vampiric count from Transylvania, was hardly the first vampire story ever written, but it is beyond a doubt the grandfather of modern vampire literature in English-speaking countries, as well as a source for innumerable vampire stories that followed in its wave of success. Although Stoker researched the myths of the vampire, as an author he justifiably used artistic license to create his own vampire, one that would be more suitable and terrifying to his audience.

In regards to species, Dracula was not any one particular type of vampire, but a conglomeration of several different types, many of which were not even native to the part of the world that the vampire comes from.

In the novel, for the few pages that he actually appears in it, Dracula is described as a tall, pale man, sporting a thick, white Victorian moustache. He has a very full and substantial head of HAIR, bushy eyebrows, and even HAIR on the palm of his hands. His teeth are caninelike, his fingernails overly long, and his beautiful blue eyes turn red whenever he grows angry. Dressed in black, he is initially old when first encountered in the book; however, as the story progresses, he becomes increasingly younger looking.

The count has an array of vampiric abilities, such as weather control; shape-shifting into a bat, dog, and wolf; and "control over the meaner things," such as bats, foxes, owls, rats, and wolves. He can also procreate his species in that he can create other vampires, such as his vampiric brides. Although it is not truly an "ability," it is a misconception that Count Dracula would shrivel up and die if exposed to sunlight. This is not true; daylight has no such ill effect on the Count.

Like one might expect, holy items have an adverse effect on Dracula as they do with many species of mythical vampires, items such as rosary beads with a CRUCIFIX, and the EUCHARISTIC WAFER. Many types of vampires must return to their graves or some dark place in which to spend their daylight hours. This is not the case for Dracula, who is unaffected in that respect by sunlight, but yet, he is still linked to his grave. The Count must lie in rest in his native soil, and so travels with COFFINS lined with Transylvanian soil. Dracula also requires an invitation to enter someone's home, somewhat reminiscent of the GREEK VAMPIRE BARABARLAKOS, if not quite as literal. Of all the vampires that the various histories and mythologies have offered us, only one lore speaks of any type of vampire that casts no reflection in a mirror—the ZEMU from the Moldavia region of Romania. This distinct and unique disability is so obscure, compounded with the fact that the ZEMU is such a little-known species of vampire, it causes one to wonder if it is at all possible that Stoker heard of this tale or if it was a creation by the author himself.

It is a popular misconception that at the novel's end Count Dracula was staked through the heart with a nicely shaped sliver of wood. The truth is that Dracula was simultaneously beheaded by Jonathan Harker and stabbed in the heart with a bowie knife by Quincey P. Morris.

Source: Eighteen-Bisang, *Bram Stoker's Notes for Dracula*; Leatherdale, *Dracula: The Novel and the Legend*; Senf, *Science and Social Science*; Stoker, *Dracula*

El Broosha (EL BROO-sha)

In the Judeo-Christian folklore of Spain, el broosha is a vampiric demon that appears as a large black cat. By night, it hunts for infants to drain dry of their blood.

Source: Conybeare, *Jewish Quarterly*, xi, 30; Howey, *Cat in Magic*, 173; Rose, *Giants, Monsters, and Dragons*, 382; Thompson, *Semitic Magic*, 42

Broucolaque, Ancient (BROW-co-look)

Variations: Broncolakas, Broucolaca, Broucolacchi, Broucolacco, Broucolokas, Broucoloques, Broukolakes, Brukulaco, Brukolak, Burcolakas, Drakaena, Drakos, Mulo, TIMPANITA, Tumpaniaïoi, VRYKOLAKA

The stories of ancient Greece are a place alive with heroes and the tales of their adventures (see GREEK VAMPIRES). When a hero or brigand is so intent on staying alive, they will return as a vampiric REVENANT called a broucolaque. Condemned to wander the world as an undead being, this bloodthirsty creature is gluttonous in its blood-drinking needs and revels in its atrocities (see UNDEATH). For hundreds of years this belief was held as a steadfast truth. In fact, it was so ingrained in Greek society that even the Catholic Church did not try to dissuade its belief, but rather added onto the mythology. The Church promised protection to its followers if they made offerings to the Church and paid to have masses

said for the broucolaque on the anniversary of his death. Over the centuries the broucolaque changed and evolved in order to remain culturally comprehensible to the people who feared it.

Source: Guiley, *Complete Vampire Companion*, 55; Masters, *Natural History of the Vampire*, 169; Stewart, *Romantic Movement*, 137; Voltaire, *Philosophical Dictionary*, 560–61

Broucolaque, Modern (BROW-co-look)

Variations: Broncolakas, Broucolaca, Broucolacchi, Broucolacco, Broucolokas, Broucoloques, Broukolakes, Brukulaco, Brukolak, Burcolakas, Drakaena, Drakos, Mulo, TIMPANITA, Tumpaniaïoi, VRYKOLAKA

The broucolaque of today is the end result of the social evolution from the broucolaque of ancient times. This modern-day vampiric REVENANT rises from the grave of particularly evil individuals, such as those who have been excommunicated from the Church.

Like most other GREEK VAMPIRES, the broucolaque is described as looking like the person it did in life but with its skin drawn tightly over its body, so tight in fact that when it is slapped, it sounds like a drum (see GREEK VAMPIRES). Also like other Greek vampires, it will knock on the doors of those it knew in life, trying to lure them out so that it can attack them, draining them of their blood. The modern broucolaque is something of a stalker, for if it cannot get an answer at a person's home, it will then go to the field where he works or try to intercept him on the way to work. If it should meet a person during its travels, it will ask him a question. Should that person answer, he will die of some means the next day.

Perhaps in an attempt to appeal to the minds of a more modern people, the broucolaque is able to rise from its grave without disturbing the ground.

Source: Encyclopedia Americana, vol. 6, 504–5; Whitelaw, *Popular Encyclopedia*, 778

Brown, Mercy

First reported in 1892 by *The Providence Journal Newspaper*, this was the highly editorialized story of the alleged vampiric REVENANT known as Ms. Mercy Lena Brown of Exeter, Rhode Island. This story broke a full four years before Bram Stoker's novel, *Dracula*, was even published.

Mercy Brown had consumption (pulmonary tuberculosis), just like her mother, Mary, who had already died of the disease, and her sister, Mary Olive, who died in 1888. In 1890 Mercy's brother, Edwin, began to grow sick, and after watching her family grow ill and die all around her, Mercy herself began to show signs of the illness in 1891. Mercy lost her strength, her skin grew pale, and she stopped eating. At night her condition always seemed to worsen. From time to time in the morning she would awaken with traces of blood on her mouth and bedsheets, and panting heavily. Pale, thin, and half dead with blood on her lips, 19-year-old Mercy must have looked like a vampire even before she died on January 17, 1892.

Mercy's father, George, after having lost a wife and two daughters in such a short period of time, was seriously concerned about the health and well-being of his only son and last remaining family member, Edwin, whose health had been failing for so long.

On March 17, 1892, George led a mob of fellow farmers and townsfolk to the Brown family's graves, convinced that one of the deceased had to be a vampire and was the cause for all the pain and suffering that he and his son had endured. Both Mary and Mary Olive's bodies had decomposed to the mob's approval. However, when Mercy's body was revealed, it was in their opinion that she was too well preserved for the length of time she had been deceased. Mercy's body was then cut open and it was noted that her liver and heart were both full of blood. Deciding that Mercy had to be the vampire, her heart was removed rendered down to ash, then given to Edwin to consume in hopes that it would cure him of the curse that his sister had laid upon him. Sadly, Edwin died two months later.

Source: Bell, *Food for the Dead;* Belanger, *World's Most Haunted Places,* 121–25; Brennan, *Ghosts of Newport,* 113–16; Stefoff, *Vampires, Zombies, and Shape-Shifters,* 17

Broxa (BEHROXAH)

Variation: Broxo, BRUJA, Bruxa, Bruxsa

In Jewish folklore, the broxa was a bird that suckled goats for their milk. It has been speculated that over time the broxa bird evolved into the broxa VAMPIRIC WITCH of medieval Portugal.

In the Portuguese lore, the broxa was a vampiric, demonic witch that looked like a typical human being. Created through witchcraft, the broxa flies through the night sky in search of people to attack and drain dry of the blood it needs to survive. It has an array of abilities that one might suspect a typical witch to have, such as divination, hypnotism, reading minds, and shape-shifting, but the demonic broxa is impossible to kill no matter what form it assumes.

Source: Gaster, *Myth, Legend, and Custom,* 580; Masters, *Eros and Evil,* 181; Monaghan, *Women in Myth,* 51; Trachtenberg, *Jewish Magic,* 43

Brucolaco (BRUKE-oh-lock-oh)

Variations: Broucalaque, Brucolak, Bruculaco, BRUCULACAS, TIMPANITA

Strictly from the lore of the Epirus and Thessaly regions of Greece, this vampire would seem to answer the age-old question of "Can a werewolf be a vampire?" (See GREEK VAMPIRES.)

In life, the person accused of being a brucolaco can fall into a state of being where all the muscles in his body will become rigid and remain in a fixed position. This person will show no reaction to painful stimuli and the limbs are said to feel "waxy." Today we know this to be a nervous condition called catalepsy that is caused by disorders such as epilepsy or Parkinson's disease. However, it was once honestly believed that this was a curse sent by God. It was said that while a person was in such a state, a wolf spirit left his body and went on the hunt, seeking human flesh and blood. When the person with the catalepsy eventually died, or when a person who was excommunicated by the Church died, he would then rise up as a vampiric REVENANT. It was described looking the way many GREEK VAMPIRES do, with its skin pulled so tightly over its body that it sounded like a drum when slapped. At night, it lets loose with a piercing cry, akin to the wail of the BANSHEE. Whoever answers its call the brucolaco will then kill with the plague.

Fortunately, the vampire can be destroyed if the Church can be convinced to recant the excommunication. If this is not possible, than the brucolaco must first be captured and beheaded. Then the head must be boiled in wine. Finally, it and the body must be rendered to ash. Because it was so firmly believed that a werewolf would become a vampire upon death, the Church made it common practice to burn at the stake anyone who was convicted of being a brucolaco in the attempt to prevent vampiric resurrection. Because of this canon, over 30,000 people were burned as werewolves during the Inquisition.

Source: Calmet, *Dissertation sur les apparitions,* 237; Riccardo, *Vampires Unearthed,* 5; Volta, *Vampire,* 148

Bruculacas

A vampiric REVENANT from the Greek Isles, the bruculacas looks like a corpse with tightly drawn, red skin (see GREEK VAMPIRES). A foul-smelling and filthy creature, its body cavity is filled with slime and excrement, spreading the plague wherever it goes. It preys on humans for their blood.

Source: Maberry, *Vampire Universe,* 57

Bruja (BREW-ha)

Variations: Brujavampyre, Bruxa, Bruxae, Bruxas, Cucubuth, Jorguinas, Xorguinae

In Spain there is a living VAMPIRIC WITCH known as a bruja ("witch"). By day she is a beautiful woman living an ordinary life (see LIVING VAMPIRE), but by night, through the use of her magic, she hunts for children and lonely travelers to attack and drain of blood. The bruja is most powerful between the hours of midnight and 2 A.M. She also regularly meets with others of her kind every Tuesday and Friday at a predetermined crossroad. Once gathered together, they will worship the devil and develop their various evil powers such as use of the evil eye ("mal occhio") and shape-shifting into various animals like ants, doves, ducks, geese, and rats.

Before the introduction of Christianity to Portugal, the bruja could be warded off with iron. Keeping some nails under a child's bed or a pair of scissors in a pocket was protection enough. After the arrival of Christianity, talismans of protection against the evil eye could be purchased. There were also various incantations that could be recited as well, but the simplest means of protection was to regularly consume GARLIC. Some folks even went as far as to sew GARLIC into their clothes.

Should a child actually survive an attack from a bruja, the mother must boil the infant's clothes and jab them with sharp iron instruments. By doing so, she is actually inflicting harm upon the witch, ensuring that she will leave her child alone, but the retaliatory assault will not kill her. There is no known method of destruction for a bruja.

There are a few regional bits of lore that tie the bruja with lycanthropy and the demonic SUCCUBUS, but that is most likely due to the witch's shape-changing ability and her beauty.

If the witch is a male, then it is called a brujo. Like his female counterpart, he can cause the evil eye but shape-shifts into a barn owl, cat, coyote, or turkey. He is also something of a supernatural matchmaker, causing one person to fall madly in love with any other. Only by having a priest offer up prayers and masses can a victim of a brujo be saved.

Source: Bryant, *Handbook of Death,* 99; Kanellos, *Handbook of Hispanic Cultures,* 228; Minnis, *Chile,* 276–77; Ramos, *The Aswang Syncrasy,* 5; Shoumatoff, *Legends of the American Desert,* 234

Buau (BWOW)

Variations: Buo

The Dayak people of Borneo have a vampiric spirit that they fear called a buau. Created when an enemy of theirs is slain in battle, the spirit returns as a warrior ghost to haunt those who caused its death, attack them, and drink their blood.

Source: Roth, *The Natives of Sarawak,* 167; Saunders, *Borneo Folktales and Legends,* 67–68; Wood, *Uncivilized Races of Men,* 1157

Bucolacs

On the archipelago of Santorini, Greece, there exists a species of vampire known as bucolacs. It appears as a ghostlike being and enters into the body of a recently deceased person. Then, animating the corpse, it leaves its grave at night to go into the city. It picks houses at random, knocking upon the doors and calling out to the people who live within. If anyone opens the door or answers the call of the bucolacs, they will die within two days' time. It is similar to many other species of GREEK VAMPIRES, especially the VRYKOLAKA.

Source: Theosophical Society, *Theosophist,* vol. 36, 92; Wright, *Book of Vampires,* 38

Bullet (Bull-it)

Variations: Sacred Bullet, Silver Bullet

Romanian Gypsies believe that firing a bullet into the ground and penetrating the COFFIN is a legitimate way to kill the vampire that lies within. Bram Stoker mentioned this method of vampiric destruction in his novel *Dracula*; however, he added to the mythology to further enhance the flavor of his fictionalized story. In Stoker's account, it was claimed that the bullet must be made of silver and was referred to by the descriptive and somewhat creative name "sacred bullet." (See BRAM STOKER'S *DRACULA.*)

Source: Cavendish, *Man, Myth and Magic,* 2926; Day, *Myths and Metaphors,* 15; Stuart, *Stage Blood,* 150

Burach-Bhaoi (BUICK BOY-ah)

Variations: Burach, Burach Bhadi, Wizard's Shackle

In the western Highlands of Scotland there lives a type of vampiric fay that resembles an eel with nine eyes. It lives in bodies of water near roadways, although there have been sightings of it in Badenoch, Loch Tummel, and some streams in Argyll.

The burach-bhaoi lies in wait for a horse, with or without a rider, to pass near enough by so that it can strike out, wrapping itself around the animal's feet. Then it pulls tight, dragging the horse, rider and all, into the water, where it will drown its prey before draining it dry of blood.

Source: Barber, *Dictionary of Fabulous Beasts*, 31; Covey, *Beasts*, 182; Dekirk, *A Wizard's Bestiary*, 26; Rose, *Giants, Monsters, and Dragons*, 62; Spence, *Magic Arts in Celtic Britain*, 95

Bushyasta

Variations: Buyasta

In the Zoroastrian belief, the bushyasta is a demonic ENERGY VAMPIRE that feeds off a person's efficiency and physical energy. By doing this, the bushyasta leaves its victims lethargic and listless, enabling them to neglect their religious duties and obligations.

Source: Alexander, *Mythology of All Races*, 261; Anonymous, *Zend Avesta*, 54, 216, 264–65; Jobes, *Dictionary of Mythology*, 262

Caballi (Cab-ALI)

Variations: Cabales

This is a vampiric being of the astral plane that preys on other astral beings, the occasional human passing through the astral plane, and sexually driven mediums (see ASTRAL VAMPIRE). The caballi, similar to the INCUBUS and SUCCUBUS, seeks out those who share its passion for satisfying its voracious needs, latching on to those humans and utilizing their bodies during sexual activity.

These beings are created when a man dies before it is his natural time to do so. His soul travels to the astral plane, retaining its intellect and a desire to do nothing more that interact with the world again. For this purpose a caballi will possess a psychic medium so that for a little while at least it will have some sense of sensation. Fortunately, the caballi in this instance will only remain as such until the day arrives that it would have died naturally.

Source: Drury, *Dictionary of the Esoteric*, 40; Gaynor, *Dictionary of Mysticism*, 31; Masters, *Eros and Evil*, 181; Rulandus, *Lexicon of Alchemy*, 77

Cai Cai Filu (KY KY FEE-loo)

The Mapuche people of Chile have a rich folklore that is reflected in their religion. Within its pantheon is an immortal, godlike, vampiric leviathan named Cai Cai Filu. Its natural form is that of a tsunami or tidal wave, but it can shapeshift into an ox and a horse. Living on the bottom of the ocean, it is constantly, ravenously hungry for human flesh and blood. Regular sacrificial offerings made to this monster can stave off its attack—a tidal wave crashing down upon the Mapuche.

Cai Cai Filu is one of the old gods, worshipped before the introduction of Christianity. After the Mapuche began to meld this new religion with their traditional one, changes had to be made. Cai Cai Filu was made into a demon by early missionaries and was described as a consumer of sinners.

Source: Benjamins, *Death of 4 European Gods*, 19; Maccoby, *A Pariah People*, 192; Tierney, *The Highest Alter*, 132

Callicantzaro (Cal-ah-KIN-zaro)

Variations: Kalikandsaros, Kallicantzaros, KALLIKANTZAROS, Kapaconcolos, Karaconcolos

The callicantzaro is different from the other vampires that hunt the Greek islands, most obviously in its method of creation (see GREEK VAMPIRES). It does not matter how good a life someone lived or even if he was a devout Christian—all that matters is when he was born. Any child who had the misfortune of being born between Christmas Day (December 25) and the Feast of the Twelfth Night (January 5) will rise from its grave as a callicantzaro when it eventually dies. These children are called "Feast Blasted" and are pitied by all who know the circumstances of their birth. The only method of saving the child of its UNDEATH fate is to hold the newborn's feet over a fire until its toenails burn and blacken. If this is not done, there is no chance of later salvation.

If the child was not saved from its fate and returns after death as a callicantzaro, it can only survive in our world on the days between Christmas and either New Year's Day (January 1) or the Feast of the Epiphany (January 6). It is an old belief that the callicantzaro can only live on earth these few days of the year, going back to the times of antiquity. With that in mind, it seems obvious that these dates are Christianized and the original times that the vampire would have been allowed back to roam the earth was probably something along the lines of from winter solstice to the next full moon.

Nevertheless, when the callicantzaro does return, it is now a horrific creature, looking nothing like the other numerous vampires that roam the Greek countrysides. Half human and half animal, it has a black face, red eyes, very long ears, clawed hands, and sharp teeth. The first time that it returns it will seek out its surviving family members, ripping them apart, limb from limb, with its clawed hands. Although blood drinking is not a requirement for its survival, that is something the callicantzaro most certainly revels in. As soon as its family members are slain, it will move on to targets of opportunity.

As the time for it to return to its own dimension draws near, the male callicantzaro will try to capture a woman to take back to its home plane with it. Its goal is to have children by this woman, forcibly if necessary. The offspring of this union will be born callicantzaro. When not seeing to its parental duties, it sleeps in caves by day and terrorizes villages by night.

Source: Barber, *Dictionary of Fabulous Beasts*, 34; Bryant, *Handbook of Death*, 99; Georgieva, *Bulgarian Mythology*, 90; Jackson-Laufer, *Encyclopedia of Traditional Epics*, 321; Senn, *Were-wolf and Vampire in Romania*, 30

Camazotz (CAM-ah-zots)

Variations: Cama-Zotz, H'ik'al, Sotz, Zotz, Zotzilaha Chimalman

Camazotz, a greatly feared blood drinker, was the vampiric bat god of the ancient Mayan people of Central America, the Quiche Maya of Guatemala around 100 B.C., and the Zapotec Indians of Oaxaca, Mexico. His name translates in a number of befitting nomenclatures, such as "black man," "death bat," "neckcutter," "the sudden bloodletter" and "Snatch Bat." In art he is depicted as a large man-bat creature sporting a knife in one hand and a human sacrifice in the other.

In chapter three of the *Popol Vuh*, the Mayan's sacred book, it was Camazotz who slew the first race of man; in chapter ten it was he who beheaded the hero Hunahpú. Ultimately, Camazotz was defeated in the battle between the gods and man.

Each year, the planting of the corn is timed with Camazotz's descent into Xilbalba, the Mayan equivalent of hell. He is feared by the Zotzil people of Chiapas, Mexico, to this day.

Source: Allardice, *Myths, Gods and Fantasy*, 50; Nicholson, *Mexican and Central American Mythology*, 37; Spence, *Myths of Mexico and Peru*, 172, 226, 344–45; Stefoff, *Vampires, Zombies, and Shape-Shifters*, 17

Cambion (CAM-bee-in)

Variations: Campion

In post-medieval Europe, belief in INCUBUS and SUCCUBUS attacks were commonly accepted. Naturally, it stands to reason that if a human is having sexual relations with a demon, willfully or not, there is bound to eventually be offspring from such an unholy union. These demonic hybrid progeny were called cambion and for the most part, developed as normally as any other child would. Typically, a child born with a physical defect was suspected of being a demonic half-breed, especially twins. Unfortunately for the poor cambion child, it was not considered to be a living being until it reached the age of seven years. Until that time, it was perfectly acceptable for a witch hunter to kill one without any fear of repercussion whatsoever. A common test that was performed to see if a child were a cambion or not was to have a holy man simply touch it. Being demonic, a cambion would cry out in pain. Naturally, should it survive, a cambion adult was oftentimes prejudiced against because of its lineage.

Incredibly dense and weighing more than it looks like it would, a cambion grows into a tall and well-muscled individual who may have an apparent physical defect of some description. Its nature is to be arrogant, bold, and wicked and will have some sort of supernatural ability; most develop a talent for using magic spells and go on to become sorcerers.

King Arthur's very own Merlin was said to have been a cambion—his mother a nun and his father an INCUBUS. The founding twins of Rome, Remus and Romulus, were also supposed to be cambions, as was Alexander the Great, Caesar Augustus, Martin Luther, Plato, Scipio Africanus, and the father of William the Conqueror. In 1275, a woman by the name of Angela de Labarthe of Toulouse was burned at the stake for giving birth to a child who allegedly had the head of a wolf and a tail that resembled a snake. It was deduced that only an INCUBUS could have fathered such a child as hers, and therefore came from Hell.

Source: Gettings, *Dictionary of Demons*, 65; Kramer, *Malleus Maleficarum*, 26; Spence, *Encyclopaedia of Occultism*, 93; Wedeck, *Dictionary of Spiritualism*, 186

Canchus (Can-CHUS)

Variations: PUMAPMICUC, Rumapmicuc

In ancient Peru there existed a class of devil-worshipers called canchus. They believed that by drinking the blood of children, they would retain their youth and bolster their own life-energy (see ENERGY VAMPIRE). Oftentimes, they would sacrifice the children to the devils that they worshiped.

Source: Florescu, *Dracula: A Biography*, 164; Hickey, *Sex Crimes and Paraphilia*, 123; McNally, *In Search of Dracula*, 117; Trumbull, *Blood Covenant*, 115

Carrickaphouka Castle (Carric-POO-ka Cas-el)

Variations: McCarthy Castle

Today, Carrickaphouka Castle ("the rock of the pooka") in Ireland stands in ruins, but its reputation of being haunted remains. Back in 1601, it was widely believed that a pooka (a type of fairy creature) haunted the grounds. It lived within one of the large boulders that were on the land that was then used to build McCarthy Castle. Like many of the fay, pooka can shape-shift, and this one preferred the forms of an eagle, a large horse, and a wild goat.

After the Battle of Kinsale in 1601, Cormac Mór MacDermot Tadhg McCarthy, Lord of Muskerry, was made High Sheriff of Cork County. The new ruling English were having trouble bringing the defeated Irish lords under control and McCarthy was tasked with the duty of rounding up those who opposed English rule. One of these "rebel lords" was a popular man by the name of James Fitzgerald. He had a very large following, most of whom were displaced nobility themselves. Under the pretense of making peace, the High Sheriff invited Fitzgerald to McCarthy Castle.

The meal that was served to Fitzgerald was poisoned, but death of a rebel was not enough for the High Sheriff, who sought to impress the English. McCarthy had the body drained of blood and then cooked. Much to the horror of his English masters, he then set about the act of cannibalism in front of them, eating the flesh and drinking the blood.

All of Ireland was shocked and outraged at his behavior. His clansmen tried to say that the High Sheriff had been possessed by the pooka. The High Sheriff apparently left for France shortly after the incident and disappeared into obscurity. However, after his death, his spirit returned to his ancestral home, now a demonic and vampiric spirit. The sounds of painful wails and screams of terror are heard at night coming from the ruins. Anyone who walks by the ruins at night will be viciously attacked by unseen, spectral claws that will cut deep enough to draw blood, which is then lapped up. Fresh blood is also often seen on the remnants of the castle's gate.

Source: Cork Historical and Archaeological Society, *Journal*, 135, 145; Curran, *Vampires*, 58–59

Catacano (Cat-ah-CO-no)

Variations: Catacani, Catakano, Kathakano, "The Happy Vampire"

On the Greek isles of Crete and Rhodes there is a vampiric REVENANT that smiles all the time, showing off its teeth. It is known as the catacano (see GREEK VAMPIRES). Strong and fast, it is able to instill trust in its human prey, making it arrogant by nature. The catacano has a singularly unique way of creating more of its own kind—it

spits regurgitated blood on people. Should this sticky and burning discharge hit the intended target, that person will become a vampire.

The catacano can be killed in a number of ways: decapitating and boiling its head in vinegar, trapping it and isolating it behind saltwater (see SALT), or by burning its nails off.

Source: Haining, *Dictionary of Vampires*, 50; Volta, *The Vampire*, 150

Cauchemar (KOSZ-mare)

Variations: Cauquemare, Chauche Vieille, Coche-Mares, Cochomaren, Cochomares, Couchemache, Couchemal, GAUKEMARES, Macouche, "Pressing Demon," Quauquemaire, "Witch-Riding"

Cauchemar is the French word for "nightmare," and it is also the name of this species of vampiric demon or witch.

At night the cauchemar shape-shifts into either an INCUBUS or a SUCCUBUS and slips into the bed of what it perceives to be an evil person. Then it has sexual relations with him, enslaving the person to its will and draining him of some of his life and sexual energy (see ENERGY VAMPIRE). In the morning, the victim will awake with drool descending from either side of his mouth and with evidence of having experienced a nocturnal emission. Other signs include feeling overly tired and suffering leg cramps.

To prevent the cauchemar from attacking, a person can place some SALT under his pillow or dried beans or stones under his bed every night. A broom propped in the corner will offer protection, as will sleeping on one's stomach. Saying prayers before going to bed and keeping religious items in the room will prevent it from entering. If all else fails, one can put screens on the windows.

If the cauchemar cannot be prevented from entering the room and attacking, it is vital that no one ever so much as touches the victim during one of the assaults. To do so can cause the cauchemar to kill the victim as it flees.

Source: *The Living Age*, vol. 4, 495; Mackay, *Gaelic Etymology*, 305; Masters, *Eros and Evil*, 181; Rose, *Spirits, Fairies, Gnomes*, 212

Cel-Rāu (Cell-ROO)

Variation: Concealmentrāu, Ieli, Orgoï, Strigoii

In Romania, people are careful not to say the true name of this vampiric REVENANT aloud. The cel-rāu ("the bad") is easily summoned; as it has amazing hearing, it can hear its name uttered from any distance. The cel-rāu will appear near the person who has said it within moments.

Source: Cremene, *Mythologie du Vampire en Roumanie*

Cercopes

Variations: Kerkopes

Ancient Greeks believed that the twin sons born of Oceanus and Theia were vampiric creatures. Collectively referred to as the Cercopes, meaning the "tailed ones," they were renowned as being liars and thieves. The names of the brothers vary depending on the source—some say that their names were Acmon and Passalus, another claims that their names were Eurybatus and Olus, and a third claims the names were Sillus and Triballus. However, all the sources do agree in that the cercopes' physical appearance is that of short and squat monkeylike beings that lives in the forest. Very fast and particularly dangerous if trapped, the cercopes will use their amazing stealth to creep into the room of a sleeping child, where they will drink blood from the child's arms and legs.

Source: Barber, *Dictionary of Fabulous Beasts*, 37; Hesiod, *Hesiod, the Homeric Hymns, and Homerica*, 153–54, 539; Lurker, *Dictionary of Gods and Goddesses*, 348; Mahaffy, *History of Classical Greek Literature*, 114, 116; Rose, *Giants, Monsters, and Dragons*, 73

Chedipe (CHA-dippy)

Variations: ALVANTIN, CHUREL, Jakhai, Jakhin, Mukhai, Nagulai

In India when a woman dies in an unnatural way, such as in childbirth or by suicide, she may return as a vampiric REVENANT known as a chedipe. Riding upon a tiger at night, the chedipe selects a home and places all of the inhabitants within into a deep sleep. Then it drains the blood from all the men by biting a hole in their big toes. The chedipe, whose name means "prostitute," is associated with a discriminated caste of people known as the *devadasi*, those who work in the sex industry.

Source: Crooke, *Religion and Folklore*, 194; Duprae, *The Vampires*, 61; Riccardo, *Liquid Dreams of Vampires*, 51; Thurston, *Omens and Superstitions*, 261–62

Chesme (Chez m)

The chesme of Turkey is a vampiric fountain spirit that looks like a cat. However, it has the shape-shifting ability to appear as a corpse surrounded by mice. Its name, chesme, is quite appropriate as it translates to mean "fountain cat." Sitting on a rock near a source of water, the vampire sings a sirenlike song that lures men to it. When one answers the call and appears, the chesme will attack and try to drown him by draining him of his life-energy (see ENERGY VAMPIRE).

Source: Byrne, *Unbearable Saki*, 32; Leland, *Gypsy Sorcery and Fortune Telling*, 166; Spence, *Encyclopedia of Occultism*, 160

Chevêche (CHE-vig)

Variations: Chevche, Chevecsch, Chevesche

The chevêche is a VAMPIRIC WITCH from France that preys on little children, drinking their blood.

Source: Wilgowicz, *Le Vampirisme*

Children of Judas

Considered to be the worst of the Bulgarian species of vampires, the Children of Judas is the clan name for a family of vampires alleged to be the direct descendants of Judas Iscariot. All the vampires in this clan have a full head of bright red HAIR just as it is believed Judas had. Found throughout Bulgaria, Romania, and Serbia, when a Child of Judas attacks its victims, it leaves behind a scar that looks like the Roman numeral 30: XXX. The scar is thus shaped to signify the 30 pieces of silver that were given to Judas for his part in betraying Christ to the Romans. Almost exclusive to this species of vampire, its bite is referred to as a kiss.

Source: Masters, *Natural History of the Vampire*, 189; Summers, *Vampire: His Kith and Kin*, 183; Tannahill, *Flesh and Blood*, 122

Ch'ing Shih (Cha-ing SHE)

Variation: Chiang-Shi, Chiang Shih, Ch'iang-Shih, Ch'ing-Shih, Ch'ling Shih, Gaing Shi, "The Hopping Vampire of Asia," Kiang-Kouei, Kiang Shi, Kiang-Shi, Kiangshi, Kouei, Kuang-Shi, Kuang-Shii, Kyonshi, Xianhshi

Known the world over as the "hopping vampire," the mythology specifically regarding the ch'ing shih originates in the lands between Siberia and China. This vampiric REVENANT is created in the typical fashion of most Chinese vampires—when a cat jumps over a corpse, if a person has been cursed to rise as the undead, or if a person has the misfortune of dying far from home and not being returned there for burial (see UNDEATH). No matter how it is created, the ch'ing shih will return with red eyes, curved fingernails, serrated teeth, and pale GREEN-white skin that gives off a phosphorescent glow. As it ages, its HAIR continues to grow and changes from whatever its current color is to pure white. When it has a long and full mane of HAIR, it is considered physically matured. The ch'ing shih feeds off the blood of men, but with its voracious sexual appetite it is well known to first rape and then devour the bodies of women.

After it rises from the dead as a vampire, the ch'ing shih will have the ability to shape-shift into a CORPSE CANDLE. However, once it reaches maturity, it will have the ability to fly of its own accord, track its prey by scent, and shape-shift into the form of a wolf. Its breath is so foul that it can kill a person if it exhales directly on someone.

The ch'ing shih is blind and it has difficulty crossing running water. Its power is derived from the moon, so during the day and on moonless nights it stays in its underground dwelling. Although it is afraid of thunder and loud noises, the only thing it is truly fearful of is the White Emperor, to whose court it must pay homage.

To destroy an adolescent ch'ing shih, it must first be captured. There are two proven methods that can be used. The first is to trap it in a magical circle that is made by encircling the vampire with iron filings, red peas, or rice. The other method is to throw handfuls of grain on the ground as soon as one is spotted. An adolescent ch'ing shih is mystically compelled to count these grains and will cease its attack. Then, using a broom, a person can begin to sweep the grain back to the creature's resting place. It will follow, if for no other reason than to begin to recount the grains as soon as the sweeping stops.

Once an adolescent ch'ing shih has been captured, it can be destroyed by taking Buddhist or Taoist death blessings that have been written on a piece of paper and slap it against the vampire's forehead. Another method is to take the captured ch'ing shih to an ancestral burial ground and once there, after a proper burial rite is given for the creature, Buddhist or Taoist magic spells must be used to bind the vampire to its new grave.

A mature adult ch'ing shih can only be destroyed by the noise of a BULLET being fired or the sound of a large enough thunderclap. As soon as it falls over, the body must be burned to ash.

Source: New York Folklore Society, *New York Folklore Quarterly*, vol. 29–30, 195; Summers, *Vampire: His Kith and Kin*, 237; Thompson, *Studies of Chinese Religion*, 91; University of Puerto Rico, *Atenea*, 93

Chonchon (CHON-chin)

Variations: Piguechen ("vampire")

The Araucanian Indians of Chile have the belief that through a mere act of will, a person can become a chonchon, growing wings out of its ears and flapping so hard that it rips the head free of the body and flies away. Some sources say that this only happens after the person is deceased. The Mapuche Indians in the same area say that the chonchon is a bird with the head of a kalku,

a sorcerer. Its cry sounds like "tui-tui-tui." Whether it is a flying head or a bird, it feeds on human blood and can shape-shift to look like a person with large ears.

Source: Alexander, *Latin-American*, 329; Edwards, *My NativeLand*, 395; Van Scott, *The Encyclopedia of Hell*, 287

Chonchonyi (Chon-CHUN-ly)

A vampiric spirit from Argentina, the chonchonyi looks like a human with big ears, which it uses to fly to the home of sick people. It sneaks inside their homes and, when no one is looking, drains them dry of their blood.

Source: Carlyon, *Guide to the Gods*, 58; Rose, *Giants, Monsters, and Dragons*, 80; Turner, *Dictionary of Ancient Beings*, 127

Chordeva (Core-DEV-ah)

Variations: Chordewa, Cordewa

There is a VAMPIRIC WITCH or vampiric demon that terrorizes the Oraon hill tribe in Bengal, India, known as a chordeva. By shape-shifting its soul into the form of a cat, the chordeva ("thief-demon") sends it out to prey on the old and sick by stealing their food and poisoning what little morsels it leaves behind. While using its cat form, it can kill a person merely by licking the person's lips. This is why all cats are kept away from anyone who can be perceived as a potential victim, even though the chordeva can be detected by the particular type of mewing it makes. Although it can also shape-shift into a were-cat, a chordeva is only as strong as an average person; however, it has the ability in its were-cat form to place its victim in a trance by direct eye contact.

The chordeva is repelled by water of any kind, as well as HAWTHORN. Anything that would kill a normal cat will destroy the chordeva's cat form, and the physical damage that is delivered will instantly become visible on the chordeva's human body. When it is in its human guise, a wooden or iron stake driven through the heart will kill the vampire, as will prolonged exposure to sunlight. However, it is completely indestructible in its were-cat form.

Source: Briggs, *The Chamārs*, 134; Crooke, *Religion and Folklore of Northern India*, 208; Meyer, *Sexual Life in Ancient India*, 392; Sinha, *Religious Life in Tribal India*, 41

Chuiaels (CHEW-ee-ales)

Variations: Cijurreyls

There is a vampiric demon in Hindu lore that is called a chuiaels. Created when a woman dies in childbirth, the chuiaels returns as a beautiful woman that lures men into its bed. Akin to the SUCCUBUS, it has a reputation of being an excellent lover from the few men who survived this experience to report upon it. They claim that during the act of fellatio, it literally drains away their life (see ENERGY VAMPIRE).

Source: Masters, Eros and Evil

Chupacabra (Chew-pa-COB-rha)

The chupacabra, the well-known "goat sucker" of Mexico, is one of the best-known vampiric creatures. The first recorded sighting of the beast was by the governor of New Galicia in April of 1540. He described one as being a small, dark-scaled man who carried a torch and a spear, and when it attacked, it did so in large numbers. It was also reported that the creature was an excellent jumper and could cover a great distance in a single leap. As time passed, the description of the chupacabra changed, and each one varied widely from a foxlike animal with bat wings, cat eyes, and blue skin to a thick-bodied, furless, quadruped-type canine. There have also been a number of different theories as to what the chupacabra is exactly. Ideas range from an extraterrestrial creature and escaped genetic hybrid to the more mundane explanation that it is merely an animal of the natural world that has previously been unrecorded or is simply suffering from a bad case of mange. What is not in dispute is that the chupacabra, regardless of what it is or where it came from, is a blood-drinking creature.

So far, all of the known victims of the chupacabra have been an array of domestic animals: chickens, cows, goats, and sheep. The chupacabra uses its amazing stealth to sneak up on the animal, killing it quickly and from surprise before it can sound an alarm. In the morning, the animal carcass is found with the smallest of bite marks on its body and completely drained of blood, with not a single drop to be found anywhere on the ground. Interestingly, in the year 2000 campers and other nature enthusiasts claimed to have seen the chupacabra in their campsites at night and when they awoke in the morning, they discovered that their water bottles had been stolen.

This creature, as steeped in folklore and mystery as it is, has also been attributed to having other supernatural powers, such as never leaving tracks or a scent trail, the ability to shape-shift into an old man, and it cannot be photographed or trapped. Fortunately, all the myths and stories surrounding this bloodthirsty creature describe it as being afraid of humans, running off as soon as opportunity presents itself.

Source: Burnett, Conspiracy Encyclopedia, 311; Candelaria, Encyclopedia of Latino Popular Culture, 161–62; Davis, Ecology of Fear, 268–70; Szasz, Larger Than Life, 197–98

Chupa-Chupa

Variations: The Animal, The Apparatus, The Beast from the Sky, The Bug, Chupa, Chupa Sanguine, Disco Voador ("Flying Saucer"), The Fire, The Light, The Machine, The Thing, Vampire in the Sky, Vampire UFO

In South and Central America, often accompanying reports of CHUPACABRA sightings, are witnesses claiming to have seen red beams of light coming from the sky and targeting a person's chest. These lights are commonly referred to as chupa-chupa, Brazilian for "suck-suck." Once the lights have locked on, they begin to burn and boil away a "significant" amount of blood. Victims, both animal and human alike, are left feeling numb and weak, running a low-grade fever, and suffering from lingering headaches. Also, there are the telling burn marks that are seared onto their chests. Oftentimes, these burns will have three small puncture marks within them that form a triangle.

Source: DiAntonio, Brazilian Fiction, 134; Icon Group International, Inc., Foresters, 191; Slater, Dance of the Dolphin, 258

Churel (CHUR-el)

Variations: ALVANTIN, CHEDIPE, Churail, Churreyls, MUKAI, Nahulai

In India, when a woman dies an unnatural death or in childbirth, she will return as a type of undead (see UNDEATH). However, if she should do so during the five-day Festival of Diwali, she returns specifically as the vampiric REVENANT known as a churel.

Churels are an extremely ugly species of vampire in their true form, having backward-facing feet; a black tongue; sagging breasts; thick, rough lips; and wild HAIR. However, the churel has the ability to shape-shift as it is occasionally described as being a beautiful woman who carries a lantern.

A bitter creature, carrying the anger of her early and tragic death, the churel starts its vampiric life by attacking the male members of its family. Beginning with the youngest and most handsome man in its family line, it will seduce him and drain him dry of his blood, leaving only a shriveled husk of an old man behind. Once the men of its family are used up, it will move on to others, stalking the roadways and luring lone male travelers astray. Sometimes it will capture a man and take him back to its lair in a graveyard. There, it will keep him prisoner, feeding off him a little at a time.

In some places to the south, there is the practice of making a Stonehenge-like structure at the entryway to the village that is blessed in order to keep a churel from entering.

Source: Briggs, *The Chamārs*, 129–31; Crooke, *An Introduction to the Popular Religion*, 69–70, 72, 168–71; Kiev, *Magic*, 135, 136; Taylor, *Death and the Afterlife*, 67

Cihuacoatl (Chee-AH-co-til)

Cihuacoatl is the vampiric goddess of the Aztec people from ancient Mexico and one of the four princesses who accompany the goddess Tlalteuctli. Cihuacoatl means "Serpent Woman," the name no doubt having been derived from the cloak she is depicted as wearing, as it looks like the hood of a snake. She is shown holding a rattle in her left hand and a serpent in her right, but she has also been rendered as holding a baby in one hand and a knife in the other. Always thirsting for human blood, she painted her body with chalk and donned a white gown to go wandering the streets calling out for the people to go to war, as prisoners were sacrificed to her. When not using so direct a method in demanding sacrifice, she would leave an empty cradle with a knife in it at a well-used source of water. Perhaps she was sending the message that if prisoners of war were sacrificed to her, then she would not have to start taking children.

Source: Aguilar-Moreno, *Handbook to Life in the Aztec World*, 86–87, 147, 148, 191, 192; Markman, *The Flayed God*, 217; Salas, *Soldaderas*, 5; Turner, *Dictionary of Ancient Deities*, 129

Cihuateteo (Chee-who-ta-TAY-oh)

Variations: Ciuatateo, Ciuateteo, Civapipltin, Civatateo

A type of vampiric, demonic demigoddess of the Aztec people of ancient Mexico, a cihuateteo is created when a mother dies in childbirth or a child is a stillborn. Cihuateteo, a name meaning "right honorable mother," fall under the dominion of the goddess of evil, lust, and sorcery, Tlazolteotl, and all of the cihuateteo are considered to be her followers. They are depicted as having arms, faces, and hands white as chalk and they live in the jungle, keeping to the dark places, as they were susceptible to sunlight; long-term exposure to it will destroy them. Although cihuateteo will feed off lone travelers who they happen upon as they fly on their brooms through the jungle, they prefer the blood of infants. Their

bite has a paralytic effect, which enables the cihuateteo to feed in silence.

Source: Aguilar-Moreno, *Handbook to Life*, 147, 199, 258; Kanellos, *Handbook of Hispanic Cultures*, 227; Salas, *Soldaderas*, 5–6, 34, 95; Stefoff, *Vampires, Zombies, and Shape-Shifters*, 17; Turner, *Dictionary of Ancient Deities*, 129

Ciuapipiltin (Chi-ap-AH-pil-ton)

Variations: Totecujiooan Cioapipilti

In ancient Mexico, when an Aztec noblewoman died giving birth to her first child, she would become a type of vampiric, demonic demigoddess called a ciuapipiltin, a word that translates to mean "princess honored woman." Like the CIHUATETEO, the ciuapipiltin fall under the domain of the goddess Tlazolteotl, and like all of her followers, paints their arms, faces, and hands white. In fact, they are similar to the CIHUATETEO in every way save for the fact that the ciuapipiltin are considered nobility and therefore can be beseeched not to attack. If offerings of bread or bits of meteorites are left near an infant, the ciuapipiltin will accept the gifts and leave the baby in peace. Temples were once constructed to honor them at crossroads and at places where horrific murders were committed. Offerings of bread and meteorites were left in these places too to stave off attacks on wandering travelers.

Source: Bancroft, *Works of Hubert Howe Bancroft*, 362, 364, 366; Kanellos, *Handbook of Hispanic Cultures*, 227; Turner, *Dictionary of Ancient Deities*, 130

Coatlicue (COAT-la-que)

Coatlicue ("Serpent Skirt") was a vampiric goddess worshiped by the ancient Aztec people of Mexico. As her name implies, she wore a skirt made of live snakes as well as a necklace of human hearts offset by an actual human skull pendant. Her hands and feet were clawed and her breasts were described as being long and flaccid from excessive nursing.

The goddess Coatlicue was an expert grave digger and preferred the blood of infants over all. She was one of the four princesses who accompanied the goddess Tlalteuctli, the others being CIHUACOATL, CIHUATETEO, and Itzpapalotl.

Source: Aguilar-Moreno, *Handbook to Life*, 142, 162, 191, 257; Davis, *Don't Know Much about Mythology*, 470–71, 474; Leeming, *Goddess*, 41–43; Salas, *Soldaderas*, 4–6

Cocoto (CO-co-toe)

Cocoto was a vampiric god of the West Indies who preyed exclusively on women. Like an INCUBUS he would have sexual intercourse with all the women in his area of influence, taking just a little bit of life-energy from each one of them in turn (see ENERGY VAMPIRE). Victims eventually grew weaker and weaker and would in the end die.

Source: Levack, *Witchcraft Sourcebook*, 81; Pareto, *Mind and Society*, 550; Summers, *Examen of Witches*, 34

Coffin (Cof-fin)

Variations: Casket, Kophinos, Pall

The words *coffin* and *casket* are often used interchangeably, but in truth they are two different things. Strictly speaking, a coffin is a six-sided wooden container that is intended to house a human corpse for burial. A casket has four sides and can be made of metal or wood.

Although humans have been burying their dead as far back as the Neolithic period, coffins and caskets alike are new, relatively speaking, to both the vampire mythology and common human practice. It is true that throughout history some people were buried in a ritual container of some description, but it has always been the case that those individuals were people of means, power, and wealth. Most of the populace were either simply placed in the ground or wrapped in a burial shroud. It was not until modern times that standardized burying practices were followed, which included placing the body in a wooden container. As mankind and his culture evolved, so did the vampire mythology. As coffins became more and more common, vampires began to use them.

Source: Bunson, *Vampire Encyclopedia*, 49; Colman, *Corpses, Coffins, and Crypts;* Metcalf, *Celebrations of Death*

Colo-Colo (COL-o COL-o)

Variations: Basilisco

A vampiric creature in the mythology of the Araucanian tribe of Chile, this monstrous creature, which is born of an egg from a cockerel, preys on those asleep. At night, it hovers over them, drinking up their saliva and thereby draining the body of all moisture. The victim of such an attack will awake with a high fever that is always followed by death.

Source: Edwards, *My Native Land*, 395; Guirand, *Larousse Encyclopedia of Mythology*, 453; Rose, *Giants, Monsters and Dragons*, 86

Con Tinh (SON TENTH)

This type of vampiric REVENANT of the Orient is created when a woman dies before her time, specifically if her death occurred because of an illicit love affair or if she were a virgin who dies a violent death. Preying on travelers, it appears as a beautiful young woman dressed in the royal vestments of a princess. It will carry a fan and a basket of fruit. Usually its familiar, a pair of cranes or doves, accompany it. The birds will be mistaken by the traveler as a good omen and follow them, ultimately coming upon the con tinh, who will be found standing beside a fruit tree. Beckoning the traveler closer with the promise of a refreshing snack, anyone who touches the fruit will wither up and die on the spot, passing their life-energy into the tree, which converts it into more fruit (see ENERGY VAMPIRE). The con tinh, desirous only of killing and consuming life, lives off the fruit of the tree and cannot leave its immediate area.

Source: Fjelstad, *Possessed by the Spirits*, 65–66; Leach, *Funk and Wagnalls Standard Dictionary of Folklore*, 284; Stein, *The World in Miniature*, 84, 97, 300, 302

Corpse Candle (Corps Can-del)

Variations: Brünnlig, Buchelmännle, Corpse Sans Âme, Dichepot, Draulicht, Dröglicht, Druckfackel, Dwallicht, Dwerlicht, Earthlights, Erlwischen, FEU-FOLLET ("Foolish Fire"), Flackerfür, Flämmstirn, Follet, Friar's Lantern, Fuchtel-Männlein, FÜERSTEINMANNLI, Ghost Lights, Heerwisch, Huckepot, Ignis Fatuus ("Foolish Fire"), Irdflämmken, Irdlicht, Irrlüchte, Irrwisch, Jack-o'-Lantern, Lichtkedräger, Lidércfény, Lopend Für, Lüchtemannchen, Pützhüpfer, Quadlicht, Schäuble, Schwidnikes, Spoklecht, Spooky Lights, Stäuble, Stölten, Stöltenlicht, Tückebold, Tückebote, Tümmelding, Will-o'-the-Wisp, Willy Wisp, Wipplötsche, Zunselwible

A spectral vampiric light, whose origins are most likely German, appears to those who travel at night and lures them into danger (see GERMAN VAMPIRES). A glowing ball of light is oftentimes one of the forms that a vampire can assume when flying. Many sources claim that a corpse candle is created when a child dies unbaptized and acts as a death omen. Some corpse candles are also guardians of treasure.

Vampires who have the ability to shapechange into a corpse candle are the ADZE, ASEMA, ASIMAN, CH'ING SHIH, HAHN SABURO, JUMBIES, LEYAK, LIDERC NADALY, LIOGAT, LIVING VAMPIRE, OBOUR, SAMPIRO, SUCOYAN, and the TLACIQUES

Source: Ellis, *Mainly Victorian*, 305–6; Folklore Society of Great Britain, *Folklore*, vol. 6, 293–94; Masters, *Natural History of the Vampire*; Radford, *Encyclopedia of Superstitions*, 58–60

Craitnag Folley (CRAIG-nag FAWL-a)

Variations: SOODER FOLLEY ("blood sucker")

On the Isle of Man, the Gaelic words *craitnag folley* ("blood bat") are used when describing a vampire.

Source: Kelly, *Fockleyr Manninagh as Baarlagh*, 54, 110; Maberry, *Vampire Universe*, 82

Craqueuhhe (Crack-COAL)

Variations: Chan Hook, Craqueuhle, Father Tôsô, Jean Crochat, Kaperman

In the Lorraine region of France, *craqueuhhe* is a word that is used when referring to a vampiric REVENANT. It is created when a person dies unbaptized. Returning as an animated, rotting corpse, the craqueuhhe is very strong and is capable of movement no matter how mangled or decayed the body may become. Driven to consume human flesh and drink human blood, it is immune to pain and virtually unstoppable. Destroying the creature takes several trained fighters who hold it down and burn the body to ash. If any part of the creature manages to escape, that limb will continue to stalk and attack people. Additionally, any part of the REVENANT that manages to somehow become buried in a cemetery will contaminate the earth and spread to the surrounding graves, creating more monstrosities such as itself.

Source: Maberry, *Vampire Universe*, 87

Croglin Grange Vampire (CROG-lynn GRANGE Vam-pire)

In Crumbria, England, there is a vampire tale that began on the estate of Croglin Grange. Although the tale takes place in the early nineteenth century, it most likely originated in the seventeenth century. At that time both a chapel and a burial vault were visible from the house. Both had long since been demolished by the time history shows that the Cranswells (or Cromwells, sources vary) rented the property; nevertheless, it is an enduring tale. Miss Amelia (or Anne, sources vary) Cranswell, a survivor of the vampire's attack, described it as being a tall man smelling like death and decay, whose skin was nearly a translucent, dried-out brown. Its shriveled-up face had red eyes and lips. Its hands were long, thin, and clawed. Despite its appearance, it was fast and have the agility of a cat.

The Fisher family had owned and lived in the Croglin Grange estate up until the time it was rented out to the Cranswells: two brothers and a sister. One summer night as Miss Cranswell was preparing for bed, she noticed out of her bedroom window (which overlooked the ancient cemetery in the distance) two points of light moving between the stones. She could just make out a dark form, and the whole sighting left her feeling uneasy. She closed and locked her window and retired to bed for the evening. Just as she was about to drift off to sleep, she opened her eyes to see a horrid face staring at her through the window, the eyes burning red, and instantly she knew that the dots of lights she had seen earlier had to have been the eyes that were looking at her now. She tried to scream but found that she was frozen with fear, unable even to move. She sat there helplessly as she watched the creature use its clawed hands to pluck away at the lead window sealing and knock the glass out of place so that it could slip its arm inside and undo the latch. The window swung silently open and the monster climbed in with startling ease. She was still unable to move as it crossed the room, grabbed her up by the HAIR, and pulled her face close to its as if it were preparing to kiss her. Only when it bit down into the flesh of her neck was she able to scream. Her brothers awoke and immediately dashed to her room. Finding the door locked, they had to waste precious time smashing it down. When they finally broke into the room, their sister lay on her bed, blood pumping from her neck. The smell of mold and decay filled the room, and one of the brothers just saw something flit out the window. He raced to it in time to see something dashing across the cemetery in the distance. The rest of the long night was spent bandaging their sister's neck and barely managing to save her life.

As soon as Miss Cranswell was well enough to travel, the brothers whisked her away to Switzerland to recover. There she told them of the events that had occurred and the brothers swore revenge on the monster. The three returned to Croglin Grange and laid a trap for the vampire. The sister insisted that she act as bait and the brothers lay in wait. Not long after their trap was set, the vampire returned, but this time the brothers were prepared and shot it several times. With a howling wail it fled back out the window and into the night. The brothers waited until morning to try and track it.

With first light they took their sister to a safe place and rounded up some of the local residents to help them search the graveyard for evidence of their sister's attacker. With a thorough search they noticed that one of the crypt doors was ajar. Looking inside they came upon a grizzly sight. All the COFFINS, save one, were smashed to bits. Bones were scattered everywhere and showed signs of having been gnawed upon. They opened the one COFFIN that was intact and found a corpse of a tall man who was sporting what they considered several fresh gunshot wounds. Assuming that this had to be the vampire, the COFFIN and the body within were taken outside of the crypt and moved to the churchyard. There it was set ablaze and watched, making sure it burned down to ash.

Source: Copper, *Vampire in Legend*, 51–54; Farson, *Man Who Wrote Dracula*, 108; Masters, *Natural History of the Vampire*, 132–35; Summers, *Vampire in Lore and Legend*, 112–15

Crucifix (Crew-sa-fix)

A crucifix is a religious item in the Christian faith, a Latinized cross with the figure of the Christo Mortuis (the dead Christ) upon it. Stoker employed the use of the iconic crucifix in his book on a number of occasions. In the first chapter of the novel *Dracula*, a woman gives Jonathan Harker a rosary that she was wearing around her neck when she learned of his destination. Harker, a Protestant, was amused by the gift and wore it as a polite gesture. Later in the book, the sternsman of the *Demeter* is found tied to the wheel, a rosary still clutched in his hand; the vampiric Lucy was locked in her tomb with a crucifix and GARLIC; and it was also used to drive Dracula back when he came for Mina.

Stoker used artistic license when he combined the Catholic idea of holy objects and the medieval tradition that vampires fell under the domain of Satan. Prior to *Dracula*, vampires were not affected by either crosses or crucifixes. However, it was by Stoker's creation that this bit of fiction, the idea of the crucifix having the power to repel a vampire, found itself woven into the vampire's lore. (See BRAM STOKER'S *DRACULA*)

Source: Heldreth, *Blood Is the Life*, 61–62; Johnson, *Restless Dead*, 4; Richardson, *Existential Joss Whedon*, 15, 125–26

Cundalai Madan (CON-da-eye-lie MAID-en)

Variations: Kundalini Madan

Cundalai Madan is a vampiric god from Hindu lore. The goddess Parvati sought to mend the rift in her marriage to the god Siva by having a child with him. She descended into hell and took a spark from the sacred lamp. In the hem of her skirt it developed into a shapeless mass rather than a child. Parvati complained to her husband, who turned it into a child. But before she could feed it milk, the child consumed some flesh from a corpse, earning his name Cundalai Madan

("Coiled-Up Infatuation"). Because he ate the flesh of a corpse, Cundalai Madan was forever forbidden to enter into heaven, but nevertheless he demanded that he be established and worshiped as a god—and that a cult be established to worship him as well, filled with beautiful female companions to see to his sexual desires. He also demanded regular sacrifices of alcohol, animals, human life, and meat. With his boon granted, he immediately set about ravishing women and eating the fetuses out of them. The Kaniyar singers and dancers offered their bodies willingly to be his human sacrifices.

Source: Bhattacharyya, *Path of the Mystic Lover*, 188; Madan, *Non-renunciation*, 40

Curco (CUR-co)

Variations: Curoï, Orgoï

Curco as well as *curoï* and *orgoï* are Romania words that mean "vampire."

Source: Cremene, *Mythology of the Vampire in Romania*; Folklore Society, *Publications*, vol. 87–88, 429; Znamenski, *Shamanism in Siberia*, 46

Čuval

In the folklore from the regions of Montenegro and Serbia, vampires are particularly fond of consuming fingers. To be rid of a vampire in a community, a severed finger is placed into a bag called a čuval, tied tightly up, and thrown off a bridge and into a river. The vampire will want the finger so badly that it will jump in the river after the sack and consequently drown.

Source: Lincoln, *Myth, Cosmos, and Society*, 41–63; McClelland, *Slayers and Their Vampires*, 70

Dachnavar (DAC-na-var)

Variations: Dakhanavar, Dashnavar

In 1854 in Armenia, there were reports of a lone PALIS vampire named Dachnavar that was living in a specific valley near Mount Ararat. By species, it was a palis. Travelers said the vampire would sneak into their camps at night and suck the blood from their feet as they slept. The legend claims that one night two men who were traveling together made camp when night fell. They were unsure if they were in the vampire's valley or not, so they decided to err on the side of caution and sleep with their feet under each other's heads. Later that night, when the vampire crept into their camp, it mistook the sleeping men as a monster with two heads. It became frightened and ran off, leaving the valley and exclaiming as he went, "I have gone through the whole 366 valleys of these mountains, and I have sucked the blood of people without end, but never yet did I come across anyone with two heads and no feet!"

Source: Huss, *Focus on the Horror Film*, 59; Jones, *On the Nightmare*, 119; Suckling, *Vampires*, 29

Daitja (DATE-ja)

Indonesian lore tells of a vampiric creature that is essentially a SUCCUBUS with eyes the exact shade of deep blue that the lotus has when it is in bloom. This creature is called a daitja.

Source: Making of America Project, *Harper's New Magazine*, vol. 10, 685; Suckling, *Vampires*, 29; University of the Philippines, *Diliman Review*, 413; Williams, *The Historians' History of the World*, 491

Dakin (DA-kin)

Variations: Khandro

The Dakin of Tibet are a race of demonic vampire attendants to the goddess KALI. Their name, Dakin, has been translated by different sources to mean different things depending on the role they are fulfilling. Common translations are "celestial woman," "cloud fairy," "sky dancer," and "space-goer."

Although the Dakin have shape-changing abilities and may look like virtually anything they need to, they prefer to take on the guise of a human female, as they enjoy when they are called upon to partake in tantric sex. Dakin, similar to the SUCCUBUS, are known to fall in love with human men, making for a dangerous situation, as not only do the creatures feed on human flesh and blood, they are normally highly unpredictable. Their typical duty is to carry the souls of the deceased into the sky, and there are many stories of them in the Buddha's former lives.

Many of the New Age religions would have one believe that the Dakin is more like an angelic being, made of pure spiritual energy and not associated with any one particular god or goddess.

Source: Blavatsky, *The Theosophical Glossary*, 95; Bryant, *Handbook of Death*, 99; Lurker, *Dictionary of Gods and Goddesses, Devils and Demons*, 88

Danag (Dhu-NAG)

The Danag are an ancient vampiric species said to be as old as the Philippine islands that they come from. Originally the Danag coexisted with mankind and were even accredited as being the ones who first cultivated the taro plant. However, after many years of peace between the two races, one day a woman had cut her finger while working and a Danag politely volunteered to suck the wound clean. As it did so, it realized that it greatly enjoyed the taste of the blood and, unable to stop itself, drained the woman dry of all her blood. Ever since then, the Danag carried on the vampiric practice.

Source: Bryant, *Handbook of Death and Dying*, 99; Raedt, *Kalinga Sacrifice*, 220; Ramos, *Creatures of Philippine*, 116, 117, 327

Deamhan Fola (DJOW-agn FUL-ah)

Variations: Diabhal Fola ("Blood Devil"), Deamhain Fhola, DEARG-DUE, Vaimpír

In Ireland, *deamhan fola* is a term that is used to refer to a vampire. It translates to "blood demon."

Source: Haining, *Dictionary of Vampires*, 69

Dearg-Due (DEER-rig DUEL)

Variations: Deamhain Fhola, DEAMHAN FOLA, Dearg-Dililat, Dearg-Diulai, Dearg-dul, Dearg Dulai, Derrick-Dally, Headless Coach ("Coach a Bower"), Marbh Bheo ("night walking dead")

The dearg-due is a type of vampiric REVENANT from Ireland that has been feared since the days before the introduction of Christianity. These ancient creatures are described as looking like a beautiful yet pale woman who can be seen strolling aimlessly through graveyards at night. It uses its beauty to lure men to it and then kisses them on the mouth. When it does so, it drains them of their blood.

To stop a dearg-due from continued assaults, its grave must be found and a cairn erected on top of it, trapping it beneath. Ireland's most famous dearg-due is said to be buried beneath a strongbow tree. About four times a year it is able to escape from its grave and feed.

Source: Jones, *On the Nightmare*, 123; MacHarris, *Folklore and the Fantastic*, 135; Stuart, *Stage Blood*, 15

Death Coach

Variations: Cóiste Bodhar

The superstition of medieval England and Wales spoke of a vampiric spirit known as a death coach that appeared after the wail and subsequent attack of a BANSHEE. The death coach would then descend from the sky, looking rather like a funeral coach drawn by a black horse. It gathers up the soul of the BANSHEE's victim, traveling without a sound. The death coach may be the transmuted concept of Charon, the Ferryman from Greek mythology, and is similar to the vampiric species called DULLAHAN.

Source: Keegan, *Legends and Poems*, 131; Leach, *Funk and Wagnalls Standard Dictionary of Folklore*, 300; Radford, *Encyclopedia of Superstitions*, 70–71, 101–2; Wentz, *The Fairy-Faith in Celtic Countries*, 71

de Morieve

Variations: Viscount de Morieve

One of the few members of the French nobility who retained their estate and survived the French Revolution, Viscount de Morieve took it upon himself to enact revenge. Described as a tall man with a tall, thin forehead and protruding teeth, he donned an air of kindness and sophistication around his staff and the peasantry who worked his lands, all the while biding his time. After the revolution ended, he maintained his façade for a while longer, lulling those around him into a sense of false security. Then, one day, the Viscount de Morieve sent for those in his employ one by one. He beheaded each retainer he spoke with in an attempt to enact a type of justice that he imagined was denied to his fellow noblemen. De Morieve was stopped before he slew his entire household staff and was himself beheaded for the crime by his own retainers.

Shortly after the Viscount was placed in his tomb, children in the area started to die, each one of their throats bitten into, the obvious sign of a vampire attack. As many as nine deaths happened in a single week. These attacks continued for the next 72 years until the Viscount's grandson, Young de Morieve, was given the title. It was decided that the new viscount would have to do something about his murderous grandfather, the vampire. A priest was consulted and it was decided to hire a vampire hunter and have de Morieve's tomb opened before witnesses. Every other COFFIN in the tomb showed signs of decay and deterioration except for de Morieve's. When opened, his body showed no signs of decomposition whatsoever; the face was rosy, the skin soft. New growth was visible on his hands and feet, and most telling was that blood was in his heart and chest. A stake of HAWTHORN was driven through the vampire's heart, causing the Viscount to scream out in pain and shock as blood and water gushed from the corpse. As soon as the remains were taken to the seashore and burned to ash, the child deaths ceased.

Subsequent research into the family's lineage proved that the Viscount had always had the curse of the vampire in his blood, as he was in fact born in Persia. There he married an Indian woman, after which they came to France and became naturalized citizens.

Source: Keyworth, *Troublesome Corpses*, 258; Summer, *The Vampire in Lore and Legend*, 125–26

Dhampire (DOM-peer)

Variations: Dhampir, Dhampyr, Dhampyri, LAMPIJEROVIC (feminine), Vamphile, VAMPIJEROVIC (masculine), VAMPIR (masculine), VAMPIRDZHIJA, Vampiritc, Vampirovitch, Vampuiera (feminine), Vampuira

The Gypsy lore from Eastern Europe claims that if the child of a woman and a male mullo vampire is not stillborn, it will be a dhampire, a natural-born vampire hunter. In almost all cases the dhampire is male (females are called dhampiresa), but no matter the gender, they tend to have a shorter lifespan than humans. This is because a dhampire does not have any bones in its body but rather a thick rubberlike substance instead. Usually the dhampire has a restless spirit and becomes a wanderer, and because of this, and the fact that he is also the child of a vampire, he is generally distrusted. Even if he should be an established member of a community, his ability to hunt and destroy vampires will be respected, but he will have no social or political power among his people.

The dhampire does not have any of the vampiric abilities of his vampire father. He has no enhanced senses, regenerative abilities, nor is he a shape-shifter; not only is he not immortal, he does not even have slowed ageing. What he can do is see a vampire for the creature that it is, even if it is invisible. He is also able to destroy a vampire without having to use a special weapon. For instance, if a vampire can only be slain by being stabbed through the heart with a stake made of ash, the dhampire can use a stake made of any material. He can even extend this ability to his gun and shoot a vampire while it lies at rest in its grave.

For more stubborn cases of vampiric attacks, a dhampire may be hired. Once he has arrived at the infested town and money has changed hands, the dhampire will go to the center of town and call out a challenge for the vampire to meet him there the next day at a certain time. The next day, the dhampire will show up early and wait for the vampire to arrive, and when it does, it usually does so invisibly. If it is hiding, the dhampire will be able to feel its presence or catch its scent on the wind, allowing him to track it. Usually the dhampire can see a vampire without any assistance, but occasionally he needs to perform a simple magical ceremony to do so. Usually this ritual is as simple as looking through a shirtsleeve, putting his clothes on backward, or whistling. Once the dhampire is ready, he will physically confront the vampire, grab it, and wrestle with it. Eventually, the dhampire will be able to overcome the creature and manage to stake it or shoot it or even run it out of town with a banishment.

In 1959 there was a dhampire who was still actively working in Kosova. The last time he was ever heard from was when he was performing the last known vampire removal ceremony later that same year.

A dhampire, because of the conditions of his birth, must make arrangements to have a proper funeral held for him when he dies. If not, he will return to unlife as a vampire himself.

Source: Gypsy Lore Society, *Journal of the Gypsy Lore Society*, 44; MacGillivray, *Stoker's Spoiled Masterpiece*, 518–27; Richardson, *Psychoanalysis of Ghost Stories*, 427–28; Senf, *The Vampire in Nineteenth-Century English Literature*, 165; Twitchell, *Living Dead*, 11–12, 46, 50, 52, 89

La Diablesse (LA DEE-ah-bless)

Variations: Lajables

There is a vampiric spirit that exists in the folklore of France, and Trinidad and Tobago that tells of a beautiful vampiric woman wearing a large hat and carrying a fan. Known as La Diablesse ("Devil Woman"), it roams the quiet roads in the form of a woman wearing a long billowing dress to hide her one leg that ends in a cloven hoof.

Any man that La Diablesse meets, it will attempt to charm and lure off the path with sweet promises of a discrete indiscretion. If it succeeds, it will drain the man dry of his blood, leaving his nude body to be found up in a tree or atop a grave in a cemetery. More modern tellings of this vampire say it no longer is content to wander down seldom-used roads but rather has learned that it can slip relatively unnoticed into local celebrations to hunt for men.

Vampires that are very similar to La Diablesse are the LANGSUIR, LEANHAUM-SHEE, MATI-ANAK, ONOSCÈLES, PONTIANAK, SKOGSFRU, VELES and the WHITE LADIES.

Source: Besson, *Folklore and Legends*, 12; Cartey, *The West Indies*, 43; Jones, *Evil in Our Midst*, 122; Parson, *Folk-lore of the Antilles*, 75

Djadadjii (DA-dad-gee)

In Bulgarian vampire lore there is a type of vampire hunter known as a djadadjii, who specializes in the destruction of a specific type of vampire called a KRVOIJAC. The djadadjii is an expert in the BOTTLING technique used to capture and destroy vampires. First he takes a bottle and baits it with blood. Next he carries it with him as he seeks out the vampire's hiding place. As he searches, he uses the image of Jesus, the Virgin Mary, a saint, or a holy relic to flush the vampire out of its hiding place. When the icon starts to shake of its own accord in his hand, the vampire is near. The djadadjii will use his religious icon to herd the vampire into the bottle (see BOTTLING) and then quickly cork it and throw it in a blazing fire. The explosion of the bottle will be powerful enough to destroy the vampire within. If for some reason the djadadjii is unable to herd the vampire into the bottle, the creature will retreat into its corpse. Now the djadadjii must unearth the corpse, pierce its heart with thorns, and burn the remains in a fire fueled with HAWTHORN branches.

Source: Georgieva, *Bulgarian Mythology*, 98; Gregory, *Vampire Watcher's Handbook*, 113; Ronay, *The Dracula Myth*

Dockele (DOC-el)

Variations: Alpdaemon, Dochje, Dockeli, Doggi, Toggeli

In the vampiric lore of Germany, the dockele is a vampiric creature similar to the ALP (see GERMAN VAMPIRES). It looks like a common house cat and it kills its victims by draining their blood through their mouth.

Source: Culebras, *Sleep Disorders*, 86; Magyar Tudományos Akadémia, *Acta ethnographica*, 34; Meyer, *Vampires of Germany*, 131, 134

Dodelecker (Doe-DE-lic-er)

Variations: Dodeleker, NACHZEHRER

The dodelecker is a unique and interesting vampire. It is as aggressive as any of the vampires one can imagine; however, it lacks the coordination, manual dexterity, and speed to actually catch anything. Its cries of hunger can be heard as it lies in its grave, chewing on its burial shroud and its own body, struggling to free itself. If it ever manages to escape its tomb, the dodelecker innocuously shambles about, moaning and making whimpering noises as it feebly attempts to catch something. It would love to feed on fresh human flesh and blood, as most REVENANTs do, but because of its physical inability to successfully hunt, it is forced to settle for living a GHOUL-like lifestyle and consuming the rotting flesh it is able to find and scavage. If it were not for the fact that it is a plague carrier, it would be completely harmless. After nine years of nightly risings and wanderings, it will finally lie down in its grave and rise no more (see GERMAN VAMPIRES).

Source: Barber, *Vampires, Burial, and Death*, 95; Conway, *Demonology and Devil-lore*, 51–52; Guiley, *Complete Vampire Companion*, 25; Lindahl, *Medieval Folklore*, 1017

Dogirs (DOG-ers)

In the Egyptian village of Dabod there is a vampire that normally lives peacefully with its human neighbors called a dogirs. A type of vampiric spirit, it looks just like a human during the day but with a lump on its lower back. This lump is in truth the dogirs' tail hidden under the skin. In its true form, which it can assume at night by rolling in ashes, the vampire looks like a werewolf with glowing eyes.

In 1929 the police of the village were called to conduct an official search for a dogirs. Law enforcement officials cited having a lump on a person's back as grounds for arrest.

Source: American Anthropological Association, *American Anthropologist*, vol. 69, 689; Beshir, *Nile Valley Countries*, 139; Grauer, *The Dogri*, 114–24

Dogrose (Dog-rose)

Variations: Brier Hip, Brier Rose, Dog Berry, Eglantine, Gall, Hep Tree, Hip Fruit, Hogseed, Hop Fruit, "The Queen of Flowers," Rose Hip, Sweet Brier, Wild Brier, Witches' Brier

The dogrose shrub, found commonly in Europe and across Asia, is a bushy plant with small white or pink flowers and thorny branches. The folklore in these regions has woven this plentiful plant into their vampiric lore. Dogrose petals can be collected and thrown at a vampire, as the monster will then be mystically compelled to stop what it is doing and count the blooms. The petals are oftentimes strung together to make long garlands that are then wrapped around a COFFIN to mystically chain it shut, trapping the vampire within. A dogrose plant placed on top of a vampire's grave will keep it from rising.

Source: Bostock, *Natural History of Pliny*, vol. 6, 84; Gypsy Lore Society, *Journal of the Gypsy Lore Society*, 27; Hughes, *Celtic Plant Magic*, 63–64; Perkowski, *Vampires of the Slavs*, 176

Doppelsauger (DOP-ool-saug-er)

Variation: Doppelgänger, Double Auger, Dubblesüger, Dubbelsuger

In eastern Germany, the Wends, who occupied the land between the Elbe and Oder Rivers, used the word *doppelsauger* to describe a vampire (see GERMAN VAMPIRE). Later the word was applied to the Germanic imagery of what a vampire was.

A doppelsauger is created when a mother allows her child to breast-feed long after it should have been weaned. Eventually the time will come when that person will one day be near death. When this happens, a gold coin must be placed in his teeth prior to his passing to prevent him from rising as an undead monstrosity (see UNDEATH). If the person dies before the coin is placed, then some sort of propping device must be employed to keep the chin from resting against the chest. This preventative method must be taken to see to it that the deceased does not rise up as a vampiric REVENANT. In either event, after the body has been removed from the home, the sill of the doorway must be removed and immediately replaced. This will prevent the vampire from being able to find and return to its old home.

If every preventative method was taken and still the deceased returns as a doppelsauger, it can still drain the life from its victims, starting first with its own family before moving on to others, without ever leaving its grave. When the vampire does leave its grave, it will look like a bloated corpse whose lips have not decomposed. It will drain the life essence from its victims through their nipples, occasionally biting them off (see ENERGY VAMPIRE).

The only way to destroy a doppelsauger is to strike it in the back of the neck with a spade. The creature will cry out in pain just before it falls over, finally at rest.

Source: Barber, *Vampires, Burial, and Death*, 37; International Society for Folk Narrative Research, *Folk Narrative and Cultural Identity*, 300; McClelland, *Slayers and Their Vampires*, 197; Perkowski, *The Darkling*, 106

Dousheta (SHETTA)

Variations: Opyri, Oupir

Bulgarian folklore claims that if a child dies before it can be baptized, then it will become a vampiric demon known as a dousheta.

Source: Bryant, *Handbook of Death*, 99; Georgieva, *Bulgarian Mythology*, 102; MacPherson, *Blood of His Servants*, 25

Drakul (DRA-cool)

Variations: Dracul

In the Moldovan and Romanian languages the word *drakul* means "the dragon" or "demon nearly," and it is used to describe a type of vampiric demon that possesses the body of a deceased person and animates it. Once the demon has possession of the corpse, it makes it walk around naked, carrying its COFFIN on its head while looking for humans to prey upon. Fortunately, if the burial shroud of the person is destroyed, the demon will lose its hold on the body.

Source: Andreescu, *Vlad the Impaler*, 183; McNally, *In Search of Dracula*, 21; Twitchell, *Living Dead*, 16

Drakus (DRA-cus)

In southern Bulgaria, in the Rhodope mountain region, the word *drakus* is used to describe a vampire.

Source: Georgieva, *Bulgarian Mythology*, 95; MacDermott, *Bulgarian Folk Customs*, 67; McClelland, *Slayers and Their Vampires*, 104

Draskylo

There are many species of vampires that are created when an animal, such as a cat, jumps over a corpse. *Draskylo* is a Greek word that means "to step across," and it is used only when referring to the causality of vampiric creation.

Source: Bunson, *Vampire Encyclopedia*, 113; Dundes, *Vampire Casebook*, 93

Drauge (DRAW-ged)

Variations: GIENGANGER

In the lore of the ancient Norse people, a drauge was created when a powerful necromancer died and returned as a vampiric REVENANT. It was an exceptionally physically strong being, killing anyone who entered its tomb with a single blow to the head. Eye contact with a drauge must be avoided at all cost, as it could steal vital önd ("breath") and kill someone.

Once a drauge comes into being, it is simply avoided by never entering into its burial chamber. Runes can be carved onto the gravestone to keep it trapped in its chamber, preventing it from leaving. It is very rare to hear stories of a drauge wandering the countryside.

After the introduction of Christianity, the drauge was able to be destroyed if it was reburied in a Christian cemetery or had a mass said for it. Eventually, it was replaced altogether with the DRAUGR, an evil undead corpse of someone who had drowned at sea (see UNDEATH).

Source: Crabb, *Crabb's English Synonymes*, 287; Curran, *Vampires*, 93; Henderson, *Norse Influence on Celtic Scotland*, 106; Vicary, *An American in Norway*, 119

Draugr (Daw-gr)

Variation: Aptgangr ("one who walks after death"), Aptrgangr, Barrow Dweller, Gronnskjegg, Haubui, Haugbui ("Sleeper in the Mound")

The draugr is a type of vampiric REVENANT from Iceland. Its name is derived from the Indo-European root word *dreugh*, which means "to deceive" or "to damage." The word *draugr's* more modern literal translation means "after-goer" or "one who walks in death," but is usually taken to mean a type of undead creature (see UNDEATH). There are two types of draugr, those of the land and those of the sea (see DRAUGER, SEA).

Land draugr are created when a very greedy and wealthy man is buried in a barrow with all of his possessions. To prevent this from happening, traditional lore says to place a pair of iron scissors on his chest or straw crosswise under the burial shroud. Additionally, as a precaution it is wise to tie the big toes of the deceased together so that the legs cannot move. As a final precaution, pins are driven partway into the bottom of his feet to prevent him from getting up and walking anywhere, as it would be too painful to do so.

A draugr jealously guards its treasures and viciously attacks anyone who enters its tomb. It uses its supernatural strength to crush them to death or strangle them with its bare hands. It is impervious to all mundane weaponry and a few stories say that it can even increase its body size two to three times. Some draugr are able to leave their tombs and wander off into the night with the intent of crushing or rending anyone they happen across. If one should be encountered, an elderly woman must throw a bowl of her own urine at it to drive it away.

In addition to its physical abilities, a draugr has an array of magical abilities as well. It can control the weather, move freely through stone and earth, and see into the future. It can also shape-shift into a cat, a great flayed bull, a gray horse with no ears or tail and a broken back, and a seal. In its cat form it will sit on a person's chest, growing heavier and heavier until the victim suffocates to death, much like the ALP of Germany may do.

The draugr's skin is described as being either hel-blar ("death-blue") or na foir ("corpse pale"). It smells like a rotting corpse, although even after many years it may show no real signs of decay. It retains the personality and all the memories of the person it once was. It longs for the things it had in life—food, loved ones, and warmth, but unable to have these things, it destroys property and kills livestock and people. The only pleasure it has in death is taken through its violence.

After the introduction of Christianity, the draugr was destroyed if it was exhumed and given a Christian burial in a churchyard or if a mass was said for it. Also, burning the body to ash would destroy it. However, the traditional method of destroying a draugr must be undertaken by a hero, who defeats it in hand-to-hand combat, wrestling it into submission and then beheading the creature. Some of the traditional tales say that after the beheading, the hero must then walk three times around the head or body. Other stories say that a stake must also be driven into the headless corpse. Additionally, the sword that is used in the beheading must be some sort of ancestral, special, or magical sword; typically this sword is already in the tomb somewhere in the draugr's treasure hoard.

It has been speculated by some scholars that the monster GRENDEL from the heroic epic poem *Beowulf* was a draugr. Also dragons and draugrs may well be interchangeable in some stories, as they are both greedy guardians of treasure, which is kept in an underground chamber; they act violently when motivated by greed or envy; they are shape-shifters; and they were both important enough to be Christianized when times changed.

The oldest, best-known story of a draugr is that of Glam from the *Grettis Saga*. In it, after Glam died he became a draugr, killing many men and cattle. He was defeated by the outlaw hero Grettir in a wrestling match. Grettir promptly beheaded the creature and burned the body to ash.

Source: Chadwick, *Folklore*, vol. LVIL, 50–65; Grimm, *Teutonic Mythology*, 915; Houran, *From Shaman to Scientist*, 103; Marwick, *Folklore of Orkney and Shetland*, 40

Draugr Sea (DAW-gr See)

Variations: Sea Trow, Trowis

According to Icelandic lore, a draugr of the sea is created whenever a person drowns in the ocean. They have been described as being "black as hell and bloated to the size of a bull," their bodies covered with curly HAIR and seaweed. Their penis and testicles are also noted as being overly large.

This draugr, a REVENANT vampiric creature, preys on seamen using an array of supernatural abilities. It can shape-shift into rocks along a shoreline, is impervious to mundane weaponry, and has supernatural strength. Like the draugr of the land that it thoroughly hates, it too retains its personality and all of its memories. Usually, it only makes itself visible to its victims, sailing the sea in half a boat.

There is a draugr story that takes place on Christmas Eve back in 1857. On the Norwegian Isle of Lurøy, all the farmhands were celebrating the holiday. When they ran out of drink, everyone was too afraid to go out to the boathouse to retrieve more alcohol for fear of encountering a draugr—except for a young boy. He made it there, filled his jug, and on the way back to the celebration, a headless draugr confronted him. The boy attacked the draugr, knocking it off balance, which gave him just enough time to escape. As the boy ran for his life, he looked back over his shoulder and saw that not one but a great num-

ber of draugr were rising from the sea behind him, ready to give chase. The boy pressed on and jumped over the churchyard wall, hollering as loudly as he could, "Up, up, every Christian soul, save me!" As he landed in the churchyard, the church bell tolled the midnight hour and draugr began to rise from the earth. Within moments the two species of draugr were engaged in battle. The land draugr clutched the wood from their COFFINS to use as weapons; the sea draugr made whips of their seaweed. The boy fled to the servant quarters and told the tale of what had happened. Christmas morning everyone looked to the graveyard. It looked like a battlefield. Bits of broken COFFINS, seaweed, jellyfish, and slime were everywhere.

Source: Grimm, *Teutonic Mythology*, 916; Marwick, *An Orkney Anthology*, 261–62; Mckinnell, *Runes, Magic and Religion;* Shipley, *Dictionary of Early English*, 686

Dreach-Fhoula (DROC-OLA)

Variations: Dreach-Shoula, Droch-Fhoula

In ancient Ireland dreach-fhoula ("tainted blood") was a type of vampiric fay. However, in modern times, the word is now used to refer to a blood feud between families. There is a castle in Kerry County, Ireland named DU'N DREACH-FHOULA ("the place of tainted blood").

Source: Curran, *Vampires*, 64

Drude (DROOD)

Variations: Drudenfuss ("Drude's foot"), Drudenstein ("Drude's stone"), Drute, Nachtmahr, Törin, Trud, Trude, Trut, Walriderske

A VAMPIRIC WITCH well versed in the black arts, from the folklore of Austria and Bavaria, the drude has been reported as far back as the twelfth century. Almost always a woman, it will shape-shift into a bird at night and seek out a man, as they are powerless against her, to inflict horrible nightmares and terrible visions upon. She can be warded off with a drudenstein ("drude's stone"), a stone with a naturally occurring hole in it, or with a drudenkreuz ("drude's cross"), essentially a pentagram.

Source: Grimm, *Teutonic Mythology*, 1041; Jones, *On the Nightmare*, 218; Pearson, *Chances of Death*, 181

Drujas (DREW-ha)

Variations: Drujes

There is a Persian belief that if a person dies while harboring a great rage, or while seeking revenge, or was otherwise simply an evil person, they will remain an earthbound, vampiric spirit called a drujas. These beings live in colonies in dark places and have no other goal or purpose beyond causing physical pain, committing acts of depravity, and being the catalyst that causes the complete ruin of a man.

Drujas are similar to the SUCCUBUS and are typically described as beautiful women with insatiable lust, and, using their powers of corruption and deceitfulness, take pleasure in witnessing crime and corruption. The only way to save oneself from the attack of the drujas is to first realize that one is being attacked. Then, the victim must call out to God to help empower him to resist its temptation. There are 45 different passages that mention the drujas in the Zoroastrian text, *The Avesta*. The drujas are also mentioned in the Old Testament's Book of Judgment, chapter 1, verse 9: "And thou shalt suffer evil spirits and all manner of drujas, and vampires, and engrafters, to come, and manifest unto mortals, that they may know, whereof My revelations unfold the matters of earth and heaven."

Source: Bleeck, *Avesta*, 22, 26, 27, 65, 114, 122, 125, 143, 176; Moffat, *Comparative History of Religions*, 191, 214

Drunken Boy

Variations: SHUTEN-DOJI

Asian lore tells us of a gigantic, vampiric ogre called Drunken Boy. Dressed all in scarlet, Drunken Boy can be found in his cave lair where he and his demon companions drink vast quantities of alcohol. Within his lair are also any number of beautiful women who were kidnapped and held as his sex slaves. In the Japanese version of the myth, a hero named Raiko (or Yorimitsu, sources conflict) fought and beheaded the ogre. Drunken Boy was such a ferocious combatant that he continued to fight on for some time after the fatal blow was delivered, but eventually succumbed.

Source: Allan, *Realm of the Rising Sun*, 82; Davis, *Myths and Legends of Japan*, 45; Jackson-Laufer, *Encyclopedia of Traditional Epics*, 633; Japan Society of London, *Japan Society of London*, 3

Dschuma (SHOE-ma)

The dschuma is a VAMPIRIC WITCH spirit from Romanian lore. Looking like either a young virgin or an old hag, it is covered with cholera that it spreads wherever it goes. At night, it can be heard wailing in pain, as the disease is worse then. The dschuma cannot be destroyed, but it can be made to leave an area. Seven old women must spin, weave, and sew a scarlet shirt all in one night, without speaking, and then leave it in the woods for the dschuma to find. The vampire has a particular vulnerability to the cold and very often has no clothes of its own. As soon as it finds the shirt, the dschuma will put it on and leave the region, perhaps as a token of appreciation. If seven old women are not available, seven maidens can be used in their place. However, the dschuma will take its time when it decides to leave.

Source: Gerard, *The Land Beyond the Forest*, 202; Guiley, *The Complete Vampire Companion*, 81; *The Nineteenth Century*, 140

Duendes (DO-end-days)

In Spain, there is a type of vampiric fay called a duendes that looks like a middle-aged woman, small and slight of build, wearing GREEN robes. Occasionally it will appear as a young girl on the brink of womanhood wearing a showy suit of red and GREEN topped off with a straw hat. In either case, it will have fingers made of icicles.

A seductress and corruptor of men, the duendes will use its persuasive powers to overcome and dissuade all concerns its victim may have about enjoying a quick indiscretion with it. It takes a certain sadistic delight in making a man break his wedding vows or a vow or chastity, but the highest achievement it can obtain is to successfully seduce a man while in its childlike form. Duendes are angry at mankind because they so desperately wish to be human themselves, but fortunately, there is only a handful left.

Source: Jones, *On the Nightmare*, 82; Kanellos, *Handbook of Hispanic Cultures*, 235; Roth, *American Elves*, 174

Dullahan (DAH-hool)

Variations: Dullaghan, Far Dorocha, Gan Ceann, Headless Horseman

The Headless Horseman was popularized in 1820 by Washington Irving's American retelling of the German folklore short story "The Legend of Sleepy Hollow."

No such being existed in Irish lore or folktales until after the potato famine started in 1845. Suddenly, people started to say that on occasion the BANSHEE was being accompanied by a headless man riding upon a horse, particularly at midnight on Feast Days. The man was carrying his head, which was smiling ear to ear and was the color and texture of moldy cheese. The head was sometimes in hand or tied to the saddle. Even the horse was said to be headless by some. There were also claims that the headless man drove a coach made of human thigh bones and was pulled by six black horses with skull heads, their eyes lit by candles in their sockets. (This version is akin to the DEATH COACH.) Whether by coach or on horseback, the dullahan races down roads, spreading disease as it travels and causing entire households to suddenly fall ill. The horseman uses a bullwhip to lash out the eyes of anyone on the roadside who sees him, as he is cursed with poor eyesight himself. The lucky victims only get covered with a bucket of blood he throws at them as he charges by. The dullahan is exceedingly greedy and any momentary offering thrown to it will be accepted.

Source: Curran, *Vampires*, 57; *Indian Antiquary*, 300; Leatherdale, *Dracula: The Novel and the Legend*, 79

Du'n Dreach-Fhoula (DO-in DROC-OLA)

Variations: Dune Droc-Ola ("Castle of the Blood Visage")

In a place called Magillycuddy Reeks in Kerry County, Ireland, stands a castle named Du'n Dreach-Fhoula ("the place of tainted blood"). Originally it was intended to be a fortress to stand guard over a mountain pass, but the area was seldom used for travel as it was rumored to be inhabited by blood-drinking fay.

It is argued by some that this castle's name was the inspiration for the name of BRAM STOKER'S *DRACULA* rather than the Wallachian prince, Vlad Dracul III. Despite the fact that Stoker's own journals say otherwise, the debate continues. The basis for this argument is that Stoker had never traveled to Eastern Europe and relied entirely on the secondhand descriptions of travelers who had been to those areas for descriptions he would need for his novel. Coincidentally, during the time that Stoker would have been writing *Dracula*, Geoffrey Keating's *History of Ireland* was on display in the National Museum in Dublin. It was filled with tales and descriptions of the undead (see UN-DEATH). Additionally, it is possible that Stoker could have also read a then-popular novel about an ancient Irish chieftain named ABHARTACH that was written by Patric W. Joyce in 1880. It has been theorized that Stoker may have taken the name of Du'n Dreach-Fhoula, the historical blood-drinking chieftain ABHARTACH, and the tales of the undead gathered from Keating's book, melded them all together, and created the character of Dracula we all know today.

Source: Briggs, *Encyclopedia of Fairies;* MacKillop, *Dictionary of Celtic Mythology*, 180; Rose, *Giants, Monsters and Dragons*, 86

Dus (DUCE)

In Celtic lore there is a vampiric demon called dus ("specter") that consumes the flesh and blood of humans.

Source: Gettings, *Dictionary of Demons*, 84; Turner, *Dictionary of Ancient Deities*, 159

Dux-Ljubovnik (DO-ex La-JOB-nick)

The dux-ljubovnik ("demon lover") is a type of vampire known to the Slavic people of Eastern Europe.

Source: Lecouteux, *History of the Vampire*, 59; Schmalstieg, *Introduction to Old Church Slavic*, 94; Terras, *Supernatural in Slavic*, 124

Dvadushni (Va-DOSH-nee)

Variations: Opiri

Dvadushni is a word that translates to mean "vampire" in the Ukraine.

Source: Barnhart, *Barnhart Dictionary of Etymology*, 1193; Georgieva, *Bulgarian Mythology*, 99

Dvoeduschnik

Dvoeduschnik is an old Slavic word that translates to mean "vampire."

Source: Lecouteux, *History of the Vampire*

Dwaallicht (WILL-ict)

Variations: CORPSE CANDLE

Dwaallicht is a Dutch word used to describe a being from the Netherlands that is essentially a CORPSE CANDLE.

Source: Cordier, *T'ung pao*, 43; Foundation, *Writing in Holland*, 5, 7; Mladen, *Dutch-English, English-Dutch Dictionary*, 209

Dybbuk (DIB-ick)

Variations: Gilgul ("clinging soul")

The concept of the dybbuk first entered into Judaism by means of the mysticism that was practiced in the eighth century. Jews were forbidden to practice the art of mysticism for fear that it could weaken one's faith. However, by the twelfth century mysticism was an accepted part of the Kabbalah, and by the sixteenth century, mysticism was completely embraced.

The dybbuk ("cleaving"), an evil and restless vampiric spirit, was said by some sources to be one of the children born of LILITH; others say that it is created through an act of sorcery. Earliest beliefs in the dybbuk claimed that it was a demon, but later that origin was changed to be the soul of a person attempting to escape final justice. Its description remained the same, that of a hairy, unclean, goatlike demon (see HAIR).

For the dybbuk to survive, it must gain entry into a human body. It may allow itself to be breathed in through incense or it may embed itself in a piece of food about to be eaten, but typically it will make its own way into the body, by force if necessary through the nostril, although any orifice will suffice. Once it has gained access, the dybbuk will possess the person and begin to feed off the person's life-force, taking up residence in one of the pinky fingers or one of the toes (see ENERGY VAMPIRE).

While it is in the body, the dybbuk will drive the person to consume candy and other such treats, as it has a sweet tooth. The person will begin to tire and soon fall ill. They may even develop a twitch and start to vomit a foamy white substance. After a little while the dybbuk will start to cause mental illness, and with the person weak and broken down, the dybbuk will become the dominant personality. Eventually the vampire will leave the body, as it can only stay inside a person for a limited time. The possessed person may possibly be saved by a rabbi who has the specialized training to perform a complex ritual to drive the dybbuk away.

Amulets made of wax or iron may be worn or hung in the home to ward it off. Repeating certain ritual incantations may work as well. Red ribbons and GARLIC tied to a baby's crib will protect a child. Leaving almonds, candy, raisins, and the like for the dybbuk to find will cause it to leave a baby alone as well.

When not possessing a person, dybbuk live in caves, dust storms, whirlwinds, and buildings that have been abandoned for some time.

Source: Dennis, Encyclopedia of Jewish Myth, 72–73; Loewenthal, Religion, Culture and Mental Health, 119–20; Mack, Field Guide to Demons, 241; Schwartz, Reimagining the Bible, 72–77

Earl of Desmond (ERL of DEZ-min)

Variations: Gearoid Larla Fitzgerald

In Limerick County, Ireland, there once stood a castle overlooking Lough Gur (or Loch Gair in Irish). It was the home of a count who professed to be a scholar and a user of magic. He always conducted his magical ceremonies behind closed doors and never permitted anyone entry while he was at work practicing his art. His wife begged him to let her watch, and eventually, he allowed it with the conditional provision that she did not make a sound, no matter what she may see. Only after securing her vow to obey did he begin to conduct a ritual. The earl began to assume various shapes and forms, and eventually he assumed a form so horrific and ghastly that his wife let loose with a scream. As she did so, the entire castle began to quake and sink into the nearby lake. No one escaped the disaster. However, the Earl now a vampiric REVENANT occa-

sionally leaves his watery home to travel about the surrounding countryside and capture whatever young adults he can find to bring back to his castle. He uses them, draining away their life-energy through sexual intercourse (see ENERGY VAMPIRE and INCUBUS). The Earl is forced to live this existence until such a time comes that he may return and "restore all to as it was."

Source: Ellis, Dictionary of Irish Mythology, 135; McCormack, Earldom of Desmond, 20, 32, 39, 40, 46, 54; Spence, Encyclopædia of Occultism, 299; Summers, Geography of Witchcraft, 92

Ekimmou (ECK-ay-moo)

Variation: Edimmu ("Hollow"), Ekimmu ("Robber"), Ekimu, "Evil Wind Gusts," Lamassu ("Bullgod"), Shedu

Dating as far back as 4000 B.C., a type of vampiric spirit called an ekimmou was first written of in ancient Assyria, making it one of the first and oldest myths known to mankind. The lore of the ekimmou spread and survived over the years, as the ancient Babylonians, Egyptians, and Inuit all developed this same type of vampire myth in parallel evolution (see ANCIENT BABYLONIAN AND ASSYRIAN VAMPIRES).

The ekimmou is bitter and angry, doomed to stalk the earth, unable to find peace, desperately wanting to live again. Ghostlike in appearance, it attacks humans relentlessly until they are dead. Then the ekimmou possesses the body and does with it as it will. It has been known to stalk a person for years, leaving them alone for long periods of time and then returning suddenly, taunting with its telekinetic ability.

One is created when burial procedures are not followed, such as when a person is not buried properly, when the family of the deceased does not make the proper funeral offerings, when funeral offerings are not plentiful enough, or simply when the body is not being buried at all. An ekimmou can also be created if a woman dies while pregnant or giving birth, if love is never realized, or if a person dies of starvation, heat exhaustion, or leaves behind no surviving family.

Source: Mew, Traditional Aspects of Hell, 12; Muss-Arnolt, Concise Dictionary of the Assyrian Language, 20, 36, 489; Perrot, A History of Art in Chaldæa and Assyria, 345; Thompson, Semitic Magic, 9, 39

Elbe (EL-baa)

Variations: Ottermaaner

The elbe of Germany is a species of ALP (see GERMAN VAMPIRES). It looks like a transparent humanoid and lives in ponds, lakes, and rivers. It is very protective of its home and will attack anyone who fouls the water or picks night-blooming plants by sending them horrific nightmares. Wherever there is bad fishing an elbe lives. They will not tolerate each other's presence and attack one another.

Source: Ennemoser, History of Magic, 114; Grimm, Teutonic Mythology, 1073; Polomé, Perspectives on Indo-European Language, 322; Reventlow, Vampire of the Continent, 96

Empouse (Em-POO-say)

Variations: Demon du Midi ("Mid-Day Demon"), Empusa, Empusae, Empusas, Empuse, Empusen, Moromolykiai, MORMO ("terrible one"), "She who moves on one leg"

In Greek, the word empouse translates as "vampire," but technically, it is considered a demon by the ancient Greeks' own mythological standards of classification. They define a demon as any creature born in another world but that can appear in ours as a being of flesh. Nevertheless, the word was completely understood to mean a vampire, therefore, the empouse is considered by some to be the oldest recorded vampire myth and not the EKIMMOU (see GREEK VAMPIRES).

In Greek mythology an empouse, or empousai as they are referred to collectively, are born the red-headed daughters of the witch goddess Hecate and act as her attendants. Their legs are mulelike and shod with bronze shoes. Along with its powers of illusion and shape-shifting, an empouse will also use its persuasive abilities to convince a man to have sexual relations with it. However, during the act it will drain him of his life and, on occasion, make a meal of his flesh, much like a SUCCUBUS.

Avoiding an attack from an empouse is fairly easy, as long as one does not fall victim to its allurements. A thin-skinned and sensitive creature, it will shriek in pain and flee as quickly as it can if confronted for what it is with use of insults and profanities. Outrunning the vampire is also possible, as all references describing its fastest gait depict it as being comically slow.

In Russian folklore, the empouse appears at harvesttime as a widow. It breaks the arms and legs of every harvester it can lay hands on.

Source: Challice, French Authors at Home, 240; Curl, Egyptian Revival, 403; Oinas, Essays on Russian Folklore, 117; Time-Life Books, Transformations, 110

Energy Vampire

Variations: EV, Pranic Vampire, P-Vampires, Psy-Vampires, Psychic Vampire (PV)

Both modern-day psychologists and self-help gurus have each subscribed to the idea of the existence of energy vampires, or EVs as they are often called. However, after that, their opinions on accounts, appearance, descriptions, and details tend to vary widely.

Essentially an EV is a being, human or supernatural, that feeds on the energy of another living being. This action can be accidental, conscious, willful, or uncontrollable. Many people interchange psychic vampire with energy vampires, but they are in fact two different beings. A psychic vampire is a vampire who has one or more psychic abilities, such as telekinesis or telepathy. A psi-vampire is an energy vampire, a vampire that feeds off the bio-physical energy of living beings.

Energy vampire is a very broad term. EVs need to feed off the energy they collect in order to survive, whether they are aware of it or not. The word vampire is used because historically it was well documented that they could drain the life and sexual energy from their victims. With no other being capable of such a method of feeding, it was most likely deemed appropriate when the terminology was developed.

Typically vampires drain life-energy or sexual energy, but that is not the only type of energy that can be tapped into. Depending on the type of EV, virtually any sort of energy can be drained: creative energy, fear, happiness, rage, suffering—any emotion that can be named.

The being drained of the energy is not necessarily a victim so much as a vessel, as there are cases where the exchange is a mutual and even a pleasurable experience. No matter how the energy transfer is made, the person who experiences the energy loss will feel tired and empty of the specific type of energy or emotion that was drained. If allowed time to recuperate, the person should be able to make a full recovery.

Source: Ahlquist, White Light, 19–24; Hort, Unholy Hungers; Nyarlathotep, Ardeth, 171–72; Ramsland, Science of Vampires, 36, 116, 176, 182; Slate, Psychic Vampires

Eng Banka (ING Ban-CA)

The peaceful Chewong tribe of Malaysia has in its mythology a vampiric spirit hound known as an eng banka. It hunts humans, ripping their souls from their bodies and devouring them. The victim of an eng banka attack will die within a few days.

Source: Curran, Vampires, 135; Howell, Society and Cosmos, 122

Ephata (Epp-HA-ta)

Variations: Targumic

In Aramaic lore there is a vampiric demon, an ephata, that appears as a shadow. It is formed when the body of a deceased person did not properly decay, forcing their spirit to stay with the body, bound to this world. At night, the spirit leaves the corpse and seeks out humans to drain of blood. If the corpse should ever be destroyed, then the ephata will be released to pass on to the next world.

Source: Cross, *Phoenician Incantations*, 42f; Donner, *Kanaanaische*, 44; Fauth, *S-s-m bn P-d-r-s-a*, 299f; Hurwitz, *Lilith, the First Eve*, 67

Ephélés (Eff-ee-YAHL-teas)

Variations: Éphialte, Ephialtes ("Leaper")

First conceived in ancient Greece and later adopted by ancient Rome, the ephélés ("one who leaps upon") was a vampiric demon with hooked talons. Created when a person died before his time or by murder, the ephélés was a bringer of nightmares. At night it would sit on a sleeper's chest, grabbing hold tightly with its hooks and sending forth bad dreams.

The ephélés was identified with the gods Artemis and Pan (Diana and Faunus in Roman times) as well as the satyrs, sirens, and Silvani. During the reign of Augustine, the ephélés were directly tied to the INCUBUS, SUCCUBUS, and the god Pan, who, apart from having dominion over flocks and shepherds, was also the giver of bad dreams.

Source: Hillman, *Pan and the Nightmare*, 97; Hufford, *Terror That Comes in the Night*, 131, 229; Rose, *Handbook of Greek Mythology*, 62; Royal Anthropological Institute, *Man*, 134

Eretik (Eh-reh-teak)

Variation: Elatomsk, Erestan, Erestun, Erestuny, Eretica, Eretich, Ereticy, Eretiku, Eretitsa, Eretnica, Eretnik, Eretnitsa (female), Xloptuny

In Russian folklore, if a dying person is possessed before passing away and then is reanimated by a witch or sorcerer, the body becomes a type of LIVING VAMPIRE called an eretik ("heretic"). Be that as it may, there are other ways a person can become this type of vampire, such as being deemed a heretic, selling his soul to the devil, sleeping on a grave, or making inappropriate noises in a bath house.

However it is that the vampire is created, it will immediately set out to consume the flesh and blood of mankind, starting with its family members first. It causes a person to wither away, eventually dying, but it can glare at a person with such hate and malice that it can kill with a mere look (see ENERGY VAMPIRE). It is most active at night in spring and fall, living in dry riverbeds where it routinely performs Black Masses.

In truth, the eretik is a living being (see LIVING VAMPIRE), but it must be slain as if it were a true vampire: staked through the heart with a wooden stake, beheaded, and then burned to ash.

Source: Dundes, *Vampire Casebook*, 53; McClelland, *Slayers and Their Vampires*, 81; Oinas, *Essays on Russian Folklore and Mythology*, 121; Ryan, *Russian Magic at the British Library*, 34

Erinnye

Variations: Dirae, Ériyes, Érynies

A vampiric spirit from ancient Greece, the erinnye is always female, distinguished by her fiery eyes and snakes living in her HAIR. Her name, erinnye, translates to mean "to punish, punisher," and she is indeed very good at this task, as the erinnye specializes in killing only those who commit murder. The erinnye will first drive the murderer insane before killing him, making a meal of his remains. Erinnye were seen by the ancient Greeks as performing a public service. In ancient Roman times they were called *dirae*, which means "the terrible."

Source: Morris, *Sorceress or Witch*, 165; Rose, *Giants, Monsters and Dragons*, 420; Summers, *Vampire in Lore and Legend*, 268

Ermenki (Er-MIN-key)

A vampiric spirit from Bulgaria, the ermenki feeds exclusively on young or new mothers and their babies.

Source: Georgieva, *Bulgarian Mythology*, 102–3; MacDermott, *Bulgarian Folk Customs*, 81

Estrie (ES-tray)

The estrie is from the lore from the medieval era. Considered a vampiric demon or vampiric spirit, the estrie is a noncorporeal mass of evil that can assume human female form. It will take up residence in a community to ensure a constant supply of blood. At night the estrie will engage in sexual activity, draining its victim dry of blood. As long as it continues to eat human flesh and drink human blood, it will be able to maintain human form.

If the estrie should ever become injured or seen in its true form by a human, it must eat some of that person's bread and SALT or it will lose its abilities and be rendered helpless. Eating bread and SALT will also heal any damage that its form has taken.

Should a woman ever be suspected of being an estrie, when she dies, her mouth must be filled with dirt, as this will prevent her from rising from her grave.

Source: Hurwitz, *Lilith, the First Eve*, 43; Masters,

Eros and Evil, 183; Robinson, *Myths and Legends of All Nations*, 197; Trachtenberg, *Jewish Magic and Superstition*, 43

Eucharistic Wafer (You-CUR-wrist-tic WAY-fur)

Variations: Bread, Blessed Sacrament, Holy Communion, The Wafer

Until blessed and transformed through religious service, the Eucharistic Wafer is merely a piece of unleavened bread. The Roman Catholic Church considers the Eucharistic Wafer to be a holy object, the embodiment of the flesh of Jesus Christ, the symbol of His purity. The Bible says that during the Last Supper "The Lord took bread," and without any further information to go on it can thereby be assumed that the bread being used was wheaten bread, as Jesus, being Jewish, would have used unleavened bread.

Source: Rubin, *Corpus Christi*, 118, 130; Sofer, *Stage Life of Props*, 31–32; Stephens, *Demon Lovers*, 221–40

Farkaskoldus (Far-KISS-ole-dis)

In Hungary, werewolf and vampire stories were not uncommon, so it would not be wholly inconceivable that the two mythos would cross. If a werewolf ever ate the flesh of an executed person, when it died, it would rise up as a REVENANT vampire called a farkaskoldus. It rises from its grave at night, and using its ability to shape-shift into a cat, dog, or goat, it makes its way discreetly through town looking for its next victim. When it has found someone suitable, it lies on top of its prey, drinks his blood, and returns to its grave before the sun rises. If a deceased person is suspected of being a farkaskoldus, his grave must be exhumed. If he is in fact a vampire, the corpse will show little or no signs of decomposition nor will it smell like death or decay; rather the body will be filled with fresh blood.

Once a farkaskoldus has been discovered, there are a number of ways it can be destroyed. The simplest way is to burn the body to ash or soak the corpse in holy water. However, if it is felt that a more severe method is necessary, a stake can be driven through the heart or a nail through the head, after which the body must be burned to ashes. An even more extreme method of destruction is to sever the arms, legs, and head, remove the heart through the vampire's back, and then burn everything to ash. Finally, place the remains in a sack and throw it into a deep river.

Source: Inge Heinze, *Proceedings*, 270; Kenyon, *Witches Still Live*, 39, 52; Volta, *The Vampire*, 144

Fear Gortagh (FEAR GOR-ta)

Variations: Fair-Gortha, Fairy Grass, Féar Gortach, Fód Gortach, Foidin Mearuil ("Stray Sod"), Grave Grass

In Ireland there are patches of earth that have vampiric tendencies. Known as fear gortagh ("hungry grass"), it is the spot where a person has died from starvation. Looking like the grass all around it, there is nothing to give it away for what it is until another person happens to walk upon it—suddenly he will find that he has become very hungry. Retreating from the spot will not reverse the effects, as the fear gortagh has already begun the process of eating away at his life-energy. In order to save himself, the victim must quickly eat and drink something or he will succumb to hunger pains and die (see ENERGY VAMPIRE).

Source: Jones, *New Comparative Method*, 70, 73; Kinahan, *Yeats*, 73; Royal Society of Antiquaries, *Journal of the Royal Society*, vol. 72–73, 107; Wilde, *Ancient Legends*,183, 226

Feu-Follet (FEW FOL-et)

Variations: Fifollet, Foolish Light, Swamp Lights, Will-o'-the-Wisp

The Cajun people of Louisiana, Tennessee, and Virginia in the United States say that the feu-follet is the harmless, returned soul of a family member who escaped purgatory in order to beg its family for prayers and masses said in its name. The Irish people who settled near the Cajuns believe that the feu-follet are elves and fairies dancing, while the Basque claim that it is their guardian spirit warning of danger.

However, the African-Americans in the same areas believe that it a vampiric spirit. They say the feu-follet ("dancing light") is the soul of a person that God sent back to earth to do penance, but rather than doing good, it decided to do evil instead. If a person sees it (a glowing orb of electricity that occasionally emits a lightning bolt), he must quickly stab his knife in the ground, as it may buy him just enough time to run home and change his clothing. If he does not, he will be struck by its lightning. Should he go back the following day to collect his knife, the blade will have blood on it.

Mischief makers, feu-follet also have INCUBUS- and SUCCUBUS-like tendencies in which they draw blood to drink. There is the belief that if a feu-follet can consume enough human blood, it will become a physical vampire.

Source: Boatright, *The Golden Log*, 115; Bryant, *Handbook of Death*, 99; Senn, *Were-wolf and Vampire in Romania*, 71; University of Missouri, *University of Missouri Studies*, vol. 10, 75, 104

Fir Gorta (FUR GORTA)

The Irish Potato Famine lasted about six years, beginning in 1845. In those desperate times in the areas hit hardest, some people turned to the eating of relish cakes—a small cake made with oatmeal, turnip greens, and fresh blood let from the necks of animals. After the blight ended, it was believed that some people had developed a taste for relish cakes and did not give them up. It was only then, in the years after the Irish Potato Famine had ended, that the vampiric creature known as the fir gorta ("hungry man") came into existence, a skeletal being carrying a staff in one hand and a begging cup in the other. Stories of the creature warned that it would go to the back door of a home where these cakes were still being eaten. Then, in a weak and feeble voice, it would ask for money or food. If nothing was given, sickness befell the home's occupants.

Source: Curran, *Vampires*, 57; Macafee, *Concise Ulster Dictionary*, 119; McLean, *Event and Its Terrors*, 73; Tuke, *Visit to Connaught*, 18–19

Flygia (FLY-ja)

This invisible tutelary spirit from Norway, the flygia, only appears to people in their dreams. If the flygia is seen while the person is awake, then it is regarded to be a death omen. There are a few stories connecting the flygia to the DOPPELSAUGER. The notion of a spirit connected to a person for his entire life is not uncommon. In fact, it was a well-accepted concept in Roman times when it was called a *daimonion*.

Source: Einarsson, *Saga of Gunnlaug*, 40; Grimstad, *Volsunga Saga*, 88

Flying Heads (Fly-ing Heds)

The Iroquois tribes of the northeastern United States have a vampiric creature in their folklore aptly named the flying heads. It is a large head with fiery red eyes, stringy HAIR, and rows of sharp teeth within a huge mouth that has locking jaws. It has wings where its ears should be. Flying heads glide through stormy skies, keeping aloft by the undulating of their HAIR while they look for prey. Once a suitable victim is found, the head dives down, biting into the person, its jaws locking into place.

Luring in a creature capable of flight so that it can be close enough to kill would be a difficult thing to do in the best of circumstances; fortunately, flying heads are not exceeding bright. The Iroquois would roast chestnuts over a fire made of many small coals. Then, they would eat them, making loud exclamations of how delicious the nuts tasted. The flying heads, wanting to eat something as wonderfully tasting as the nuts, would swoop down and grab up a mouthful of the red-hot coals. Once the jaws locked shut, the coals would begin to burn, and soon, the flying heads would ignite and burst into flames.

Source: Beauchamp, *Iroquois Trail*, 95; Canfield, *Legends of the Iroquois*, 125–26; McLeish, *Myths and Legends*, 199; Rose, *Giants, Monsters and Dragons*, 124; Wonderley, *Oneida Iroquois Folklore*, 92

Forso

In New Guinea and the islands off the coast of northern Australia, there is a vampiric ghost known as a forso. An ENERGY VAMPIRE, the forso feeds off the emotions, life energy, and sexual energies of its victims, in addition to cursing them with bad luck and depression. Intangible and invisible, the forso seldom travels far from its gravesite but will take advantage of any opportunity to attack anyone who comes close to its grave. Charms and prayers can be used to ward off its attack but only if in life the forso was an immoral yet religious individual. Papuans consider the forso a being to be pitied, a lonely soul looking for attention. Therefore when a forso is discovered, its burial mound is located and its bones exhumed and taken into a family's home. By adopting the forso and making it feel welcome, it no longer feels the need to feed off or curse people.

Source: Frazer, *Belief in Immortality*, 152, 164, 174, 451; Maberry, *Vampire Universe*, 121

Füersteinmannli (Few-er-STINE-man-lee)

Variations: Feux Follet, Treasure Light

In Switzerland there is a type of vampiric spirit named füersteinmannli. Essentially, it is a male CORPSE CANDLE.

Source: Dyer, *Popular Science Monthly*, vol. 19, 74; Meyer, *Mythologie der Germanen*

Fyglia (FIG-lee-ah)

In Iceland there is a type of flesh-eating REVENANT known as a fyglia ("following spirit") who has the odd behavior of climbing onto rooftops and kicking shingles loose when looking for its victims. To destroy this vampire it must first be captured, beheaded, and then reburied with the head positioned under its body.

Source: Dillon, *Winter in Iceland*, 272

Gaki (GA-key)

Gaki are doggedly persistent vampiric spirits from Japan that are created when an exceedingly greedy person dies. They are returned to earth and forced to wander with an unquenchable thirst for blood. Gaki are described as having a cold body, hollow features, and pale skin. A gaki's stomach is enormous but its neck is narrow. Although they can shape-shift into mist, gaki enjoy attacking people in one of the physical forms they can assume, that of an animal, a red-skinned humanoid with horns, or a specific person.

Gaki need not physically assault their prey; just being near them is enough to drain them of blood. They chatter incomprehensibly up until the point they actually attack. Once they do, the gaki enter into a feeding frenzy, completely fixated on their target.

The gaki are impervious to damage in mist form unless attacked by weapons especially designed to affect a ghost. Although such a weapon will cause harm, it will not destroy a gaki. The only way it can be destroyed is while it is in a physical form. The best chance of success is to attack while it is feeding, as it will not have the presence of mind to defend itself.

There are several species of gaki and each has a specialized diet. The most dangerous gaki consumes flesh, human blood, and souls. Another dangerous type feeds on a person's thoughts while they meditate. Other gaki feed on samurai topknots or tattoos. Still others eat incense, paper, sweat, or tea. These less dangerous gaki can be saited by Zen monasteries making small offerings of food to them.
Source: Ashley, *Complete Book of Vampires*; Covey, *Beasts*, 96; Davis, *Myths and Legends*, 388; Smith, *Ancestor Worship*, 41

Gandarva (Gan-DAR-ah)

Variations: Gandarwa, Gandharva, Kundrav

In the Hindu religion there is a vampiric demigod named Gandarva ("ecstatic" or "music"). He preys only on a very specific type of women—those who married for love without the permission of their family or a proper ceremony; and then, he only attacks when they are home alone and asleep. Extremely stealthy, he sneaks into their bedrooms, raping and draining them of their blood.

Legends of Gandarva go back more than 2,000 years, making him at least as old as the PISACHA vampire.
Source: Barber, *Dictionary of Fabulous Beasts*, 64; Greiger, *Civilization of the Eastern Iranians*, 45–46; Rose, *Giants, Monsters, and Dragons*, 132; Turner, *Dictionary of Ancient Deities*, 186

Garlic (Gar-lik)

Variations: *Allium sativum*, Chaios ("shepherd's crook"), Gaesum ("heavy javelin"), Garleac, Garlick, *theriacum rusti-corum* ("country man's cure-all")

Humans have cultivated garlic for at least 10,000 years. It has been theorized that it originated in southcentral Asia and northwestern China. Some anthropologists speculate that it was most likely the very first plant product intentionally cultivated by mankind. Sanskrit writings dating back 5,000 years refer to garlic as the "slayer of monsters," because its odor warded off evil creatures. The ancient Egyptians said it could increase a person's physical strength. In Transylvanian lore, placing garlic and a silver knife under one's bed would keep vampires away.

It has been speculated that vampires, generally speaking, have two universal consistencies: they will always prey upon what their specific cultural people consider most valuable and they will always be repelled by an inexpensive and common item. Considering how widespread and accessible garlic has always been, it is small wonder that vampires from all over the world and from every time period have been thwarted by this remarkable herb.
Source: Barbe, *Vampires, Burial, and Death*, 48, 63, 100, 131–32, 157–58; McNally, *In Search of Dracula*, 120–22; South, *Mythical and Fabulous Creatures*, 243, 246, 277; Summers, *Vampire: His Kith and Kin*, 187–88

Gaukemares (GOW-ca-mares)

A VAMPIRIC WITCH from France, the gaukemares assaults sleeping people. The witch shape-shifts into an INCUBUS or SUCCUBUS and drains its prey of their life-energy and sexual energy a little each night (see ENERGY VAMPIRE and LIVING VAMPIRE). The victims will be weak and have leg cramps at night, growing more and more tired as the nightly assaults continue; if the witch is not stopped, the victims will eventually die. Placing SALT under one's pillow and saying prayers at night keeps the witch away.
Source: Praetorius, *Blockes-Berge Verrichtung*

Gayal (GA-yal)

Variations: Geyal, UT

A vampiric spirit from India, the gayal, whose name means "simple," is created when a man dies and has no sons to properly perform his funeral rites or when someone dies with a great wrong committed against them. When the gayal returns, it will start attacking the sons of the people it knew in life, eating their flesh and drinking their blood. It is especially fond of attacking pregnant women. It enters into a woman's body when she opens her mouth to eat. Then, from within, the gayal drains away her and her child's life-energy until they both die (see ENERGY VAM-PIRE).

When not assaulting people, the gayal can be found in cemeteries eating the flesh off corpses at night and hiding in its grave during the day. Young boys can be saved from a gayal attack by wearing a necklace of coins. A gayal cannot be destroyed, but it can be made less aggressive if someone performs the proper burial rites for its body, a process that involves cremation. To keep the gayal from rising from its grave, place cups filled with a combination of milk and water from the Ganges River around it. Placing burning lamps around the grave at night may trick the gayal into thinking it is daytime and keep it in its grave.

Source: Asiatic Society of Bengal, *Bibliotheca Indica,* 415; Briggs, *The Chamārs,* 131; Crooke, *Introduction to the Popular Religion,* 69–70, 72, 168–71

Gello (GEL-oh)

Variation: Drakaena, Frakos, Gallu, Gelloudes, Ghello, Gillo, Gyllou, Gylo, Lamis, the Lady of Darkness.

As early as 600 B.C. the story of Gello has been with us. The ancient Greek poet Sappho mentions this earliest vampire in her poetry. By the Byzantine period (A.D. 330 to A.D. 1453) Gello was transformed into the demon Gylu and was written of in an ancient text entitled *Apotrofe tes miaras kai akazartu Gyllus* ("*Averting of the wicked and impure Gylu*"). The text is a story as well as a spell to be used against her.

Gello, as the story goes, was once a maiden from the Isle of Lesbos who died without leaving an heir or having any living descendants, causing her to return as a vampire who consumed female children. In direct opposition to divine law, Gello uses her willpower and magic to get her way. She plays with kidnapped girls until she tires of their company and then consumes them. If captured, she will become complacent and do whatever is asked of her, pleading for her life the whole while. The one thing she will not do willingly is tell her 12½ names, for that information would have to be beaten out of her. If ever the opportunity presents itself, she would escape from her captor and flee, not stopping until she is 3,000 miles away. According to her story, it took the angels Sansenoy, Senoy, and Semangeloph to finally defeat her. First they learned her names, and then they forced her to breastfeed from the tit of a woman whose child she consumed. After the feeding, Gello vomited up all the children she ever consumed. With the children rescued, the angels killed her by stoning her to death.

If the story is being told from the later Byzantine era, the three angels are changed to three saints: Sines, Sinisius, and Sinodorus; otherwise, the story is exactly the same.

Gello's 12½ names are Anavadalaia ("soaring"), Apletou ("insatiable"), Byzou ("bloodsucker"), Chamodracaena ("snake"), Gulou, Marmarou ("stony-hearted"), Mora, Paidopniktia ("child strangler"), Pelagia ("sea creature"), Petasia ("winged one"), Psychanaspastria ("soul catcher"), Strigla, Vordona ("swooping like a hawk").

Source: Bremmer, *Early Greek Concept,* 101; Cumont, *Afterlife in Roman Paganism,* 128–47; Hartnup, *On the Beliefs of the Greeks,* 110; Oeconomides, *International Congress for Folk Narrative,* 328–34

German Vampires

Germany has a great number of species of vampires, about fifty, and most of them are REVENANTs. Truth be told, the vampires of Germany are fairly similar to what is considered by many to be the "traditional" vampire. They are repelled by GARLIC as well as HAWTHORN. To destroy one, a person must stake it through the heart or behead it. But that is where the similarity ends.

German vampires cannot create more of their kind, at least, not simply. To actually "make" another vampire may be beyond their capability. Generally speaking there is little evidence to suggest that they have more than basic animal instincts, if that. But if this type of vampire were so inclined to seek out a person to create as a fellow REVENANT, there would only be three ways to do so. The first would be to train someone to be a witch and enable them to live as such. The second would be to select a person and cultivate him into leading an immoral lifestyle. The third option would be to drive someone to commit suicide. Only through these methods can a person elect to become a vampire. All other methods of creation are beyond control. Children who are born with a red caul, dying before a person's time or in childbirth, and dying without being baptized are the other creation methods.

No matter how it came into being, the German vampire is a nocturnal hunter, stalking the streets by night. By day, it chews ravenously on its burial shroud in its grave. It is amazingly simple to stop a German vampire before it can do anyone any harm. When a person dies, if there is the slightest suspicion that he may become a vampire, all that has to be done to keep him in the ground is place a rock in his mouth or tie his mouth closed prior to burial.

Source: Dundes, *Vampire Casebook*, 5; Leatherdale, *Dracula: The Novel and the Legend*, 41, 52, 95; Taberne, *German Culture*, 121, 126

Ghîlân (GE-lan)

Ghîlân is an Arabic word that means "vampire."

Source: South, *Mythical and Fabulous Creatures*, 373

Ghole (GOOL)

Variations: Gholi, Ghoûl, GHOULAS, Goule, Gouli, Labasu

Covered in thick HAIR, the ghole from Arabic lore also has long tusks, one large cyclopean eye, and a long neck like an ostrich. Using its ability to shape-shift into a human of either sex, it lures lone travelers to a secluded place where it may then consume the flesh and drink the blood. On occasion it has been known to fall in love with a human, and when it does, it will capture that person and take him or her on as a mate. The offspring from such couplings produces a new type of ghole, a monstrous being that is a fast, savage, extremely effective predator that takes delight in killing and raping.

Source: Colin de Plancy, *Dictionnaire Infernal; Encyclopædia Metropolitan*, 70; Gustafson, *Foundation of Death*, 32–33; Jones, *On the Nightmare*, 112; Smedley, *The Occult Sciences*, 70; Summers, *Vampire: His Kith and Kin*, 204

Ghoul (GOOL)

Variations: KASHA

The Arabic stories of the ghole spread east and were adopted by the people of the Orient, where it evolved as a type of vampiric spirit called a ghoul ("grabber") that possesses corpses. Once it has claimed a corpse, it animates it in order to consume the other bodies in the cemetery in which it lives; it is particularly fond of the liver. In art the ghoul is rendered to look like a three-year-old boy with reddish-brown HAIR and a mouth full of black teeth and blood. Its eyes are rendered to make it look as if it is insane.

To prevent a ghoul from taking a corpse as its own, a vigil must be maintained over the newly deceased with bells, drums, and gongs constantly sounding off. The ghoul is particularly frightened of loud noises and can be easily frightened away in this manner. Carefully woven talismans of crimson thread can be used to ward it off, as well as the use of Passover bread and metal plates with the Tetragammaton inscribed on them. Should a ghoul manage to capture a body, there is no way to remove it. To destroy it, the ghoul must be captured and burned to ash.

Source: Scarborough, *Supernatural in Modern English*, 158–59; Summers, *Vampire: His Kith and Kin*, 204; Thompson, *Devils and Evil Spirits of Babylonia*, 35–37

Ghoulas (GOOL-ahs)

The word *ghoulas* may be the feminine form of the word GHOLE. In Algerian lore, however, the ghoulas is a vampiric creature that appears to men as a beautiful woman, luring them into her castle in the mountains where she will either consume them or turn them into her sex slaves.

There is a popular tale told involving a ghoulas. There once was a prince who was taken on a hunting trip by his jealous brothers. They had hoped to lure him near enough to a castle that they believed was occupied by a ghoulas who would at the very least devour him. Just when the brothers decided they had gotten as close to the castle as they dared and were about to abandon the young prince, they suddenly found themselves surrounded by beautiful women on every side. With no way to escape, they thought they would bide their time and make camp for the night. While the brothers slept, the prince went and tended to his horse. While he was gone, the ghoulas descended upon the sleeping brothers en masse and carried them farther up the mountain to an even larger and more inaccessible castle. The young prince returned to his people and told them what happened. It is said that the band of brothers are still being held by the ghoulas, forced to be the mates of the ghoulas forever.

Source: Knappert, *Aquarian Guide*, 97; Melton, *The Vampire Book*, 258

Ghul (GOOL)

In Muslim folklore there is a female vampiric demon known as a ghul that eats only the flesh of the dead. It breaks into the graves of those properly buried and feeds off their corpses. If it cannot find an easy meal in a graveyard, it shape-shifts into a beautiful woman in order to trick male travelers into thinking that it is a prostitute. Then, once alone with a man, she kills him.

Source: Delcourt, *Oedipe*, 108–9; Gibb, *Shorter Encyclopaedia of Islam*, 114, 159; Stetkevych, *Mute Immortals Speak*, 95–99; Villeneuve, *Le Musée des Vampires*, 368

Giang Shi (GANG Gwa)

Variations: Chang Kuei, Chiang-Shih, Kiang-Shi, Kuang-Shii, Xianh-Shi

As far back as 600 B.C. there are records of a vampiric demon called the giang shi. Taking possession of the new corpse of a person who died a violent death or committed suicide, it leaps up out of the grave, attacking travelers.

The giang shi is described as having two different forms. The first is that of a tall corpse with GREEN or white HAIR. It has red eyes, serrated teeth, and long claws on its fingertips. Its other form passes for human until it does something to give itself away, such as obviously retreating from GARLIC or shape-shifting into a wolf.

The breath of the giang shi is so foul that it will literally send a man staggering back a full 20 feet. If it is successful enough to mature, as told by when its HAIR is long and white, it will develop the ability to fly. Once it has achieved maturity, only the sound of an extremely loud thunderclap can destroy it.

Since there is no way to prevent a giang shi from possessing a corpse, destruction is the only option. The vampire cannot cross running water, and during moonlit nights, it can be trapped in a circle made of rice. Once captured, it must be reburied and given proper burial rites.

Source: Bush, *Asian Horror Encyclopedia*, 96; Glut, *Dracula Book*, 25; Groot, *Religion of the Chinese*, 76–77; Summers, *Vampire: His Kith and Kin*, 213

Gienganger

Variations: Gienfärd

A REVENANT from Denmark, a gienganger is the vampiric spirit of a person who was laid to rest but is not at peace. It returns to its family to haunt them, feeding off their fear (see ENERGY VAMPIRE).

Source: Gaster, *Thespis*, 334; Grimm, *Teutonic Mythology*, 915; Palgrave, *Collected Historical Works*, 193; *The Quarterly Review*, vol. 29, 460–74

Gierach (GEAR-ruck)

Variations: Gierrach, Girrach, Givach, Stryz

In what is now northern Poland, the gierach is very similar to the VIESCZY of Russia. A REVENANT with long teeth and red eyes, it smells like death and decay. Hunting between noon and midnight, the gierach is easily distracted and confused fairly easily.

To prevent a gierach from rising from its grave, place fishing net over its COFFIN. The vampire will busy itself trying to untie all of the knots. Another method is to put poppy seeds into its grave, as the gierach will be compelled to count them, but will eventually drift off to sleep before it finishes. When it awakes, it will start over. Even a simple sock placed in the grave will occupy its attention. The gierach will not leave the grave as long as the sock is intact, but it will not undo more than a single stitch a year.

Preventing a gierach from rising is a safer method than trying to destroy one. As with many vampires, it can only be destroyed if burned to ash, but with a gierach one must be very careful. Every single piece of the vampire must be completely destroyed. If so much as one bit survives the fire, the gierach will return, focused and vengeful.

Source: Aristotle, *Aristotle's History of Animals*, 45; Barber, *Vampires, Burial and Death*, 151; Maberry, *Vampire Universe*, 138

Gierfrass (GEAR-firss)

In Germany, when a person commits suicide or is buried in clothes that still have his name sewn into them, he may return as a disease-carrying vampiric REVENANT known as a gierfrass (see GERMAN VAMPIRES). It attacks all of its family and friends first before moving on to strangers.

Source: Briggs, *Encyclopedia of Fairies*, 206; Curtin, *Hero-Tales of Ireland*, 482; Gaelic Society, *Transactions of the Gaelic Society*, 236; Lecouteux, *History of Vampire*; O'Donnell, *Confessions of a Ghost Hunter*, 124, 132

Gjakpirës

In Albania, the reanimated corpse of a deceased Albanian of Turkish descent is called a gjakpirës, loosely translated to mean "sanguineous." Upon sight it is instantly recognizable for the species of vampiric REVENANT because only the gjakpirës wears both its burial shroud and high-heeled shoes as it hunts for human blood. Once made aware that one is hunting nearby, a person can go to the cemetery and look for the CORPSE CANDLE. Whichever grave it is hovering over is the one that the gjakpirës is occupying. A stake or nail driven into its chest will pin it to the ground and keep it in its grave.

Source: Drizari, *Albanian-English Dictionary*, 38; Maberry, *Vampire Universe*, 138

Glaistig (GUL-stig)

Variations: Elle Maid, Glaistg, Gruagachs, *Oinopôlê* ("She with an ass's leg"), ONOSCÉLES

One of the vampiric fay, the glaistig of Scotland is a member of the Tuathan race. Always female, the glaistig is usually a benign water spirit, although it is known for having an erratic and somewhat unpredictable personality. Often seen wearing a long GREEN dress that hides its goat-like legs, it waits patiently for a man to come too close to the water it jealously protects. For the most part, the glaistig only attacks men, as it tends to act as a protector of cattle, children, and pregnant women. It shape-shifts into a beautiful, gray-faced maiden (the word *glaistig* means "gray") and pretends to be drowning, calling out for help. When the man comes to its rescue, the vampire turns and attacks, drowning him as it drains him of his blood and life-energy (see ENERGY VAMPIRE). Like all fay, it has an aversion to iron, and if the man has the presence of mind to defend himself with an iron knife, he may be able to escape. Glaistig will sometimes "adopt" a person and decide to protect her in the area that it has claimed as its own. When this mortal eventually dies, the mournful cry of the glaistig can be heard for miles.

Vampires that are similar to the glaistig are LA DIABLESSE, LANGSUIR, LEANHAUM-SHEE, MATI-ANAK, PONTIANAK, SKOGSFRU, VELES and the WHITE LADIES.

Source: Campbell, *Superstitions of the Highlands*, 155–83; Davidson, *Roles of the Northern Goddess*, 27–28; Fleming, *Not of This World*, 92–94; Maclean, *Highlands*, 42–49; Spence, *Magic Arts in Celtic Britain*

The Gleaner (GLEEN-er)

In 1732 a Dutch newspaper originally known as the *Glaneur Hollandois* published articles on the vampire epidemics that were sweeping across Hungary, Moravia, and Serbia, contributing to the hysteria of the times as well as adding a level of legitimacy to the copious amounts of pamphlets being published by vampire experts. *Gleaner* is a Dutch word that means "vampire."

Source: Bunson, *Vampire Encyclopedia*, 108; Calmet, *Phantom World*, 54, 56; Perkowski, *Vampires of the Slavs*, 92, 99; Southey, *Thalaba the Destroyer*, 110

Glog (plural glogve)

The glog is a vampire slayer from Bulgaria and uses traditional tools to destroy the vampire, such as a wooden stake made of black HAWTHORN wood that he carves himself.

Born from the unnatural union between a vampire and his human mother, the glog himself is half vampire and inherits some of his father's supernatural abilities, such as being able to see and therefore destroy vampires (see LIVING VAMPIRE and DHAMPIRE). The vampire who is said to have fathered the child is usually the deceased husband of the child's mother. Because the child's parents would have otherwise been married if not for the fact that the father was undead, the child is not considered to be illegitimate and suffers from no social stigma. There are no female glogve.

Source: American Association, *Balkanistica*, 125, 140; Keyworth, *Troublesome Corpses*, 142; Lodge, *Peasant Life in Yugoslavia*, 266; McClelland, *Slayers and Their Vampires*, 110

Gnod-Sbyin (KNOB-SIGN)

Variations: Gnod Sbyin Mo, Gnodsbyin, Yaksha

The gnod-sbyin of Tibet preys exclusively on people who live a holy or spiritual life. Its name, gnod-sbyin, translates literally to mean "doer of harm," and this demonic, vampiric spirit does everything it can to live up to its name. Apart from its immense strength and its ability to cause and spread disease on an epidemic scale, it has a wide array of unspecified supernatural powers at its disposal. It has INCUBUS- and SUCCUBUS-like behaviors that it indulges in whenever the opportunity presents itself. Although it takes great pleasure in the hurt it causes people, it delights in making noises that disrupt the meditation of the monks and nuns, but it should be noted that its silence can be purchased with the regular offerings of proper sacrifices. Described as having black skin, the gnod-sbyin is usually found living in difficult to reach and isolated places in the mountains.

Source: Bellezza, *Spirit-Mediums*, 292; Beyer, *Cult of Tara*, 252, 253, 293, 294, 342, 416; Dagyab, *Tibetan Religious Art*, 19, 70; Nebesky-Wojkowitz, *Oracles and Demons of Tibet*, 30, 32

Goulekon (GOOL-kin)

The goulekon, a type of vampire, was mentioned in an ancient Arabic treatise.

Source: Dumas, *A la Recherche des Vampires*

Le Grand Bissetere (LA GRAND BIS-eat-er)

In France, there is a vampiric creature called the *le grand bissetere* ("the great bissetere"). It makes a sound like a screech owl just before it attacks its prey—anyone who happens to be in its vicinity. It lives in wooded areas and walks the roads near woodland pools. Anyone who is anywhere near it is automatically drained of his life-energy and will die unless he can get far enough away from it quickly (see ENERGY VAMPIRE).

Source: Curran, *Vampires*, 72

Greek Vampires

There are over a dozen words in the Greek language that translate to mean "vampire," and it is no wonder, as Greece has more species of vampires and vampiric creatures than any other country.

Just like the great white shark, which over the eons has changed very little, evolutionarily speaking, so too has the Greek vampire. For the most part, their mythos was consistent up until the introduction of Christianity, then, after a slight adaptation was made in order to keep their monster, their vampire has remained unchanged ever since. Naturally, there are slight variations from region to region as to who can become a vampire, how it happens, what it looks like, the preventative methods that can be taken to prevent a corpse from rising up from its grave, and that notwithstanding, how the creature is consequently destroyed.

To begin, there are oftentimes a number of ways to spell a single vampire's name. This is most likely due to Greece being an island nation; even from its earliest times natives traveled freely between them. Just as each island developed its own variation in language, it is natural that the spelling of words would also have slight variations to them as well.

Greek vampires are almost always REVENANTS and usually come to be so because in life a person was particularly evil and was excommunicated from the Church. Having committed suicide was also grounds for returning as an undead (see UNDEATH), for in the Catholic religion the act of taking one's own life prohibits a person from having mass said for one's soul and being buried in hallowed ground. It automatically closes the gates of Heaven to that person. Other ways Greeks can become a vampire is by having the misfortune of being murdered, having eaten a piece of meat that was killed by a wolf, or allowing an animal to jump over a corpse.

All REVENANT Greek vampires are described the same way—as a corpse whose skin has been tanned and pulled so tightly over its body that when slapped it feels and sounds like a drum. This skin condition is called timpanios. Other than the occasional species that is said to be bloated, the body shows no sign of decomposition whatsoever.

According to the Church of Saint Sophia at Thessalonica, Greece, there are four types of bodies that do not decay. The first type is preserved in the front but its back has obvious signs of decay. This happens when a person dies under the effects of a curse or has left unfulfilled a specific request made by his parents. The second type has turned yellow and its fingers are wrinkled but is otherwise preserved, the sign of a person who has died in the midst of a scandal. The third type looks pale but is otherwise preserved, and this happens only to people who have been excommunicated from the Church. The fourth and final type is that of a person who has been excommunicated from the Church but only at the local level, such as by a bishop. The body is whole, but its skin has turned black.

As it hunts for human prey, something it can do anytime during the day or night, it begins by going door to door, knocking loudly. If no one answers after the first knock, it will not linger long enough to knock a second time.

The Greek REVENANTS can rise and return to their graves without disturbing the dirt. To see a Greek vampire is enough to kill a person instantly, and if that were not awful enough, their presence alone is harmful to nearby humans. The need to consume human blood is not a requirement for their continued existence, so the fact that they hunt and kill at all only adds to the evilness of their nature.

If the vampires of Greece were to have a weakness, it would be that they are so well known and consistent that they can be avoided and defeated. They have no physical disabilities or susceptibilities that can be exploited. By not answering the door when it knocks or by having the Church recant the excommunication will outsmart and undo the vampire.

Vampires from the folklore include the ALA; ALITOS; ALYTOS; ANAÏKATOUMENOS; ANARRACHO; BARABARLAKOS; BROUCOLAQUE, ANCIENT; BROUCOLAQUE, MODERN; BRUCOLACO; BRUCULACAS; CALLICANTZARO; CATACANO; CERCOPES; EMPOUSE, ERINNYE; GELLO; HARPPE; KALIKANDZARE; KATAKANAS; KATAKHANA; KATAKHANÁS; KER; LAMIA, STORIES; LAMPASMA; LAMPASTRO; NOSOPHOROS; ONOSCÈLES; REVENANT, TIMPANITA; VRYKOLAKA; and the VYRKOLATIOS

Source: Melton, Vampire Book; Szigethy, Vampires, 4, 6, 59; Summers, Vampire in Lore and Legend, 18, 43, 217–220

Green

The color green has played a part in Celtic and Chinese vampire lore from early beginnings. Usually in their stories, if green is mentioned as being the color of someone's clothing or HAIR, it is something of an early indicator to the listener or reader that the person is in fact some sort of vampire. Lamps are narrated as suddenly burning with a green flame when a vampire enters a room. This ancient custom has found its way into modern storytelling; H. P. Lovecraft, Edgar Allan Poe, and Bram Stoker have all used this color to point out the undead to their readers (see UNDEATH).

Some vampires known for their green clothes, HAIR, or skin are the BANSHEE, BAOBHAM SITH, CH'ING SHIH, DUENDES, DUS, GIANG SHI, GLAISTIG, GWRACH Y RHIBYN, HAMEH, HANNYA, KAPPA, KARASU TENGU, LANGSUIR, MASAN,

RUSALKA, SAMODIVA, TOYOL, VETALA, and the VODYANIK.

Source: Bush, *Asian Horror Encyclopedia*, 96; Davidson, *Roles of the Northern Goddess*, 137, Kanellos, *Handbook of Hispanic Cultures*, 235; MacKillop, *Dictionary of Celtic Mythology*, 30; Thompson, *Studies of Chinese Religion*, 91

Green Ogress (GREEN OH-griss)

In France, there is a type of vampiric fay called a green ogress who appears to men as a supernaturally beautiful woman. Using its feminine guiles, it lures a man into sexual intercourse, during which it drains him of his blood. Like all of her kind, the green ogress is susceptible to iron.

Source: Lang, *Blue Fairy Book*, 61–63; MacDonald, *Storyteller's Sourcebook*, 119; Moilanen, *Last of the Great Masters*, 60; Sue, *Mysteries of Paris*, 8, 11–12

Grendel (GREN-del)

Grendel, the monster from the legendary epic saga *Beowulf*, is often overlooked in vampiric lore, but in truth it is a vampiric creature. In the saga, Grendel is a descendant of Cain; a gigantic monster, he is half man and half water troll. At night he would leave his watery cave, located in Dark Lake, and attack the men of King Hrot's court and all who served him. Grendel would rip them apart with his bare hands, drinking their blood and eating their flesh. A vicious warrior already, he was rendered impervious to swords by a spell cast upon him by his mother, a witch. His only pleasure is killing. Beowulf is asked by the king to slay the beast, which the hero does, by ripping off one of his arms in a wrestling match.

If the story of Beowulf and his encounter with Grendel sounds familiar, it should. It is similar to many ancient Norse stories regarding the vampiric REVENANTS known as DRAUGE and DRAUGR. Both of these vampires are described as being large and exceptionally strong, as Grendel was. Both vampires were able to kill a man in a single swipe, as Grendel did. The DRAUGE was created by magic, and Grendel was protected by the witchcraft his mother placed on him. The DRAUGE was re-imagined when Christianity was introduced; the story of Beowulf was written during the time when the old religion was giving way to the new. DRAUGR wanted what they had in life—warmth, food, and family; and since they could not have it, they got what pleasure they could through death and destruction. Grendel, who also had none of those things, only found pleasure in killing as well. Neither a DRAUGR nor Grendel could be harmed by mere weapons. A DRAUGR could only be defeated by a hero in a wrestling match, which was exactly how Grendel was defeated.

Source: Hoops, *Kommentar zum Beowulf*, 163; Olsen, *Monsters and the Monstrous*, 79; Perkowski, *Vampires of the Slavs;* Robinson, *Tomb of Beowulf*, 185–218; Tolkien, *Beowulf*, 278

Groac'h (Grow-LICH)

Variations: Grac'h

In the Breton region of France comes Groac'h, a vampiric fay that looks to be a beautiful woman. Groac'h lives deep in the woods; although she will venture out to find children so that she may eat their flesh, she oftentimes finds herself having to protect her treasure from men who come seeking to steal it. Using her beauty to entice a man into letting his guard down, she seduces him, then suddenly attacks, draining him of his blood.

There is a story of a young man named Houran Pogamm. He went out into the world to seek his fortune so that he could afford to marry his love, a maiden named Bellah Postik. Houran had heard that that there was a beautiful yet evil woman named Groac'h who lived on the Isle of Lok. It was said that the woman had a large fortune hidden there. Houran traveled to the island and soon came across Groac'h. She took particular delight in capturing young men and finding new ways of imprisoning them, as she believed herself too clever to ever be caught or tricked. Houran she transformed into a toad. Fortunately for the young couple, Bellah came to rescue her love. She was able to outsmart Groac'h, trap her under a net, and push her into a deep hole that was then plugged with a large boulder. Once Groac'h was imprisoned, the spell was broken, Houran was restored, and the treasure was revealed to them.

Source: Breton Legends, *Breton Legends Translated*, 132–149; Krappe, *Balor with the Evil Eye*, 44–46, 77–79; Lang, *Lilac Fairy Book*, 315–26; Markale, *Women of the Celts*, 128, 228, 230

Grobnik (GRUB-nic)

Variations: Gromlik

In the Kukush, Ohrid, and Struga districts of Bulgaria, there is a vampiric REVENANT known as a grobnik ("of a grave"). It is created when either a person is strangled to death or is simply predisposed to becoming a vampire. After the body is buried, for the first nine days, the vampire is an invisible spirit. It is capable of only pulling off small pranks. Then, after 40 days, it can leave its grave and pass itself off as a human who has only one nostril. The only other telltale sign that it is not human is that its shadow will have sparks in it. The grobnik is very dense and strong, and it feeds on cattle, draining off their blood, and consumes the carcasses of animals it can find. Talismans can be worn to ward off the vampire, but if it can be captured and destroyed, all the better, as left unchecked, it will destroy all the cattle in a village. Once it is caught, it must be tied to a pyre of thorn bushes and burned to ash. If the vampire is detected during its first nine days of unlife, a DJADADJII can be hired to bottle it (see BOTTLING).

Source: Georgieva, *Bulgarian Mythology*, 95; Gypsy Lore Society, *Journal of the Gypsy Lore Society*, 131; Perkowski, *Vampires of the Slavs*, 206

Guédé (GLIED-ah)

Variations: Ghede, Guede

In Haitian voodoo, there is a vampiric ioa named Guédé. He is one of 30 different spirits who are members of the spirit family headed by Baron Samdi. Guédé, who dresses like an undertaker, presides over death, sex, and tomfoolery. He is a healer to the sick and protector of children, as well being a font of knowledge when it comes to death and those who have died. Guédé also has the power to return a zombie back to a living human. During ceremonies he freely possesses his followers, particularly those who cross-dress or wear the traditional elaborate costuming consisting of dark glasses, large hats, and walking sticks.

Source: Deren, *Divine Horsemen*, 267; Huxley, *The Invisibles*, 220; Laguerre, *Voodoo Heritage*, 100; Rigaud, *Secrets of Voodoo*, 67–68

Gwaenardel (Gway-ah-NAR-dil)

A vampiric fay from the Isle of Man, Gwaenardel looks like a beautiful woman. She is attracted specifically to poets, feeding off their blood. In exchange she gives them inspiration and a magnificent but short life (see ENERGY VAMPIRE).

Source: Pughe, *Dictionary of the Welsh Language*, 169; Rhys, *Celtic Folklore*, 197–206; Trevelyan, *Folk-lore*, 65–68

Gwrach Y Rhibyn (GOO-rack UH HREE-bun)

Variations: Cunnere Noe, Gwrarch Er Hreebin, Hag of Warning, Witch Rhibyn

A vampiric fay from Wales, Gwrach Y Rhibyn is described as having two different forms. The first guise is that of a hunchbacked being beneath a GREEN cloak. Under the hood only darkness can be seen. The other description says that under the hood of the GREEN cloak is a being so hideous and ugly that it causes madness to anyone who looks at it. A constant string of drool, either saliva or blood, hangs from the corners of its mouth. It has one tusklike tooth, a hooked nose with one nostril, webbed (or clawed) feet and hands, ridiculously long thin breasts, a long, barbed tongue, long, thin, gray HAIR, and skin with a greenish or bluish tint to it. It also has a pair of large, leathery bat wings that hang at its side.

Gwrach Y Rhibyn attacks sleeping people, especially the bedridden, children, and the old. It drains blood from them, but not so much that the victim dies. Rather, it returns to the person several times, only taking a little more than they can fully recover from, until the person eventually becomes too weak and dies.

Living in secluded forest glades or along waterways, Gwrach Y Rhibyn can tell when someone of pure Welsh descent is about to die. It will turn invisible, find the person, and travel alongside them, waiting until they reach a crossroads. There, Gwrach Y Rhibyn cries out a warning to the person: "My husband!" if a man, "My wife!" if a woman, or "My child!" if a child. Usually, upon being so suddenly surprised, the person who Gwrach Y Rhibyn was trying to warn of imminent death drops over dead or goes insane with the shock of the experience.

Source: Jacobs, *Celtic Fairy Tales*, 259–64; Motley, *Tales of the Cymry*, 88; Rhys, *Celtic Folklore*, 453; Trevelyan, *Folk-lore*, 65–68

Gyonshee

Gyonshee is the Chinese word for a type of vampire that has both the characteristics of a traditional Chinese vampire as well as aspects taken from nontraditional and Western vampires. The word *gyonshee* is based on the Japanese pronunciation of the word *jiangshi*, which is one of the names that are used to refer to the HOPPING CORPSE of China.

Source: Bernardi, *Persistence of Whiteness*, 154; Ho, *Abracadaver*, 29–35; Jones, *Essential Monster Movie Guide*, 163; Strassberg, *Chinese Bestiary*, 53–55

Habergeiss (HABBER-gies)

Variations: Schrattl, Ziegenmelker

A vampiric demon from Serbia, the habergeiss is a three-legged, birdlike creature. It uses its shape-shifting ability to appear like various types of animals. In its disguised form it attacks cattle during the night to feed off their blood. The cry of the habergeiss is considered to be a death omen.

Source: Folkard, *Plant Lore*, 84; Friend, *Flowers and Flower Lore*, vol. 1, 64; Hillman, *Pan and the Nightmare*, 127; Jones, *On the Nightmare*, 108; Róheim, *Riddle of the Sphinx*, 55

Hahn Saburo (HAN SA-burro)

Variations: Hanh Saburo, Hantu Saburo

A vampiric spirit from India, the hahn saburo is normally invisible, unless it is on the hunt; then, it resembles a ball of light. Much like a CORPSE CANDLE, it lures travelers into the forest, but the hahn saburo does so by making strange noises. If the lure of noises fails, the hahn saburo will then employ the use of its hunting dogs and drive its prey deep into the woods. Once the victim is driven far enough away from any type of help, the vampire attacks, draining him of his blood. The rest of the body is left for the dogs to devour.

Source: Bastian, *Die Voelker*, 41; Bastian, *Indonesien*, 55, 128; Bunson, *Vampire Encyclopedia*, 33; Wright, *Book of Vampires*, 64

Hahuelpuchi (Ha-hool-POO-chee)

Variations: BRUJA, "the bloodsucking witch of Mexico"

The hahuelpuchi ("witch") originated in Spain, but it traveled to Mexico during Spain's occupation. It is a LIVING WITCH who has the ability to shape-shift into different animals. In its new form, it hunts out children to feed on (see VAMPIRIC WITCH).

Source: Butts, *Witches*, 15; Just, *Conflict Resolution*, 107; Stewart, *Witchcraft*, 7; Thomas, *Folk Psychologies*, 227

Haidam (HADE-em)

In 1720, Count de Cadreras was ordered by the emperor to send investigators to a town called Haidam near the Hungarian border to look into reports of vampiric activity. It was said that some of the undead sighted had died some thirty years previously. The Count ordered the bodies of several of the accused exhumed and examined for signs of UNDEATH. None of the bodies of the accused showed signs of decay, and when cut open they oozed with ample fresh blood. The Count ordered that all the bodies of those accused vampires be gathered together, beheaded, and burned to ash.

A report was written, submitted, and is still on file at the University of Fribourg. Unfortunately, the town was never properly identified nor has it ever been seen on a map or proven to exist by being mentioned on any official documentation beyond the report filed by Count de Cadreras.

What is interesting is that the Ukrainian word for "outlaw" and "freebooter" is *haidamak*. To be haidamak was to be a member of a society of loosely organized individuals who survived off the land by any means necessary. Eventually, they were hired to be guardians of the frontier. It is possible that there was a miscommunication as to what or who was attacking the town. It could be that those who were attacking the village were socially dead, a haidamak, and not literally dead.

Source: Fanthorpe, *World's Most Mysterious Places*, 238–39; Summers, *Vampire in Lore and Legend*, 107; Wilson, *Occult*, 446–77

Hair

It has long been believed that people with red hair are, after their death, highly susceptible to rising from the grave as a vampiric REVENANT; more so if in addition to having red hair, their eyes are either hazel or blue. Having red hair is also considered to be a mark of a werewolf. These are ancient beliefs dating as far back as ancient Greece but became more popular with the onset of Christianity. Early editions of the Bible described Judas Iscariot as being a redhead. Austria, Finland, Italy, Poland, Romania, Russia, Sweden, Ukraine, and the lore of the Gypsies all have this idea tied in with some, if not all, of their national vampiric species.

Source: Broster, *Amagqirha*, 60; Day, *Vampires*, 50; Paglia, *Sexual Personae*, 339

Hameh (Hay-MA)

A vampiric bird with beautiful GREEN or purple feathers from the mythology of Arabia, the hameh is created from the blood of a murder victim. The hameh has a monotonous cry, "iskoonee," which translates to mean "give me blood." It will also cry out if it sees a murder about to happen. The vampire will tirelessly seek out its own murderer, never stopping until it has drunk its fill of his blood. Once the hameh has tracked down its killer, it will fly off to the land of spirits and gladly announce that its murder has been avenged.

Source: Hulme, *Myth-land*, 140–41; Lane, *Selections from the Ḳur-án*, 35; Muir, *Songs and Other Fancies*, 157–59; Reddall, *Fact, Fancy, and Fable*, 250

Hannya (HAN-ya)

Variations: Akeru, Hannya-Shin-Kyo ("emptiness of forms")

A vampiric demon from Japan, the hannya ("empty") feeds exclusively off truly beautiful women and infants. It is described as having a large chin, long fangs and horns, GREEN scales, a snakelike forked tongue, and eyes that burn like twin flames.

Normally, the hannya lives near the sea or wells, but it never too far from humans, as it can sneak unseen into any house that has a potential victim, a sleeping woman, inside. Just before it attacks, the hannya lets loose with a horrible shriek. While the woman is in a state of being startled, the vampire possesses her, slowly driving her insane, physically altering her body into that of a hideous monster. Eventually, it drives her to attack a child, drink its blood, and eat its flesh.

There is no known potential weakness to exploit, but there is a Buddhist sutra that renders humans invisible to spirits and demons. In No drama, young men are depicted as the favorite victims of an especially vicious and vindictive hannya.

Source: Louis-Frédéric, *Japan Encyclopedia*, 287–88; Pollack, *Reading Against Culture*, 50; Toki, *Japanese Nō Plays*, 40

Hant-Pare (HANT-PAR)

Variations: Han Parl, Hantu Pari, HANTU PENYARDIN

In Indian lore the hant-pare is a vampiric spirit that attacks people from the safety of its home on the astral plane (see ASTRAL VAMPIRE). Described as looking like a three foot-long leech, it reaches into our dimension and, invisibly, attaches itself to an open wound on a person, draining away his blood.

Source: Berdoe, *Origin and Growth*, 12; Leatherdale, *Dracula: The Novel*, 17; McHugh, *Hantu Hantu*, 124; Skeat, *Pagan Races of the Malay Peninsula*, 234

Hantu Dodong (HAN-too Do-DONG)

Variations: Hántu Dondong, Hantu Dor Dong

The hantu dodong of India feeds off the blood of wild pigs as well as the blood of humans, like many vampires do. However, this vampire comes into existence in a rather unique way—the evils of humanity give it form and allow it to physically manifest. Once it has a form, when not living in its cave, it hunts for its prey.

Source: Christen, *Clowns and Tricksters*, 44–45; Dennys, *Descriptive Dictionary*, 151; Skeat, *Pagan Races of the Malay Peninsula*, 323

Hantu Langsuir (HAN-too LANG-surz)

Variations: Hantu Pennanggalan

A vampiric demon from Malaysia, the hantu langsuir looks like a beautiful woman or as a floating woman's head with a tail made of entrails and spinal column that hangs down from its sev-ered neck. It is most difficult to keep this vampire from entering into a home, as it can squeeze through even the smallest opening or crack.

A picky eater, the hantu langsuir has a very specific order to the victims it preys on. Of all the sources of blood that a vampire can choose from, the hantu langsuir prefers the blood of a newborn male child. If none is available, then the blood of a newborn female will suffice. The entrails of either gender are consumed as well. When the hantu langsuir manages to find a suitable victim, it bites a tiny hole in his neck from which it draws the blood.

On occasion, it will drink milk from any available source and lick the blood off a sanitary napkin. If it does so, the woman to whom the pad belonged will start to grow weak as her life-energy is being mystically drained away.

Should the hantu langsuir be caught in the act of feeding, the head will detach from its body and fly off to safety as it shape-shifts into an owl, emitting an ear-piercing screech as it flees. Both parts of the vampire, the discarded body and the head, must be captured and burned to ash if the creature is ever to be destroyed.

There are some women who have the ability to see the hantu langsuir, as it is invisible during the day. (See BRAHMAPARUSH.)

Source: Annandale, *Fasciculi Malayenses*, 23; Guiley, *The Complete Vampire Companion*, 24; Laderman, *Wives and Midwives*, 126; McHugh, *Hantu-Hantu*, 125–28, 131, 201; Skeat, *Pagan Races of the Malay Peninsula*, 697

Hantu Penyardin (HAN-too Pen-YAHR-dean)

Originally a Malaysian vampiric demon, the hantu penyardin has spread to the Polynesian Islands. It looks like a dog-headed demon and lives in caves in and near the sea. The hantu penyardin feeds off human souls.

Source: Aylesworth, *Story of Vampires*, 5; Flynn, *Cinematic Vampires*, 2; Spence, *Encyclopædia of Occultism*, 220

Harppe (HARP)

Variations: The Vampire of Milos

Chevalier Ricaut, in his study of the Greek Church, was told a tale of a vampiric REVENANT by a monk named Sophrones. The monk was very well known in his parish, the Turkish town of Smyrna, and it is from there that the story of the Vampire of Milos originates. Although no year was given as to when the story was supposed to have unfolded, Dom Augustin Calmet included the story in his book titled *Dissertation of*

Revenants, the Excommunicated, and the Ghosts of Vampires, which was published in 1751.

In the town of Smyrna, a man by the name of Harppe was excommunicated by the church. When he died, his body was interred in unhallowed ground. Shortly thereafter, Harppe rose to unlife as a vampire. The townfolks wanted to dispose of it in the traditional way—beheading and quartering the body followed by boiling the parts in wine. However, the parents of the REVENANT begged the local monks not to allow that to happen, at least until they had the chance to go to Constantinople themselves, where they hoped they would be able to obtain absolution for their son. The monks agreed, but erring on the side of caution, moved the vampire inside the church while it was at rest in its COFFIN. There, daily morning mass was said over it as well as the continuous prayers being said throughout the day that were offered up to Heaven toward the restoration of Harppe's soul.

One day, during mass, a great noise was suddenly heard from inside the coffin. The monks opened it up, expecting to see Harppe's bloated body, full of blood, and showing no obvious signs of decomposition. Instead, the monks were shocked to see that the body had suddenly withered up and was in a stage of decay that would have been consistent with the length of time that Harppe had been deceased. It was later discovered when the parents returned that at the very moment the monks heard the noise from within the coffin, absolution was granted for Harppe's soul.

Source: de Plancy, *Dictionary of Demonology*, 101; Dundes, *Vampire Casebook*, 65; Masters, *Natural History of the Vampire*, 184–86; Summers, *Vampire: His Kith and Kin*, 304, 344, 410

Hawthorn (HAW-thorn)

Variations: Bread and Cheese Tree, *Crataegus oxyacantha*, Gaxels, Hagthorn, Ladies' Meat, Mayblossom, Mayflower, Quickset, Sceach, Thorn-Apple, Tree of Chastity, White Hawthorn

With its short trunk, dense reddish leaves, thorned branches, and distinctive white blossoms, the hawthorn shrub is a native of Northern Europe. Its durable, hard, and heavy wood makes it a perfect and natural weapon to be used for the staking of vampires. Hawthorn is considered to be a sacred plant as it was said in the medieval period that not only was it the burning bush of Moses but also that it was used to make the crown of thorns for Christ. For these reasons hawthorn is the preferred wood used for funeral pyres as well, as its smoke carries the souls of the dead quickly to the afterlife.

Source: Barber, *Vampires, Burial and Death*, 72; McClelland, *Slayers and Their Vampires*, 109; Summers, *Vampire in Lore and Legend*, 16; Taylor, *Death and the Afterlife*, 385, 393

Hayopan

In the Philippines when an ASWANG decides that it no longer wishes to hunt for its human prey itself, it moves to the swampy regions of the country and becomes a hayopan. Physically, nothing has changed and the vampire is still an aswang in every way. The only thing that has changed, other than its new geographic location, is how it hunts. Still desirous of consuming human blood, the hayopan raises and trains a float of crocodiles to hunt and return with food for it.

Source: Gardner, *Philippine Folklore*, 7; Redfern, *Strange Secrets*, 153; Rodell, *Culture and Customs*, 31

Hefnivargar (Heff-NA-vig-or)

Hefnivargar is a type of vampiric activity. In Iceland it is customary to never let a baby sleep in the same room as an elderly person because they could unintentionally steal away the baby's life-energy (see ALFEMOE and ENERGY VAMPIRE).

Source: Sluijter, *Ijslands Volksgeloof*, 72, 80

Hexe (HEX)

Variations: Gabelreiterinner ("pitchfork riders"), Tochter des Donners, Truten, Unholdinnen, Wettermacherinner, Wickhersen ("seer"), Zauberinnen ("magicians")

In Germany, witches are oftentimes suspected of practicing acts of vampirism (see GERMAN VAMPIRES). The hexe, whose name means "witch," can send her soul out from her body to meet with other witches on their Sabbaths. Once the hexe have gathered, these red-eyed witches shape-shift into various forms and summon ghosts. Hexe are most active on Saint George's Day (April 23) when evil in all forms are most active. Although the hexe is a LIVING VAMPIRE, the preferred method for killing one is to burn her at the stake.

Source: Durrant, *Witchcraft*, 244; Grimm, *Teutonic Mythology*, 1040; Pearson, *Chances of Death*, 14, 35, 55, 62, 130, 181–82, 227; Sebald, *Witchcraft*, 33–34, 46

Hili (HIL-ee)

Variations: TIKOLOSHE, Tokoloshe

The Xhosa people of Lesotho, Africa, tell of a vampiric bird called a hili. Large and skull-headed, it drips bile and fecal matter from its body as it flies. If so much as a single drop lands on a person, he will contract a disease so powerful that only the strongest magic can cure it. To keep the illness from spreading throughout the community, the infected person must be driven out. As the victim grows sicker and sicker, the hili returns to be near so that it may be the first animal on the scene when the person dies.

Source: Broster, *Amagqirha*, 60; Bud-M'Belle, *Kafir Scholar's Companion*, 82; Doyle, *Francis Carey Slater*, 38, 121; Theal, *Faffir*, 149–50

Hminza Tase (MENS-za TAY)

In Burma, there is a vampiric spirit that attacks the people in the village where it used to live. The people it pays particular attention to are those who caused it the most strife during its human life. The hminza tase will possess the body of a crocodile, dog, or tiger and use it to attack people. There are death dance rituals and sacrifices that can be made to prevent its return, but these do not always work. If the spirit returns, a person can remove its grave marker in the hopes that the vampire will forget who it was since it only haunts the place it used to live and attacks the people it used to know.

Source: Burma Research Society, *Journal of Burma*, vol. 46–47, 4; Hastings, *Encyclopedia of Religion*, 30; Jobes, *Dictionary of Mythology*, 1537; Leach, *Funk and Wagnalls*, 1104

Hopping Corpse (HOP-ing KORPS)

Variations: Jiangshi ("stiff corpse"), Pinyin, XI XIE GUI ("blood-sucking ghost")

The myth of the hopping corpse of China comes from a story titled *The Corpse Who Traveled a Thousand Miles*. It is a tale about a wizard who enchants corpses to hop home so that they may receive proper burial and their P'O (soul) can be laid to rest. It has been speculated that if smugglers did not invent the tale, they most certainly capitalized upon it by dressing up as these corpses and hopping to scare away superstitious local law enforcement.

According to the myth, a corpse that has had its yin shocked and its P'O disrupted will become a vampiric REVENANT. Events that can cause this to happen are if a cat jumps over a corpse, moonlight falls on it, or the body was not sent back to its home for proper burial. If the P'O will not leave the body, the soul cannot be laid to rest.

A hopping corpse is described as wearing burial clothes from the Qing Dynasty and is accompanied by monks, mourners, and Taoist priests. Its eyes are bulging out of its sockets and its tongue is lolling from its mouth. Its arms are outstretched and it smells horrible enough to make a man fall unconscious.

A hopping corpse hunts by its sense of smell, and when it finds someone, it goes right for the throat, either biting right in the jugular or strangling the person to death. It has the power to kill a person instantly with a single touch, never grows tired, and can fly if need be.

Yellow and red Chinese death blessings placed on its forehead will slow it down, as will throwing long-grain rice at it, since it will be compelled to count them. It can be warded off for a while, as it is afraid of chicken blood, straw brooms, and Taoist eight-sided mirrors. However, to destroy a hopping corpse, only long-term exposure to dawn's light or by burning it and its COFFIN to ash will work.

Source: Chiang, *Collecting the Self*, 57, 98–101, 106, 113, 169–70, 173, 250; Hauck, *International Directory of Haunted Places*; Journal Storage, *Chinese Literature*, 140, 143; Yashinsky, *Tales for an Unknown City*, 142, 145

Hsi-Hsue-Kue

Variations: Hsi-Hsue-Keui

The hsi-hsue-kue is a type of vampiric demon from China. Its name translates to mean "suck-blood demon."

Source: Bunson, *Vampire Encyclopedia*, 126; Colloquium on Violence and Religion, *Contagion*, 32; Crowell, *Farewell My Colony*, 182; Maberry, *Vampire Universe*, 152

Huitranalwe (Hoot-TRA-nal-we)

Variations: Piguechen ("vampire")

The huitranalwe is a species of vampiric REVENANT that comes from the lore of Chile.

Source: Darwin, *Naturalist's Voyage Round the World*, 22; Summers, *The Vampire*, 124; Tierney, *Highest Altar*, 146

Huli Jing

Variations: Kitsune, Kumiho

In China, a type of vampiric spirit known as a huli jing (fox fairy) is invisible in its grave by day, but at night it becomes apparent, and its bushy fox tail is easily seen unless great measures are taken to hide it. Each evening it rises from its grave and shape-shifts into an appropriate form in order to find its prey, preferring to look from a perch up on a rooftop. Huli jing are particularly fond of the life-energy of scholars because of their virtue (see ENERGY VAMPIRE). It seduces them, and during sexual intercourse, drains them of their life-energy. One of its hunting tactics is to shape-shift into a person who has died a long time ago and return to their home, haunting it.

Huli jing can shape-shift into a number of forms, including a beautiful woman, a scholar, or an old man. It can live to be over 1,000 years old, has the ability to see miles away, and can pass through solid walls as if they were not there. It has been known to possess a person and drive him insane, as well as bestow the gift of flight onto a person who worships it.

The vampiric spirit can be bribed with offerings of food and incense. Also a potion can be made and consumed to keep the huli jing away. To make it, take prayers that have been written on rice paper, burn them to ashes, and mix them into tea.

Unfortunately for the huli jing, all of its powers reside in its tail, so if it is cut from its body, it becomes powerless. A female huli jing can be easily tricked into drinking too much alcohol, which will cause it to reveal itself for what it truly is. From time to time, a female will fall in love and take a human as its husband; it will even have children with him. It will tire of the relationship and leave as soon as its tail is discovered. It should be noted that if someone attempts to cut the tail off and fails, the huli jing will haunt him and his entire family line forever.

Source: Brill, *Nan Nü*, 97; Jones, *Evil in Our Midst*, 158–61; Leonard, *Asian Pacific American Heritage*, 452; Pomfret, *Chinese Lessons*, 143

Iara (EE-yara)

Variations: Mboiacu

An iara is a vampiric spirit or VAMPIRIC WITCH from Brazil, depending on the way it died. If a person dies violently, or before his time, or outside the Catholic Church, or if a body is not given a proper Catholic burial or is buried in the jungle, that person will become the vampiric spirit type of iara. However, if a living person sells his soul to the devil for power, he will become the VAMPIRIC WITCH kind of iara (see LIVING VAMPIRE).

The iara, no matter how it came to be, can, in its human guise, sing a beautiful, sirenlike song that will lure men out into the jungle. There is a protective chant that can be uttered as soon as a man hears the iara's song, but he must be quick, otherwise he is doomed to fall prey to it. Once the iara has secured a victim, it shape-shifts into a snake with red eyes and, using a form of mesmerism, hypnotizes its prey, after which it will drain off his blood and semen. It leaves the bodies of those it has killed near waterways.

Source: Bryant, *Handbook of Death*, 99; de Magalhães, *Folk-lore in Brazil*, 75, 81; Prahlad, *Greenwood Encyclopedia*, 160

Ichanti (It-CHANT-e)

The Xhosa people of Bantu descent in southeast South Africa must contend with the VAMPIRIC WITCHES of the region (see AFRICAN VAMPIRE WITCH). In doing so, they must also confront the ichanti, a snake that is often summoned and kept as a generational familiar; there is a saying that accompanies this idea—"Witchcraft goes through the breasts."

Ichanti snakes tend to be very beautiful, their skin patterned in many attractive colors, and they make for one of the best familiars a witch could ever want. They can shape-shift into any object that is desired and some even have telepathic abilities. Ichanti also have a powerful hypnotic stare that they use to paralyze their prey; even a brief glance into their eyes can cause this effect. Touching one can also be dangerous, as it may drive a person insane, if not killing him outright. Only the person who controls the snake knows the antidote to its poisonous touch and how to naturalize the effects of its glare.

The snake seldom leaves its river home, unless its witch sends it forth to do some harm. If a person is ever attacked by an ichanti, the only way to protect himself is an earnest prayer to God for assistance. If He blesses him, then any means that would normally kill a typical river snake will also kill an ichanti.

Source: Broster, *Amagqirha*, 60; Hammond-Tooke, *Bhaca Society*, 285–87; Hodgson, *God of the Xhosa*, 32; Oosthuizen, *Afro-Christian Religion*, 51; University of the Witwatersrand, *African Studies*, 22; Wilson, *Reaction to Conquest*, 286

Iele (EE-lays)

Variations: "Those without"

In Romania and throughout Eastern Europe there exists a vampiric, bipedal cat known as an iele. Standing about four feet tall and built rather lithe and thinly, it travels in small groups of three to seven members, looking for prey near crossroads, fields, village fountains, woods, or anyplace where they may find a person alone and fairly well isolated. Although it feeds mostly on human and sheep blood, it will also entice children into dancing with it, and as it does so, drains away their life-energy (see ENERGY VAMPIRE).

Fond of music and dancing, the iele are occasionally taken to falling in love with a beautiful young person, taking one as its lover and placing itself completely under the person's control. Shepherds who play their pipes exceptionally well are placed under the protection of the iele, whether they know it or not. The iele have their own music ability and are known to join in and play along with the shepherds. Iele are also known to set fields on fire and can cause insanity and paralysis in people.

Source: Ankarloo, *Early Modern European Witchcraft*, 211, 213; McNally, *In Search of Dracula*, 68; Senn, *Werewolf and Vampire in Romania*, 24, 41; Stratilesco, *From Carpathian to Pindus*, 185–86

Ikiryoh

A vampiric spirit from Japan, the ikiryoh has a most uncommon method of creation. It comes into being when a person has evil thoughts and bad feelings about another person for a long time. Eventually, these thoughts can gain enough power to become an entity and leave to possess the person its host hated (see ASTRAL VAMPIRE). Once it has done so, it begins to drain away his life-energy (see ENERGY VAMPIRE). An ikiryoh is exceptionally difficult to exorcise from a person. Rites involving the reading of Buddhist teachings are necessary.

Source: Maberry, *Vampire Universe*, 155

Impundulu (Im-PON-do-lou) plural:

iimpumdulu

Variations: Ishologu

From the Cape region of South Africa comes the impundulu (see AFRICAN VAMPIRE WITCH and VAMPIRIC WITCH). A vampiric creature only about three inches tall in its true form, it usually stays in its shape-shifted form—that of a bird with a red bill, legs, and tail. In addition to its shape-shifting ability, it can also spread "the wasting disease" (tuberculosis), cause infertility in cattle and men, and cause near instant death in a person through a sudden pain in his chest. In its natural form, the impundulu can fly through a small flying machine that is powered by human blood.

At night it attacks both cattle and humans, drinking their blood and consuming their flesh. A lone impundulu can kill an entire herd of cattle in a single evening, as its hunger is that insatiable. Additionally, it enjoys the pain and torment it causes.

An impundulu makes an excellent familiar for a witch, as it is loyal by nature, cannot be destroyed, and can be passed down from mother to daughter, even if the child is not a witch herself. However, if a nonwitch comes to own one of these prized familiars, it must be used or it will turn and kill its master. When bound as a familiar, it will only show itself to its master in its bird form. The impundulu must be fed every night or at least allowed to hunt for itself, or it will turn

on the witch and kill her. Obligated to protect the witch as well as her family line, the impundulu can only be passed on to the next master at the time of the witch's death. If not done so, then the impundulu is freed from its obligations and is now referred to as an ishologu and will do at it pleases.

Source: Hodgson, *God of the Xhosa*, 32, 47–48; Laubscher, *Pagan Soul*, 128, 131, 151, 153; Marwick, *Witchcraft and Sorcery*, 371, 427

In Bao A Qou

Variations: A Bao A Qu, Á Bao A Qu, Abang Aku

In Chitor, India, an ageless being known as the In Bao A Qou lives in the very spot where the *Vijay Stambh* ("Tower of Victory") was constructed in 1440 by Rana Kumbha to commerate his victory over Mahmud Khilji of Malwa.

In Bao A Qou remains invisible until someone interesting to it touches the first of the 157 narrow steps of the tower. Then, it manifests as a being made of translucent skin. As the person ascends the spiral stairs, In Bao A Qou, always staying to his right side and feeding off his courage, becomes more and more vibrant and solid (see ENERGY VAMPIRE). If an individual can reach the top of the stairs and has previously achieved nirvana, he will cast no shadow and In Bao A Qou will completely physically manifest.

If someone should make it to the top of the stairs and has not achieved nirvana or casts a shadow, In Bao A Qou will moan in horrible pain and disappear. Nevertheless, the person will still be rewarded with a view of one of the most beautiful landscapes in the world. Legend has it that only once has anyone made it all the way to the top of the stairs, although there is no report as to what, if anything, happened or who the person was.

Source: Borges, *Book of Imaginary Beings*, 15–16; Leee, *Tanah Tujuh*, 49–51; Manguel, *Dictionary of Imaginary Places*, 689

Incubus (IN-cue-bus)

Variations: Ag Rog ("old hag"), Agumangia, ALP, AUFHOCKER, Barychnas ("the heavy breather"), Buhlgeist, Cauchmar ("trampling ogre"), Da Chor, Dab ("nightmare"), Ducci, DUENDES, EPHÉLÉS, Haegte, Haegtesse, Haehtisse, Hagge, Hegge, Hexendrücken, Hmong, Ka wi Nulita ("scissors pressed"), Kanashibara ("to tie with iron rope"), Kikimora, Kokma, Mab, Maere, Mair, Mar, MARA, Mare-Hag, Molong, More, Morúsi, Móry, Muera, Ngarat, Nightmare, Phi Kau ("ghost possessed"), Phi Um ("ghost covered"), Pnigalion ("the choker"), Preyts, Raukshehs, Tsog ("evil spirit"), Tsog Tsuam ("evil spirit who smothers"), Ukomiarik, Urum, Védomec, Zmora

All cultures from all over the world and from all time periods have reports of a type of vampiric demon that feeds off the sexual energy of humans (see ENERGY VAMPIRE). The incubus is generally described by its female victims as "feeling" male. At night this vampire assaults a woman while she is asleep, stealing her sexual energy from her. She seldom awakes during the attack but rather will experience the event as if it were an erotic dream.

Once an incubus has locked on to a woman (it prefers nuns), it can be very difficult to drive away, although there are many recommendations that the church offers in order to ward it off, such as performing an exorcism, relocating, repeatedly making the sign of the cross, or, as a last resort, performing an excommunication on the woman being assaulted. Traditional lore says that to hang GARLIC and a Druidstone (a stone with a natural hole through it) next to one's bed will keep an incubus away.

Incubi can father children with their female victims; these offspring are known as CAMBIONS. There is a report of a man from Bologna, Italy, who staffed his entire brothel with incubi and the female equivalent of this vampiric creature, SUCCUBUS.

Source: Cohn, *Europe's Inner Demons*, 235; Doniger, *Britannica Encyclopedia of World Religions*, 503; Jones, *On the Nightmare*; Robbins, *Encyclopedia of Witchcraft and Demonology*, 28, 125

Inovercy (In-o-VER-see)

In Russian the word *inovercy* means "nonbeliever," as in someone who is not a practicing member of the Russian Orthodox faith. Already ostracized by the community, when this person dies, he may rise up as an undead creature, typically a vampiric REVENANT (see UNDEATH).

Source: Jackson, *Compleat Vampyre*; Oinas, *Essays on Russian Folklore*, 127–28; Senf, *Vampire in Nineteenth-Century*, 21

Invunche (Een-IWN-che)

Of all the vampiric beings, creations, and creatures, the invunche is perhaps the most pitiable. In Chile a witch will kidnap a firstborn male child while it is an infant and take it back to her cave, a place accessible only through an underground lake entrance. Once the baby is in her lair, the witch first breaks one of its legs and twists it over the baby's back. The other leg,

arms, hands, and feet are broken and disjointed and twisted into unnatural positions. A hole is cut under the right shoulder blade and then the right arm is inserted through it so that the arm will look as if it is growing off the child's back. The baby's head is gradually bent and shaped over time as well so that it will be misshapen. After the procedure is completed, the witch then rubs a magical ointment over the mangled infant, causing it to grow thick HAIR all over its body. Finally, its tongue is cut down the center so that it resembles a snake's forked tongue. A baby no longer, the invunche is from then on fed a diet of human flesh, completing the transformation.

The creature is never able to leave the witch's cave lair, as it does not have the physical capability of swimming due to the imposed deformities of its body, unless the witch chooses to use her magic to fly it out. Otherwise, its primary duty is to act as a guardian of her cave, killing all who enter it, unless they know the secret to entering the cave without violence—kissing it on its ass. The creature can emit a blood-curdling scream, a talent it gained in lieu of the ability to speak. The sound is enough to freeze a man with fear, permanently.

The invunche has control over a lesser being, a trelquehuecuve. The invunche uses it to lure young girls to the water, abduct them, and bring them back to him so that it can then drain them dry of their blood. Only a hero can kill a trelquehuecuve and an invunche.

Source: Beech, *Chile and Easter Island*, 324; Minnis, *Chile*, 276–77; Roraff, *Chile*, 98; Rose, *Giants, Monsters, and Dragons*, 190

Isithfuntela (EYES-it-von-tel-la)

In West Africa witches are known to disinter the bodies of those who have committed suicide (see AFRICAN VAMPIRE WITCH and VAMPIRIC WITCH). Through a magical ceremony, the witch cuts out the person's tongue and embeds a wooden peg into his head, thus enslaving her construction, a zombielike REVENANT vampire known as an isithfuntela, into doing her bidding. It makes up for its lack of physical strength by having an array of abilities at its disposal, including shape-shifting into bats and rats and the power of hypnosis. Its most powerful ability is it can raise the dead and command them until the sun rises, after which the animated corpses will turn into dust.

The isithfuntela must feed off human blood to survive, but it is not strong enough to take a healthy person on its own. Rather, it uses its powers of hypnosis to make a person stand still while it drives a wooden peg into his brain, killing him. Then it feeds at its leisure from the corpse.

Wolves hate the isithfuntela and will rip it apart should a pack ever come across one. Otherwise, a stake driven through its heart or decapitation will destroy the construct.

Source: Hammond-Tooke, *Bhaca Society*, 287

Istral (Its-TRILL)

Variations: USTREL

In Bulgaria, when a child born on a Saturday dies before it can be baptized, it will rise from its grave nine days after its burial as a vampiric REVENANT known as an istral ("lost heart"). It attacks livestock, killing five or more a night, by drinking their blood. Only a VAMPIRDZHIJA ("vampire hunter") can slay it.

Source: Bryant, *Handbook of Death*, 99; Frazer, *Leaves from the Golden Bough*, 37; Keyworth, *Troublesome Corpses*, 68

Itzapapalotl (Its-za-PUT-till-ot-tle)

The ancient Aztec people of Mexico worshiped a vampiric goddess of agriculture named Itzapapalotl ("Obsidian Knife Butterfly"). She could shape-shift into a butterfly and was described as being a beautiful winged woman with jaguar claws on her fingertips and carrying a stone knife in her hand, the symbol of her personification as the ritual knife. Although she was not as bloodthirsty as other gods in her pantheon, she was slain by Mixcoatl with an arrow and her body burned to ash.

Source: Carrasco, *Oxford Encyclopedia*, 105; Lurker, *Dictionary of Gods and Goddesses*, 172; Sal, *Soldaderas*, 2; Vaillant, *Aztecs of Mexico*, 181

Jaracas (Ja-ROCK-ka)

Variations: Jaracaca

In Brazil there is a vampiric demon known as a jaracas. It assumes the form of a snake when it is time to feed, slithers up to a mother while she is asleep, and attaches itself to her breast, draining her breast milk. During the attack, the jaracas slips the end of its tail into the baby's mouth to prevent it from crying and waking its mother. When it attacks a sleeping man, it will bite him in his upper arm, taking a survivable amount of blood. Victims will eventually begin to grow weaker as the attacks continue, and will never be able to fully recover until the jaracas has moved on to other prey. Mothers will discover that their milk has dried up.

A jaracas can only be driven off if one hopes to save its victims, as it cannot be destroyed.

Catholic prayers to the saints work, as will the blessing of a Catholic priest. There are also several ancient and traditional incantations, spells, and talismans that can be purchased or made to ward it off.

Source: Masters, *Natural History of the Vampire*, 51; Volta, *The Vampire*, 85

Jé Rouge (J ROUGE)

Haitian vampire lore tells us of a werewolf-vampire hybrid called jé rouge ("red eyed"). When an evil person dies, he can rise from the grave as a wolf that feeds only on human blood. The only known way to destroy this creature is to behead it using a new sexton's spade. Once this is accomplishled, the head must be thrown into a river.

Source: D'Argent, *Voodoo*, 42–43; Desmangles, *Faces of the Gods*, 95, 145; Métraux, *Voodoo in Haiti*, 89–90; Stein, *Encyclopedia of the Paranormal*, 801

Jéci (DZET-si)

Variations: OPI, Opji, Oupire ("bloodsucker")

In Kashubia, Poland, the word used to describe a vampire is jéci. It translates to mean "empty hallway."

Source: Canadian Centre for Folk Culture Studies, *Paper: Dossier*, 25; Perkowski, *Vampires of the Slavs*

Jedogonja (YA-dog-in-ya)

Variations: LAMPIR, LAPIR, Upir, VUKODLAK

In Slavic regions, Serbia in particular, there is a species of vampire known as a jedogonja. It has a hairy body, red eyes, and sharp teeth (see HAIR). It feeds on animals and the blood of the people it knew in life through a hole that it bites into their chests. It spreads an epidemic wherever it goes and anyone who is killed by a jedogonja or died because of the disease it carries may come back to unlife as this type of vampire. Horses and oxen are particularly sensitive to this vampire and become nervous when one is near. If someone leads one of these animals around a cemetery, it will balk and refuse to pass over the grave of a vampire. Once the resting place of the vampire has been found, the body can be exhumed during the day and burned to ash.

Source: Georgieva, *Bulgarian Mythology*, 100; Hastings, *Encyclopaedia of Religion*, 624; Khanam, *Demonology*, 251; Pócs, *Fairies and Witches*, 56

Jigar Khoy (JIG-ger COY)

Variations: Jigar Kohr, Jigogonja

In the North Indian nomadic tribes of the Bhils, Kols, and Santals there exists a type of

VAMPIRIC WITCH called a jigar khoy, or a JI-GARKHWAR if a woman. The jigar khoy uses his hypnosis skills to place a person into a trancelike state. Then, using magic, he steals a small seed from inside the person's body that contains his life-energy (see ENERGY VAMPIRE). The witch implants the seed into his own calf muscle and uses his telepathic ability to call other jigar khoy to a meal. The witch will roast his leg over a fire; this causes the seed to grow in size. When it is large enough, he cuts out the seed and serves it as a meal to his guests, along with some of his own flesh. After the meal has been completely eaten, the person from whom the seed was taken dies. It is suspected that by use of magic the leg muscle is somehow healed or replaced.

The jigar khoy witch can seek out an appropriate apprentice to learn the evilness that is the witch's purpose for being. After learning the spells, the student must then eat a cake that has bits of human liver in it. Once the cake is eaten, the student is no longer fully human but rather a fellow jigar khoy, which translates to mean "liver eater."

Among the basic acts of evil the jigar khoy will commit when the opportunity presents itself, it will also be able to steal the intestines of a person, chew on them, and then place them back inside the person. Jigar khoy do this to feed off the pain it causes.

Having a jigar khoy in one's tribe in very dangerous. If someone is suspected of being a jigar khoy witch, he is bound hand and foot to a large boulder, which is then rolled into a body of water. The belief is that no matter how large the stone is, the jigar khoy will not allow the rock to sink.

Once the VAMPIRIC WITCH has been discovered, the matter of his human restoration is at hand. First, two and half days must have passed from the last time the witch has eaten a human liver. To be certain, the jigar khoy is typically made to fast during its first three days of incarceration. After the fast, the jigar khoy is then branded with a specific glyph on either side of his temple and again on each and every joint. Next, his eyes are rubbed vigorously with SALT to cleanse out all of the evil things he has seen. Once the body has been prepared, the jigar khoy is taken to a cave and suspended from the ceiling for forty days. During that entire time special prayers and incantations are constantly said over it. At the end of the forty days, if there is still life in the body, the person is declared cured and human once again.

Source: Crooke, Introduction to the Popular Religion, 349–50; Franklyn, Dictionary of the Occult, 153; Masters, Natural History of the Vampire, 65; Spence, Encyclopedia of Occultism, 225

Jigarkhwar (JIG-are-quor)

Oftentimes called the female equivalent of the JIGAR KHOY, the jigarkhwar of the Sindh region of India is, although similar in many ways, distinctively different enough to be its own type of VAMPIRIC WITCH. The jigarkhwar uses her power of hypnosis to place a person into a trancelike state in order to steal his liver. After the organ has been stolen, the witch returns to her home and cooks it. While this is occurring, the victim falls suddenly ill. As soon as the last bite of the liver is eaten, the person's life-energy has been consumed, and he die (see ENERGY VAMPIRE).

The spell can be reversed as long as a single bite of the liver remains uneaten. As soon as it is eaten, the person's fate is sealed.

Source: Crooke, Introduction to the Popular Religion, 69–70, 72, 168–71; Hodivala, Studies in Indo-Muslim History, 460; Pakistan Historical Society, Journal, vol. 26, 153–54

Jiki-Ketsu-Gaki (GEE-key-KETS-oo-GAC-ee)

Variations: GAKI

When a person who has made numerous mistakes in his life dies, according to the Japanese Buddhist doctrine, his soul is condemned to reincarnate as a vampiric creature known as a jiki-ketsu-gaki. It is described as a gaunt humanoid with dark, oily skin; deep-set bloodshot eyes; ragged clothes; and sharp yellow teeth and claws. It is cunning and intelligent and has an utterly unquenchable thirst for human blood. The only way to stop such a creature is to destroy it; a wooden stake must be driven through its heart, as wood is the only material both strong enough to penetrate the body as well as porous enough to absorb all of its blood.

Source: Hearn, Kottō, 189; Hearn, Kwaidan, 209, 212; Hurwood, Passport to the Supernatural, 94; Watson, Rural Sanitation in the Tropics, 186

Jikininki (Ji-ki-NIN-key)

Buddhist text tells tales of a vampiric REVENANT with large, blood-filled eyes and thick fingernails called a jikininki ("corpse-eater demon"). Created when a greedy, materialistic, and selfish priest dies, it returns and scavenges in the night for human corpses to feed upon, keeping any valuables it may find for itself at night. By day, a jikininki lives what would pass as a normal life. Jikininki hate themselves for what they have become, the lowest-ranked creature in its religious order of being. By making offerings to its spirit, the jikininki can be convinced to gather up its found treasures and seek out a brave warrior to kill it in battle.

Source: Bush, *Asian Horror Encyclopedia*, 88; Chopra, *Dictionary of Mythology*, 155; Hearn, *Kwaidan*, 72

Joachimken (YO-ack-im-kin)

A joachimken is a type of vampiric demon from Germany (see GERMAN VAMPIRES).

Source: Sturm, *Von denen Vampiren oder Menschensaugern*

Jumbies (JUM-bees)

Variations: Heg, SOUCAYANT

In the Caribbean islands, the word *jumbies* refers collectively to any and all vampiric creatures of the night. They are described as looking like a CORPSE CANDLE flying through the night sky as they seek out those who travel alone in the dark or children to drain dry of their blood. Apart from their desire to drink blood, jumbies also "RIDE" a person, much the way an ALP or INCUBUS does, draining the victim of his life, sexual energy, and sperm (see ENERGY VAMPIRE).

Jumbies can be good or evil and have been seen in populated downtown areas where the streetlights happen not to reach. Oftentimes one will hover just outside a window, peeking in as it hunts for prey. Because of this hunting technique, one should never throw water out a window because a wet jumbie is a special kind of dangerous and vengeful creature.

Jumbies move by their ability to fly, but they can do so only over continuous ground; it cannot fly across water, off a cliff, or over a hole. What they can do that other vampires of their type cannot, such as the CORPSE CANDLE, is steal the voice of a child in order to have a voice so that it may speak.

The jumbie by day wears a faux human skin and can pass as a person, but at night the skin is removed and the CORPSE CANDLE is free to go hunting. If the skin can be found and rubbed with SALT, it will cause it to shrivel up. When the jumbie returns just before daybreak, it will find that its skin does not fit and the creature will perish when exposed to the light of day.

Source: Abrahams, *Man-of-Words*, 45, 179; Allsopp, *Dictionary of Caribbean English Usage*, 317; Bell, *Obeah*, 121–26, 144, 158; Philpott, *West Indian Migration*, 49, 154, 158

Kaibyou (KI-be-you)

In Japanese lore there is a vampiric cat with two tails that slowly drains its victims of their life-energy (see ENERGY VAMPIRE), which causes them to have bad dreams, although, on occasion, the cat will simply strangle its victims to death. This highly intelligent creature, called a kaibyou ("cat"), can shape-shift into the forms of its victims, but even that is not enough to mask the sense of uneasiness that its very presence emits. It also has the capability to put large numbers of people to sleep at one time.

There is a Japanese legend called *The Cat of Nabeshinia* that is about a vampire cat. Back in 1929 a Japanese periodical called the *Sunday Express* reported that the cat of Nabeshinia was tormenting the wives of the descendants of a samurai.

Source: Copper, *Vampire in Legend*, 49–50; Davis, *Myths and Legends of Japan*, 265; Howey, *Cat in Magic*, 176

Kali (COL-lee)

Variations: Cause of Time, Force of Time, Kalaratri, Kali Ma ("Black Mother"), Kalikamata, Kottavei, Maha Kali, Mother of Karma, Nitya Kali, Raksha Kali, She Who Is Beyond Time, Shyama Kali, Smashana Kali ("Lady of the Dead"), The Terrible

Kali is the vampiric goddess of Change and Destruction in the Hindu religion. She is attended to by the DAKIN collectively known as the ASRAPAS. Kali is described as having an exceptionally long tongue that she uses to drink blood with, eyes and eyebrows the color of blood, jet-black skin, and long, loose HAIR. She has four arms and each hand wields a sword. The only thing she wears is a necklace of human skulls and a belt made of severed arms.

Kali, whose name means "black," became a blood drinker only out of necessity. She was fighting a demon named Raktavija, and each time a drop of his blood was shed, a thousand new demons came into being and added themselves to the confrontation against the goddess. Finally, in order to defeat Raktavija and his ever-increasing horde of minions, she had to drain him dry of his blood.

Kali is a destroyer of ignorance and only kills in order to maintain the cosmic balance to things. Whenever she acts in violence, change comes in her wake. It is said that her image can be seen on a battlefield after a particularly long and bloody engagement.

As recently as the 1880s a tribe called Thugee worshiped Kali with human sacrifice. It was estimated that they were responsible for some 30,000 deaths each year that were offered in honor to the goddess. Thugee garroted their victims, rob them of any valuables, drain their blood, and roast the bodies over an open fire before an image of Kali. The British claim that they were able to put a stop to that brand of worship by something short of tribal genocide. However, it has been alleged that small pockets of worshipers still practice human sacrifice to their goddess in remote areas of India.

Source: Crooke, *Introduction to the Popular Religion*, 31, 43, 50, 78, 81–82, 91–92, 105, 152; Leeming, *Goddess*, 22–25; Masters, *Natural History of the Vampire*, 171; Turner, *Dictionary of Ancient Deities*, 257

Kalikandzare (Kal-la-CAN-dare)

Variations: Kallikanzaros

In ancient Greece there is a vampiric REVENANT called a kalikandzare (see GREEK VAMPIRES). When a werewolf-like wild man dies, he will rise up to unlife as this type of vampire.

Source: Durrell, *Greek Islands*, 138–39; Georgieva, *Bulgarian Mythology*, 90; Gimbutas, *Realm of the Ancestors*, 257; Young, *Greek Passion*, 64

Kallikantzaros (Kal-la-CAN-droze)

Variations: CALLICANTZARO, Kalkes

The myth of the vampiric creature kallikantzaros is specific to the Aegean, Crete, and Messenia regions of Greece (see GREEK VAMPIRES). When a child is conceived on the Day of the Annunciation (March 25), a holy day, that exactly nine months later on Christmas Day (December 25) or anytime during the Feast of Saturnalia (December 17–23), a kallikantzaros child will be born. If the child is not immediately bound up in GARLIC and straw and then held over a fire until its toes are blackened, it will quickly develop into this type of vampiric creature. It will have black skin, fangs, horns, hooves, a tail, talons, or any combination of animal parts. In the Greek language, *kallikantzaros* translates to mean "beautiful centaur."

Once a year, starting on the winter solstice and then every night for the next sixteen days, the vampire is free to roam the world doing evil. By day it will hide in an underground lair away from the lethal rays of the sun. By night, it will "RIDE" people, much the same way that the ALP of German folklore does, stealing their sexual energy (see ENERGY VAMPIRE). It is also blamed for putting out hearth fires, urinating on the food stores, and sawing away at the roots of the Tree of the World.

Fortunately, for as dangerous a kallikantzaros can be, it is balanced by having a great number of weaknesses. It is most susceptible to sunlight, and any direct exposure will kill it, as will throw-

ing it into a bonfire. It will only willingly count as high as two, but if it can be tricked into counting to three, a holy number, it will combust into flames. Placing a colander or a knotted ball of string on the doorstep will prevent it from entering one's home, as it is compelled to count the holes in the colander and untie the knots. The idea of this is to occupy its attention long enough for the sun to rise and destroy it.

The sound of church bells or Christmas carols will drive it away. Burning a handful of SALT and an old shoe in the fireplace will keep it from entering one's home through the chimney, as the smell of these objects burning will keep it at bay. Also, hanging the jaw of a pig on the door or over the chimney will ward it off as well.

Source: Anthiasm, *Cyprus Village Tales*, 11–12; Blum, *The Dangerous Hour*, 46, 120; Ginzburg, *Ecstasies*, 168–69; Jackson, *Compleat Vampyre*

Kappa (KAY-pah)

Variations: Kawako

In Japan there is a vampiric creature that lives in ponds called a kappa ("river child"). It looks like a GREEN child with a long nose, round eyes, tortoise shell on its back, and webbed fingers and toes, and smells like fish. However, its most interesting physical feature is a dent in the top of its head deep enough to hold water. The water that sits in the dent is representative of its power. Should a kappa attempt to attack a person, he must quickly bow to it. As it is a stickler for courteousness and ritual, the kappa will take pause to return the bow. When it does so, the water in the dent will spill out, rendering the creature powerless.

The kappa hunts from its home in the water. It waits until a cow or horse comes to drink and then it pulls the animal down into the water. As the animal drowns, the kappa bites into the animal's anus to drain it of its blood. The only time a kappa will leave its watery home is to steal cucumbers and melons, rape women, and to rip the livers out of people.

The kappa is incredibly strong and a highly skilled sumo wrestler. It is also a skilled teacher in the art of bone setting and medical skills.

It may well be that the kappa is the only vampire that has a cucumber fetish. No matter what may be happening all around it, a kappa will stop whatever it is doing to steal away with one should the opportunity arise. By writing one's family name on a cucumber and giving it to a kappa, the entire family will be temporarily protected from its attacks.

Kappas can be surprisingly courteous, honorable, and trustworthy beings. They are highly respectful of ritual and tradition, even going so far as to challenge one of its would-be victims to a wrestling match. A kappa can even be bargained with, willing to enter into contractual agreements not to attack certain people.

Source: Davis, *Myths and Legends of Japan*, 350–52; Mack, *Field Guide to Demons*, 17–18; Rowthorn, *Japan*, 511

Kara-Kondjiolos (CARA Con-GEE-ah-lows)

Variations: Karakondjoula, Karakondlo, Karkantebokis

A VAMPIRIC WITCH from Turkey, the kara-kondjiolos rides through the night sky on uprooted trees looking for victims to drain of blood.

Source: Georgieva, *Bulgarian Mythology*, 90; Jackson, *Compleat Vampyre*

Karasu Tengu (KA-rah-shoe TEN-goo)

Variations: Demonic Crow Tengu, Kotengu, Minor Tengu

Originally, there were two types of tengu ("sky dog") demons in Japan, the karasu tengu and the yamabushi tengu. However, as time passed the two species of tengu demons became intertwined and developed into a singular entity.

The karasu tengu is a demon in the truest sense of the word in that it was never a human; it was always an immortal being. It looks rather like a small humanoid with a GREEN face but has the beak, claws, and wings of a crow. It lives in the mountains and is malicious and fiercely territorial, attacking anyone who enters; it is particularly fond of the flesh of children, stealing them to get them if it must.

Able to shape-shift into the forms of a man, woman, or child, it is often seen carrying a ring-tipped staff called a *shakujos* that aids it in exorcisms and protects it from magic. Known for its unusual sense of humor, the karasu tengu can possess people and speak through them. Fortunately, an offering of bean paste and rice can appease it.

Source: Blomberg, *Heart of the Warrior*, 35; Davis, *Myths and Legends of Japan*, 170; Louis-Frédéric, *Japan Encyclopedia*, 958; McNally, *Clutch of Vampires*

Kasha (KAH-shuh)

Vampiric REVENANTS of Japan, the kasha are the returned bodies of those people who were not properly cremated. Whenever opportunity presents itself, the kasha, with its unquenchable desire for human flesh, will dig up and steal a corpse, COFFIN and all. Then, it will run off with its prize to consume it in solitude. Keeping a guard at a gravesite will keep it at bay, and should a kasha begin to creep forward, making loud noises will frighten it away.

Source: Bush, *Asian Horror Encyclopedia*, 95; Dorson, *Folk Legends of Japan*, 45

Katacan (CAT-a-can)

Variations: Katachanas, Katakhanes

In Sri Lanka there is a species of vampiric GHOUL known as a katacan.

Source: Baskin, *Dictionary of Satanism*, 184; Carter, *Vampire in Literature*, 17; Masters, *Eros and Evil*, 108

Katakanas (CAT-ah-can-nas)

Variations: Barkomenaos

From the Greek island of Crete comes a vampiric REVENANT known as a katakanas; it is created when a person commits suicide and once it rises as an undead being (see UNDEATH), preys on the blood of children (see GREEK VAMPIRES). To destroy this vampire, a priest can perform an excommunication rite over the body if time permits. Once completed, the katakanas must be burned to ash. If necessary, the religious rite can be skipped, but it lessens the chance of complete success.

Source: Gypsy Lore Society, *Journal of the Gypsy Lore Society*, 125

Katakhana (Ka-TAC-ah-na)

Variations: Katakhanádes, Katalkanas, Katalkanás

On the mountainous Greek island of Crete there is a vampiric demonic spirit called a katakhana; its very name means *vampire* (see GREEK VAMPIRES). It is created when an evil person or someone who has been excommunicated by the church dies. After burial, a demonic spirit inhabits the body and for the next 40 days is able to occupy the corpse and use it to attack islanders.

Although it can be frightened off by gunfire, the katakhana must be found, decapitated, and the head boiled in vinegar as quickly as possible. After 40 days, the vampire is otherwise indestructible.

Source: Belanger, *Sacred Hunger*, 21; Neale, *History of the Holy Eastern Church*, 1021; Rodd, *Customs and Lore*, 197; Summers, *Vampire in Europe*, 268

Katakhanás (Kay-TAC-han-ahs)

In the Greek islands of Crete and Rhodes, a type of vampire called a katakhanás must be killed by hitting it in the head with a sharp-edged weapon and then throwing boiling vinegar on top of it (see GREEK VAMPIRES).

Source: Fielding, *The Stronghold*, 197; Keyworth, *Troublesome Corpses*, 64; Rodd, *Customs and Lore*, 196, 291; Summers, *Vampire in Europe*, 261

Katanes (Kay-TINS)

In the Islamic mythology from Montenegro, the katanes is a type of vampire that is described as being thin, very hairy, and having sharp teeth (see HAIR).

Source: Knappert, *Encyclopaedia of Middle Eastern Mythology*

Kephn (CALF-inn)

Variations: Swamx

The Karen people of Burma fear a demonic vampire called a kephn. It is created through the use of dark or evil magic. It is described as looking like both the floating head of a wizard, dangling its stomach beneath, or as a dog-headed water demon. Both versions are always hungry for human blood and souls.

Source: Conway, *Demonology and Devil-lore*, 41–43; Spence, *Encyclopædia of Occultism*, 421; Summers, *Vampire: His Kith and Kin*, 224

Ker (CARE)

Variations: Letum, Tenebrae

In ancient Greece a ker was the vampiric spirit of a deceased person who had escaped the funeral jar that it was buried in (see GREEK VAMPIRES). Keres (plural for *ker*) were hideous women wearing red robes over their dark-skinned bodies. They had black wings and long white fangs and nails.

The keres were under the control of the Fates, killing only those that they are permitted to kill. The vampires began their attack with a blood-curdling scream, then they dived down and drank the blood of the dying on the battlefield and ripped the souls from the bodies of the dying. Vengeful, plague-carrying beings, the keres were known to control heroes on the battlefield. It was said that the Olympian gods themselves would stand invisibly on the battlefield and swat at incoming keres to keep them off their favorite heroes.

Tar was often painted on doorways to keep a ker from entering into a home. The idea was that the tar would stick to the ker if it tried to enter into the home and it would be stuck in the doorway. To destroy one, it must be exorcised by ritual incantations.

Keres played a prominent role in Homer's *The Iliad*. On March 4, a three-day ritual called *Anthesteria* was held to honor the keres, keeping them from attacking.

Source: Berens, *Myths and Legends*, 149; Lawson, *Modern Greek Folklore*, 290; Turner, *Dictionary of Ancient Deities*, 266; Widengren, *Historia Religionum*

Kharisiri (Hris-EAR-ee)

Variations: Cholas, ÑAKAQ, PISHTACO

The Kallawaya tribes of the Andes Mountains in Bolivia never had a vampire in their mythology or lore until they encountered the Spanish and were invaded. From the start of the Spanish occupation, the Kallawaya suddenly had vampiric attacks upon their people, and the vampiric demon they named kharisiri suddenly became woven into their culture and mythology.

A kharisiri attacks when a person is intoxicated. It will cut a small hole near a person's liver and enter into his body. Once inside, it eats away at the fatty tissue. What it does not eat, the kharisiri gathers together and sells to bishops and hospitals.

If a person has this vampiric demon inside of him, he will run a high fever and behave oddly. Sometimes there is also a small scar on his body near the liver. Chewing on cocoa leaves has the magical ability to ward off a wide variety of evil beings, including the kharisiri.

Source: Crandon-Malamud, *From the Fat of Our Souls*, 119–23; Jones, *Evil in Our Midst*, 67–70; Kolata, *Valley of the Spirits*, 25–26; Wachtel, *Gods and Vampires*, 52–71, 146

Khmoch Long (CA-muck LONG)

Variations: Khleng Khmoch, Khleng Srak, Preay ("vampire")

In Cambodia there is a vampiric bird that looks like an owl but is not. Khmoch Long ("ghost owl") flies into a village and lets out a call that causes disease and brings death to those who are already dying. Fortunately, the vampire can be easily driven off by yelling vulgarities and insults at it or by throwing firewood or cheese made from cheese at it.

Source: Fong, *Culturally Competent Practice*, 201; Frazer, *Fear of the Dead*, 189; Maberry, *Vampire Universe*, 175

Kiang-If (KANG-IF)

According to Chinese legend, if the light of the moon should fall upon a corpse, it will return to unlife as a vampiric REVENANT known as the kiang-if (see UNDEATH).

Source: De Quincey, *Confessions*, 206

Kilcrops (KIL-crops)

In France, a child born of the union between an INCUBUS and a mortal woman is a type of CAMBION called a kilcrops. It looks thin and fragile; even eating great quantities of food will not cause it to gain weight. As an adult it will become a rapist.

Source: Chaplinpage, *Dictionary of the Occult*, 91

Kishi (KEY-she)

The Kimbundu people of Angola believe in a fast and agile vampiric demon named kishi. In its true form it has two heads or appears as a hyena with large teeth and powerful jaws. It can shape-shift into a man or a skull. In its human guise it will take a wife and impregnate her as quickly as possible. After she gives birth to its child, the kishi will kill her. It will then raise the two-headed monstrosity (one of a man and the other of a hyena) in its home under the sea, where the child will become a flesh-eater like its father.

Source: Chatelain, *Folk-Tales of Angola*, 57, 85, 97; Mack, *Field Guide to Demons*, 70–71; Stookey, *Thematic Guide*, 138

Kiskil-Lilla

Variations: Ki-sikil-lil-la-ke, Ki-sikil-ud-da-ka-ra ("the maiden who is as the light"), LILITH

In ancient Sumeria Kiskil-Lilla was a female, vampiric demon of the night. She is mentioned in the prologue to the *Epic of Gilgamesh*. Her name, Kiskil-Lilla, translates to mean "Lila's maiden," as in the "beloved companion of Lila." Gilgamesh's father, Lila (or Lillu, sources conflict), was said to have been an INCUBUS and was known for assaulting women as they slept.

Source: Gray, *The Mythology of All Races*, 362; Lurker, *Dictionary of Gods and Goddesses*, 192, 208; Rose, *Spirits, Fairies, Gnomes*, 181

Koldun (Coal-DUNE)

In Russia, a koldun is a vampiric sorcerer whose name means "one who uses magic." (The female form of the word is koldun'ia.) Generally speaking, he is a poor man of marginal social status among his people, who victimize him while simultaneously asking for his assistance. The koldun, in life, uses his magic to do harm to others, either by evil inclination or because he was hired to do it, accepting jobs out of whimsy if not financial necessity.

Kolduns are carefully watched by the people of the community that they live in or near, as they are both feared and respected. A koldun who has accumulated a great amount of magical knowledge has the ability to "spoil," a power that causes crops to fail and causes illness and death to livestock and people. Apart from his herbal lore, the sorcerer has a power source that he can tap into—a vampire that gives him the ability to cast spells.

Although the koldun is a human, it may be possible that he is a LIVING VAMPIRE, but after his death (particularly if he dies by committing suicide, dies by drowning, or was never baptized), he will return to unlife as a vampire himself.

Source: Oinas, *Essays on Russian Folklore*, 121; Paxson, *Solovyovo*, 165–66; Ryan, *The Bathhouse at Midnight*, 39, 43, 50–52, 68, 73–90; Warner, *Russian Myths*, 65

Kosac (CO-sac)

Variations: Orko, Prikosac

In Croatia, when a member of the community returns to unlife, its face red and with an elastic body, it is called a kosac. By day it lies helplessly in its grave. However, at night the vampiric REVENANT returns to its former hometown, knocking on doors, and drinking the blood of anyone who answers; it is especially interested in attacking its former spouse. Victims remember only falling into a deep sleep and awakening feeling tired and drained of energy (see ENERGY VAMPIRE). Kosacs can also spread a mysterious and fatal disease. Although it is impervious to being staked, it can be destroyed by beheading.

Croatia was the site of the first "modern-day vampire epidemic." In 1672 it was reported that Giure Grando of Khring, located on the Istrian Peninsula, returned to unlife and was responsible for causing many deaths.

Source: Bryant, *Handbook of Death*, 99; Dundes, *Vampire Casebook*, 145; Jones, *On the Nightmare*, 114; Perkowski, *The Darkling*, 86, 92

Kosci

Variations: Koscima (masculine); Koscicama (feminine)

Kosci is a Croatian word that is used to describe all vampires in general, but there is also a specific species of vampiric REVENANT that is called by this name as well. The kosci, as a species, is created when a person dies by drowning or was an adulterer or murderer in life. Its first victim is always the last person it argued with in life. When it returns, the kosci will relentlessly seek him out, consume his heart and soft tissue organs, and drain his body completely dry of blood. After this victim is killed, it will move on to others, sneaking into their homes, raping women, eviscerating anyone it can, and consuming their organs. It spreads a variety of nonfatal illnesses in its wake, predominantly of which is diarrhea.

Only a stake made of BLACKTHORN wood is strong enough to pierce the skin and penetrate into the heart of a kosci. Then the body must be decapitated and have its knees destroyed with either an axe or a sword.

Source: Perkows, *The Darkling*, 87–88, 92; Riccardo, *Liquid Dreams*, 46

Kozlak (CAUSE-lack)

Variations: Kuzlak, Orko, Ukodlak

In the Dalmatian region of Croatia, the kozlak is the vampiric spirit of a child who was weaned before its time and then died. When it returns to unlife, it acts much like a poltergeist, breaking dishes and throwing pots and pans. It can also shape-shift into a bat or a small carrion animal so that it can attack livestock, draining the animals of some blood (it can assume a solid yet nondescript form as well). While in this physical state, the kozlak can be hypnotized with a branch of HAWTHORN, and once it has been lulled into a trancelike state, it can be stabbed through the heart with a stake made of HAWTHORN or a ritualistically blessed dagger. It is best if a Franciscan monk performs the destruction.

Source: Bunson, *Vampire Encyclopedia*, 146; Dundes, *Vampire Casebook*, 70; Perkowski, *The Darkling*, 38

Krappa (CRAP-pa)

A vampiric creature and REVENANT from Japanese lore, the krappa is created when a woman dies in childbirth. When the creature returns, it looks just like a normal woman until it separates its head from its body and flies out, dangling entrails, in search of its favorite prey—children and women in labor. As it flies, it drips a toxic bile that, if comes in contact with human flesh, will cause blisters and infectious open sores. The krappa hates children and takes great delight in terrorizing them as it feeds. It has a long, serpentine tongue that it inserts into the child's anus and drains their blood from inside their body.

The krappa usually hunts by night when it is impervious to attack, but it can hunt during the day if it chooses. There is only one way to destroy the vampire. First it must be discovered who the vampire is. Then, one must wait until such a time comes that the head goes off hunting during the day. While the head is detached, the body must be discovered and destroyed. When the head returns, there will be nothing left for it to reattach to and it will die.

Source: Dorson, *Folk Legends of Japan*

Krassy (CRAS-ee)

In Laos and Thailand the word *krassy* is a slang word that means "vampire."

Source: Guiley, *The Complete Vampire Companion*

Kravyad (CRAV-yad)

In India the word *kravyad* ("flesh eater") refers to anything that consumes flesh, including animals, cannibals, and funeral pyres. There is also a type of vampiric sprit that is called kravyad because it feeds off human flesh. It is a hideously ugly thing with teeth made of iron.

Source: Dowson, *Classical Dictionary of Hindu Mythology*, 160; Macdonell, *Vedic Mythology*, 164; Roy, *The Later Vedic Economy*, 223–34; Singh, *Vedic Mythology*, 117

Krsnik (KRES-nic)

Variation: Crusnik, Kresnik

In Slovenia when a child is born with a clear or white caul, the child is destined to be a protector of his people with shamanlike abilities, a vampire hunter called a krsnik ("protector of the clan"). Although he can combat any type of vampire, he specializes in the slaying of two specific types of vampires: the KUDLAC and the VUKODLAK. The krsnik has the ability to shape-shift into a white or multicolored boar, bull, dog, or horse in order to combat the vampire, as it will also have the ability to shape-shift into the form of a solid black animal.

Other natural-born vampire hunters are the DHAMPIRE, dhampiresa, DJADADJII, LAMPIJEROVIC, VAMPIJEROVIC, and the VAMPIRDZHIJA.

Source: Bunson, *Vampire Encyclopedia*, 146; Oinas, *Essays on Russian Folklore*, 116; Perkowski, *The Darkling*, 31

Kruvnik (CREW-nic)

In Slavic vampire lore, if a person is not properly mourned or does not have the proper burial rites said over his body, he can return as a type of vampiric REVENANT known as a *kruvnik* ("bloodsucker"). A person who committed suicide died a violent death, or led an evil life can also return as this type of vampire as well. At night, it will return and attack the people from the town where it used to live. It sometimes even tries to return to its wife and continues to live there as if it never died. If the wife accepts the vampire, takes it in and loves it, at the end of three years the kruvnik will become a human man again. Any children that are conceived from their union will be born a DHAMPIRE. However, if the vampire returns home and the wife does not want the vampire's attention or affections, it can be warded off with prayers to the god Troyan.

The kruvnik can be destroyed by beheading it and then placing it back in its grave with its head between its legs. Then its hands and feet must be severed as well. Finally, a stake of aspen wood must be driven through its heart.

Source: Alexander, *Mythology of All Races,* vol. 3, 232; Senn, *Were-wolf and Vampire in Romania,* 66; Taylor, *Death and the Afterlife,* 392

Krvoijac (Kra-VOY-jac)

Variations: Kropijac, Krvopijac, Obors, Obours, Opiri

In Bulgaria, *krvoijac* is a generic word used to describe a vampire as well as a specific species of vampiric spirit. It is believed that if a person drinks wine or smokes during Lent, he will become a krvoijac when he dies. For the first 40 days of UNDEATH, the vampire remains in its grave because when the person died his bones became a soft gelatinous substance. It needs this time for its new skeleton to grow. After its bones have grown, the body that the spirit occupies looks like a person who has only one nostril. Its tongue is barbed to allow it to drink blood from its victims, but it prefers not to attack humans. The krvoijac does not have fangs like many other vampires, but it does not necessarily need them, as it can eat regular food. When it moves, it creates sparks that give it away for what it truly is.

Compared to other vampires, the krvoijac is hardly a real threat to humanity, but should one turn violent and need to be found, it rests by day in its grave. A nude adolescent of proven virginity is placed on the back of a black foal, which is led through a graveyard. The grave that the foal balks at is the one that the krvoijac occupies. Wild roses placed in the COFFIN with the body and additional strands of the garland used to tie the COFFIN shut will trap the vampire within. Next, a vampire slayer such as a DJDADJII must be hired to bottle the vampire's spirit and destroy it in fire (see BOTTLING).

Source: Ronay, *Truth about Dracula,* 22; Triefeldt, *People and Places,* 21; Volta, *The Vampire,* 144

Kudlac (CUD-lac)

Variation: Kudlak

Kudlac is the abbreviated form of the Russian word *vorkudlak,* which is used in the Istrian Peninsula in Slovenia, but each word also represents a separate species of vampire. A kudlac is a person who is born with a red or dark-colored caul (see LIVING VAMPIRE). Predisposed toward evil, he will develop the ability to leave his body

at night to fly through the air looking for victims of opportunity to drain life-energy from (see ENERGY VAMPIRE). He will also have the ability to cast magic that he will use to harm the people of his community. Eventually, he will learn how to shape-shift into a black boar, bull, and horse. When he ultimately dies, he will return to unlife as a vampiric REVENANT. In death, as in life, the kudlac takes great pleasure in the pain and suffering it causes, relishing every moment. Fortunately, it is relentlessly hunted by a highly focused vampire hunter that specializes in slaying kudlacs—a KRSNIK.

If a KRSNIK is not near or to be found, anyone can exhume the corpse of a person who is suspected of being a kudlac and cut the tendons behind the knees to prevent it from rising from its grave. Then impale it with a stake made of HAWTHORN wood.

Unlike other vampires who are born destined to become vampires, the kudlac has a way to escape from the curse of UNDEATH if he truly seeks it. While still alive, he must confess all his sins in earnest to God and be forgiven for them. After absolution, he must then never hurt another living soul for as long as he lives.

Source: American Association for South Slavic Studies, *Balkanistica,* vol. 16, 121; McClelland, *Slayers and Their Vampires,* 105; Oinas, *Essays on Russian Folklore,* 116; Senn, *Were-wolf and Vampire in Romania*

Kuei (GWA)

Variations: K'UEI

In China, there is a vampiric demon known as a kuei. Horrific in appearance, it possesses and animates the corpse of the recently deceased. It seeks out bodies that did not have proper burial rites said for them or performed properly. As it ages, the kuei gains the ability to fly with its corpse, but until that time, it is limited as to how it can attack. The kuei is incapable of climbing over even the simplest of walls or fencing.

Source: Latourette, *The Chinese,* 36, 164; Strickmann, *Chinese Magical Medicine,* 24–26, 72–75; Summers, *Vampire: His Kith and Kin,* 237; Werne, *China of the Chinese,* 231–33

K'uei (GUAY)

In Chinese vampire lore there are a number of blood-drinking REVENANT and the word that is used to describe them collectively is *k'uei,* which translates to mean "deficient." The idea of a k'uei being an undead entity stems from the belief that every person has two souls (see UNDEATH). The first soul, hun, is considered to be the superior soul. A person does not receive it until he is born;

it enters into his body with his first breath. The second soul, P'O, is seen as the inferior soul. It is present in a human even when he is a fetus, but it merely exists in the body; it is what makes a person alive until he receives his superior soul. When a person dies, his P'O is supposed to leave the body. However, through a variety of methods or reasons, should the P'O not leave the body or if any amount of it stays behind, the k'uei that is created at the time of death will interact with the P'O, causing unlife to occur.

Source: Bunson, *Vampire Encyclopedia*, 147; Ouellette, *Physics of the Buffyverse*, 4; Rose, *Giants, Monsters and Dragons*, 424

K'uei, Revenant (GUAY Rev-a-nint)

According to Chinese lore, this type of k'uei is a vampiric REVENANT that looks like a skeleton with a demonic face. It is created when a person did not achieve enough goodness in life to be deserving of the happiness of an afterlife. An angry and vicious being, it attacks those who commit sins. What is most interesting about this vampire is that it can only move in straight lines; that is to say, it cannot walk in a circle or even climb a spiral staircase.

Source: Adams, *Encyclopedia of Religion*; Ouellette, *Physics of the Buffyverse*, 4

K'uei, Spirit (GUAY SPEAR-it)

This vampiric spirit from Chinese lore looks like a transparent, dark humanoid with black HAIR and dark eyes. It is created when a person's P'O does not leave his body because he led a dishonest or sorrow-filled life or committed suicide. Events that can occur after death that can cause some of a person's P'O to be left behind are failure to be given proper funeral rites, letting direct sunlight or moonlight fall across the body, or letting a cat jump across the corpse. If any of these events should occur, this type of k'uei, a vampiric spirit, lives off the evil aura that some people generate.

The k'uei is an agile and intelligent being, and as long as it is left alone, it will not harm anyone—unless someone tries to prevent it from feeding. Should this happen, the k'uei will first resort to using its limited magical ability to curse that person, as it is somewhat cowardly and shies from physical attacks.

K'uei can easily be found on a battlefield because any place that has been touched by the chaos of war will attract them. They are repelled by holy artifacts and will not enter onto holy ground.

Source: Belanger, *Sacred Hunger*, 122; Hodous, *Folkways in China*, 78; Latourette, *The Chinese*, 163

Kukudhi (Coo-COD-ee)

Variations: Kukuthi, LUGAT

This vampiric REVENANT from Albania begins its life cycle as a type of vampire known as a lugat. Some accounts say that it takes a mere 30 days for it to develop into its adult form, although 40 days is the most frequently cited amount, and there are a scant few sources that claim it takes 40 years. No matter the actual length of time it takes for the lugat to mature into a kukudhi, when it does it can pass for a human being. Usually the vampire takes on the guise of a merchant so that it can always be on the move. While this seems to be a practical means of self-preservation, the kukudhi is in fact compelled by its wanderlust. Truth be told, the kukudhi seldom needs to feed, and when it does, it takes a very small amount of blood from its victim. In almost every case it leaves the person alive and with a brief recovery period, he will be back to full health, able to return to his normal activities.

Kukudhi can be a vicious combatant and it is well advised not to provoke one into a physical confrontation. Under normal circumstances the kukudhi is invulnerable to any sort of attack unless it is facing a wolf, its only natural enemy. Wolves hate kukudhi, as well as the other species of Albanian vampires. Luckily for mankind, they are the only thing that can damage or destroy one. If a kukudhi should manage to escape wolf attack, it will retreat to a grave and if so much as a single limb is destroyed, the vampire will never rise again.

Source: Elsie, *Dictionary of Albanian Religion*, 153; Lurker, *Dictionary of Gods and Goddesses*, 197; Rose, *Spirits, Fairies, Gnomes*, 359

Labartou (La-BAR-too)

Labartou was a word that was used in ancient Babylon to mean "vampire."

Source: Dechambre, *Dictionnaire Encyclopédique*, 677; Pottier, *Catalogue des Antiquités Assyriennes*, 116

Lamašhtu (La-MOSH-too)

Variations: Dimme, Lamashto, Lamastu, Lamatu; in incantations Lamashtu is referred to as "the Seven Witches"

At least 4,000 years ago in ancient Babylon, there was a vampiric, demonic goddess by the name of Lamashtu. She was born the daughter of the sky god Anu and was described as a woman with a hairy body, the head of a lioness (or bird), the ears and teeth of a donkey, wings, and long eagle talons for fingers (see HAIR). She rode upon an ass, carrying a double-headed snake in each hand. In art she was depicted as suckling dogs and pigs at her breasts.

If crops failed or rivers ran dry it was her doing. When Lamashtu grew hungry she would seek out a pregnant woman and touch her belly seven times, causing the woman to miscarry. Then Lamashtu would eat the aborted fetus. If opportunity presented itself, Lamashtu would kidnap a newborn child and nurse it from her own poisoned breast.

The most feared goddess of her time because she was known as a remorseless baby-killer, Lamashtu would also strike down men at random, as well as send haunting nightmares and fatal diseases.

Pregnant mothers would often wear the amulet of Pazuzu, a wind demon, as he would often clash with the goddess. Mothers who did not want the protection of a demon had the option of offering Lamashtu gifts of broaches, centipedes, combs, and fibulae. These gifts, along with a clay image of the goddess, would be put in a model boat, and in ritualistic fashion be set adrift down a river in the hopes that it would reach Lamashtu in her underworld home.

For all the fear the goddess inspired, archeologists have never discovered any evidence of a single sanctuary, shrine, or temple erected to her; not even a mention of one exists in any writings that were left behind. There have, however, been numerous prayers that can be said to invoke against Lamashtu.

Source: McNally, *Clutch of Vampires;* Nemet-Nejat, *Daily Life in Ancient Mesopotamia,* 128–32; Schwartz, *Tree of Souls,* 216; Turner, *Dictionary of Ancient Deities,* 285–86

Lamia (LAY-me-uh)

Variations: Lamie, Lamien, Lamies, Leecher, Swallower, Vrukalakos

In ancient Greece there was a vampiric being known as Lamia. Her name was used in early versions of the Bible to mean "screech owl" and "sea monster." She was a monstrous creature that fed exclusively on the flesh and blood of children each night. There are a number of vampiric beings, creatures, REVENANTS, and the like throughout ancient times that share the name *Lamia,* which translates as "dangerous lone-shark."

Source: Flint, *Witchcraft and Magic in Europe,* 24, 131, 293; Thorndike, *History of Magic,* 515–17; Turner, *Dictionary of Ancient Deities,* 286

Lamia Stories (LAY-me-uh Stor-ees)

In ancient Babylon, there were tales told of Lilatou, a vampiric being who fed off the blood of children. Its name translated to mean "vampire." In Assyria and late period Babylon, she was called Lilats. Later, throughout ancient Greece, there were stories of a vampiric being, creature, REVENANT, or what-have-you by the name of Lamia. The stories are all strikingly familiar, but each has its own variant to it. Even ancient Rome, after it conquered the Greeks, took not only the land and holdings, but also the people, their culture, gods, and monsters. The Romans called her Lemuren.

In ancient Greece Lamia disguised itself as a wealthy Phoenician woman. In doing so, it would wander the streets of the city that the story happened to take place in, looking for handsome young men it could lure into a secluded place and drain them of their blood in peace.

In the first century in Corinth, Greece, there was a popular Lamia tale of how it was setting out to seduce a particularly fine-looking young man by the name of Menippos. In the story the man is saved when the highly respected sage and holy man, Apollonios of Tyana, was able to expose the creature for what it was and drive it out of town before anyone was hurt.

Another story of a Lamia-like vampire is the tale of a beautiful young girl named Philinnion. When the story opens, she has already died and risen up as a vampiric REVENANT. Each night she would leave her grave and meet with a man named Makhates, who happened to be visiting her parents. One night the mother happened upon the young people speaking together in a rather secluded place, and upon the discovery, Philinnion fainted back into death. Her parents had the body publicly burned at the stake, rendering the corpse down to ash. After the cremation, Makhates, even knowing what Philinnion now was and what she had intended to do to him, was so stricken with grief over the loss of his love, he committed suicide.

Sybarias was another vampiric REVENANT compared to Lamia. In the ancient Greek tale of *Sybarias* ("She who bears herself pompously"), the vampire lived in a cave on Mount Kriphis, preying regularly on the men and sheep of the towns of Delpoi and Phokis. This went on until a hero named Eurybaros grabbed Sybarias up and threw it off the mountain, killing it. On the spot where Sybarias's head hit the ground a fountain sprang up. A city was built around the fountain and it and was named Sybaris, after the vampire.

Lamia, the Libyan Queen, was also a vampiric being, and something of a cautionary tale. Her story is an ancient tale from Greece as well. Lamia was born the daughter of Belus, Queen of Libya. She was a beautiful young woman, so beautiful that she attracted the attention of the god Zeus and became his lover. Unfortunately, the affair was discovered by the god's very jealous wife, Hera, who decided to punish Lamia by stealing her children. Lamia literally went insane with the grief of the loss of her children and went on a killing spree. All across her country she murdered the babies of her people. Additionally, she would seduce men and lure them into a private place where she would then kill them during sex, draining them of their blood. As time passed, Lamia lost her beauty and grew to look every bit as monstrous as the murderous acts she was committing. She learned how to shape-shift and became nearly invulnerable to any sort of attack. Zeus saw what had happened to his former lover, and, moved by pity, did what he felt he could to soften the blow his wife had dealt—he gave Lamia the ability to remove her eyes so that she would have the option of not having to look at her new, hideous appearance. As part of the gift, when her eyes were removed, she was vulnerable to attacks and could be slain. Lamia, in her embittered state, aligned herself with a group of demons known as the EMPOUSE, the wicked children of the goddess Hecate.

There was also a race of vampiric beings called Lamia. It was made up of hermaphrodites, many of which were some sort of creature from the waist down, usually a snake. They fed on the flesh and blood of infants and lived in cemeteries and the desert. Their children were collectively referred to as the Lamiae. They too were half man and half animal, and the combination of characteristics they could have were endless. The Lamiae fed on young and handsome foreigners who traveled alone.

In the Basque region of Spain the LAMIA, or lamiak as they are called when they gather together in numbers, are very much like their Greek cousins. They are described as being vampiric creatures who from the waist up are beautiful women with long golden HAIR. However, from the waist down they have the body of a snake or the legs of a bird. They could be found sitting near streams or standing in running water combing out their HAIR, singing alluring songs, attracting men and killing them to consume their flesh and drink their blood. It may be that the Lamiak are the progenitor of the mermaid legend.

Source: Fontenrose, *Python*, 288; Plutarch, *Lives*, 20, 23, 28, 32–33, 144; Turner, *Dictionary of Ancient Deities*, 286; Wright, *Vampires and Vampirism*

Lammikin (LAMB-ah-kin)

Variations: Balcanqual, Ballkin, Lambert Linkin, Lamkin, Lankin, Lantin, Long Lankin, Long Lankyn, Longkin, Lonkin, Rankin and similar variations

In a Scottish cautionary ballad from 1775, a mason named Lammikin was hired to build a castle for a nobleman. He was never paid for the work and thereby embittered, he enlisted the help of the nobleman's nursemaid. She let him into the castle one night and Lammikin set about killing the lord and his entire family. Lammikin and the nurse were captured, tried, and executed for the crime. The moral of the story was perhaps that noblemen should pay their bills and keep their house staff loyal.

As time wore on and the ballad traveled, it changed a little with each telling and no doubt was adapted to the region and local events that it was currently being sung in. In all, there were 22 different variations of the story that have been saved, and in one of them Lammikin was not a mason seeking revenge but rather a vampiric creature who fed off mothers with young children. The story goes that at night it would slip silently into a home with a child. Once the child was found, Lammikin would then poke it until it cried and its mother came to see what was wrong. Then Lammikin would attack, draining the mother dry of her blood and filling a bowl with blood from the baby. Some scholars believe that Lammikin the vampire had leprosy, as washing with human blood was once thought to be a cure for the disease and this cure was still in practice at the time the ballad was popular.

Source: Child, *English and Scottish Ballads*, 307–12; M'Dowall, *Among the Old Scotch Minstrels*, 84–91; Rose, *Giants, Monsters, and Dragons*, 220

Lampasma (Lamb-PAS-ma)

In Cythera, Greece, this is a word used to describe a vampire (see GREEK VAMPIRES). *Lampasma* translates to mean "a brightness" or "an entity."

Source: McClelland, *Slayers and Their Vampires*, 197; Summers, *Vampire: His Kith and Kin*

Lampastro (Lamb-PAS-trow)

In the Greek language, *lampastro* is a word that means "vampire" (see GREEK VAMPIRES).

Source: Summers, *Vampire: His Kith and Kin*

Lampiger (Lamb-PIG-er)

Variations: Lampijer

In Montenegro and Serbia, *lampiger* is a word that translates to means "vampire."

Source: Gypsy Lore Society, *Journal of the Gypsy Lore Society*, 131; Indiana University, *Journal*, vol. 14, 252; Perkowski, *Vampire of the Slavs*, 206

Lampijerovic (Lamb-PER-jovic)

In the lore of the Balkan Gypsies, a *lampijerovic* ("little vampire") is the child of a human woman and a type of vampire known as a MULLO. Born a natural enemy to vampires, this fated hunter can see a vampire for what it is, even if the vampire is invisible. Sometimes this is an innate ability of the person; other times he must first perform a ritual to temporarily gain the ability.

Other vampire hunters that are similar to the lampijerovic are the DHAMPIRE, DJADADJII, KRSNIK, STREGONI BENEFICI, VAMPIJEROVIC, and the VAMPIRDZHIA.

Source: Bunson, *Vampire Encyclopedia*, 169; Indiana University, *Journal of Slavic Linguistics*, 66; Masters, *Natural History of the Vampire*, 143

Lampir (LUM-peer)

Variations: LAMPIGER, Lampijer, LAMPIJEROVIC, Lepir, Tenac, VUKODLAK

In Bosnia, Montenegro, and Serbia there is the belief that the first person who dies from an epidemic or a plague will rise from the grave and become a vampiric REVENANT known as a lampir. It lies motionless in its grave by day, but at night it will return to those it knew in life and attack them, draining their blood through a small hole it bites in its victims' chests. The lampir looks exactly as it did in life, except that now its skin has a red cast to it and its body looks to be somewhat bloated, a condition that is more noticeable after it has fed. The only other change to its physical aspect is that it now has seven fangs in its mouth, four on the top row of teeth and three on the bottom. Anyone who survives an attack from a lampir will become this sort of vampire himself. If someone were inclined to become this sort of vampire, it is possible—by eating the flesh of a person who has been executed.

To destroy a lampir, its body must be exhumed during the day and burned to ashes.

Source: Durham, *Some Tribal Origins*, 260; MacDermott, *Bulgarian Folk Customs*, 67; Perkowski, *The Darkling*, 37; Royal Anthropological Institute, *Man*, 189–90

Langsuir (LANG-sure)

Variations: Langsuior, Langsuyar

There is a vampiric REVENANT in Malaysia that is created when a woman dies giving birth. Forty days after the death, the dead will rise up as a langsuir. If the child died with her, then it too will come back in UNDEATH as a type of vampire—a PONTIANAK. To prevent a woman from rising as this type of undead creature (see UN-

DEATH), glass beads must be placed in the corpse's mouth, a chicken egg put in each armpit, and needles stuck into the palm of each hand.

The langsuir does not have fangs like nearly all other types of vampires; rather, it drains the blood it wants from its victims through a hole in the back of its neck, which its ankle-length black HAIR hides. It also has very long fingernails and commonly wears a GREEN robe. By night, the vampire shape-shifts into an owl and then flies out seeking its favorite prey, children. As it flies, it occasionally lets loose with a powerful wail known as an *ngilai*. By day it can be found sitting in trees or by a river catching and eating fish.

Unlike many other vampires, the langsuir can be captured and domesticated. Once tamed, it makes for a wonderful wife and a good mother, living a happy and full life doing nothing other than caring for its family. However, if the langsuir is allowed to dance or show any signs of its happiness, it will quickly revert to its wild and murderous ways. Once this happens, it must be captured, and then its HAIR and fingernails cut off and stuffed into the hole in the back of its neck. This will force it to change back into a mortal woman.

Source: Laderman, *Wives and Midwives*, 126; McHugh, *Hantu-Hantu*, 74; Skeat, *Malay Magic*, 325–28

Laousnicheta (La-sha-NET-ah)

In Bulgaria, when a child dies before it can be baptized, it will become a type of vampiric demon known as a laousnicheta.

Source: Georgieva, *Bulgarian Mythology*, 102

Laousnitsi (La-SNIT-she)

In Bulgaria, when a woman dies in childbirth, she will become a type of vampiric demon known as a laousnitsi.

Source: Georgieva, *Bulgarian Mythology*, 102; Institut za balkanistika, *Études Balkaniques*, 40–41

Lap (LAP)

Variations: Opji, Oupire ("bloodsucker")

In Kashubia, Poland, the word *lap* translates to mean "vampire."

Source: Calmet, *Treatise on Vampires and Revenants*, 59; Canadian Centre for Folk Culture, *Paper*, 25; Pacific Northwest Conference, *Proceedings*, vol. 18–25, 253; Perkowski, *Vampires of the Slavs*, 186

Lapir (LA-peer)

Variations: JEDOGONJA, LAMPIR, Upir, VUKODLAK

In the Balkans, Serbia, and Ukraine there is a

type of vampire called a lapir. It is completely covered with HAIR, has long sharp teeth, and red eyes. It feeds on both animal and human blood each night. Its presence can be sensed by horses and oxen, causing them to act anxiously.

Source: Georgieva, *Bulgarian Mythology*, 100; Khanam, *Demonology*, 251; Perkowski, *Vampires of the Slavs*, 196; Pócs, *Fairies and Witches*, 56

Larva (LAR-va)

Variations: LAMIA, Lemures, Lemurs, Umbrae

In ancient Roman mythology there was a type of vampiric spirit known as a larva. It was created when a person died in some violent fashion or while bearing a burden of guilt. The larvae (the plural form of the word) were the evil, feminine version of the Lares, the protective, male ancestral spirits that safeguarded families and their homes. Larvae ("hungry ghosts") attack nightly, frightening and tormenting the living. They cause erotic and explicit dreams that generate nocturnal emissions, which they carry back to their nests, incubate like an egg, and hatch out horrific monsters.

The ancient Romans celebrated the Feast of the Lemuria on May 9, 11, and 13. The Vestal Virgins made offerings of black beans and of a sacred SALT made into cakes. The food was offered to the larvae at midnight in the hopes that they would accept the gifts and leave their family alone. Loud noises were made throughout the celebration, oftentimes scaring the larvae away before the offerings were made. During this festival all other temples were closed, no legal action could be taken, marriages were forbidden to take place, and voting was not allowed.

Source: Bulfinch, *Bulfinch's Greek and Roman Mythology*, 9; Leach, *Funk and Wagnalls Standard Dictionary of Folklore*, 196, 605; Steuding, *Greek and Roman Mythology*, 145

Latawiec (La-TA-vec)

Variations: Potercuk

In Poland and Ukraine there is a vampiric creature, a huge bird with a child's face, that is called a latawiec. The word *latawiec* translates to mean "vampire falcon." It flies down from the sky and with a blood-freezing shriek grabs up children, livestock, and women; it carries its prey back to its roost to consume.

Source: Bonnerjea, *Dictionary of Superstitions and Mythology*, 148; Jobes, *Dictionary of Mythology*, 975; Lecouteux, *History of the Vampire*

Leanhaum-Shee (LEE-awn-SHE)

Variations: Leanan-Sidhe, Leanhaun-Shee, Leanhaun-Sidhe, Lhiannan Shee

On the Isle of Man, located in the middle of the northern Irish Sea, there is a type of vampiric fay that appears to its victims as a beautiful young woman but to everyone else is invisible; it is called a leanhaum-shee. It will try to seduce a man, and if it is successful, its magic will cause him to fall in love with it. If he does, the leanhaum-shee will take him as a lover; if he does not, it will strangle him to death and then drain his corpse of blood. Little by little it will drain off its lover's life-energy during intercourse (see ENERGY VAMPIRE). The leanhaum-shee also collects his blood and stores it in a red cauldron, which adds to its magical properties. (The cauldron is the source of its power, that it is what gives the leanhaum-shee its ability to shape-shift into a white deer and keeps it looking young and beautiful.) The vampire also feeds small amounts of the blood to its lover so that he will be inspired to write love poems. Eventually, the man will become nothing more than a used-up husk and die.

Source: Jones, *On the Nightmare*; Moorey, *Fairy Bible*, 162–65; O'Connor, *Book of Ireland*, 50–52; Wilde, *Ancient Legends*, 169, 257–59

Leeton (LAY-tin)

In Latvia, there is a type of vampiric spirit that is similar to an ALP. The leeton literally rides horses to their deaths during the night, draining them of their life as it makes them race around the field (see ENERGY VAMPIRE).

Source: Meyer, *Mythologie der Germanen*

Lehoussi (LAY-house-ee)

In Bulgaria there is a vampiric spirit that feeds exclusively on young mothers and their children, but only for the first 40 days after the birth. This vampire, called a lehoussi, can be warded off with herbs and magical charms.

Source: Georgieva, *Bulgarian Mythology*, 102–3

Leyak (LEE-ack)

Variations: Leak

On the Indonesian island of Bali, there is a type of VAMPIRIC WITCH called a leyak. By day, the witch looks and acts like everyone else in its community, but at night, it will search through the local cemeteries for human entrails that it will use to make a magical formula (see LIVING VAMPIRE). If there are no suitable corpses in the cemetery that can be pillaged, the leyak will harvest what it needs from a sleeping person. The elixir that it brews will give it the ability to shape-shift into a tiger, as well as being able to rip its head free from its body so that it may fly off in search of prey, dragging its entrails behind it, much like the PENANGGLAN and the numerous other vampires who use that method for hunting. The leyak can also cause crops to fail, as well as start epidemics and famine. In addition to shape-shifting into a tiger, it can also become a bald-headed giant, a ball of light (CORPSE CANDLE), a monkey with golden teeth, a giant rat, a riderless motorcycle, or a bird as large as a horse. Should a leyak possess a person, that person is called *pengeleyakan*. No matter what form the leyak is in, it should always be considered a highly dangerous and unpredictable monster.

A leyak drinks the blood of both animals and humans, but it is particularly fond of the blood of women who just gave birth and newborn babies. One is often seen wandering along back roads, crossroads, cemeteries, forests, ravines, and the seashore. If on a moonless night dogs begin to whimper, a leyak is near. Gourmet food left outside one's house is usually offering enough to appease one.

The leyak can be restored to harmony with nature through an elaborate, high-level ceremony called *mecaru* (see MECARU CEREMONY). The ceremony requires blood sacrifice. However, according to Balinese lore, the leyak's magic only works on the isle of Bali. Java and the other small islands are safe from its attack, and if the witch can be moved there, it would be rendered impotent.

There is a temple built in the town of Pura Dalem Penataran Ped, Bali, in honor of Ratu Gede Mecaling, the patron saint of all leyak witches.

Source: Howe, *Gods, People, Spirits and Witches*, 23, 90, 168, 195; Jennaway, *Sisters and Lovers*, 204; Mack, *Field Guide to Demons*, 240

Lidérc (LIED-ric)

Variations: LÜDÉRC

In Hungary there is a vampiric creature that is very similar to the INCUBUS and SUCCUBUS in that it drains off the blood and life energies of a person through sexual intercourse. Called a lidérc, it is created in the most interesting way—by placing the first egg laid by a black hen under one's armpit and keeping it there until it hatches. The lidérc also acts as something of a familiar, as it is known for its ability to find treasure. It can shape-shift into a chicken or into a person who has one foot that is a chicken's foot. The lidérc will ask to do odd jobs for the person who hatched it. It is always asking for more to do, never satisfied with its given task and wanting to move on to the next one as quickly as possible.

Keeping a lidérc out of one's home so that it cannot assault one during the night while asleep is as easy as hanging GARLIC on the bedroom doorknob. Killing a lidérc is also easy, for those who know how. They simply give it an impossible task to complete, such as cutting an odd length of rope or dehydrating water into a powder. The little vampiric creature will try its hardest, but eventually it will become so frustrated that it will suffer a stroke and die.

Source: Dömötör, *Hungarian Folk Beliefs*, 83; Hoppál, *Eros in Folklore*, 129; Pócs, *Between the Living and the Dead*, 48–49

Liderc Nadaly (LIED-rick NAD-lee)

Variations: FARKASKOLDUS

In Hungary there is a type of vampire known as a liderc nadaly. It hunts by appearing to lone travelers, using humor to gain their trust, and seduction to lure them into a secluded place. During sexual intercourse, it drains victims of their blood. It is especially fond of the blood of infants. It will also sneak into a home by shape-shifting into a ball of light, looking much like a CORPSE CANDLE, and flying down the chimney.

The liderc nadaly is created when a person eats the flesh of a man who was executed, and it can be destroyed by either staking it through the heart or driving a nail through its forehead. As it dies, the liderc nadaly changes into a werewolflike creature.

Source: Haining, *Dictionary of Vampires*, 259; Ronay, *The Truth about Dracula*, 22

Lihousnitsi (Lay-how-SNIT-see)

In Bulgaria there is a vampiric spirit called a lihousnitsi that, like the ERMENKI, preys on young mothers and their children.

Source: Georgieva, *Bulgarian Mythology*, 102

Lik'ichiri (LICK-cherry)

In the Andes Mountains, the Aymara, Quechua, and other native peoples in the region speak of the lik'ichiri ("fat stealer"). Originally, the lik'ichiri was a vampiric spirit that harassed people but, as was recorded in 1550 by the invading Spanish, the lik'ichiri started to kill. In modern times, it has come to be seen as a vampiric being or a group of vampiric beings working hand-in-hand with American businessmen tied to the plastic surgery industry. Even in modern-day Peru, accusations that the lik'ichiri are destroying the pistachio crops abound. "Eye Stealers," as they are called by some, troll the streets of the the very capital, rounding up children by the score and surgically removing their eyes to be sold "overseas."

Described as a tall, white man, the lik'ichiri attacks people in the highlands while they sleep, using its magical powers to place its victim into a deep sleep so that it can remove strips of body fat without causing any pain. The wound then heals up almost instantly and in most cases the victim never even knows he was assaulted. If it should be discovered that a person was attacked, there is a magical potion called *achacachi* that is administered as treatment.

The people of the Andes believe that eating GARLIC dilutes a person's fat, rendering it low quality and thereby undesirable to the lik'ichiri. Vampires that are very similar to the lik'ichiri are the KHARISIRI, LIQUICHIRI, ÑAKAQ and the PISH-TACO.

Source: *American Anthropologist*, vol. 100, 332, 334, 337; Bathum, *Ayamara Women Healers*, 8, 18, 78, 80; Stephenson, *Gender and Modernity*, 166, 199–202; Van Vleet, *Performing Kinship*, 81; Weismantel, *Cholas and Pishtacos*

Lilim (LILIM)

Variation: Lilin, Lilis, Liln

According to Jewish folklore, LILITH, the first wife of Adam, left her husband and their children to be with the demon Sammael. Together they dwelt in and near the Red Sea where LILITH became a demon herself. Every day she gave birth to one hundred demonic offspring. These vampiric demons, her children, are called *lilim*, although some sources say that all of her female children, even those she had with her first husband, Adam, were called the lilim. Some sources say that if the demon was male, it was called lili or SHAITANS. The ancient Greeks called these beings lilim lamiae, EMPOUSE, and the daughters of Hecate (see GREEK VAMPIRES). Ancient Christians referred to them as the Harlots of Hell and SUCCUBUS.

Lilim feed their bloodlust by attacking children, deer, fish, menstruating women, pregnant women, and men who have sex with their wives while fantasizing about other women. Lilim also have the right to plague newborn male children for eight days or until they have been circumcised, as well as are allowed to attack newborn females until they are 20 days old, kidnapping them to consume if the opportunity presents itself. When lilim attack adults, they have SUCCUBUS-like tendencies. They also have the interesting ability to look into a person's eyes and see what, if any, doubts he may have about anything.

To prevent attack, monks who have taken a vow of celibacy must sleep with their hands over their genitals, clutching a CRUCIFIX. Wearing Hasidic amulets of protection work as well. Lilim can only be destroyed by God, as He had decreed that 100 lilim a day will die until LILITH returns to her husband.

Source: Eason, *Fabulous Creatures*, 26–27; Koén-Sarano, *King Solomon and the Golden Fish*, 63; Koltuv, *Book of Lilith*, 35; Turner, *Dictionary of Ancient Deities*, 166

Lilith (LIL-ith)

Variations: Abeko, Abito, Abro, Abyzu, Ailo, Alio, Alu, Alû, Amiz, Amizo, Amizu, The Ancient, Ardad Lili, Astaribo, Avitu, Bat Zuge, Batna, Bituah, Bogey-Wolf, Chief of the Succubi, Daughter of Night, The Devil's Consort, Dianae, Eilo, The Flying One, The Foolish Woman, Gallu, Gelou, Gilou, Gilû, Grand Duchess of the Eighth Hell, Heva, Hilthot, 'Ik, 'Ils, Ita, Izorpo, Kakash, Kalee', KALI, Kea, Kema, Kokos, Labartu, Lamassu ("Bullgod"), Lavil, Lilatou, Lilats, Lilitu, Lilla, Lilu, Maid of Desolation, Night Hag, Night Jar, The Night Monster, The Northerner, Obizuth, Odam, Partasah, Partasha, Patrota, Petrota, Podo, Pods, Princess of Demons, Princess of Hell, the Queen of Hell, Queen of the Succubi, Queen of Zemargad, Raphi, Satrina, Satrinah, Talto, Thilthoh, WERZELYA, Zariel, Zephonith

From the earliest records of man, there is a story of an ancient being that preyed upon children. It was suspected to be female and demonic, and killed not only children but also women who were with child and men, seducing them and draining them of their blood. Over the eons, it has had many names and many titles, but today, we call it Lilith.

In ancient Assyria she was called Lilitu and described as a demoness with wings and a hairy body, much like the djinn of Arabic lore (see HAIR). In the Babylonian tradition, she was one of a trio of demons. Lilith had aligned herself with the other two demons after she had been banished from the Sumerian goddess Innana's garden. She is mentioned in the Sumerian telling of Gilgamesh and lived in a willow tree.

In Hebrew texts King Solomon had at first mistaken the Queen of Sheba for Lilitu, as she had unshaven legs, reminding him of the djinn of Arabian tales. In the Hebrew bible, Psalm 91 called her the "terror of the night." In Isaiah 34:14, she was called the "night devil."

In the *Talmud*, it is not Lilith's hatred for infants that causes her to kill them, but rather her love for them. Infertile and unable to have a child of her own, she slips into a nursery and gently picks up the infant to hold against her breast. Eventually her desperation to be a mother to a child of her own becomes much too distressing and Lilith accidentally smothers the baby to death as she presses it against her.

Because there are so many ancient texts and beliefs that have Lilith in their mythology, her story is a difficult one to exactly set straight. But the most familiar story of Lilith, as well as the oldest record of her, comes from the anonymously written Hebrew text *The Alphabet of Ben Sira*. There has been much speculation as to when the text was originally written. Some sources claim that it is as old as the seventh century and as young as the eleventh century, but most scholars are content to split the difference and say the ninth.

The text tells the story of the birth and education of Rabbi Ben Sira. The final section of the text is written as taking place in the palace of the Babylonian King, Nebuchadnezzar. The king asks the prophet a series of questions that must be answered by telling a story. There are 22 questions posed, one for each letter of the Hebrew alphabet, hence the name of the book. In the fifth passage, King Nebuchadnezzar demands that his son, who is suffering from a mysterious illness, be cured. Ben Sira responds with the tale of Lilith, the first wife of Adam.

It says that she was Adam's first wife, created from filth and mud. They were joined physically back to back, but she complained so insistently that God separated them. Still, she was not content with her lot as Adam's subservient wife and mother to their children. Wanting equality, she left her husband to live with a group of demons outside of Paradise. By crying out the name of God, she was given the ability to fly, and did so, leaving Adam far behind. God was not pleased with Lilith's new life and sent three angels to speak with her: Sanvi, Sansanvi, and Semangalef. Their job was to persuade Lilith to return to Adam and their children. She adamantly refused and was punished for it—cursed so that none of her children would survive their infancy. With Lilith on the brink of suicide, the angels took pity on her and a compromise was struck: she would be given power over newborn boys for the first eight days of their lives, and the first twenty days of life for newborn girls. In exchange, she promised not to harm any child who had the names of the angels written near them. Lilith wandered the world and came to be near the Red Sea, where she met the demon Sammael. Bound by their mutual hatred for humanity, they spawned a race of demonic beings, the LILIM.

There are as many variations to the story of Lilith as she has aliases and titles combined. Many believed that it was Lilith and Sammael who plotted the downfall of Adam and Eve. In fact, numerous pieces of art depict a woman, Lilith, offering the Forbidden Fruit to Adam and Eve.

There have been hundreds of books written about Lilith, who she was, what she means, and how to interpret her story; equally as numerous are the points of view accompanying each. Some are Christian, some Jewish, some are from a purely historic point of view, while others yet have taken such a wild interpretation and speculative spin that she has become lost in their message. Suffice it to say that no matter what a person is looking for in the Lilith story, there is an interpretation of it to suit his needs.

Source: Conybeare, *Jewish Quarterly*, xi, 30; Leeming, *Goddess*, 111–15; Turner, *Dictionary of Ancient Deities*, 291

Liogat (LIE-og-gat)

Variation: Liougat, Liugat, Ljugat, Ljuna, Ljung, Llugat, LUGAT, SAMPIRO

A sixteenth century church decree declared that all Albanians of Turkish descent would become a vampire after their death, no matter how good or spiritual a life they may have led. Later, in 1854, the vampiric REVENANT known as the liogat was officially described as meaning "dead Turks in winding sheets," a fitting description, as when this vampiric REVENANT returned from the grave, its burial shroud was wrapped around its body and it wore high-heeled shoes. Spreading disease wherever it went, the liogat was also considered to be a death omen when seen.

Just as wolves are the natural enemy of the vampire known as the KUKUDHI, they equally hate the liogat. Should a vampire manage to survive a wolf attack, it will retreat into its grave, too ashamed to rise up again.

In lieu of awaiting wolf attack, one can look for a CORPSE CANDLE and follow it, carefully, as it will go to the grave that the vampire sleeps in by day. A wooden stake driven through the heart of the vampire will pin it to the ground, and although not destroying it, will render it incapable of doing further harm.

Source: Abbott, *Macedonian Folklore*, 216; Ashley, *Complete Book of Vampires*; Summers, *Werewolf in Lore and Legend*, 149; Taylor, *Primitive Culture*, 311

Lioubgai (LOW-guy)

Variations: Lioubgaï

An Albanian vampiric REVENANT, the lioubgai is created when a person dies on the battlefield and his body is badly burned but not wholly destroyed. Rising up as a lioubgai, it will return to the battlefield at night where it will feed off the blood of dying men.

Source: Le Musée des Vampires

Liquichiri (Lay-GUEE-chi-ree)

In Peru there is a vampiric spirit that feeds off the body fat and blood of sleeping people called a liquichiri ("vampire"). It has the ability to shape-shift into a variety of different animals, which it uses in order to slip into homes silently and unseen. Vampires that are similar to the liquichiri are the KHARISIRI, LIK'ICHIRI, ÑAKAQ and the PISHTACO.

Source: Tierney, Highest Altar, 235, 291, 300, 316, 325

Living Vampire (Liv-ing Vam-pire)

Variation: Moroancă, Moroaica, Moroi, Moroii, Muroaïcă, Strigoii Viu ("Live Vampire")

In Romanian vampire lore, there are such people who are considered to be living vampires. Indicators of this condition are present at birth, such as being born with a caul or a tail. Usually, this circumstance of birth happens most often to females, and they are called moroaica ("living female vampire"). They are described as having red HAIR, blue eyes, twin hearts, and red patches of skin on their faces. The rarer moroi ("living male vampire") can easily be detected by his male pattern baldness that occurs even at a very young age. Although there is no doubt that they are living people and fully human, they display both vampiric tendencies as well as supernatural abilities, such as draining the life-energy from animals, crops, and people. They gather with others of their kind, both living and undead (see UNDEATH), to teach each other the black magic they have learned. They can also drink honey from a hive, which will cause all of the bees that live there to die. Although they rarely drink blood, they still have the ability at night to shape-shift into a cat, dog, glowing ball of light like a CORPSE CANDLE, hen, raven, or wolf. When one dies, it will rise up as a type of vampiric REVENANT called a strigoica unless a stake has been driven through its heart or the body has been decapitated and burned to ash.

There is another interpretation of the term "living vampire." There are people who claim to have been born vampires and have specific nourishment needs that must be met in order to live. Oftentimes, people who are energy vampires will say that they are living vampires, in that they require feeding on specific types of energy in order to feel healthy (see ENERGY VAMPIRE). There are also certain individuals who make a similar, albeit eccentric, claim in which they profess a need to consume blood in order to survive. Although there are individuals who have a medical condition where there is a scientific reason for craving blood, known as Hemophagia (although not specifically human blood), there is no biological means by which the human body can process raw, uncooked blood in such a way that life-sustaining nourishment can be drawn from it. In truth, it will make a living human being very sick.

Source: Ashley, Complete Book of Vampires, 344; Broster, Amagqirha, 60; Day, Vampires, 14, 70–73, 109, 116; Summers, The Vampire in Europe

Loango (LOAN-go)

The Ashanti and Asanbosam people of Africa believe that when a person who used magic in life dies, he will become a vampiric REVENANT.

Source: Haining, Dictionary of Vampires, 159; Le Roy, Religion of the Primitives, 95, 162; Masters, Natural History of the Vampire, 47; Volta, The Vampire, 152

Lobishomen (Low-biz-SHOW-men)

Variations: Loberia (feminine), Lobishumen

In Brazil there is a vampiric creature called a lobishomen, which is created through the use of witchcraft or is born through an incestuous relationship. It is one of the smallest types of vampires, standing only two inches tall. It has black teeth, bloodless lips, a hunched back, yellowish skin, a white beard, and the overall appearance of a monkey. It prefers to feed off sleeping women and will have a group of several that it will rotate through. It seldom kills its victims, taking a survivable amount of blood from each and letting enough time pass between feedings so that she can fully recuperate. Eventually, overuse will cause the women to become nymphomaniacs.

The lobishomen can shape-shift into small animals, but it should not be confused with the lobishomen of Portugal, which is a race of werewolves.

Source: Critchfield, Villages, 348; Folklore Society, Folk-lore Record, vol. 3, 143–44; Knowles, Nineteenth Century and After, 78; Woodward, Werewolf Delusion

Loogaroo (LOU-ga-roo)

Variations: Ligaroo, Loup-Garou

Throughout the Caribbean, Central Africa, Haiti, and the West Indies, there is a female VAMPIRIC WITCH that gained her magical abilities by having sold her soul to the devil (see AFRICAN VAMPIRIC WITCH). Known as a loogaroo, by day, she disguises herself to look like a feeble old woman so as not to draw attention to herself. At night, she removes her skin, hangs it on a cotton plant, and shape-shifts into a CORPSE CANDLE. There is no obstacle that can prevent her from entering into a home, and once inside, she will drain blood from her victim. Some of it she will consume, but some of it must be offered up to the devil that she made her pact with or she will lose her magical ability (see LIVING VAMPIRE).

As is the case with many of the vampires who can remove their skin (such as the ASEMA), if the loogaroo's hide is found, rubbing it with SALT will cause it to shrink. Although the witch will not die when exposed to direct sunlight, as is the case with the JUMBIES of the Caribbean Islands, it will leave the loogaroo exposed for what she is. Oddly enough, scattering rice or sand on the ground will compel the loogaroo to stop whatever she is doing in order to count the grains. Should she still be counting when the sun rises, she will be destroyed.

This vampire is oftentimes confused with a French creature called a loups garou. Although the word is pronounced the same way (no doubt due to the French influence in the area), it is not a vampire at all, but rather a werewolf.

Source: Bell, *Obeah*, 165–71; Muller, *Among Caribbean Devils and Duppies*, 449; Summers, *Vampire: His Kith and Kin*, 234; Welland, *Sand*, 66–68

Loup Carou (Lou CA-roo)

Variations: Letiche ("carnivorous, aquatic humanoid")

In the Honey Island Swamp in Louisiana, United States, there is a bipedal, hairy, vampiric creature known as the loup carou (see HAIR). Said to stand over seven feet tall and thought to weigh in excess of 400 pounds, it smells of death and has piercing, sickly yellow eyes that are set wide apart on its head. The loup carou was once a child that was either lost in the swamp or abandoned there, but in either event was saved and rescued by a mother alligator that raised it as one of her own. The loup carou lives in an area that is only accessible by boat, but routinely finds its way to civilization where it feeds on humans and livestock.

Source: Dickinson, *Haunted City*, 184–87; Holyfield, *Encounters*, 10–15; Nickell, *Mystery Chronicles*, 165–75; Simpson, *Loup Garou*, 219–22; Summers, *The Werewolf*, 12

Loups Garou (LOO GA-roo)

Variation: Lupo Mannaro (Italian)

The Cajun folklore of Louisiana, United States, tells of a vampiric sorcerer who has the ability to shape-shift into a werewolf called a loups garou (see LIVING VAMPIRE). He rubs a salve over his body, which transforms him and gives him the ability to control bats. He uses the bats to lift him up and carry him through the air, depositing him on the roof of a house. From there he climbs down the chimney and bites the neck of a sleeping person, draining him of his blood.

The loups garou is impervious to gunshots, as BULLETs pass right through him. However, he can be killed. Place a sifter over the chimney, as he will be compelled to count the holes. As he does so, sneak up behind him and pour SALT on his tail—the loups garou will instantly catch on fire. As soon as he does, he will step out of his skin and run away. He is also terrified of frogs. If someone throws a frog at him, the loups garou will flee in terror.

Source: Métraux, *Voodoo in Haiti*, 58, 75, 89, 117; Phillpotts, *Loup-Garou!*, 20; Summers, *The Werewolf*, 94

Ludak (Loo-DAC)

In the Finnish providence of Lapland, the word *ludak* translates as "vampire."

Source: Huss, *Focus on the Horror Film*, 57; Jones, *On the Nightmare*, 116

Lüdérc (Lu-DER-ric)

Variations: LIDÉRC, Ludverc

In Hungry, there is a vampire called a lüdérc that looks like a shooting star in the night sky. Specializing in preying on people whose spouses have just died, it enters into the home of the bereaved and shape-shifts into the deceased. Then, it seduces the grieving spouse and engages in sex, draining him of his blood much like an INCUBUS or SUCCUBUS.

Source: Dégh, *Legend and Belief*, 103; Dundes, *Vampire Casebook*, 94; International Society, *Folk Narrative and Cultural Identity*, 305; Pócs, *Between the Living and the Dead*, 48–49

Lugat (Loo-GAT)

Vatiation: Kukuthi, Liugat

A vampiric REVENANT of Albania, the lugat is created when a person dies suddenly, as in a murder, suicide, or sudden illness. This is the first of a two-stage life cycle for this species of vampire. Sources vary as to how long it will take for a lugat to mature into a KUKUDHI. Some claim it is a mere 30 days but others say it takes 40 years. Most commonly 40 days is given as the length of time.

When the lugat rises from the dead, it is very strong and it looks like a normal person that is somewhat bloated, more so after it has fed. Its skin is reddish but shows no signs of decomposition. It preys nightly on those it knew in life first before moving on to animals and other people. By day it remains in its grave.

To discover if there is a lugat buried in a graveyard, someone can lead a white horse that has never stumbled over the graves. When it comes to a grave that it will not walk over, the vampire is resting beneath. The corpse must be exhumed and burned to ash. Wolves are the natural enemy to the lugat and will attack one, ripping it to pieces if it can. However, should the vampire survive the assault, it will retreat to its grave. If any limb has been mauled too badly, the vampire will not rise up again.

Source: Bonnefoy, *Old European Mythologies*, 253; Elsie, *Dictionary of Albanian Religion*, 162–63; Haase, *Greenwood Encyclopedia*, 24

Lupi (Lou-PEA)

Variations: Opji, Oupire ("bloodsucker")

The Kashubian people of north-central Poland use the word *lupi* synonymously to mean both "wolf" and "vampire" in their language.

Source: Indiana University, *Journal of Slavic Linguistics*, 252; Perkowski, *Vampires of the Slavs*, 186

Lupi Manari (Lou-PEA Ma-NAIR-ee)

Variations: LUPIRZ, Orko, Vuc, Vuk ("wolf")

In Croatia, *lupi manari* ("wolf plea") is a term that is used to mean a vampire.

Source: Bryant, *Handbook of Death*, 99; Perkowski, *The Darkling*, 99; Tuke, *Dictionary of Psychological Medicine*, 753

Lupirz (Lou-PREZ)

In the Polish language, *lupirz* is a word that translates to mean "vampire."

Source: Indiana University, *Journal of Slavic Linguistics*, vol. 14, 164; Perkowski, *Vampires of the Slavs*, 185

Ma Cá Rông

Variations: Ca Rong Ghost

The Vietnamese vampire known as the ma cá rông in similar to the ASWANG, BRAHMAPARUSH,

HANTU LANGSUIR, and the KRAPPA in that it takes on the guise of a flying head dangling its entrails. However, this vampire feeds exclusively off cow dung. It only attacks humans when it cannot find its natural food source. It rips out its victims' throats, but it only does so in anger; the ma cá rông never consumes any part of the people it assaults.

Source: Maberry, *Vampire Universe*, 206; Nguyen, *Vietnamese Family Chronicle*, 278

Mahasohon (Ma-HA-so-on)

Variations: Maha-sohon

In Sri Lanka there is the belief in a gigantic, hairy vampiric demon known as the mahasohon, which hunts not only humans but elephants as well (see HAIR). The mahasohon waits at the crossroads at night for someone to pass by; when he does, it leaps out and attacks, draining him dry of his blood and then eating most of the corpse. There is a demon dance ceremony that can be performed to drive it away called Maha-sohon Samayama.

Source: Goonatilleka, *Masks*, 10, 15, 19–20; Jayatilaka, *Dictionary of the Sinhalese Language*, 762; Kapferer, *Celebration of Demons*, 206; Pranāndu, *Rituals*, 180

Mahr (MAR)

The Carpathian Mountains arch through the Czech Republic and then turn east, continuing on through Poland, Romania, Slovakia, and Ukraine before finally ending near the Danube River in Serbia. It is here in this mountain range that there lives a species of vampire known as a mahr. Living off the consumption of human souls, the mahr swoops down upon its victim in the form of a moth, taking a bite or two before flying off. The more often a mahr attacks a single victim, the easier it becomes for the vampire to do so in the future. Eventually the prey is killed and the soul consumed. Fortunately, there are two ways in which a mahr can be slain. The first is to drive a wooden stake through its heart. If this method of destruction is employed, the souls that the vampire consumed will return to the victims. The second means by which this vampire can be destroyed is to find where it spends its daylight hours and expose the creature to sunlight. The rays of the sun will render it to ash.

Source: Hastings, *Encyclopaedia of Religion*, 590; Jones, *On the Nightmare*, 144; Lurker, *Dictionary of Gods and Goddesses*, 215; Pócs, *Between the Living and the Dead*, 22

Majky (MOCK-ee)

Variations: Navjaky, Navje, Nejky

In Ukraine there is a vampiric spirit that is

called a majky. It is described as looking like a beautiful and voluptuous young maiden. It lives in the forest and survives on the blood it drinks from the men it seduces.

Source: Grey, Mythology of All Races, 253–54; Konrad, Old Russia and Byzantium, 131; Perkowski, Vampires of the Slavs, 40

De Man Met De Haak (DE MAN MET DE HACK)

Variations: Man Met De Haak, Mannet Jé Met De Haak ("Man of the Hook")

In the Netherlands, in the province of Limburg, there is the local belief of a vampiric water creature that lives off the blood of children. De Man Met De Haak ("the man with the hook") is a small, ugly, black-skinned being that lives in ponds and other sorts of waterways. It has a beard made of water plants and webbed feet like a frog. With its hook, it waits for a child to pass near enough for it to lash out, hook it, and pull it down into the water, drowning him. It is a matter of opinion as to whether the De Man Met De Haak drains the blood from its victim while it is drowning or after.

Source: Anon, English Fairy Tales, 159–60

Manducation

The technical term for the practice of a corpse chewing upon or eating its burial shroud is called an act of manducation. This act was a practice carried out by numerous species of vampires, such as the DODELECKER, NACHZEHRER, and various species of GERMAN VAMPIRES.

Experts throughout the seventeenth and eighteenth centuries agreed that the Devil was trying his best to make the living hate their beloved departed by convincing them their deceased family members had led immoral lives—and a burial shroud that was obviously chewed upon was generally proof enough.

Source: Bunson, Vampire Encyclopedia

Mandurugo (Man-dur-RUGO)

In the Capiz province of the Philippines, there is a vampiric creature that looks like a very beautiful woman called a mandurugo ("bloodsucker"). It only appears at night and uses its beauty to lure men into marrying it so that it will have a constant supply of blood. The vampire has the ability of flight, but it is particularly susceptible to sword and knife attacks.

Capiz province's capital is Roxas City, where the annual ASWANG FESTIVAL is held. Back in 1992 during the presidential elections, word

quickly spread that a mandurugo had been sighted wandering the streets. Although no reliable sources have admitted to making this statement, the vampire's presence was enough to keep many potential voters at home.

Source: Lopez, Handbook of Philippine Folklore, 227; Ramos, Creatures of the Philippine Lower Mythology, 116; University of San Carlos, Philippine Quarterly, vol. 10–11, 213

Maneden (Man-DIN)

The Chewong people of Malaysia say that there is a vampiric creature or spirit that lives in the pandan tree called the maneden. If anyone attempts to harm the tree, even so much as to cut the leaves that grow on it, the vampire will violently protect its home and defend its territory. If the attacker is a man, the maneden will latch on to his forehead or elbow; if it is a woman, her nipple. Once it has a firm grip, it will begin to drain the person's blood. Before the person loses too much blood and dies, the maneden can be lured off if offered a nut or some other suitable replacement.

Source: Howell, Society and Cosmos, 108; Melton, The Vampire Book; Royal Asiatic Society, Journal, 108

Mantindane (MAN-tin-dane)

Variations: Chitauli, TIKOLOSHE

The people of Kenya tell of a vampiric creature that stands two or three feet tall called a mantindane ("fairy man" or "star monkey"). Its very wide body is covered with brown-orange fur. It has a narrow head, pointed ears, and dark, slitted eyes. Because it never wears any clothes, we also know that it has a long, serpentine penis.

Often bound to a witch and used as her familiar, the mantindane is well suited for this purpose. It knows how to use magic, as well as the secret to brewing its own type of poison. Often asked to kill the witch's enemies, the mantindane will make a batch of its special poison and sneak into a person's home completely undetected, as it also knows how to turn invisible. Its poison is carried through the air and soon enough will kill everyone inside. Just a few drops of the toxin in the local water supply will kill anyone who drinks from it.

Mantindanes drink the blood they need to survive mostly from cattle. They have a compulsion to drink milk directly from the animal, so when they look for a cave near water to live in, preferably right along the riverbank, they like to be sure that cows frequent the area. Otherwise, if opportunity presents itself, and there is no danger or risk in doing so, the mantindane will feed off a sleeping child or woman. Fortunately, for cows and humans alike, it can easily be warded off with iron.

Mantindane are often blamed for spreading a mysterious sickness in a community, and because of this, a witch doctor is often employed to make a magical trap to capture the vampire, paralyze it, and remove all of its powers. However, one can never point at one of these traps and say, "Look, it's captured!" or something similar, as that will break the spell, free the mantindane, and restore its powers.

It is advised that women should sleep in an elevated bed so as not to attract the attention of a mantindane, should one sneak into the home invisibly and wander around looking for some mischief to cause. There is a growing belief that the mantindane is not a vampire at all, but rather an alien that is trying to use the women of Africa to perpetuate its own species.

Source: Chidester, *Religion, Politics, and Identity*, 80; Connor, *Shamans of the World*, 136–37; Jacobs, *UFOs and Abductions*, 225

Mara (MA-rah)

Variations: Mora, Morava, Morina

In Canadian and Scandinavian folklore there is a type of vampire that is similar to both the ALP and the SUCCUBUS. The mara is created when a child dies before it could be baptized. At night, it finds sleeping men and, sitting upon their chests, crushes them to death by pressing down harder and harder. If the mara should drink the blood of a man and he survives the experience, the vampire will fall hopelessly in love with him, returning to feed from him nightly. Unfortunately, its presence will give the man nightmares and, eventually, he will die (see ENERGY VAMPIRE).

Source: Billington, *Concept of the Goddess*, 42–55; Mackay, *Gaelic Etymology*, 305; Thorpe, *Northern Mythology*, 169–70

Maroc (Ma-ROCK)

Variations: Oustrel

In the Strandja Mountains of Bulgaria, *maroc* is a regional word that means "vampire."

Source: Georgieva, *Bulgarian Mythology*, 104

Märt (MART)

In Germany, the märt is a variation of the vampire known more commonly as the ALP (see GERMAN VAMPIRE). A vampiric spirit similar to a SUCCUBUS, at night it hunts for a man who has fallen asleep in a fetal position. Once he has, the märt sits upon his chest, rendering him completely immobile. Then, it mounts him in a sexual fashion and drains away his life-energy and some blood (see ENERGY VAMPIRE).

The approach of a märt sounds like a mouse gnawing on something, and if the man is wearing a glove that was inherited, he will be able to grab and hold the märt before it attacks.

Source: Senn, *Were-wolf and Vampire in Romania*, 42; Sha, *Occultism*, 225; Summers, *Vampire in Lore and Legend*, 49

Masabakes

From the lore of northern Spain comes the masabakes, an ENERGY VAMPIRE. It keeps a familiar, a species of imp known as a tentirujo, that it sends off nightly to find a sleeping virgin. When it does, the tentirujo rubs the girl's thighs with a piece of mandrake. The next day the girl is overcome with sexual desire and will seek out a man to have intercourse with. The masabakes feeds off the lustful desire that builds up throughout the day in the virgin and then feeds again as her sexual energy is released during intercourse.

Source: Maberry, *Vampire Universe*, 210–11

Masan (MA-san)

Variation: Masand

The masan is a vampiric spirit from India, created when a child from a low caste, who was a bully in life, dies. An oppressor in life, the masan now delights in tormenting and killing children, slowly draining away their life as it turns their bodies horrid shades of GREEN, red, and yellow (see ENERGY VAMPIRE); any child who walks through its shadow will die immediately.

The masan is attracted to households that use water to put out cooking fires or to people who pinch out candle flames with their fingers and then wipe the grease on their clothes. If a woman allows her gown to drag along the ground, the masan will follow her home. The only way to save the life of a child who is being harassed by this vampire is to have the child weighed in SALT.

Source: Bunson, *Vampire Encyclopedia*, 170; Crooke, *Introduction to the Popular Religion*, 80, 161–62; Crooke, *Popular Religion and Folk-lore of Northern India*, 260; Turner, *Dictionary of Ancient Deities*, 311

Masani (Man-SAA-nee)

Variations: MASAN

Although the masani is also known to some as a masan, the two are in fact different types of vampires. The masani is a vampiric spirit from India, like the masan, but that is where the similarity ends. The masani has jet-black skin and an overall monstrous appearance. It lives in burial grounds, and at night, it rises up from the ashes of a funeral pyre and attacks the first person it sees.

Source: Bunson, *Vampire Encyclopedia*, 170

Mashan

Variations: Chudel

The mashan is a demonic vampire known to the people of India and Nepal. Residing in another dimension, the mashan seldom if ever comes to our world because it is very difficult to find a place where the barrier that separates dimensions is weak enough to allow the demon to pass through. On occasion, a sorcerer, by use of geomancy, will discover such a location and summon a mashan to our world with the intent of binding the demon to do his bidding. This is a very dangerous prospect because if the sorcerer makes even the slightest mistake the mashan will drain him dry of his blood and then immediately set out on a killing spree, spreading plague everywhere it goes. Only prayers said to the god Shiva can send the demon back to the realm where it belongs. Shiva uses his influence and encourages the demon to return of its own accord.

Source: Dube, *Untouchable Pasts*, 67; Fauna and Flora Research Society, *Scientific Results of the Japanese Expeditions*, 149; Saletore, *Indian Witchcraft*, 40; Sarkar, *The Folk Element in Hindu Culture*, 89–90

Massâcet (Ma-saa-CHET)

In the country of Turkey, the word *massâcet* translates to mean "vampire."

Source: Theosophical Society, *The Theosophist*

Mati-Anak (MANTI-AH-nac)

Variation: Mati Ânak, Mantianak, PONTIANAK

A vampiric spirit from Malaysia, the mati-anak ("child dead") is created when a child is stillborn or dies at birth. It has the ability to shapeshift into an owl, the form which it will use when hunting down unsuspecting animals and people to prey upon for their blood. To prevent the spirit of a stillborn child from rising as a mati anak, it must be buried facedown in its grave. Glass beads must be placed in the mouth, a hen's egg in each armpit, and pins pierced through its palms of its hands.

Source: Benedict, *Study of Bagobo Magic and Myth*, 270; Clifford, *In Court and Kampong*, 231; Masters, *Natural History of the Vampire*, 60; Skeat, *Malay Magic*, 328

Mavky (Mov-KEY)

A vampiric fay from Ukraine, the mavky lives in the forest. The nymph lures its victims to a secluded place by using beautiful music and its own melodious singing voice. Once it has its prey alone and has won his confidence, it will literally tickle him to death, feeding off his joy until he is dead (see ENERGY VAMPIRE).

Source: Grey, *Mythology of All Races*, 253; Kubiĭovych, *Ukraine*, 329–30, 358; MacCulloch, *Celtic Mythology*, 253; Wagner, *Aspects of Contemporary Ukraine*, 276

Maw Du (MAW DO)

In Thailand, there is a type of Buddhist monk known as a Maw Du ("Seeing Doctor"). All throughout Thailand, these monks work out of shops and stalls set up in marketplaces, waiting for their services to be hired out. In addition to divining the future, fortune-telling, healing the sick, and selling charms for every occasion, they can also be hired to destroy a vampire. They cast spells and recite specific religious and magical incantations to do so.

Source: Graham, *Siam*, 545; Cambridge University Press, *Modern Asian Studies*, 781; Keown, *Buddhism and Abortion*, 44

Mecaru Ceremony (Me-CAR-oo)

In the Balinese Hindu religion, achieving balance in all things is key, and by making *yadnya* (holy sacrifices), this goal may be achieved. One such ceremony is called Bhuta Yadnya (the Holy Sacrifice to the Bad Nature Spirits). The Mecaru ceremony is especially designed to heal the rift between man and nature, in particular, placating the more malign spirits that reside in or near bridges, crossroads, and trees. Usually this sacrifice is made every 15 days.

There are three levels at which the Mecaru ceremony can be performed. At the lowest level, the head of a household will give offerings of flowers, ginger, onions, raw meat, and shrimp paste. Then he will acknowledge and honor the spirits who will then have no need to attack or otherwise cause harm to humans. An additional offering of alcoholic beverages made with rice, such as arak or brem, may also be made.

Mecaru ceremonies made at the middle level give offerings of black, red, white, and yellow rice seeds, as well as the sacrificial blood of a chicken or duck poured on the ground. The number of animal sacrifices is not as important as the color, which can vary depending on the need and this decision is made by the pinandita, a low-ranking holy person.

Only a pedanda, or high-ranking holy person, can perform the highest-level Mecaru ceremony. Hundreds of animal sacrifices are made consisting of buffalos, cows, pigs, and puppies. Again, color is important and the animals chosen must be deemed worthy of sacrifice, as they are insured a higher place in their next reincarnation.

Source: Bakan, *Music of Death*, 77; Danandjaja, *Parallelsacht*, 6; Jensen, *Balinese People*, 22; Moeljo, *Bali, the World's Belonging*, 132

Mei (MY)

The mei ("to bewitch men with feminine charms") is a vampiric creature from Chinese lore that feeds off the souls of humans.

Source: Kang, *Cult of the Fox*, 76; *Nan Nü*, 86

Le Mercure Galant

Le Mercure Galant ("The Gallant Mecury") was a late seventeenth-century newspaper similar to *The GLEANER* in that it reported in shocking detail stories of vampires and their recent activities. Many scientists and theologians alike referenced it when writing their treatises on vampires.

Source: Merrett, *Man and Nature*, 3; Muchembled, *History of the Devil*, 191; Perkowski, *Vampires of the Slavs*, 98; Rickels, *Vampire Lectures*, 15

Mermaid Vampire

Variations: Siren

Mermaids ("sea women") were not always the sweet, HAIR-combing, lovelorn beauties of the sea as we think of them today. The mythology of the mermaid is dark, and the ancient Celts had good reason to fear these vampiric creatures. A beautiful woman from the waist up, it had the body of a fish or seal from the waist down. They lived in lakes and rivers as well as the sea, luring fishermen into danger using nothing more than their beautiful singing voices (much like the sirens of ancient Greece), causing them to wreck their ships on unseen rocks. As the men fell into the water, the mermaids would swim in, grab up the drowning men, and drag them even deeper under the water. Then the mermaids would begin to drain the men of their blood while they were still alive. Usually there was nothing left to let the tale of what happened to the ship be known except for the remaining flotsam and jetsam along the coastline along with the uneaten remains of a few sailors. There are numerous tales of mermaids living in the English Channel and along the Channel Islands, as well as all along the coast of Normandy. Some of these stories, such as *The Laird of Lorntie*, date back as far as the Middle Ages.

Source: Day, *Vampires*, 45; Gardner, *New Woman and Her Sisters*, 30; Rose, *Giants, Monsters, and Dragons*, 220; Silver, *Strange and Secret Peoples*, 177–78

Mictecaciuatl (Mic-tay-ca-OO-til)

Variations: Lady of the Place of the Dead, Mectecaciuatl

The ancient Aztec people both feared and revered the vampiric moon goddess Mictecaciuatl. She was seen as both a creator and a destroyer. Her arms, face, and hands were painted white with chalk, just like the other vampiric women in Aztec lore, CIHUACOATL and CIHUATETEO. Mictecaciuatl lived with her husband, MICTLAMPA, in the dark but restful underworld known as Mictlan. Their home plane was filled with the souls of men who drowned or did not die in battle and women who died in childbirth. When a person died in such a way that they were bound for Mictlan, along with their personal possessions, they were buried with bribes specifically for Mictecaciuatl; it was hoped that by her accepting them, she would in turn make their afterlife as comfortable as possible.

Source: Seler, *Codex Fejérváry-Mayer*, 52, 105, 191–92; Soustelle, *Daily Life of the Aztecs*, 107; Turner, *Dictionary of Ancient Deities*, 321

Mictlampa (Mick-LAMP-ah)

Variations: Lord of the Mictlampa, The Taker of Life

Mictlampa ("The North Side") was a vampiric god to the ancient Aztec people. His body was the color of jet and he had a skull for a head; in art he is portrayed as pouring fire into a vessel of blood. He is the husband to MICTECACIUATL, and together they rule an underworld called Mictlan, which was thought to be to the north of Aztec lands. If an Aztec ever said that a person had "traveled north," it was to say that they had died.

Source: Aguilar-Moreno, *Handbook to Life in the Aztec World*, 138, 218; Brundage, *Jade Steps*, 189–90; Seler, *Codex Fejérváry-Mayer*, 7, 21, 103, 147; Summers, *Vampire: His Kith and Kin*, 241, 314

Milos (ME-los)

Variations: Mulo

There is Gypsy lore that says if a child is stillborn but is still moving as if it were alive, it is a type of LIVING VAMPIRE known as a milos. This condition of birth can also occur in a colt and ramling. The vampire will continue to grow until it is about eight years old, and although it will not get any larger at that point, it will continue to live on. A milos has a clothing fetish and will wear only all-white clothes. It is most active at noon and midnight, preying on the women of the community that it likes the most. The milos will kill them if it can and boil their bodies in order to make them easier to eat. It has a weakness for wine, and if a person can get it drunk, he can cut its head off, boil it, and then cut it into four equal pieces. The best way to destroy a milos, however, is to hire a professional DHAMPIRE. He will confront it in hand-to-hand combat or by the use of magic.

Source: Gypsy Lore Society, *Journal*, vol. 31–33, 125; Masters, *Natural History of the Vampire*, 184–86; *Roma*, 9, 11

Mjertovjec (Mm-jer-TA-veck)

Variation: Mjertojec, OPER, Opyr, Upar, Vupar

In Belarus when a traitor, werewolf, or witch dies, it will rise from its grave as a type of vampiric REVENANT known as a mjertovjec. Only active between midnight and sunrise, this purple-faced vampire is a blood-drinker and does not specialize in any particular sort of prey. To destroy this vampire, one must make a trail of poppy seeds that leads back to its grave, as it will be compelled to follow them. Once it is in its grave, it must be nailed through the chest so that it is forever pinned to the ground, or be burned to ash.

Source: Haining, *Dictionary of Vampires*, 176; Hertz, *Der Werwolf*, 124; Volta, *The Vampire*, 143

Mmbyu (MM-bouy)

Variations: Lord of All Night Entities, PACU PATI

Mmbyu ("Death") is a singular entity from the lore of India. He is considered to be the utmost mischief maker of all the various types of undead beings (see UNDEATH), creatures, and deities India has to offer. He is described as being surrounded by the visages of all his victims, as well as a cortege of demonic servants. At night, he can be found wandering cemeteries or places where excitations are held.

Source: Bunson, *Vampire Encyclopedia*, 133; Cuppiramaniyan, *Philosophical Heritage of the Tamils*, 16–17; Forlong, *Faiths of Man*, 401; Masters, *Natural History of the Vampire*, 65

Moloi (MUL-oy)

Variations: Moloica

A vampiric spirit from Romanian lore, the moloi is created when an illegitimate child is killed by one of its parents. Human hearts are the only food that the moloi can eat that will sustain it.

Source: Barber, *Vampires, Burial, and Death*, 30; Senn, *Were-wolf and Vampire in Romania*, 115

Moravia (Moe-RAY-vee-ah)

From the vampire lore of Czechoslovakia, this REVENANT leaves its grave at night and hunts for its nightly blood in the nude. The moravia, as it is known, can be laid permanently to rest if its burial shroud is destroyed.

Source: Dundes, *Vampire Casebook*, 180; McNally, *In Search of Dracula*, 119; *Strange Stories*, 432; Varner, *Creatures in the Mist*, 94

Moribondo (More-uh-BON-do)

From the Brittany region of France, ancient Celtic lore tells of the moribondo vampire. It feeds strictly on the blood of cattle, but they can be protected from it easily enough. Walking the herd between two pyres will magically protect them from the vampire.

Source: Haining, *Dictionary of Vampires*, 177; Volta, *The Vampire*, 150

Moribund (Mor-uh-BOND)

In Brittany, France, as well as in Cornwall, England, there is a vampiric REVENANT called a moribund. It is created when a person is killed by a werewolf.

As a word, *moribund* is used from time to time in vampire lore, as it means "to be in a state of dying."

Source: Keyworth, *Troublesome Corpses*, 274; McClelland, *Slayers and Their Vampires*, 178

Mormo (MORE-moe)

In ancient Greece, there was a monstrous vampiric creature known as a mormo ("terrible one"), or, when gathered in numbers, they were referred to as mormolykeia ("terrible wolves"). In its true form, it was covered in its own blood and blisters, though it was not as ugly as an EMPOUSE. The mormo could shape-shift into a beautiful young lady to lure handsome young men into a fatal indiscretion, draining them of their blood and consuming their flesh. When no suitable men were available, it would settle on consuming the elderly and young children. The mormo could also shape-shift into over 1,000 hideous forms.

Montague Summers, in his book *Vampire: His Kith and Kin*, mentions only by name some vampires whose names are similar to the mormo: mormolikeion, mormoliki, mormolix, and moromolukiai. Perhaps these were regional variations of the mormo, in either singular or plural form.

Over the years the vampiric mormo became something more akin to a common nursery bogey, as children are now told that if they misbehave during the day, at night the mormo will sneak into their room and bite them.

Source: Buxton, *Imaginary Greece*, 18; Fontenrose, *Python*, 116; Summers, *Vampire: His Kith and Kin*; Suter, *Lament*, 214–15

Morobondo (Moro-BON-do)

Variations: MORIBONDO

The northwest peninsula of France that is known as Brittany is home to a species of vampire known as a morobondo. Assaulting primarily cattle, it can be driven off as easily as driving the victimized cattle between two raging bonfires.

Source: Haining, *Dictionary of Vampires*, 177; Volta, *The Vampire*, 150

Moroiu (More-OY-you)

Variations: Orgoï

In Romanian vampire lore, the moroiu ("spirit") is a type of vampiric spirit.

Source: Davis, *Literature of Post-Communist Slovenia*, 148; Hurwood, *Passport to the Supernatural*, 248; Jones, *On the Nightmare*, 177; Skal, *Hollywood Gothic*, 81

Motetz Dam (Mo-tehz DAHM)

An ancient Hebrew word, *motetz dam* translates as "bloodsucker" and was used to refer to vampires.

Source: Bunson, *Vampire Encyclopedia*, 139

Moura (Mo-YOUR-ah)

Variations: Morava, Murrain, Murrain Mora, Opyri, Oupir

This vampiric spirit from Bulgaria, the moura attacks people nightly as they sleep.

Source: Georgieva, *Bulgarian Mythology*, 103; Gypsy Lore Society, *Journal of Gypsy Lore Society*, 117; Shashi, *Roma*, 103; Summers, *Vampire in Lore and Legend*, 158

Mrart (MA-art)

The Aboriginal people of Australia have in their mythology a vampiric spirit called a mrart ("ghost"). They believe it to be the restless spirit of a member in the community. Looking like a ghost, at night when its powers are at their strongest, the mrart grabs its victim and pulls him out of the light of campfire into the surrounding utter darkness. The Aborigines believe that spirits can possess a body, even if there is still another soul in it. To make sure that the body of a deceased person never rises again, the Abo-

rigines tie rocks to it when placed in its grave. Oftentimes, the limbs are broken, the person's possessions destroyed, and their personal campsite is never used again.

Source: Charlesworth, *Religion in Aboriginal Australia*, 224–25, 230; Howitt, *Native Tribes of South-East Australia*, 389, 437–39, 444, 635; Jones, *On the Nightmare*, 77; Massola, *Bunjil's Cave*, 143

Mukai (Moo-KIE-ee)

Variations: ALVANTIN, CHUREL, Jakhin, Nagulai

In India, there is a type of vampiric spirit that is known as a mukai. Created when a woman dies in childbirth or by some other unnatural way, it is easily detected for what it is, as the feet of a mukai are turned backward. At night, it attacks the men in its family first, draining them of their blood before moving on to others. If a mukai should give a man a piece of food and he accepts it, by morning all his HAIR will have turned white.

Source: Bombay State, *Gazetteer of Bombay State*, vol. 20, 125; Crooke, *Introduction to the Popular Religion*, 168; Crooke, *Religion and Folklore*, 194; Jones, *On the Nightmare*, 119

Mule (MULE)

In Gypsy lore the vampiric spirit known as a mule looks exactly as it did in life, but it does not return in its old body. Rather, it creates an exact duplicate that it uses. The mule, which is only viable between midday and midnight, is not a blood drinker and truly wants little else than to rejoin the community and reunite with its wives. Any children that are conceived and born from this union are called LAMPIJEROVIC, VAMPIJEROVIC, and vampiric; boys are sometimes called *VAMPIR* and girls *vampirera*, but in reality, they are all DHAMPIRE. The women are raised to believe that should a vampire come to them seeking intercourse, they should not resist or cry out. If a woman fights back or calls out for help, the community will not help her.

Source: Clébert, *The Gypsies*, 150; Masters, *Natural History of the Vampire*, 142; Summers, *Vampire Lore and Legend*, 271

Mullo (MOO-low)

Variations: Mulo, Vlokoslak

The Gypsy lore of Serbia tells of a vampiric REVENANT that is called a mullo ("one who is dead") or a muli if it is a female. It is created when a person dies suddenly of some unnatural cause, or the person did not have proper funeral rites performed over his body. Usually, the mullo dresses in all-white clothing, has HAIR that reaches down to its feet, and looks exactly as it did in life, except for one physical oddity. This trait varies from region to region and can be anything from missing a digit on the pinky finger to having an obvious animal-like appendage, or even flame-red HAIR. The mullo spends a good portion of its time seeking out the people it did not like in life and harassing them. The other half of its time it tries to satisfy its various appetites. When it attacks, and it will do so by day or by night, it usually strangles its victim to death and drains the blood to drink after the person has died. The mullo has the power to shape-shift into a horse or a ram and can become invisible at will.

The mullo can be destroyed, but it can be tricky business. A hen's egg can be laid out in the open and used as bait, as the vampire is partial to them. One must watch the egg carefully, because the mullo, suspecting a trap, will turn invisible in order to snatch up the egg. The moment the egg disappears, shoot at the spot where the egg was in the hopes of hitting the vampire. With the vampire wounded, it can more easily be tracked and identified. Once the mullo is captured, its toes must be cut off and a nail driven through its neck in order to kill it.

Source: Bryant, *Handbook of Death*, 99; Masters, *Natural History of the Vampire*, 142; Shashi, *Roma*, 8–9, 100

Muroï (ME-oy)

In Czechoslovakian lore, a vampiric spirit known as a muroï ("fatal destiny") is created when an evil person dies. To ensure that this type of vampire never has the chance to rise from its grave, remove the heart of the evil person before he is interred. If that precaution is not taken, when the muroï rises, it will have a red face and will prey upon the people of its former community each night. The muroï releases a cry that can freeze a person with fear, for whoever hears its call will be its next victim. By day the muroï's spirit is at rest in its grave. To discover which grave exactly, lead a stallion through the graveyard, as it will refuse to walk over a grave that a vampire occupies. With the body exhumed, a nail must be driven through its heart and the skin between its thumb and forefinger must be cut with a pair of iron scissors.

Source: Cremene, *Mythology of the Vampire in Romania*; Reynolds, *Magic, Divination, and Witchcraft*, 15

Muroni (ME-ron-nee)

Variations: Murohy, Muronul, MURONY, Orgoï, Varcolaco

A vampiric spirit from Romanian lore, the muroni is created when a person dies a violent death or was a magic user in life, when a child who was born out of wedlock to parents who were born out of wedlock dies, or if a person dies the victim of a muroni attack. It looks like a bloated corpse with red skin, long fingernails, and oftentimes, a mouth full of blood. It can shape-shift into a flea or a spider and prefers to use one of those forms when it attacks a person, although it can also shape-shift into a cat or dog as well. Because it hunts mostly in its insect form, there are seldom any bite marks to be found on a victim, and if any do show, they look just like an insect bite, so no one suspects that there is a vampire in the community and goes looking for it.

A person who is dying from a muroni attack cannot be saved, but fortunately it is known how to destroy such a creature. A muroni must be staked through the heart, have a nail driven through its forehead, or have its mouth filled with GARLIC.

Source: Bunson, *Vampire Encyclopedia*, 182; Peabody, *International Cyclopedia*, 60; Ridpath, *Standard American Encyclopedia*, vol. 7, 2600

Murony

In the countries of Moldavia and Wallachia there is a type of LIVING VAMPIRE called a murony. Typically male, the murony shape-shift into doglike creatures at night, their spines extending and becoming tails. Running outside the village, they act like a pack and attack cattle.

Source: *Appletons' Journal*, 188; Dickens, *All the Year Round*, vol. 5, 598; Leatherdale, *Dracula*, 77, 90

Murraue (MUR-row)

Historically, the land between Germany and Poland was once called Pomerania, and it is from there that the vampiric spirit known as a murraue originates. Essentially, the murraue is an ALP, a species of vampire that is common in this region of the world. However, the murraue has several small, unique aspects that warrant it to be recognized as its own species of vampire, if not a subspecies of ALP or INCUBUS or SUCCUBUS.

If a child is born on a Sunday, it will have a predisposition to becoming a murraue when it eventually dies. Another indicator is when a person's eyebrows are grown together.

Sometimes the needles of a pine tree curve as they grow and form what looks to be something like a small bird's nest. When it rains, water will gather in amongst the needles, and if a person should walk underneath one of these mock nests and a drop of its water falls on the person's head, they have been marked to be the next victim of the murraue.

The murraue comes at night when it is dark and its victim is asleep. It starts its assault by causing fear in the person and asserting pressure on their feet. Then, it moves up their body, toward the stomach and on up to the chest, and eventually to their head, paralyzing the whole body. Then it will straddle the person and "RIDE" them, draining their sexual energy (see ENERGY VAMPIRE).

If before someone is paralyzed he can call out the name of the person who the murraue was in life, it will immediately flee. Also, exposing it to light will harm, if not kill, it, as it is very susceptible to sunlight.

Source: Grimm, *Teutonic Mythology*, 1697; Meyer, *Mythologie der Germanen*, 131; Thorpe, *Northern Mythology*, 154–55

Mwère

Variations: Old Hag, Mora, Succuba

The Kashubian people of north central Poland are quick to baptize their children, for if one should die before the sacrament can be given it will return as a demonic vampire known as a mwère ("slowly"). Girls are particularly susceptible to this curse. It drains the life-energy out of sleeping horses and people by choking them to death (see ENERGY VAMPIRE). Should the victim reach out and successfully grab it, the demon will turn into a ball of HAIR or wool. If in shock the person should let go, the mwère will capitalize on the moment and vanish into thin air. The Mwère is the giver of nightmares and nocturnal emissions. It has the ability to fly through the night sky on a spinning wheel and can pass through the opening in a keyhole.

Plugging keyholes and keeping one's shoes next to the bed at night keep the mwère from attacking. If in the morning a person's horse is wet with sweat, it has managed to survive an attack from a mwère. Some lore says that when this is the case, the animal will sweat apples.

The mwère is similar to other vampires, such as the ALP, INCUBUS, MARA, and the SUCCUBUS.

Source: Jones, *On the Nightmare*; Keyworth, *Troublesome Corpses*, 103–4; Perkowski, *Vampires of the Slavs*, 197

Myertovets (My-er-TOE-vits)

Variations: Myertovjec, Opyr

In Russian vampire lore being born the son of a werewolf or witch is enough for a person to become a vampire upon death. Of this type of vampire, the myertovets, just about nothing is known of its abilities or hunting techniques. However, what is known about it is the very specific way in which it must be killed: a stake must be driven through its heart in a single blow. Should the stake miss or the strike was not powerful enough to penetrate all the way through, the vampire will immediately begin to kill its attacker.

Source: Bogatyrëv, *Vampires in the Carpathians*, 127, 171; Ronay, *Truth about Dracula*, 23; Summers, *Werewolf in Lore and Legend*, 15

Nabeshima (Nob-BAY-she-ma)

The nabeshima, as it has come to be called, is a vampiric cat from the folklore of ancient Japan. It looks like a common enough cat except that it has two tails. The creature can shape-shift into a specific person and uses this tactic to get close to its intended prey. It chokes a person unconscious and then drains him of his blood. It will also engage in sexual activity with its victim and drain his life-energy as well. The last report of a nabeshima attack was made on July 14, 1929, in the Japanese newspaper *Sunday Express*. The article claimed that the vampire cat of Nabeshima was harassing the wives of the descendants of a samurai. (See ENERGY VAMPIRE, KAIBYOU.)

There is an ancient Japanese tale of this vampire that takes place in Hizen, an old province that no longer exists. The prince, an honorable member of the Nabeshima family, was in love with a concubine named O-Toyo. After a lover's walk in the garden one night, O-Toyo was followed to her quarters by the vampire who killed her and buried her body beneath a veranda. Then, assuming the guise of the prince's beloved concubine, the vampire visited him each night, draining him of his blood and life, much like a SUCCUBUS does. All methods to restore his health failed and it was finally determined that something supernatural had to be the cause. Each night all the guards stationed around the prince's room would fall asleep, but one solider from the guard, a man named Ito Soda, offered to sit up with the prince one night, and eventually permission was granted. He stabbed a knife deep into his leg so the pain would keep him alert and awake. At the time when the other guards all mysteriously fell asleep, the vampire in the guise of O-Toyo entered the prince's chambers. The vampire felt the presence of another in the room, and made uncomfortable by it, was not able to drain the prince. For two consecutive nights Ito Soda stood on watch and each night the vampire was unable to draw life from him. As time passed, the prince showed signs of recovery, Ito Soda kept his vigil, and the guards were now able to stay awake. Ito Soda knew now that O-Toyo was responsible and tried to kill her one night, but the vampire dropped its guise and fled into the mountains. It harassed locals until the prince was recovered enough to lead a hunting exposition to hunt it down. He was able to do so and avenged the death of his beloved.

Source: Bushm, *Japanalia*, 43–44, 202; Dale-Green, *Archetypal Cat*, 106; Davis, *Myths and Legends of Japan*, 264–68; Howey, *Cat in Magic*, 173

Nachzehrer (NOCT-zeer-her)

Variations: Totenküsser

In the vampire lore of Germany, the nachzehrer ("night waster") is a vampiric REVENANT (see GERMAN VAMPIRES). It is created when money is not placed inside the mouth of the deceased before he is buried or when a person is buried in clothes that have his name written on them. The nachzchrer remains in its grave during the day not because it is harmed by sunlight but rather because it chooses not to confront the living who would without a doubt try to destroy it. At night it sends its spirit forth to stalk the community and drain the life from its family members before seeking out other, nonrelated victims. It is only on the rare occasion that the nachzehrer will actually rise up and physically leave the safety of its grave. But those occasions do take place and only happen for one of two reasons. The first is because it wishes to consume the flesh of those who have been buried in the graveyard. Second, with the accompaniment of a female REVENANT that has died in childbirth, it will climb up into the church tower and ring the bell. Whoever hears the bell toll will die. Although the nachzehrer has the ability to shapeshift into a pig, it will do little to draw attention to itself but rather utilize this form to scout out an area.

In the eventuality that a nachzehrer is discovered to be haunting a community, when it is exhumed, the vampire will be discovered holding its thumb in its hand, its left eye will be comically wide open, and the vampire will be busy gnawing on its own burial shroud. Some lore claims that the family will suffer and die only when the vampire has finally chewed the shroud's cloth away to nothing. To prevent the nachzehrer from rising or sending out its spirit, one must break its neck, leave food with it, remove the shroud, and sprinkle rice over the remains. The grains should keep it occupied, as it is mystically compelled to count them.

Source: Conway, *Demonology and Devil-lore*, 52; Ford, *Book of the Witch Moon*, 14, 15; Lindahl, *Medieval Folklore*, 1017

Nagasjatingaron (Na-GA-stay-sum-grun)

A vampire from the nation of Sumatra, the nagasjatingaron ("vampire") feeds off the tendi, or soul, of its human victims. Victims of this sort of vampiric attack must consult and hire a specific type of vampire-fighting witch doctor known as a BATAKS. Using a magical rub made of GARLIC and various other herbs, the salve will both repel the vampire and restore the damaged soul of the victim.

Source: Carle, *Cultures and Societies*, 257; Crawley, *Idea of the Soul*, 111 12; Rae, *Breath Becomes the Wind*, 56

Nagasjatingarong (NA-GA-stay-sum grun)

In Indonesia there is a vampiric spirit that preys on men known as a nagasjatingarong ("vampire"). The spirit possesses the body of a beautiful woman and uses her to seduce and then attack a man, biting him and drinking his blood. The only physical sign of attack is that the victim will develop ANEMIA. As recently as 1975 there was a report of a shaman who discovered a 25-year-old woman who was allegedly possessed by a nagasjatingarong. He asserted that she had already been married five times and each of her husbands had died of anemia within the first month of marriage.

Source: Koch, *Occult ABC*, 54–55; Perkowski, *Vampires of the Slavs*, 18

Ñakaq (Noc-AH)

Variations: Corta-Cuellos ("Throat-Cutters"), KHARISIRI, LIK'ICHIRI, PISHTACO

In Peru there is a vampire known as a ñakaq ("butcher of animals") that is described as looking like a tall white man that hunts women, mostly at night in the countryside. First, the ñakaq abducts and rapes her, and then it cuts off her body fat to both personally consume and to sell to white businessmen so that they may use it as a lubricant for their factory's machinery or in the production of cosmetics. Although the victim will be able to remember the incident, there will be no trace of physical evidence, especially where the ñakaq cut into her body.

Source: Benson, *Ritual Sacrifice in Ancient Peru*, 159; Meyerson, *Tambo*, 154; Wachtel, *Gods and Vampires*, 52, 72, 74, 77–83

Namorodo (NEM-road-dough)

The Aboriginal people of West Arnhem Land, Australia, have in their mythology a vampiric demon called a namorodo. It is a skeletal humanoid that is held together by ligaments and has long, razor-sharp finger bones. Inactive by day, at night it flies through the sky seeking prey. The namorodo will enter a home and when it finds a sleeping person, it attacks and drains them of their blood. If it is so inclined, it has the ability to create more of its own kind. The namorodo are associated with shooting stars and sorcery.

Source: McLeish, *Myth*, 407; Rose, *Giants, Monsters, and Dragons*, 263; Tresidder, *Complete Dictionary of Symbols*, 335

Naualli (New-WA-lee)

The ancient Aztec people of Mexico had in their beliefs vampiric sorcerers known as *nanahualtin* ("magicians"). A naualli (the singular spelling) was a human being who in addition to being able to cause a person to go insane, practiced his vampiric activities on children by first smothering them and then draining their blood. A naualli had the ability to shape-shift into an array of animals as well as being either a were-coyote or a werewolf.

Source: Brinton, *Nagualism*, 57; Soustelle, *Daily Life of the Aztecs*, 192; Spence, *Magic and Mysteries of Mexico*, 67–70, 87–95; Summers, *Vampire: His Kith and Kin*, 264

Navi (Nav-EE)

Variations: Látawci, Navj, Navjaci, Navje, Navki, Navyatsi, Opyr, Opyri, Oupir, Oupire ("bloodsucker")

A vampiric demon from Bulgaria, Poland, Russia, and Slovenia, a navi is created whenever a child dies before he is baptized or when a person drowns. It returns to the world looking like a common enough bird; it searches the countryside looking for its mother and calling out to anyone who will listen that it wants to be baptized. Never knowing its own mother's love, it will attack women who are about to give birth, cutting them just deep enough to draw blood so it may take a drink. For seven years the navi can wander the earth calling out to others to help it. If it manages to persuade someone to baptize it, its spirit will be able to rest; if not, it will forever remain a demon.

Source: Georgieva, *Bulgarian Mythology*, 102–3; MacDermott, *Bulgarian Folk Customs*, 81; McClelland, *Slayers and Their Vampires*, 110

Neamh-Mhairbh (NEAM MARE-bub)

Variations: Murbhheo, Neamh-Mairbh

In Irish folklore there a vampiric REVENANT that is created through magic; it is called neamh-mhairbh ("the undead"). It feeds off human blood. A neamh-mhairbh is not necessarily a species of vampire, but rather a vampire that has been created through the use of magic. Some versions of the story of the tyrant ABHARTACH consider him to be a neamh-mhairbh, as it was his own personal magic that allowed him to return.

Source: Fiérobe, *Dracula*, 67; Kiberd, *Irish Classics*, 384; Winn, *I Never Knew That about Ireland*, 255

Neamma-Parusha

A vampiric spirit from India, the neamma-parusha wears a wreath of human intestines on its head. It tears the skull out of its victim, consumes the brains, and drains the blood from the body.

Source: Ashley, *Complete Book of Vampires*; Crooke, *Introduction to the Popular Religion*, 69, 322

Necurat (Na-coo-RAT)

Variations: Orgoï

In Romania, the word *necurat* translates to mean "accursed" or "dishonest." It refers collectively to all evil, vampiric creatures. It is used in place of the name of a specific vampire so that the demon does not hear its name and be drawn to the person who said it.

Source: Cremene, *Mythology of the Vampire in Romania*; Diószegi, *Shamanism*, 146; Znamenski, *Shamanism in Siberia*, 46

Nefs

Variations: Nafs, Nefesh

In pre–Islamic Arabia, there was the belief that a deceased body could still have a soul inside of it. This animated corpse, a vampiric REVENANT, was called a nefs ("self").

Source: Bailey, *Jacob and the Prodigal*, 105; Pandolfo, *Impasse of the Angels*, 191–203, 357; Roux, *Le Sang*

Nekrštenici

According to Serbian lore, when a child dies before he is baptized he becomes a type of vampire known as a nekrštenici, which brings harm to young mothers and their newborn children.

Source: McClelland, *Slayers and Their Vampires*, 55; Stanojević, *Narodna Enciklopedija*, 45

Nelapsi (NELL-ep-see)

Variations: OPER

A vampiric REVENANT from Slovakia, the nelapsi is known to be able to destroy an entire village in a single night. With two hearts and two souls, the nelapsi is very fast, very strong. It can kill a person with a single blow and is also a plague carrier.

To prevent a person from becoming this type of vampire, place money, a religious icon, or personal items in the COFFIN with the body at the time of burial. There is also a very complex ritual that can be performed, which involves running a stake through its heart, carrying the body headfirst to its grave, and tossing a few handfuls of poppy seeds in the grave with it, just in case the ceremony did not work. Should the person rise from the dead as a nelapsi, it must be staked through its twin hearts with a stake made of HAWTHORN, iron, or oak.

Source: Belanger, Sacred Hunger, 127; Bryant, Handbook of Death, 99; Perkowski, The Darkling, 102–3

Neuntöter (New-un-TOTE-er)

Variations: Neutoter

The neuntöter is a vampiric REVENANT from German vampire lore (see GERMAN VAMPIRES). Its name, neuntöter, means "nine killer," as it takes nine days for the vampire to fully transform once it has been placed in its grave. When it does rise, it is covered with open sores and smells like excrement. It is also a plague carrier. People who were born with teeth or an actual spoon in their mouths are heavily predisposed to becoming neuntöters upon their deaths. To ensure that a person lies in rest for all time, the spoon that was in his mouth at birth must be burned to ash and then fed to the child. If this is not done, then after death, the head must be removed from the body between the hours of 11 P.M. and midnight; additionally a lemon must be placed in the mouth before the body is interred.

Source: Bunson, Vampire Encyclopedia, 188; Haining, Dictionary of Vampires, 180; Ronay, Truth about Dracula, 23

Nobusuma

In Japan if a bat can manage to live for a very long time it will become a vampiric creature called a nobusuma ("most ancient"). This ENERGY VAMPIRE flies through the night sky looking for a sleeping person to assault. When it finds suitable prey, the nobusuma lands on his chest and begins to tap on the sleeping person's chest, making him cough. When this happens, the nobusuma will take in the escaping breath, leaching off some of the person's life. Over the course of the next three days, unless the nobusuma is stopped, the victim will die, his life energy drained away. To prevent this from happening, all that has to happen is for someone to witness an attack taking place. This will drive the vampire off, never to return. The victim will instantly recover fully and go on to live a long and healthy life.

Source: Iinkai, Japan, 794; Japan Society of London, Transactions and Proceedings, vol. 9, 27–28; Poulton, Spirits of Another Sort, 64

Nocticula (Noct-TIC-oo-la)

Variations: Herodiade, "The Diana of the Ancient Gauls," "The Moon"

Nocticula is a vampiric, demonic goddess from France, a singular entity; her followers were most active during the twelfth and thirteenth centuries. Nocticula, a consort to both Asmodeus and Beelzebub, demanded human sacrifices be made in her name to the goddess Lamiae. These sacrifices, usually children, were cut into little pieces and fed to Lamiae, who devoured them but would quickly regurgitate them back up. Then Nocticula, in a show of mercy, would restore the children's bodies and place their souls back in, returning them to life. Then her followers would take the babies back to where they had been stolen from.

Nocticula followers were usually women, and while completely naked, they rode horses to their meeting place to pay homage to their goddess. Her followers wrote their names in a Book of Shadows and thereafter no longer considered themselves to be human women, but rather fay. Only one book of Nocticula has ever been found, and it was discovered in the ruins of one of her temples in the eighteenth century. Apart from the names of her followers, the book also contained the names of sorcerers and other magic users.

Some scholars have speculated that she may be a reinterpretation of a much older deity called Bensozia.

Source: Alford, Folklore, vol. 46; Clifton, Paganism Reader, 171; Gardner, Meaning of Witchcraft, 101; Grimm, Teutonic Mythology, 1057

Nora (NOR-ah)

Variations: Nore

From Hungarian vampiric lore comes a species of vampiric creature known as a nora. Humanoid, bald, and invisible, it moves about on all fours, attacking amoral and disrespectful women, drinking blood and breast milk from them. Smearing GARLIC paste over one's breasts will offer some protection from a nora attack, but the surest way to ensure one's safety is never to become a prostitute. It has been speculated that the nora was an attempt to explain sexually transmitted diseases and other such ailments.

Source: Dömötör, Hungarian Folk Beliefs, 116; Keyworth, Troublesome Corpses, 60, 111; Rihtman-Auguštin, Folklore and Historical Process, 207

Nosferat (Nos-FUR-rat)

Variations: Necuratul ("unclean one")

Across central and eastern Europe, the *nosferat* ("plague carrier") is perhaps the best-known species of all the vampires, considered by many to be the quintessential traditional vampire. There are several ways a person can become a nosferat, such as being born the seventh son of a seventh son, being born with a caul, the mother not eating any SALT during her pregnancy or having the misfortune of looking upon a vampire while pregnant, being born an illegitimate stillborn child to parents who are also of illegitimate birth, or having died the victim of a nosferat attack. The nosferat who was created because it died an illegitimate child has a deep hatred for married people, as its own parents were never married.

Nosferatu, as they are collectively called, can be either male or female, and are seen as an object of sexual desire to their victims. Shortly after nightfall, these REVENANTS rise from their graves and seek out their prey. A successful nosferat establishes itself as the sexual partner of at least one individual whom it returns to in order to feed. Over an extended period of time, the constant blood and life energy drain becomes too much and the victim dies (see ENERGY VAMPIRE). Nosferat has a veracious sex drive and there are numerous stories of it hosting orgies and having sex with a person until its victim literally dies of exhaustion (see INCUBUS and SUCCUBUS).

Usually, nosferatu cause infertility in their prey, but on occasion a male of the species can impregnate a human female. The child, called a moroi, will be born with a full head of HAIR and for all its life will continue to have a full head of wild, unkempt HAIR. Eventually, it will develop magical abilities and realize its full potential by becoming a witch.

Source: Cramer, *Devil Within*, 106; Jones, *On the Nightmare*, 117; Leatherdale, *Dracula*, 20; Riccardo, *Liquid Dreams*, 47

Nosophoros (Nos-OFF-froze)

Nosophoros ("plague carrier") is the Greek word for the Slavic word *nosferatu*.

Source: Klinger, *New Annotated Dracula*, 310; Morrow, *Halloween Handbook*, 154; Riccardo, *Liquid Dreams*, 174

Nuckelavee (NUCK-ul-leave)

In Scotland, on the Orkney Islands, there is a vampiric fay known as nuckelavee. Described as looking like a skinless centaur, it has a piglike nose that snorts steam, an overly wide mouth, and one large bloodshot eye in the middle of its forehead, which is about three feet wide. Its body is covered in thick yellow veins that pump its black blood; its overly long arms almost drag the ground as it walks.

Nuckelavee are the bane to all animals, humans, and plants; they even cause their own particular disease, *mortasheen*. Should it breathe upon a person, he will begin to wither up and die. Nuckelavee cause droughts, epidemics, and have been known to drive herds of animals off cliffs and into the sea, where they live. In fact, any area of unexplained ruin or destruction is said to be their handiwork.

Nuckelavee are repelled by the smell of burning seaweed; oftentimes it was gathered and burnt as a precaution. Like all fay, they are repelled by iron, but nuckelavee are also repelled by fresh water and falling rain, and they cannot cross running water. During the summer months, they are locked away by Mither o' the Sea, the Orcadian concept of Mother Nature.

Source: Cavendish, *Powers of Evil*, 230; Mack, *Field Guide to Demons*, 37–38; Marwick, *Folklore of Orkney and Shetland*, 22

Nutshnyk (Nut-SHIN-ski)

Variations: Opyr

In Russia there is a vampiric spirit known as a nutshnyk. It looks rather ghostlike and attacks humans at night, draining them of their blood.

Source: Summers, *Vampire: His Kith and Kin*, 18; Summers, *Werewolf in Lore and Legend*, 15; Whitney, *Century Dictionary and Cyclopedia*, 6693

Nyam Nyam (Nam NAM or Yum YUM)

Variations: Niam-Niam

Vampiric creatures from African lore, the nyam nyam are members of a mythical tribe of dwarflike people with short tails. During the period of slavery, the word came to be used as a racial slur to describe the Azande people and their allied tribes. It could have been a mispronunciation of the word *nimyam*, which means "cannibal."

Source: Battuta, *Travels in Asia and Africa*, 379; Hasluck, *Letters on Religion and Folklore*, 38; Petrinovich, *Cannibal Within*, 121; Volta, *The Vampire*, 116

Obayifo (Oh-BAY-if-oh)

Variation: Abayifo, ASEMA, ASIMAN, Obeyifo, Obayifu

The Ashanti people of the Gold Coast of Africa have in their vampiric lore a witch who uses his powers to drain the life and energy from children and crops. He is called an obayifo ("sorcery"). The Ashanti believe that people are born with the predisposition to become an obayifo, that it is not something that can be taught or passed on to another. In all respects the obayifo is human. Unless he is in a physical confrontation in front of witnesses, his secret may never be known, for when confronted with violence, his skin emits phosphorescence. This witch will oftentimes have a vampiric creature known as a SASABONSAM as a servant or familiar.

At night the obayifo, who has something of an obsession with food, leaves his body and flies off in search of prey (children and crops), but he is especially fond of the cacao bean tree, whose seeds are the primary ingredient in chocolate. When draining the life-energy from a person, it is a long, drawn-out, painful process, and it may take days or even weeks for the victim to finally die. Obayifo also has the ability, after drinking a magical elixir made of fruit and vegetable juices, to shape-shift into various animal forms in which it will adopt to kill people as well.

The Ashanti's neighboring tribe, the Dahomean, calls its version of the OBAYIFO an ASIMAN.

Source: Bryant, Handbook of Death, 99; Field, Search for Security, 35, 234–36; Stefoff, Vampires, Zombies, and Shape-Shifters, 17; Williams, Voodoos and Obeahs, 120–33

Obour (Oh-BOUR)

Variations: Opiri, Opyri, Oupir

In Bulgaria, there is a vampire called an obour that starts its reign of terror as a vampiric spirit and then develops into a vampiric REVENANT. It is created when a person is murdered and his spirit leaves the body suddenly and then tries to return, but the body is already deceased. Nine days after the body is buried, the spirit leaves the grave looking like a CORPSE CANDLE (a ball of light) and roams the community using its telekinetic ability to cause mischief. For 40 days it will harass whomever it can by biting into the udders of cows to drink blood and milk, causing shadows to move independently and look as if they are doing lewd things, making loud noises, smearing feces on holy artifacts and walls, or any number of minor acts of vandalism. If the obour becomes too troublesome or dangerous, a DJADADJII can be hired to bottle (see BOTTLING) and destroy it.

After 40 days have passed, the body of the obour rises up from its grave, looking exactly as it did in life except that it has only one nostril. Once it has risen, it will usually leave the area and try to reestablish itself in another location.

Source: Bryant, Handbook of Death, 99; Garnett, Women of Turkey, 336–37; Wolf, Dracula: Connoisseur's Guide, 24

Ogoljen (OG-ol-gen)

Variation: Ogalijen, Olgolgen, Mura

In the vampire lore of the Czech Republic there is a vampiric REVENANT called an ogoljen ("stripped bare"). When it is out hunting for humans to attack for their blood, it keeps dirt from its gravesite in its navel. An ogoljen cannot be destroyed, but it can be captured and buried at a crossroads to keep it from ever rising again.

Source: Grimm, Teutonic Mythology, 1266; Haining, Dictionary of Vampires, 191; Kessler, Demons of the Night, 13–21; Volta, The Vampire, 144

Ohyn (OH-wen)

Variations: Oupire ("bloodsucker")

In Poland any child who is born with a caul and teeth but dies soon after birth will rise up as a vampiric REVENANT called an ohyn. While in its grave it will chew upon its own body until it is able to escape. Described as looking like a red infant, the ohyn will set out initially to attack all of its family members before seeking out other prey. It hunts at night from dark places, utilizing surprise. Although very strong, an ohyn's legs are underdeveloped and therefore it cannot walk or run. However, it can levitate three or four feet off the ground and can also fly just a little bit faster than a person can run. An ohyn can be destroyed only by direct exposure to the sun for a prolonged period of time or by pulling out all of its teeth.

Source: Bunson, Encyclopedia of Vampires, 241; Point Park College, Keystone Folklore Quarterly, vol. 17, 125; Senn, Werewolf and Vampire in Romania, 66

Onoscèles (Oh-NOS-ah-clees)

The onoscèles is a vampiric creature from the Greek islands that is described as looking like a beautiful woman with one leg ending in a mule-like hoof (see GREEK VAMPIRES). It lures men into secluded places so that it can attack them and consume their blood, flesh, and sperm. It lives near the water and has the ability to shape-shift into water. The onoscèles is repelled by the root of a plant whose name has been lost to history.

Source: Cunningham, Synagoge, 355

Opachina (Oh-pa-CHEE-na)

In the Rhodope Mountains, opachina is the regional word that is used to describe a vampire.

Source: Georgieva, Bulgarian Mythology, 95

Oper (OO-pur)

Variations: Opir, Opyr, Oupire ("bloodsucker"), Oupyr, Upar, Vupar

In Belarus, eastern Poland, eastern Slovakia, Russia, and Ukraine, the word that is used to describe a vampire is *oper*.

Source: Auerbach, *Our Vampires, Ourselves*, 113; Day, *Vampire Myths*, 125; Dundes, *Vampire Casebook*, 14; Summers, *Vampire in Europe*, 307

Opi (OH-pa)

Variations: Opji, Oupire ("bloodsucker")

In Kashubia, Poland, *opi* is the Polish word that is used to describe a vampire.

Source: Indiana University, *Journal*, vol. 14, 225; Perkowski, *Vampires of the Slavs*, 196

Ornias (Oar-NEE-ahs)

In ancient Hebrew lore, there is a vampiric demon known as Ornias. It was one of many demons mentioned in the Testament of Solomon. It would appear to people in the form of fire, a lion, or a horrid winged creature. It would shapeshift into a beautiful woman and trick men into having sex with it, draining their sexual energy and potency much like an INCUBUS (see ENERGY VAMPIRE). Ornias would seek out men whose zodiac sign was Aquarius and strangle them to death, leaching off their life-energy as it did so. It did this because it resided in the constellation of Aquarius. Further the only way to save one of its victims before he died was to press the Seal of Solomon against the demon's chest.

During the construction of King Solomon's temple, Ornias appeared to one of the laborers, stealing half of his wages as well as draining the life-energy from one of his sons. The laborer sought the king for help and Solomon prayed to God for insight or intervention. His prayers were answered. The archangel Michael delivered to Solomon a ring with the seal of God upon it, giving the bearer power over demons. Solomon used the ring not only to stop Ornias from its daily muggings and assaults but also to bind other demons and use them as part of his labor force to build his temple.

Occasionally Ornias was summoned by magicians and witches who sought to divine the future, as this demon could be persuaded to fly up into the heavens and glean the future as it is written in the stars. As it would descend back to earth, Ornias looked like a shooting star. However, continued use of its abilities would cause his summoner to waste away.

Source: Ginzberg, *Legends of the Jews*, 151–53; Hanson, *Secrets from the Lost Bible*, 114–17; Rappoport, *Myth and Legend of Ancient Israel*, 88–90; Wedeck, *A Treasury of Witchcraft*, 172

Otgiruru (Ot-GOO-roo)

Variations: Owenga

The Herero people of Namibia, Africa, say that when an evil sorcerer dies, he will rise up as a vampiric REVENANT known as an otgiruru. Looking like a common dog, the otgiruru walks harmlessly about, and when no one is looking, calls out. Whoever answers the call, the otgiruru will kill, drinking his blood and consuming his soft tissue organs.

Source: Masters, *Natural History of the Vampire*, 48; Silver, *Vampire Film*, 18; Volta, *The Vampire*, 152

Ovengua (Ov-in-GUAY)

Variations: Owang, Oweng, OWENGA

The vampiric spirit of the ovengua comes from Guinea, Africa. When an evil sorcerer dies, his bones will begin to escape from the grave one at a time and gather in a secret location. Eventually, when they have all come together, the bones will reassemble themselves and become an ovengua, a skeletal spirit being that has large hooks for hands. Hiding in caves by day and wandering the forests at night, the ovengua will attack any lone traveler it sees and try to possess the person. Should the ovengua win, it will kill the person and animate the corpse to use as its own. The only way to destroy it is, unfortunately, to wait until it has claimed a body—then capture it and burn it to ash.

Source: Du Chaillu, *King Mombo*, 79–83; Wood, *Natural History of Man*, 572; Wood, *Uncivilized Races of Men*, 513

Ovengwa (Ov-in-WAY)

Variations: Owang

In Africa, *ovengwa* is a word used to describe a vampiric spirit, a "terrible catcher and eater of the dead." An ovengwa is the returned soul of a deceased man. It is described to be as tall as a tree and winking all the time. It preys on humans, draining their blood and energy (see ENERGY VAMPIRE).

Source: *Africa and Its Exploration*, 102; Bettany, *Primitive Religions*, 73; Masters, *Natural History of the Vampire*, 48

Owenga (Oh-WING-ah)

Variations: Owang

In Guinea, Africa, there is a type of vampiric REVENANT that is created when a person dies of a broken heart. The owenga lies in its grave making its plans for revenge, leaving only when it has decided upon a complete plan of action. When it rises it looks like a person with a single blood-shot eye. It only attacks or harms the people necessary to fulfill its revenge. Nothing will deter it from seeing its plan through to completion unless it is captured and burned to ash in its grave.

Source: Maberry, *Vampire Universe*, 244; Masters, *Natural History of Vampires*, 48; Volta, *The Vampire*, 152

Pacu Pati (PA-coo PA-tee)

Variation: Lords of Herds, Masters of Human Cattle, MMBYU, Pacupati, PISACHA

A race of vampiric REVENANTs from India, the pacu pati ("masters of the herd") are GHOUL-like beings that consume human flesh. Created through the vices of men and living mostly in cemeteries and places where executions are held, the pacu pati are evil and unfriendly, attacking their victims by possessing them and animating the corpses. Although they are well known to be mischief makers, as they are oftentimes referred to as being the Lords of Mischief Making, the pacu pati can occasionally be enticed to cure people of disease.

Source: Clothey, *Many Faces of Murukan*, 92–94; Cuppiramaṇiyan, *Philosophical Heritage of the Tamils*, 16–17; Forlong, *Faiths of Man*, 401

P'ai (PIE)

Variations: P'O

According to Japanese beliefs, the p'ai is the lesser of the two souls that inhabits every living person. It is present in the fetus and when the person dies; it will be the last soul to leave the deceased body. Usually, this soul only becomes active in a person when he is killed in a violent means, such as by suicide or drowning. If the p'ai of a person is particularly strong, it will use the body to fulfill its own desires, animating the corpse. When this happens, the being is called a CH'ING SHIH and is noted for its serrated teeth, long claws, and phosphorescent glow. The p'ai will not have the energy to use its animated corpse to escape the grave, so, even if possession should take place, burying the body and giving it proper burial rites will keep it in the ground and at rest.

Source: Davis, *Myths and Legends of Japan*, 226; Heinze, *Tham Khwan*, 37–40; Kuhn, *Soulstealers*, 96–97; Rivière, *Tantrik Yoga*, 92

Palis (PAL-is)

There is Persian lore of a type of vampire that is known as a palis ("licker of feet"), and as its name implies, it attacks its victims at night while they are asleep by licking the soles of their feet until they bleed. A palis by the name of DACHNAVAR once lived in a valley in the desert, and it happened upon two men who had fallen asleep foot to foot and a blanket covering them. When the vampire tried to attack, it believed that it had come upon a man with no feet and said, "I have explored 1,033 valleys, but have never seen a man with two heads."

Source: Carroll, *From a Persian Tea House*, 96–98; Cronin, *The Last Migration*, 200; Massé, *Persian Beliefs and Customs*, 272; Stookey, *Thematic Guide to World Mythology*, 135

Pelesit (Pa-LIS-it)

In Malaysia there is a type of vampiric spirit known as a pelesit ("spirit devil"). It is created with magic by a witch to be used as her familiar. She will go into the forest on the night of a full moon and, with her back to the moon and facing a hill, recite aloud the incantations that are necessary to catch her own shadow. It is a difficult process and very often does not work on the first try. When it does finally work, a child will appear and stick out its tongue. Quickly, the witch must grab the tongue, causing the child to disappear. Shortly thereafter, the tongue will turn into a small imp, the pelesit. In another version of the spell, the witch must bite the tongue out of the corpse of a first- born child whose mother was also a firstborn child and was buried at a crossroads.

Like many familiars that must be fed a special diet, the pelesit is no different. In order for the witch to keep it alive, she must feed it blood from her fourth finger mixed with saffron rice. It has the ability to shape-shift into the form of a common house cricket, a guise the pelesit will use when employed by its witch to attack the children of the woman with whom the witch suspects her husband is having an affair, a task that it takes particular joy in. The pelesit will enter into the child's body, and from within, cause an illness. The child will suffer from seizures and rant madly about cats. There is a particular charm that can be made or purchased that will ward off a pelesit, but it will do nothing for someone who is already under attack. Oftentimes a witch who has a pelesit as a familiar will also have a second familiar known as a POLONG. Very often the two familiars will work together to victimize a person.

Source: Folklore Society of Great Britain, *Folklore*, vol. 13, 150–51, 157; Masters, *Natural History of the Vampire*; Skeat, *Malay Magic*, 321, 328–30

Penangglan (PEN-non-gwen)

Variation: Pananggaln, Panangglan, Pênangal, Penanggalan, Pennanggalan, PONTIANAK

In Malaysian lore there is a type of female vampiric creature that is called a penangglan. Usually it is created when a woman dies in childbirth, but there is another circumstance that can cause a penangglan to come into being: if a woman in the process of performing religious penance is so surprised by a man that she literally dies of the shock.

A penangglan can pass as a normal woman by day, but at night it can detach its head from its body and fly off, dangling all of its soft tissue organs beneath it, everything from the esophagus to its rectum. As it hunts, it drips toxic bile that, should it touch human skin, will cause the person to break out with open sores. It flies out looking for its prey: children and women in labor. It despises children bitterly and takes great delight in killing them. The penangglan cries out, "Mangilai!" when a child is born. Only if its usual prey is not available and it is hungry enough will it settle for the blood of a man. When it returns to its home, its intestines will be bloated with the blood from its victims, so it dips them into a vat of vinegar to shrivel them up so it will fit back into its body.

To prevent the penangglan from flying near one's home, a person should place the thorny branches of the jeruju plant on the roof, as the thorns will snag on the dangling organs, trapping it. There is no known way to destroy a penangglan, but if someone manages to figure out who in the village the penangglan is, he can wait for it to detach from its body and leave. While it is gone, he must sneak into its home and destroy its vat of vinegar as well as its body. When the penangglan returns from its hunt, it will not be able to continue its ruse as its body is no more and its vinegar is not available to shrink up its organs.

Source: Laderman, Wives and Midwives, 126–27; Skeat, Malay Magic, 325–28; Wright, Vampires and Vampirism

Pey (PAY)

A vampiric demon from the lore of Sri Lanka and Tamil, India, the pey feeds off the blood of wounded warriors it finds on the battlefield. The pey drains the warrior of his blood and then takes the body back to its home to cook and eat.

Source: Hikosaka, Encyclopaedia of Tamil Literature, 67, 79, 30; Selby, Tamil Geographies, 194–95; Waghorne, Gods of Flesh, Gods of Stone, 197

Phi (PIE)

Variations: Phii, Phis

In Thailand spirits are collectively known as phi ("ghosts"). They are too numerous to be counted or fully catalogued. Their types and varieties are as varied as ghosts, undead, and fay are (see UNDEATH). There is a vampiric spirit that was first recorded from pre–Buddhist Thailand called phi. It is created whenever someone dies suddenly, as in an accident. Invisible, and usually found living in isolated places in the countryside, it attacks people by scratching them, drawing blood, and then lapping it up. Its bite can cause illness and disease. MAW DU (seers who are well-versed in occult knowledge) both sell and make charms that can protect against phi attacks. However, if there is an infestation of phi or a singularly dangerous one that is resistant to the charms, then the MAW DU can be hired to banish or destroy it.

Source: Bastian, A Journey in Siam, 158; Blanchard, Thailand, 97; Lewis, Peoples of the Golden Triangle, 260; Maberry, Vampire Universe, 247

Phi Song Nang (PEI SONG NANG)

In pre–Buddhist Thailand there was a type of vampiric phi called phi song nang that was created whenever a woman died before she married. The phi song nang looks like a beautiful woman, and at night it hunts for handsome men to prey upon. It will try to lure the man off to a secluded place with the promise of an indiscretion; once alone, it will turn and attack him, draining him of his blood.

Some men have been known to wear nail polish and women's bedclothes to bed at night in an attempt to trick the phi song nang into thinking he was a woman. Back in the 1980s in Thailand, a phi song nang was blamed for the spread of a mysterious disease that killed some 230 migrant workers. The illness was called Sudden Unexplained Nocturnal Death Syndrome. Those who claimed to be survivors of the assaults described feeling a sudden fear come over them while they slept and upon waking felt as if there was another presence in the room. They also said that there was an increasing pressure on their chest and that they were unable to move or scream. All of these symptoms are also present in an ALP attack.

Source: Bryant, Handbook of Death, 99; Graham, Siam, 544; Maberry, Vampire Universe, 247; Melton, Vampire Book, 602

Phii Krasue (PIE KRA-ows)

Variations: Phi Krasue

A type of vampiric phi from Thailand, the phii

krasue is described as a flying head with dangling entrails, a long tongue, and sharp teeth. The phii krasue drains a person's blood by inserting its tongue into its victim's anus. As it drains the blood, the vampire chews on the body, taking out bite-sized chunks of flesh.

Source: Chulalongk, *Asian Review*, 116; Phongphit, *Thai Village Life*, 54, 70; Sotesiri, *Study of Puan Community*, 44

Picacas (PEA-coc-ass)

Variations: Pisacas, Pisachi (feminine form), Pisakas, Pishachas, Pishashas

In ancient India there was a demonic race of vampiric Asuras known as picacas. They were evil by nature, chattering incessantly and, although aligned with the RAKSHASAS, were ranked beneath them. The picacas often warred against the Aryans, a race of tall, white-skinned people who migrated to India from central Asia; the Daitayas, a race of giants; and Nagas, god-like snake beings. They ate the flesh and drank the blood of both the living and the dead, being particularly fond of pregnant women. Picacas lived in abandoned places, burial grounds, and charnel houses but have been known to hunt in the jungle, spreading diseases while looking for humans to afflict with insanity or consume. Carrying iron or a piece of the neem tree will ward a picacas off.

Source: de Gubernatis, *Zoological Mythology*, 376; Keith, *Religion and Philosophy*, 384; Meyer, *Sexual Life in Ancient India*, 94; Rose, *Spirits, Fairies, Gnomes*, 261

Pihuechenyi (Pea-hoo-CHIN-ee)

The Araucanian people of Chile tell of an evil, vampiric god named Pihuechenyi. He looks like a gigantic winged snake and at night will find sleeping humans from whom to suck blood.

Source: Carlyon, *Guide to the Gods*, 64; Guirand, *Larousse Encyclopedia of Mythology*, 453; Rose, *Giants, Monsters, and Dragons*, 382

Pijavica (Pie-java-CA)

Variations: Pijawica, Pijawika

In Croatia and Yugoslavia there is a vampiric REVENANT known as a pijavica ("drinker"). Typically male, this vampire is created when a person dies who has committed an act of incest with his mother, although a person who was particularly evil in life may also return as this type of vampire. The pijavica will first attack its family and then its descendants, ultimately killing every person it can on its family tree until it is stopped. Only once it has killed its entire family line will it move on to other people. The pijavica has the ability to detect its own family members, no matter how distant the relation.

This vampire is very fast and very strong. In addition to being able to read minds, it also has the power of suggestion. Unless it is destroyed by a willful act, the pijavica is otherwise an immortal being.

Prolonged exposure to direct sunlight will eventually kill a pijavica as will staking it through the chest with HAWTHORN or burning it to ash. However, the most effective way to kill a pijavica is to decapitate it and when reburying the body, place the head between its legs.

Source: Ralston, *Songs of the Russian People*, 410; Ronay, *Truth about Dracula*, 22; Senn, *Were-wolf and Vampire in Romania*, 66

Pikulas (Pi-KOO-lis)

Variations: Piccolus, Picollus, Pikulis, Pikuolis, Piktulis, Poccolus, Velinas

A vampiric god from Lithuania, Pikulas looks like a pale old man with a long beard. A god of cattle, magic, wealth, and the underworld, Pikulas is responsible for all the death and destruction that occurs. Known to manifest to high-ranking officials during the last days of their life, Pikulas is ritualistically offered the severed head of a man and tallow is often burned in the god's honor. If angered, Pikulas must be appeased by the offender or he will die within three days. The only way to appease him is by offering him horse or human blood spilled against an oak tree. He is one of the three gods that make up the holy trinity of Lithuanian traditional religion, which was practiced until the late 1300s. After the introduction of Christianity to the people, Pikulas was reimagined to be the Christian devil, Satan, most likely because of his strikingly long beard.

Source: Bojtár, *Foreword to the Past*, 309; Fraenkel, *Die baltischen Sprachen*, 126; Golan, *Prehistoric Religion*, 112

Pisacha (Pa-SITCH-ah)

Variations: Hatu-Dhana, KRAVYAD, Pisâchâ, Pischca, Pishacas, Yaksha, Yatu-Dhana

In India, the word *pisacha* ("bloodthirsty savages" and "eaters of raw flesh") is used to collectively refer to all ghosts and vampires. There is a vampiric spirit called a pisacha that is created from human vice or as the by-product of the anger of the Brahma. Hideous in appearance, the pisacha feeds off human carcasses and is known to rape drunken women, an attack which is almost always fatal as it is very fast and strong; its blood is a contact poison. Pisacha live in cemeteries and at crossroads, and unless one wants to be found, the pisacha is unable to be detected by any means. On occasion it can be enticed to cure a person with leprosy, a disease it is known to spread; it is particularly fond of good conversation, as it is an intelligent and otherwise polite being.

Should a pisacha attack, it can be driven off by soaking it with holy water, but this is a temporary fix, as it will return as soon as it dries off. While it is gone, the victim must assume that he has contracted leprosy if not some other horrible disease. He must go to the crossroads with offerings of rice and perform a ceremony every night until the pisacha arrives. It will want to eat the rice, but the victim should offer it in exchange only if it heals him of the disease. The only way to truly destroy a pisacha is to burn it to ash.

Source: Agrawala, *India as Known to Pāṇini*, 447–48; Bkah-Hgyur, *Tibetan Tales*, 23–25; Crooke, *Introduction to the Popular Religion*, 153; Wright, *Vampires and Vampirism*

Pishtaco (Fish-TACO)

Variations: Phistako

Originally an Andean legend, it is now a Peruvian nursery bogey that represents the dark side of the cultural Latino male persona. A vampiric demon, the pishtaco looks like a tall white man wearing a long white coat, which hides the knife he carries. It sleeps too much and drinks great quantities of milk. This imagery has appeared on the ceramic work of the ancient Nazca people. The pishtaco, overly aggressive and unnaturally overendowed, captures children and severs the limbs and heads so that all that remains are the torsos. Then the pishtaco removes the body fat, which it then sells to make large bells for the church, run machinery, and contribute to paying off the country's huge international debt.

As recently as April 8, 1998, police received an anonymous tip that led them to discover the mangled bodies of two men. The bodies were described as having been flayed and all of their body fat removed. The autopsy revealed that the cause of death was due to cardiac arrest that was caused by lack of blood. The skins of the men were never found.

Vampires that are very similar to the pishtaco are the KHARISIRI, LIK'ICHIRI, LIQUICHIRI and the ÑAKAQ.

Source: Campion-Vincent, *Organ Theft Legends*, 153–56, 168; Gow, *Amazonian Myth and Its History*, 256–59; Llosa, *Death in the Andes*, 12–13, 18–19, 28, 33, 52–58, 80–85, 98–101

Pitaras (PIT-ah-rhas)

Variations: Manes

From the lore of India, the pitaras are a race of vampiric birds that feed off human life-energy (see ENERGY VAMPIRE).

Source: Blavatsky, *Isis Unveiled*, 107; Garg, *Encyclopaedia of the Hindu World*, 443, 513; Griffith, *Hymns of the Rgveda*, 158

Platnik (PLAT-nic)

Variation: Plâtenki ("fleshed out"), Plotenik, Plutenik, Plutnik

A vampiric being from Bulgaria, the platnik has a measurable and precise life cycle. After the body is buried, the spirit spends the first nine days of its unlife in the grave, and as it develops, the surface of its grave begins to sink in. As soon as that time has passed, the platnik rises from its grave as a spirit and begins attacking its family members for the next 40 days. In spirit form it looks like the shadow of a dog, hen, or person. Platnik attacks will range anywhere from breaking dishes to running off the cattle at night to vandalizing homes as well as physically assaulting people. To prevent a platnik from attacking while still in its spirit form, one must utilize the things it is afraid of: animal skulls, fire, iron, light, and wolves—it will not stay in an area where these things are present. Unfortunately, only a bolt of lightning will kill it, and the chances of that happening are rather slim. Exhuming the body on a Saturday and then piercing the corpse with a red-hot poker may also work.

If the spirit vampire can manage to drink enough blood and not get itself destroyed in the process, at the end of its 40-day rampage, it will become a platnik: a full-blown, solid-form vampire. It can now pass for a normal person except for having no fingernails and red eyes; furthermore, it will have the ability to shape-shift into a dog or wolf. Its new body does not have bones, but rather a cartilage-like substance. The first thing a new platnik will do upon developing its body will be to seek out its widow and attack her in broad daylight, torturing her to death. As soon as she is dead, the platnik will leave town and seek out a new place to live as far from its old community as possible. Once established in a place where no one will know it is a REVENANT, it will marry and have children. The offspring will be born VAMPIRDZHII. If the platnik is discovered for what it is, it can easily be killed. Any simple cut will prove to be fatal, causing it to bleed out and die. Its blood will be thick, dark, and jelly-like and is called pixtija.

Source: Georgieva, *Bulgarian Mythology*, 98; Lecouteux, *History of Vampires;* MacDermott, *Bulgarian Folk Customs*, 66, 67

P'o

Variations: P'AI

As far back as the Chou Dynasty (1027–402 B.C.) it has been believed that a person has two souls. The p'o, which first enters into a human during the development of the fetus, was characterized by yin and was associated with a person's material aspect. Normally the p'o descended into the underworld, or the Yellow Springs. However, if a person had a very powerful p'o or if a deceased body was exposed to either sunlight or moonlight, it could cause the p'o to remain, animate the body, creating a REVENANT, and use it to fulfill its own needs. When this happens, a vampiric being known as a CH'ING SHIH is created.

Source: Heinze, *Tham Khwan*, 37–40; Kuhn, *Soulstealers*, 96–97; Watson, *Death Ritual*, 8–9, 56, 193; Werne, *China of the Chinese*, 231–33

Polong (POE-long)

In Malaysia witches can create a vampiric familiar out of the blood of a murdered man. They take the blood and place it in a bottle, then perform a magical ceremony that can last as long as two weeks. During the ceremony, a bond develops between the witch and the developing familiar. Finally, when the sound of chirping is heard coming from within the bottle, the spell is complete and the vampiric familiar known as a polong is finally created. Before the creature is released from the bottle, the witch must let the polong bite her finger and drink her blood to permanently seal the bond between them. It will continue to feed from her daily. When not in use by the witch, it will stay inside its bottle home.

The polong looks like a one-inch-tall woman and is a trickster and a liar. Witches who have a polong oftentimes have another familiar, a type of vampire called a PELESIT. Together, the two familiars will attack whomever the witch sends them after. The PELESIT will cut a hole with its sharp tail in the victim and the polong will crawl inside, causing sickness and insanity in the person. A person who is ill because of a polong will have many unexplained bruises on his body as well as blood around his mouth.

A polong is resistant to the magic of other people, unless it is completely overwhelmed. It can be captured and with the use of powerful magic be forced to tell the name of its witch. Charms can also be made to neutralize and destroy a captured polong.

Source: Endicott, *Analysis of Malay Magic*, 57–59; Folklore Society of Great Britain, *Folklore*, vol. 13, 150–51, 157; Kadir, *Hikayat Abdullah*, 113–17; Masters, *Natural History of the Vampire*, 62

Poludnica (Poe-low-NICKA)

Variations: Lady Midday, Poludniowka, Polunditsa ("noon-wife"), Pszepolnica, Rzanica

In Slovenia there is a vampiric demon that looks like a beautiful, tall woman wearing white or dressed as if in mourning. In either guise, a poludnica ("noon") carries a scythe or shears. During harvesttime, right around noon, a poludnica attacks laborers who are working and not taking their proper rest, causing them to be afflicted with heatstroke or madness if they are lucky. If not, the poludnica will lure them off with her beauty and when she has them in a secluded place, attack viciously, draining them of their blood. It also will break the arms and legs of anyone it happens to come across. If a poludnica comes up to a field worker, it will start to ask him difficult questions. As soon as he cannot answer one, it will chop off his head. If a poludnica is seen, one must immediately drop to the ground and lie perfectly still until it meanders off. The male version of the poludnica is called polevoy.

Typically a bundle of grain is decorated when harvest starts to keep poludnica at bay, and when harvesttime is over, the effigy is burned.

In addition to attacking laborers, it also steals children that it found wandering unattended as the adults worked. Most likely the poludnica is a nursery bogey used by parents to keep their children from wandering off and damaging the crops. It is also an excellent story for a worker who wants to take a break.

Source: Grey, *Mythology of All Races*, 267; Oinas, *Essays on Russian Folklore*, 103–10; Rouček, *Slavonic Encyclopaedia*, 237

Poludnitsi (Pole-ah-NITS-ee)

The poludnitsi is a vampiric spirit from Czechoslovakia. It preys on young and first-time mothers and their children.

Source: Georgieva, *Bulgarian Mythology*, 103

Pontianak (PONT-ah-nook)

Variation: Buo, Kuntilanak, MATI-ANAK, Pontipinnak

In the folklore of Indonesia and Malaya there is a vampiric demon known as a pontianak. When a woman dies in childbirth, as a virgin, or as the victim of a pontianak attack, she will then transform into this type of vampire unless specific burial rites are followed. Glass beads must be placed in the corpse's mouth, an egg in each armpit, and needles driven into the palms of the hands and soles of the feet.

A pontianak can pass as a human woman except for a hole in the back of its neck and smelling exactly like the tropically sweet frangipani flower. It will also announce its presence with a call that sounds like a crying baby.

At night, it leaves its home in a banana tree and shape-shifts into a bird. Then the pontianak flies out looking for prey. Although any person will do, it truly prefers the blood of infants and pregnant women as it is filled with hatred for never having been a mother itself. When it finds a suitable target, the pontianak then changes back into its human guise and detaches its head from its body, dangling its organs beneath as it flies back to where it saw its prey. If it can, it will rip the unborn child right out of the mother's body, eating it on the spot.

The pontianak has a unique fear among vampirekind. It will flee in terror from anyone who manages to pull a HAIR out of its head. Also if a nail can be placed into the hole in the back of the neck, it will change into a beautiful woman and remain that way until someone pulls the nail back out. It is fortunate to know that the pontianak has these weaknesses, because there is no known method for destroying one.

Source: Laderman, *Wives and Midwives*, 126–27; McHugh, *Hantu-Hantu*, 74; Skeat, *Malay Magic*, 326–28

Porcelnik (Pour-SELL-nick)

In Russia, there is a type of human sorcerer that practices vampiric activities; he is called a porcelnik ("harmer") (see LIVING VAMPIRE). When he dies, the porcelnik's body must be burned to ash on a pyre made of aspen wood or else the body will rise up as a type of vampiric REVENANT known as an ERETIK.

Source: Melton, *Vampire Book*, 525

Porphyria (Poor-FEAR-ee-ah)

Porphyria is a rare hereditary medical condition in which a person's body does not produce heme, the main component in hemoglobin. Those who suffer with this disease have a sensitivity to sunlight, allergic reactions to GARLIC, excessive HAIR growth, scars that easily break back open and never heal properly, and a tightening of the skin around the gums and lips that gives the illusion of the incisor teeth being larger than normal. These symptoms certainly add up to what many

people consider being textbook vampiric traits. However, there are no vampires, mythologically speaking, that fit this profile. People who claim to suffer from porphyria and claim that their craving to drink blood stems from the disease are incorrect. Although the craving may be real, there is absolutely no medical evidence to support the idea that porphyria sufferers crave blood, human or otherwise.

Source: Bunson, *Encyclopedia of Vampires*, 210; Evans, *Porphyria*; Ramsland, *Science of Vampire*, 91

Potsherd (POT-shard)

On the Greek island of Chios (see GREEK VAMPIRES), as well as in various places throughout Europe, a piece of pottery called a potsherd was buried with a person to prevent him from rising as an undead creature (see UNDEATH). Typically placed in the grave by a priest, the potsherd was inscribed with the phrase "IXNK" which means "Jesus Christ conquers." The Kashube people of Pomerania and western Prussia would place a potsherd into the mouth of their deceased in order to give them something to chew on in lieu of their burial shroud.

Source: Argenti, *Folk-lore of Chios*, 338; Barber, *Vampires, Burial and Death*, 47; Crawford, *Antiquity*, 502; Daniels, *Encyclopedia of Superstitions*, 812

Prêt (PRET)

Variations: Bhoot, Bhot, Jakhh, Kinner

In India, the soul of a male deformed or stillborn child will return as a vampiric spirit called a prêt, or a paret if a female. When it returns, the prêt is no larger than a person's thumb, but it carries disease with it as it is compelled to wander the earth aimlessly for the next year, in a state of sorrow over not having its body any longer. It will gravitate to cemeteries, cremation grounds, and dark places. If food offerings are left for it and it is otherwise left alone, the prêt will remain nonviolent. After a year of sorrow, it will dissipate.

Source: Angoff, *Parapsychology and Anthropology*, 229; Crooke, *Introduction to the Popular Religion*, 153; Crooke, *Religion and Folklore of Northern India*, 185; Smith, *Self Possessed*, 113

Preta (Par-EE-ta)

The preta ("morbid") is a vampiric spirit from India. It appears as a fresh corpse whose stomach is bloated and large but its mouth has shriveled up, leaving only a small opening. Walking the earth lost and hungry for human blood, the Buddhist faith sees the preta's condition as a fitting punishment for a person who had too many desires in life.

Source: Crooke, *Introduction to the Popular Religion,* 153; Daniélou, *Myths and Gods of India,* 27, 213, 301, 311; Turner, *Dictionary of Ancient Deities,* 184

Priccolitsch (PRAY-co-litch)

Variations: PRICULICS, Prikolotsch

In Romanian lore, there is a man, typically a shepherd, who is a type of vampiric werewolf called a priccolitsch. He has the ability to change into a bloodthirsty wolf and then attacks his own flock, draining them of their blood.

Source: Abbott, *Macedonian Folklore,* 217; *Chambers' Encyclopaedia,* 708; Greene, *International Cyclopedia,* 804; Summers, *The Werewolf,* 147; Tozer, *Researches in the Highlands of Turkey,* 83

Pricolic, Undead (PRAY-co-lic)

A vampiric REVENANT from Romania, a pricolic is created when a child dies before it was baptized; however, if a person intentionally burns a porridge spoon or sweeps dust from the home out a doorway and into the setting sun, then when he dies, he will join the pricolici (as they are collectively called).

Upon rising from the dead, a pricolic will attack members of its family before moving on to other victims. If a person is suspected of being this type of vampire, his body must be exhumed. If the corpse is found to be facedown in its grave and blood is on its lips, then the person is a vampire. There is no known way to destroy this vampire, but there is a method that will prevent it from continuing to kill people. Some of the blood must be taken from the vampire's lips and administered to the remaining family members, thus preventing the pricolic from attacking them.

Source: Melton, *The Vampire Book*

Pricolic, Wolf (PRAY-co-lic)

In Romania, in addition to the vampiric REVENANT that is called a PRICOLIC, there is a vampiric creature that is called a pricolic, but it is born of an incestuous relationship and has a tail. This person has the ability to shape-shift into a dog, although as to whether this is a given talent or something that was gifted to the pricolic by the devil remains to be answered. While in his dog form, the pricolic mingles in the company of wolves. The person will find that it begins to spend more and more time in its other form, until eventually, one day, it shape-shifts into a wolf and, giving in to its wanderlust, joins a pack. To prevent it from attacking family and livestock, the pricolic can be kept at bay by leaving offerings of food for it to eat.

Source: Melton, *The Vampire Book*

Priculics (PRAY-co-lics)

Variations: PRICCOLITSCH, Prikolotsch, Varcolaci

In the geographic and historic region of Romania that was once Wallachia, there is the lore of a vampiric were-creature called a priculics ("wolf coat"). By day it passes as a handsome young man, but at night it has the ability to shape-shift into a large and shaggy black dog. In its animal form it will attack anyone it encounters, draining his of his blood.

Source: Baskin, *Sorcerer's Handbook,* 88; Leland, *Gypsy Sorcery and Fortune Telling,* 65; Masters, *Natural History of the Vampire,* 93; Perkowski, *The Darkling,* 40

Procolici (PRO-cal-lee-chee)

Variations: Pryccolitch, TRICCOLITCH

Another vampiric werewolf from Romanian lore, the procolici is a man who has the ability to shape-shift into a wolf by spinning in a circle three times. In his wolf form he will then hunt for animals and the occasional human to attack to drain dry of blood.

Source: Maberry, *Vampire Universe,* 251; Perkowski, *Vampires of the Slavs*

Pumapmicuc (Poo-ma-MIC-coo)

Variations: CANCHUS, Rumapmicuc

In ancient Peruvian lore, there was a sect of vampiric devil worshipers called pumapmicuc. They slipped into a home, found a sleeping child, and drank some of its blood, taking with them some of the child's life (see ENERGY VAMPIRE).

Source: de Molina, *Narratives of the Rites,* 83, 89, 114; McNally, *In Search of Dracul,* 117; Ralston, *Russian Folktales,* 311–28; Trumbull, *The Blood Covenant,* 115

Punyaiama (Pom-AH-ya-ma)

Variations: VETALA

In the Bihar and Orissa regions of India there is the belief in a vampiric creature called a punyaiama ("pure race"). It is described as looking like an old woman with black skin, poisonous fingernails, and slitted eyes. It is usually covered in the ashes from funeral pyres, as that is where it sleeps during the day. At night, the punyaiama attacks lone travelers as they walk down quiet roads. It also climbs up to the roof of a house and feeds a magical string down the home's chimney. The thread is enchanted to find sleeping women or women who are passed out drunk, insert itself into their skin, and feed blood back up to the waiting punyaiama. The vampire also has the ability to possess a corpse, and when it does so, the corpse's feet distort and bend backward.

Source: Kosambi, *Introduction to the Study of Indian History*, 35–45; Saletore, *Indian Witchcraft*, 83; Volta, *The Vampire*, 151

Rakshasas (RAK-sha-sa)

Variations: Ramayana

In the Hinduism that is practiced in India there is a vampiric race of demons known as the rakshasas, created by Brahma to protect the ocean from those who sought to steal the secret Elixir of Immortality. They are part human and part animal, but the human-to-animal ratio varies widely depending on the source being cited. Most often the animal mix is tiger. The *Vedas*, a Hindu religious text, describes the beings as having five legs and a body completely covered in blood. Modern descriptions of rakshasas add that they have fangs and the ability to use magic.

When not protecting the Elixir of Immortality, the rakshasas live in the treetops; however, they will often wander in cemeteries where they will disrupt services and religious incantations. When hunting for humans to feed upon, the male of the species will stay up in the treetops and wait for its favorite prey to pass underneath: infants or pregnant women. Then, the rakshasas will vomit down onto them, killing them. Female rakshasas, called rakshasis, have the ability to shape-shift into beautiful women, and in that guise will lure men off to a discreet location in order to attack them, draining them of their blood.

There is a belief that if a child can be persuaded to eat human brains, it will transform into this vampiric creature. A type of sorcerer exists that follows the rakshasas' activities closely, as they will consume the uneaten remains of a rakshasas kill. This act is called YATU DHANA.

Rakshasas can be killed if an exorcism is performed on them, but prolonged exposure to sunlight or burning them to ash works as well.

Source: Crooke, *Introduction to the Popular Religion*, 124, 154–58, 234, 320; Knapp, *Machine, Metaphor, and the Writer*, 161–62, 171; Pattanaik, *Indian Mythology*, 79, 86, 90–96

Ralaratri (RHA-lar-tree)

There is a VAMPIRIC WITCH in India that is called a ralaratri ("black night"). Accompanied by cats, one of which is her familiar, she is described as having eyebrows that have grown together, full lips, large cheeks, and suspiciously large and predominant teeth. Beyond having her own type of witchcraft, the ralaratri has an array of abilities, including controlling storms, prophesying, potion brewing, and shape-shifting into

a tiger. It is usually in her tiger form that the ralaratri will hunt for humans to kill, but she will revert to her human self to eat their flesh.

The ralaratri in tiger form is notoriously difficult, as well as dangerous, to kill. It is suggested that the better route would be to follow or track the tiger back to the ralaratri's home and wait until she has assumed her human form. Then, before she can cast her magic or shape-shift again, her teeth must be smashed in, as this will remove her powers. Once stripped of her magic and abilities, the ralaratri is completely helpless and can be killed by any method that would kill a human.

Source: Baskin, *Dictionary of Satanism*, 272; Masters, *Eros and Evil*, 188; Spence, *Encyclopædia of Occultism*, 226; Wedeck, *Dictionary of Magic*, 77

Ramanga (Rha-MAN-ga)

The Betsileo people who live on the southern part of the Madagascar plateau have in their mythology a ceremonial vampire known as a ramanga ("blue blood") who serves the tribal chiefs. His duty as the noble's constant companion is to eat the nail clippings as well as drinking any blood or spit that the chief or other people of high stature may shed. This is done to ensure that these vital ingredients cannot fall into the hands of a witch who would use them to make a fetish.

Source: Frazer, *The Golden Bough*, 236; Kent, *Early Kingdoms in Madagascar*, 221; Masters, *Natural History of the Vampire*; NPAP, *Psychoanalytic Review*, 6

Ravana (Rha-VAN-ah)

Variations: The King of (Sri) Lanka

Ravana, according to Hindu lore, was once the king of Lanka, faithful to his god, and ruler of a prosperous kingdom. He was brave, courageous, and smart, and knew how to use every type of weapon with a degree of skill. Only Lord Shiva himself could kill him. He was further blessed with the ability of flight and invisibility, and could make it rain water, fire, or thousands of arrows. Despite all of this, in his heart Ravana was a pleasure seeker who sought to use his abilities and gifts for his own personal satisfaction, which in turn caused him to become lustful, proud, quick to anger, and filled with jealousy. Open to corruption, he succumbed and fell from his status as human and devolved into a ten-headed and twenty-armed demon that became the king of the RAKSHASAS. As a demon, he is now driven by his compulsion to drink human blood. A highly skilled shape-shifter, he is also strong enough to split a mountain with his bare hands. Ravana can rip a man's soul right from his body, regenerate lost limbs, and is immune to all the elements of this plane of existence. Should an attack reach his only vulnerable place, his heart, Ravana can be struck dead by any blow or attack that would destroy a human heart. However, he can be resurrected by pouring blood into his mouth.

Source: Shashi, *Encyclopedia Indica*, 418–39; Summers, *Vampire: His Kith and Kin*, 300; Turner, *Dictionary of Ancient Deities*, 335

Redcap (Red-cap)

Variations: Powrie

In Scotland and Wales there lives a type of vampiric fay called a redcap. Looking like a small and twisted old man with big teeth, long fingers, and skinny arms, it wears boots made of iron with iron spikes on the soles. The redcap gets its name from the hat it wears upon its head. White originally, it has turned red because the little fay is always trying to mop up the blood of its victims.

Redcaps live in abandoned places where there was once a great amount of violence, like a battlefield or a place of execution. Highly territorial, they will attack anyone who walks too near their home by utilizing their amazing strength to drop boulders on victims' heads.

Unlike most fay, the redcap is not susceptible to iron, as its boots prove. However, reciting verses from the Bible, showing it a CRUCIFIX, or sprinkling it with holy water will drive it off.

Lord Soulis of Hermitage Castle had a redcap as a familiar (see SOULIS, LORD OF HERMITAGE CASTLE).

Source: Dorson, *The British Folklorists*, 111; IGI, *Folklore*, 248; Masters, *Natural History of the Vampire*, 140; Summers, *Geography of Witchcraft*, 205

Revenant (Rev-a-nint)

The word *revenant*, a variation of the French word *revenir* ("to return"), simply means "one who has returned after death or a long absence." It is used in vampiric lore to describe any being or creature that has died, risen up from its grave, and returned to a kind of "unlife" (or UNDEATH) among the living. Not all revenants are vampires, although many types of vampires are revenants.

Source: Ashley, *The Complete Book of Vampires*; Barber, *Vampire, Burial and Death*, 85; Day, *Vampires*, 194

Ride (Ride)

The word *ride*, when used in context of a vampiric attack, refers to a specific type of sexual assault on a victim. There are numerous species of vampires that utilize this method of assault, many of which are energy vampires, and the best known is perhaps the ALP of German lore (see GERMAN VAMPIRES).

To commit an act of riding, a vampire typically seeks out a person who is asleep. Upon entering the room, the vampire usually induces a form of sleep paralysis, rendering the victim unable to move or speak but otherwise fully aware of his surroundings. By either sitting upon his chest or straddling the victim, the vampire then causes some varying amount of pressure to the person's body. From this position the vampire may engage in some level of sexual activity with its prey, and this is done for a variety of reasons, be it attempting to cause a nocturnal emission, steal semen, or impregnate a woman. What the vampire is doing, in essence, is creating energy, sexual in this case, that it feeds off of in addition to any other activities it may be involved in. It is not uncommon for a vampire, after it has consumed its required need for sexual energy, to then attack its prey, draining him of some to all of his blood.

It should be noted that although the amount of pressure the vampire uses upon its prey may be great enough to kill in some cases, the act of riding is not about crushing a person to death but rather absorbing his vital energy and essences (such as sexual energy and related bodily fluids) (see ENERGY VAMPIRE).

Source: Botting, *Gothic*, 139; Leatherdale, *Dracula the Novel and Legend*; Krevter, *Der Vampirglaube in Sudosteurope*, 433; Williams, *Ways of Knowing in Early Modern Germany*, 65

Rolang (ROLL-ing)

Variations: Rô-Lang

A type of Tibetan magic user known as a ngagspa can perform a very precise and dangerous spell ceremony that will create a vampiric REVENANT called a rolang ("corpse who stands up"). The sole purpose for his wanting to create such a creature is to obtain the creature's tongue, a powerful magical item.

The ngagspa locks himself in a room with a corpse that he has procured. He then lies on top of it and empties his mind of all thought except for the magical incantation he is continuously repeating to himself. He will eventually place his lips on top of the corpse's lips and use his arms to keep the corpse's arms pinned down.

Sooner or later, the corpse, now a rolang, will try to rise and escape. The ngagspa must prevent this from happening while his lips maintain contact with the rolang's lips. If even so much as an instant of separation occurs, the spell will be broken, the ngagspa will lose control of the vampire, and it will rampage through the village, killing everyone it sees by ripping bodies apart. No one will survive the assault; even its touch is fatal. Nothing will remain but a decimated town littered with bodies. It is said that only a scant few lamas are still in existence who know the magical rites that will stop the rolang, causing it to lie back down and return to its former state of being, a harmless corpse.

However, if the ngagspa can maintain the spell and the physical contact long enough, the rolang's tongue will make its way out of its mouth and into the ngagspa's, who must then bite down as hard as he can, severing the tongue. As soon as this happens, the rolang will collapse dead and the ngagspa will have a powerful and hard-won magical item.

Source: Cuevas, *Travels in the Netherworld*, 95–103; David-Néel, *With Mystics and Magicians in Tibet*, 127–29; Knapp, *Women, Myth, and the Feminine Principle*, 9–10; Mead, *Primitive Heritage*, 441–43

Rusalka (Roo-SAW-ka)

Variations: Mokosh, Rusalky, Samovily

In the Republic of Slovenia there is a type of vampiric fay known as a rusalka ("shore"), said to be a member of the Unseelie Court, a spinner of Fate, and a regulator of the seasons. It is created when a child dies before it has been baptized or if an adolescent dies a virgin.

Rusalka descriptions vary slightly from region to region. In some areas it looks like a young girl on the brink of womanhood—very beautiful with long, flowing HAIR that is GREEN and decorated with poppies. In other places the rusalka wears a beautiful gown or tunic or nothing more than some strategically placed leaves. Other accounts describe the rusalka as looking like a drowned corpse or a mermaid. Its male counterpart is called a VODYANIK. It looks like a very handsome young man, but no matter where it is or what it is wearing, the left side of its body is always wet. But no matter the region one is in or the gender of the rusalka one may see, it will always be attractive and in or near the water.

On the nights of the full moon, rusalka can be found in ponds or rivers, and it will kill cattle and horses that come too close to the water's edge. If it sees a handsome man, it will lure him into the water with it, as it is looking for someone to pass the night in pleasure with. However, the man seldom survives the experience; the rusalka ends up draining him of his youth and life (see ENERGY VAMPIRE), and more often than not, forgets in the throes of passion that its human lover

needs to breathe air. However, the very few men who have managed to escape the embrace of a rusalka say that its love is literally worth dying for. Apart from men, from time to time a rusalka will want a child of its own and will snatch one up from the water's edge. It takes the child to its home under the water, where the human will inevitably drown.

Rusalka do not allow anyone to bathe in the water it calls home or even in water near its favorite dancing places. It will do everything in its power to drown them. To prevent one from attacking, one should tie ribbons and scarves to its sacred trees and leave gifts of eggs for it. Under Christian influence, the rusalka cannot stand the sight of the CRUCIFIX and will quickly flee if it hears prayers being recited.

Before Christianity came to the region, the rusalka was most likely originally the singular entity Mokosh, goddess of bounty, fertility, and moisture. Mokosh looked after women while they worked.

Source: Hubbs, *Mother Russia*, 24–35; Ivanits, *Russian Folk Belief*, 75–80; Mack, *Field Guide to Demons*, 19; Willis, *World Mythology*, 211–13

Ruvaush (ROO-vosh)

The vampire lore of the Gypsies of Romania tells of a VAMPIRIC WITCH called a ruvaush. Aside from having the ability to create more of its own kind through magic, it can also shape-shift into a wolf, but one that is much larger than a normal wolf. Grevase of Tilbury (1150–1228), a medieval chronicler, was the first person to associate the transformation of werewolves to the moon and its cycles, but his concept was never popular until it was used by modern fiction writers.

Source: Icon Group International, *Victims: Webster's Quotations*, 489; Summers, *Vampire in Lore and Legend*, 92

Sâbotnik (So-BOT-nic)

Variations: Sâbota ("Saturday"), Vâperar

From the Balkans comes a type of LIVING VAMPIRE known as a sâbotnik ("one born on a Saturday"). This individual, typically male, is marked by his community as a quasi-supernatural being who can see and identify vampires, demons, diseases, and magicians, as well as interpret dreams. Socially the sâbotnik is considered an outsider in his own community, but he is still obligated to perform his services. Although a woman may be born on a Saturday and thereby inherit the title of sâbotnik, she seldom has the actual ability of seeing vampires, let alone the ability to destroy them. Sâbotniks specialize in killing a type of vampire known as a VRKOLAK by using a gun or a knife. Like the VAMPIRDŽIA, the sâbotnik is very well paid for his services, either with actual money or with gifts.

Interestingly, dogs that are born on a Saturday are also considered to be sâbotnik. This is not because anyone believes that they were sired by a vampire but rather because they were born on Saturday, the Jewish holy day, rather than on Sunday, the Christian Sabbath. These dogs, like their human counterpart, are able to detect vampires and diseased individuals. The best sâbotnik dogs have four eyes, particularly pronounced eyebrows, or are large and solid black. Whenever possible, one of these dogs is used as a familiar by a vampirdžia. In extreme cases a sâbotnik dog may be buried with the body of a vampire that has otherwise been especially difficult to kill.

Source: AASSS, *Balkanistica*, 104; Keyworth, *Troublesome Corpses*, 131; McClelland, *Slayers and Their Vampires*, 97, 111

Salt (Sault)

Salt has long been used by man for purification, protection, and preservation; in fact, the earliest record of salt being used dates back to 2255 B.C. Among the many beliefs and truths that have been attributed to it are that salted food cannot be hexed, that making a circle of salt will protect whatever or whomever is placed inside, and that it attracts luck and money while driving away demons and witches. It is also used in some vampiric lore: it is applied to the shed skin of an ASWANG MANNANANGGAL; one can trap a CAT-ACANO behind a line of salt; an ESTRIE will eat bread and salt to heal itself of any wounds it may have taken in a fight; and salt placed under one's pillow at night will deter a GAUKEMARES from attacking, to name but a few.

Source: Barber, *Vampire, Burial and Death*, 68; Dundes, *Vampire Casebook*, 50; Gadsby, *Sucking Salt*, 67; Phillips, *Forests of the Vampire*, 62–64; Summers, *Vampire: His Kith and Kin*, 234

Samodiva (Sah-MO-de-va)

Variations: Samodivi, Samovili

A type of vampiric wood nymph from Bulgaria, the samodivi (as they are collectively called) look like young women, wearing their HAIR down and loose, and are occasionally sighted with wings. They live in old trees or in natural caves and dress in simple clothes tied with a GREEN belt decorated with feathers, a bow and quiver slung across their backs. With little to fear, as they not only have the natural ability to fly but also have control over all the elements, samodivi patrol the woods riding upon the backs of stags whose bridle tack is reined with live snakes. Should a samodiva ("divinity" or "devil") happen across a hunter, it will kill him, taking the unfortunate person's head as a trophy and draining the body dry of its blood. Should he escape, it will cause a drought in his village.

Anyone who comes across a samodiva dancing at night in the woods will not be able to resist joining it, and will enjoy its merrymaking all night long. When the sun rises, only the samodiva remains; its dance partner is never seen again.

There is a Serbian myth that a samodiva named Villa raised Prince Marko, nursing him at its own breast. Because of this, the prince developed supernatural powers. He rode upon a winged horse named Dapple and had a samodiva stepsister named Gyura.

Source: Georgieva, *Bulgarian Mythology*, 75, 81; MacDermott, *Bulgarian Folk Customs*, 68, 69; McClelland, *Slayers and Their Vampires*, 103; Perkowski, *Vampires of the Slavs*, 42

Sampiro (Sam-PEER-oh)

Variations: LIOGAT

Once any Albanian of Turkish descent would upon death become a type of vampiric REVENANT known as a sampiro, no matter how good a person he may have been or how virtuous a life he may have led. This curse also befell upon any Albanian who had committed an unnatural act, such as beastiality, homosexuality, prostitution, transvestitism, or heterosexuality with a Turkish person. Other means were attending a Moslem religious service, consuming meat handled by a Turk, or being a habitual liar or professional thief in life.

The sampiro returns from the grave three days after its death with its burial shroud wrapped around its body and wearing high-heeled shoes upon its feet. Its eyes are large and glow brightly. A small amount of dirt from its grave is inexplicably kept in its navel.

Every night it rises from its grave but is particularly fond of nights with heavy fog, as that will make its eyes glow even brighter than usual, as bright as the headlights on a car. Once it finds a victim, it follows behind the person making "kissing" sounds that can be heard clearly over the click of its high-heeled shoes. When it finally attacks, it drains a survivable amount of blood from the person and then flees the scene as quickly as it can totter away on its heels. Victims are left feeling tired and weak, and repeated assaults will eventually kill them.

On nights when it does not feed or after it has already done so, the sampiro will go out to the countryside and peek into the homes of people. Its glare alone will spread a disease that infants are particularly susceptible to. Fortunately, it will not stay long outside of town, as it is hated by wolves, which will relentlessly hunt it down once they become aware of one in their territory. Should it manage to survive a wolf attack but one of its limbs become mangled, the sampiro will retreat to its grave and never rise again. However, should there be an attempt made on its life by people and they fail, they will soon discover that the sampiro is a particularly vengeful vampire. It will seek out those who were directly involved and kill them in an extreme act of violence.

During the day, the sampiro lies at rest in its grave, which is fairly easy to spot as not only will the soil always be loose because of its comings and goings but also because there will be a blue ball of light, similar to a CORPSE CANDLE, that hovers over it. The body should be exhumed during the day when the sampiro is immobile and a stake made of yew wood should be driven with a single blow through its heart.

Source: Abbott, *Macedonian Folklore*, 216; Ronay *The Dracula Myth*, 22; Summers, *Werewolf in Lore and Legend*, 149; Taylor, *Primitive Culture*, 311

Sasabonsam (Sa-so-BUN-sum)

Variations: Kongamato

The Ashanti people of Africa have in their lore a vampiric creature called sasabonsam. This bearded man-faced creature that stands about five feet tall has a mouth full of fanged teeth, a row of scaly ridges over its bloodshot eyes, and a small horn that protrudes from the top of its head. Its very long arms are like gigantic bat wings that have a twenty-foot wingspan, its torso is skeletally thin, its legs are permanently bent, and there are three toes on each of its feet. The sasabonsam's body is covered with black and white spots, adding to its camouflage as it sits in the cotton tree, dangling its stringy legs below. When a person walks underneath and brushes against the legs, it snatches up the person, pulling him into the tree and biting off his head, then drinking up the blood. The belief that the sasabonsam lives in cotton trees is prevailing, as can be proven by the great height that these trees grow to—everyone is afraid to cut them down.

Sasabonsam can cause sickness in a person just by looking at him and are oftentimes used as a servant by an OBAYIFO.

There is an article that was written in 1939 for *The West African Review* that reported that a sasabonsam had been successfully hunted down and killed.

Source: Jahoda, *Psychology of Superstition*, 12; Rattray, *Ashanti Proverbs*, 48; Shuker, *Beasts That Hide from Man*, 103–5; Williams, *Psychic Phenomena of Jamaica*, 16–18

Sburator (SUE-but-or)

Variations: Zburător, ZBURATOR

In Romanian vampiric lore there is a vampiric creature called a sburator ("flying man"), which is essentially a variation of an INCUBUS. Described as being an extremely handsome man, the sburator is virtually custom made for the victim, making it the perfect lover. Once every seven years, at night, it attacks the woman, slipping into her home through an open window. While she is asleep, it kisses her so gently that she may not even wake up. The next day, the woman awakes feeling drained of energy, her body throbbing with pain, and she is easily agitated (see ENERGY VAMPIRE). Once a woman has had an encounter with a sburator, she is not interested in other men.

Source: Florescu, *The Complete Dracula*, 374; Senn, *Were-wolf and Vampire in Romania*, 44; Stratilesco, *From Carpathian to Pindus*, 175

Segben (SEG-bin)

Variations: Sigbin

In the Philippines there is a vampiric creature whose description varies from case to case, but generally it is a large, dark-colored, hornless, smelly goat called a segben. During the day, it is invisible.

The segben attacks its prey only at night. Although it can kill a person simply by looking at him or by biting his shadow, its mere presence will drain off the life of a dying person, consuming it for its own (see ENERGY VAMPIRE). Any child that falls prey to the segben will have its heart made into a magical amulet. It usually does not eat the flesh and blood of those it kills; it prefers to gorge itself on charcoal, corpses, and pumpkins. If seen while in its goat form, it will only be pretending to eat grass.

The segben uses its supernatural speed to prevent capture, but it has a number of forms that it can shape-shift into: a frog with extraordinarily long legs, a goat with exceptionally floppy ears whose hips are higher than its shoulders, and a locust. In all of its forms, it has a horrible smell.

The smell and sight of thick smoke is enough

to keep a segben away, as will the scent of spices and the clang of knives.

Source: Ateneo de Davao University, *Kinaadman*, 50; Paraiso, *The Balete Book*, 15; Ramos, *Creatures of Philippine*, 70; Ramos, *Creatures of Midnight*, 53, 95

Sekeht (SAH-ket)

Variations: Once there were more than 4,000 names for this goddess, and of those only a few hundred have survived. All of her titles refer to her vampiric nature, such as Devouring One, Lady of the Bloodbath, Lady of Transformations, Mother of the Dead, Pacht, and Terrible One.

Sekeht's exact origins are unknown but it is long suspected that this vampiric goddess was imported to Egypt and adopted into the religion of the ancient Egyptians. Sekeht was made a daughter of Ra, although she was older than him. She was described and pictured in art as having the head of a lioness and holding a sun disk in her hand. It was a popular belief that there were only two types of demons in the ancient Egyptian lore: those who were under Sekeht's control and those who were not—yet.

The priests and priestesses of Sekeht were very powerful people both politically and magically. Through the goddess Sekeht, her priests were empowered to heal as well as to control and banish demons. There is an Egyptian text that describes trials and tortures that people went through to become one of her clergy, including having to face down GHOULs and vampires without showing fear.

There was once a time when the people worshiped their kings and queens more than they did their own gods, which naturally angered the pantheon. It was decided to send Sekeht to enact vengeance upon the people to show them how wrongly misplaced was their worship. Sekeht was chosen because whenever this goddess killed a person, she also destroyed his soul. Sekeht descended from the heavens at night and immediately began ripping out the hearts of all the men she could find, eating their bodies and drinking their blood, and then ascending back up with the dawn. Night after night she returned and eventually Sekeht became blood drunk and would not end her assault. The god Sketi made a drug that looked like blood and left it where Sekeht would see it, knowing that the goddess' bloodlust would compel her to drink. As soon as she did, the madness passed and Sekeht regained her senses.

Source: *Eclectic Magazine*, vol. 36, 150–60; Tiele, *Comparative History of the Egyptian and Mesopotamian Religions*, 192

The Seven Demons

Variations: Seven and Seven, Seven Times Seven

In ancient Mesopotamia, Sumerian mythology claimed that The Seven Demons were the offspring of the god of the underworld and earth, An, and goddess of the sky, Ki. The Seven Demons were the personifications of the violent and deadly forces of nature. They are a collection, considered to be a single entity, and seldom act independently of one another. They are mentioned in several holy texts and demonic banishing rites. They will not go into temples because they are afraid of the images of the Sumer gods, such as Anshar, Enki, Enlil, and Ereshkigal.

Source: Dalley, *Myths from Mesopotamia*, 224; Harris, *Gender and Aging in Mesopotamia*, 133; Horowitz, *Mesopotamian Cosmic Geography*, 219; Mackenzie, *Myths of Babylonia and Assyria*, 34

Shaitans (SHE-tans)

Variations: Mazikeen, Shaytan, Shedeem, Shedim, Shehireem, Sheytan

Shaitans ("to be born violent") are vampiric beings from Arabic and Rabbinic lore, but from that lore, their pedigree is varied. Some claim that the shaitans are the male children that were born to LILITH and her demon husband, Sammael; their female counterparts are called LILIM. Other sources say that the nomenclature of shaitans also includes the children born from LILITH and her first husband, Adam. Still other sources claim that the shaitans are the children fathered by Adam during the 130 years of separation from Eve.

Regardless of their parentage, the shaitans live in deserted places and are described as being winged men with talon feet. They have the ability of divination, flight, invisibility, and shapeshifting, and are skilled magic users as well.

Source: Davidson, *Dictionary of Angels*, 270; Lewis, *Satanism Today*, 247; Messadié, *History of the Devil*, 300

Sheerree (SHRE)

Variations: Strix Nocturna

The Berber people of the High Atlas Mountains in Morocco have in their mythology a vampiric bird with a woman's breasts. Preying on newborn and nursing children, the sheerree hunts at night. The fate of the child depends entirely on which breast it is drawn to. If the child suckles from the correct breast, it will live; if it chooses incorrectly, it will die.

Source: American Philological Association, *Transactions and Proceedings*, 138; Knappert, *Aquarian Guide to African Mythology*, 39; Tate, *Flights of Fancy*, 94–95

Shtriga (STREE-ga)

Variation: Stringla

Albanian lore tells of a female VAMPIRIC WITCH known as a shtriga, which preys on children (see LIVING VAMPIRE). By day the witch lives as a normal member of the community, even attending church; but at night it hunts for children in its animal form of a bee, fly, or moth. It approaches the child while it is asleep and steals its life-energy, leaving the body completely undisturbed in the bed (see ENERGY VAMPIRE). Parents oftentimes leave a piece of GARLIC-flavored bread near their sleeping child, as GARLIC is a repellent to the shtriga.

To determine who in the community may be a shtriga, one must wait until everyone has gone into the church to celebrate mass. Then, while everyone is inside, using some pig bones, one can make a cross and hang it over the church doors. Everyone who is not a shtriga will be able to pass through the door and outside, leaving the shtriga trapped within.

Shtriga periodically spit up blood; some say that it is the blood of their victims. If a person takes some of that blood and places it on a silver coin and then wraps it in a cloth, it can be used as a charm to keep the shtriga away.

Source: American Folklore Society, *Journal*, vol. 64, 309; Kane, *The Dreamer Awakes*, 56, 59; Lockyer, *Nature*, vol. 113, 25; Royal Anthropological Institute, *Man*, 190–91

Shuten-Doji (SHOE-tin Dodge-EE)

In Japanese lore, there is a hideously ugly and deformed vampiric REVENANT known as shuten-doji ("sake-drinking lad"). Carefully using its long clawed fingers, the shuten-doji plays on its flute a mesmerizing tune that places anyone who listens to it into a trancelike state. Once the person is under its spell, the shuten-doji kills him with its long claws, drinking the blood. Usually this vampire keeps to itself, as it does not even like the company of its own kind. Beyond its remarkable flute-playing abilities and its claws, the shuten-doji has the strength and reflexes of an average human being.

Source: Asiatic Society of Japan, *Transactions of the Asiatic Society of Japan*, 67; Marra, *Japanese Hermeneutics*, 129–30, 140–41; Shirane, *Traditional Japanese Literature*, 1123; Tanaka, *New Times in Modern Japan*, 58–60

Sile na Gig (SHEE-lah na GIG)

Variations: An Chailleach Beara ("the Old Woman of Beara"), Black Annis, Clotha, Hag, Old Hag, Sheelagh na Gig, Sila na Gig

In the Celtic lore of Ireland, Sile na Gig was a type of vampiric earth spirit or mother goddess from which all life came forth. Hideously ugly with an extended vulva, pot belly, twisted face, and withered breasts, her image was commonly found even after it was outlawed by the Church. It is possible that Sile na Gig was in fact originally a little-known Celtic goddess by the name of Clotha. She was the embodiment of battle and the weaver of soldiers' burial shrouds. The goddess had similar traits to the BANSHEE and washed bloody shrouds at the riverbank much like the WASHERWOMEN OF THE NIGHT.

Source: Barfoot, *Ritual Remembering*, 185; Mercier, *Irish Comic Tradition*, 54–55; O'Driscoll, *Hidden Extras*, 36–37

Skatene (Skay-TEEN)

Variations: STIKINI

There is a monstrous, vampiric humanoid that is part of the mythology of the Choctaw Indians in the southeastern United States, called the skatene. It pretends to be a good person and gains the trust of a family with small children. Once the skatene has been taken into their confidence, it will sneak into their home one night and behead the father, taking its prize with it as it escapes off into the night. The skatene has the ability to shape-shift into a huge owl. It is only vulnerable to the attack of the wildcat, as that is the only animal that is not afraid of it. The skatene was most likely never based on any real animal or lore but rather developed strictly as a nursery bogey, a tale told to young children to teach them that it can be dangerous to talk to and trust a stranger.

Source: Gill, *Dictionary of Native American Mythology*, 129, 228; Krech, *Spirits of the Air*, 135; Rose, *Giants, Monsters, and Dragons*, 339, 382

Skogsfru (Scocks-FRU)

Variations: Huldra, Skogsra, Swor, Tallemaja, Wood Wife, Wood Woman

In Scandinavia there is a type of vampiric fay that looks like a beautiful woman with long auburn HAIR and a cow tail. It is called skogsfru. It lives in the woods and usually approaches a young man at night while he is at rest in his campsite. It tries to use its beauty to seduce him. While engaged in sexual intercourse, it will drain him of his life-energy (see ENERGY VAMPIRE). On occasion, the skogsfru will decide not to harm the man and marry him instead. Sadly, their union will not last as it is a fay, an inherently wild creature, and will eventually return to the woods. The abandoned husband will slowly begin to die, longing for its touch. It is considered an unlucky omen to see a skogsfru, as it causes madness in its lovers.

Source: Keightley, *Fairy Mythology*, 153; Klein, *Legends and Folk Beliefs*, 35–36, 188; MacCulloch, *Celtic and Scandinavian Religions*, 133; Turner, *Dictionary of Ancient Deities*, 435

Soucayant (Soo-CA-yant)

Variations: Heg, Ol' Higue, Soucouyant, Soucouyen, Soukoyan

On the island of Trinidad there is a vampiric creature called a soucayant that looks like an old woman who sleeps all day. However, at night, it removes its skin and emerges as a ball of light, resembling a CORPSE CANDLE, and flies out looking for sleeping people to attack in order to drink their blood. Victims of the attack will have two small bite marks side by side someplace on the body.

If the soucayant is seen before it attacks, the vampire can be driven off by beating it with a stick. The next day the victim can search the community for an old woman who is covered in bruises. When he finds her, he has found the soucayant. Like many of the vampires who can remove their skin and turn into a ball of light, such as the ASEMA and the ASWANG MANNANANG-GAL, if one can find its shed skin and rub it with SALT, its hide will shrivel up. When the soucayant returns, it will not be able to fit back into its skin and will die when the sun rises. Also, like the ASEMA and the CH'ING SHIH, the soucayant is compelled to count seeds it comes across. The easiest way to kill a soucayant is to toss a handful of poppy seeds down at the crossroads, as the vampire will be compelled to count them all, a feat that will take all night. The light from the rising sun will then destroy it.

Source: Besson, *Folklore and Legends of Trinidad and Tobago*, 31–33; Liverpool, *Rituals of Power and Rebellion*, 202, 210, 237; Russell, *Legends of the Bocas*, 49–51; University College of the West Indies, *Caribbean Quarterly*, vol. 45, 72

Soulis, Lord of Hermitage Castle

(SOOLS)

Variations: The Bad Lord Soulis, William Lord Soulis, Evil Lord De Soulis

Lord Soulis of Hermitage Castle in Roxboroughshire, Scotland, was believed to be a VAMPIRIC WITCH that made a pact with the devil back in the fourteenth century (see LIVING VAMPIRE). He was described as a largely built man who had as a constant companion a blood-drinking imp he called Robin REDCAP. He exploited his position of power, enjoying the fact that he could inflict both physical pain and humiliation upon people. He also terrorized the people of his lands,

kidnapping men, women, and children to torture them and use in the practice of his dark arts, both by drinking their blood and offering their lives up in sacrifice. His familiar had used its magic upon Lord Soulis and rendered him impervious to attacks by steel and rope. Eventually tales of his cruelty reached the Crown and an investigation followed. Ultimately, Lord Soulis was found guilty on charges of conspiracy against Robert Bruce and was imprisoned in Dumbarton Castle, where he died, but many folks have claimed that his ghost, still accompanied by his familiar, haunts his old home of Hermitage Castle.

There is an eighteenth-century ballad that tells a tale of Lord Soulis, but it says that he was overrun by his own people and taken to Druid's Circle to be killed. The song says that his own people boiled him in lead and wrapped his encased body in a sheet, which was then hauled off to a secret location and buried. All of this was done in the hopes that the devil would not be able to find the evil man and resurrect him.

Source: Christmas, *Cradle of the Twin Giants*, 156–57; Dorson, *British Folklorists*, 111–13; Leyden, *Poems and Ballads*, 79–93; Summers, *Geography of Witchcraft*, 205

Sriz (SHREEZ)

In the Silesia region of Poland, there is a type of vampire that is called a sriz. It climbs to the highest place in a community and calls out a person's name. That same night, the person will die. What is interesting about this vampire is that there is no method given for how the sriz comes into being and what if anything it gains from the death it causes.

Source: Maberry, *Vampire Universe*, 272; Volta, *The Vampire*, 146

Stigoi (STEE-gway)

A vampiric REVENANT from Romania, a stigoi is created when a person's soul returns to its body and animates it. Twice a day, at the noon hour and the midnight hour, it rises from its grave in an attempt to sate its insatiable appetite, seeking out humans to drain of their blood. The rest of the time the stigoi lies in its grave, chewing on its burial shroud; its COFFIN is filled with the blood of its victims.

Source: Masters, *Natural History of the Vampire*, 44; Senf, *Vampire in Nineteenth-Century English Literature*, 18

Stikini (Sta-KEY-nee)

The Seminole Indians of Oklahoma in the United States have a vampiric creature in their mythology called a stikini ("man owl"). By day, it looks like a human, but at night it vomits up all its internal organs so that it can shape-shift into a great horned owl to fly out in search of a sleeping person to prey upon. It removes his still-beating heart from his body by pulling it out of his mouth, then it takes the heart back to its home. There, it cooks the heart in an enchanted pot and eats it in secret. Before dawn, it returns to where it hid its organs and swallows them back down before changing into its human guise.

The only way to destroy this vampire is to find its intestines while it is out hunting. Then, using magical herbs and owl feathers, one must construct an arrow. When the stikini returns to consume its organs, one can fire upon it with the magic arrow, as this is the only time that the creature is vulnerable.

Source: Gill, *Dictionary of Native American Mythology*, 288; Hitchcock, *Traveler in Indian Territory*, 139–40; Howard, *Oklahoma Seminoles Medicines*, 97; Martin, *Sacred Revolt*, 26; Rose, *Giants, Monsters, and Dragons*, 346

Strega (STRAY-gah)

In ancient Rome there was a type of VAMPIRIC WITCH called a strega ("female witch"), or stregone ("male witch") if the witch was a man (see LIVING VAMPIRE). At night, the strega would shape-shift into a bird or ride upon her flying goat, looking for children to drain dry of their blood. Like many vampires who can be warded off with a common object, the strega is no different, as placing a broom in the child's room is enough to keep this type of vampire out.

Source: Grimassi, *Italian Witchcraft*, 3–8, 259–74; Leland, *Etruscan Roman Remains*, 162; Summers, *The Vampire in Europe*, 127; Symonds, *Renaissance in Italy*, 125, 143, 187

Streghoi (STRAG-hoy)

In the historical region of Romania called Wallachia, there is a female VAMPIRIC WITCH called a streghoi that drains children of their blood. Similar to the STREGA of ancient Rome, the streghoi shape-shifts into a bird and then flies out looking for its prey.

It is tradition in the Wallachia region that when a child is born, all those who are present go outside and throw a stone over their shoulder, saying aloud, "This into the mouth of the streghoi."

Source: Franklin, *Baby Lore*, 115; Jackson, *Compleat Vampyre*; Leland, *Gypsy Sorcery and Fortune Telling*, 135

Stregoni Benefici (Stra-GONE-ee Ben-ah-FEE-chee)

The stregoni benefici ("beneficial vampire") of Italy is a type of vampiric being that preys on other vampires. However, there is a great deal of confusion as to whom or what it is. Some sources say that the stregoni benefici is a living witch or LIVING VAMPIRE; others say it is a vampiric half-breed, similar to a DHAMPIRE. Still others claim that it is not a vampire living or undead, but rather a normal human being who has dedicated his life to the pursuit of slaying vampires (see UNDEATH).

Source: Bunson, *The Encyclopedia of Vampires*, 247; Drakakis, *Gothic Shakespeares*, 182; Oinas, *Essays on Russian Folklore and Mythology*, 116

Striga (STREE-gah)

Variations: Strigen

In ancient Rome there was a type of VAMPIRIC WITCH called a striga ("witch"), but it is now uncertain as to whether it was a LIVING WITCH or the returned spirit of a deceased witch. In either case, the witch was consistently described as looking like an old woman. When it took flight in its shape-shifted form of an owl, it would meet with its coven, a collection of either seven or nine strigele (the plural form of the word). As they flew about, the coven was described as looking like little dots of lights up in the night sky. These lights were referred to as "witch lights." Strigele would gather together to celebrate who and what they were, dancing at first, and then later flying out en masse to find children to feed upon. The strigele would drain the children they came across of their blood and curse others, causing them to slowly waste away and die.

Source: Alexander-Frizer, *Pious Sinner*, 21; Morris, *Sorceress or Witch*, 165; Trachenberg, *Jewish Magic and Superstition*, 37, 41–42

Strigae (STREE-gay)

Variations: Striglais

In ancient Rome there was a deformed and vicious vampiric, owl-like creature with the face of a woman called a strigae. At night it flew out into the night sky to attack children and drain them of their blood. By day, it shape-shifted into the form of an old woman. The strigae fell under the domain of Hecate. Offerings of honey-cakes and chicken hearts as well as puppies and black lambs would keep it at bay. King Stephen I of Hungary (969–1038) made it against the law for strigae to leave their home at night or to do harm to anyone.

Source: Burns, *Witch Hunts in Europe*, 96–97, 195; Levack, *The Witch-Hunt in Early Modern Europe*, 46; Russell, *Witchcraft in the Middle Ages*, 68–70, 132; Talasi, *Acta Ethnographica*, 129–69

Strige (STREE-gee)

In Romania and Macedonia there is a vampiric bird called a strige. It is created when a witch's soul returns to plague the living. Using its long sharp beak that can easily cut the skin of a person so it can drink his blood, it will attack alone or in a flock.

Source: Bryant, *Handbook of Death*, 99; Cremene, *Mythology of the Vampire in Romania*; Gaster, *Myth, Legend and Custom*, 579; Hurwitz, *Lilith, the First Eve*, 48

Striges (STREE-gis)

Variations: Striges Mormos, Strigla

In Rome, Italy, there is a VAMPIRIC WITCH called a striges that by the use of her magic can shape-shift into a crow. In her bird form the striges will then attack people, using its claws and beak to draw blood that it will then drink up. The striges is no doubt the modern incarnation of the STRIGA and the STRIGE.

Source: Day, *Vampires*, 233; Summers, *The Vampire in Europe*, 230; Wood, *The Nineteenth Century*, 52

Strigoii Morti (STREE-goy MOR-tea)

Variations: Strigoii

In Romania, a strigoii morti is a male vampiric REVENANT that is friendly toward the Gypsy clans. It is created when a person commits suicide or the seventh son of a seventh son dies and rises back up from the dead. The strigoii morti returns looking much like it did in life, a blue-eyed redhead with twin hearts (see HAIR). A blood drinker whose very presence causes fear and repulsion, it is easily repelled by GARLIC. To kill this vampire, both of its hearts must be destroyed.

Source: Konstantinos, *Vampires*, 30; Mackenzie, *Dracula Country*, 76, 87

Strigoii Vii (STREE-goy VEE)

Variations: Concealment-Rãu ("bad one"), Strigoii

In Romanian vampire lore a strigoii vii is a person who is a VAMPIRIC WITCH while alive (see LIVING VAMPIRE) and will become a vampire, most likely a STRIGOII MORTI, in death. Strigoii vii are easily recognized for what they are, as they have blue eyes and red HAIR and two beating hearts. At night the strigoii, as it is commonly called for short, sends out its soul to psychically attack animals, crops, and humans, draining them of their life-energy (see ENERGY VAMPIRE). As its soul flies in the night sky it looks like sparks, but it also has the ability to shape-shift its soul to look like an insect or small animal.

Source: Belanger, *Sacred Hunger*, 10; Keyworth, *Troublesome Corpses*, 104; Konstantinos, *Vampires*, 30

Strigoiu (STREE-goy-oo)

A vampiric REVENANT from Romania, strigoiu appears whenever someone speaks its name aloud. Described as looking like a redheaded woman, a strigoiu will usually take up residence in an abandoned house. The only way to destroy this vampire is to nail it to the bottom of its COFFIN to keep it in the ground or to burn the REVENANT to ashes.

Not as dangerous as its female counterpart, the male of this species is called a strigoiul. Uncommon for a vampire, the strigoiul will gather together and hunt in packs. The same method of detruction that is used to kill a strigoiu will not work on a strigoiul. The death of the male requires that its heart be removed and cut in half. Then GARLIC must be placed in its mouth and an iron nail driven through its head.

Source: Eliade, *Encyclopedia of Religion*, 179; Ginzburg, *Ecstasies*, 170; Masters, *Natural History of the Vampire*, 44, 92

Strigoiul Muronul (STREE-goy-ee-el Mooron-OOL)

The strigoiul muronul of Romania sounds as if the MURONI and the strigoiul (the male counterpart of the STRIGOIU) mythologies were combined. When one considers how regional the vampire species of Romania can be, it is entirely possible that this vampire came from a region located between that of the other two.

A strigoiul muronul is created when a child is born out of wedlock to parents who were each born out of wedlock. Always born a redheaded boy, this child will become a vampiric REVENANT when he eventually dies. The only way to destroy this vampire is to burn its body to ashes or drive a nail through its heart.

Source: Haining, *Dictionary of Vampires*, 179; Ronay, *Truth about Dracula*, 23

Strigol (STRAY-goal)

A vampiric REVENANT from Romania, the strigol is created when a magic user or sorcerer dies. It has the ability to shape-shift into numerous animal forms, such as a cat, dog, frog, or insect, which it uses mostly to get close to the humans from whom it intends to drain the life-energy (see ENERGY VAMPIRE).

To prevent its rising from the grave as a vampire, the sorcerer's heart must be removed, spat upon, and nailed to his forehead with an iron nail. If the sorcerer was a woman, then the heart is nailed to its eye. The body is then taken up into the mountains and abandoned in a secret place. Once at the site, GARLIC is placed in the mouth. Should this ceremony happen to take place on St. Ignatius Day, then the body must also be covered in a layer of pig's fat. The Feast Day of St. Ignatius is October 17, according to the Roman Catholic and Anglican Churches, December 20 in the Greek Church, and January 2 in the Coptic Church calendar.

Source: Folklore Society, *Publications*, vol. 79–80, 100; Senn, *Were-wolf and Vampire in Romania*, 10; Stratilesco, *From Carpathian to Pindus*, 250; Thigpen, *Folklore and the Ethnicity Factor*, 131

Strigon (STRAY-gun)

Variations: Vedavec

In Istria there is a type of vampiric REVENANT called a strigon. It is created whenever a sorcerer who drank the blood of children dies. It wanders the community during the midnight hour, knocking on doors or punching out windows. Within three days, someone in the knocked-upon houses will die. The strigon slips into homes and drains the blood of children, as well as has sexual relations with a woman while she is asleep without waking her husband.

To destroy a strigon it must be stabbed through the stomach with a stake made of ash or HAWTHORN wood, but only after its midnight wanderings are finished. When staked, the strigon will thrash about wildly and that blood will erupt from its body. While the vampire is in its death throes, it must be set on fire and burned down to ash.

The last known strigon outbreak was reported in Larbach, Germany, back in 1672; however, it is not wholly uncommon to find fresh corpses in the Istria countryside with stakes in them to this day.

Source: Oinas, *Essays on Russian Folklore and Mythology*, 116; Ralston, *Russian Folk-Tales*, 326; Summers, *Vampire: His Kith and Kin*, 185

Stryx (STREAKS)

Variation: Stryga Vel Masca, Stryge, Stryges, Strygia, Strygie, Strygis, Strygon, Stryz, Stryzga, Strzyzyz

The Roman poet Ovid (43 B.C.–A.D. 17) wrote about the stryx in his poem *Fasti*. Prior to this poem written about the various Roman holidays, there is no mention of this VAMPIRIC WITCH. However, Charlemagne recorded in his *Saxon Capitulary* of A.D. 781 a law that all stryx when discovered were to be criminally prosecuted and condemned to death.

The stryx was able to shape-shift into an owl and then fly out into the night sky looking for a child it could attack with its beak and talons so that it could drink up its blood. To prevent a stryx attack, the parents would need to appeal to the goddess Crane. If their prayers were answered, the goddess would then go herself into the home and perform the sacred rites to prevent the stryx from entering, including placing a branch of HAWTHORN in the child's sleeping area.

Source: Davenport, *Sketches of Imposture*, 276–77; Hurwitz, *Lilith, the First Eve*, 78; Stoneman, *Greek Mythology*, 163; Stuart, *Stage Blood*, 68

Succubus (SUC-you-bus)

Variations: BELILI, Buhlgeist, Compusae, DAITJA, EPHÉLÉS, Hyphialtes, Kiel-Gelal, Lilit, Pishauchees, Succuba, Unterliegerinnen

Men have been assaulted by the vampiric demon known as the *succubus* ("spirit bride") as far back as ancient Greece where it was clearly defined and described. The male counterpart to the succubus is known as an INCUBUS, and, according to medieval lore, the incubi outnumber the succubi by a ratio of nine to one.

At night succubi, as they are collectively called, appear as beautiful women. They can be very alluring and persuasive. They seek out sleeping men to have sexual intercourse with and, according to medieval lore, are particularly fond of monks. During the sex act, the succubi drain off a number of vital essences and fluids, such as blood, breath, life-energy, and semen to the point of their victims' deaths (see ENERGY VAMPIRE). A succubus need not even be physically in the room for the assault to take place, as it can visit a man in his dreams, causing his body to fall into a state of sleep paralysis. Succubi are specifically interested in semen, taking it and implanting it into unsuspecting and innocent women.

If a man wanted an encounter with a succubus, he need not wait in hopeful anticipation for one to show, as it is a demonic being and can be summoned to appear by use of magical incantations. Likewise, if a man is desirous of ridding himself of its assaults, he must seek help through the church.

If a child is conceived by a succubus, it will be born a half demonic being known as a CAMBION.

Source: Bullough, *Human Sexuality*, 298–99; Cavendish, *Powers of Evil in Western Religion*, 103–5; Doniger, *Britannica Encyclopedia of World Religions*, 503, 1035; Jones, *On the Nightmare*, 125, 243, 320

Sucoyan (Sue-COIN)

Variations: Ligaroo (masculine), SUKUYAN

In the West Indies there is a vampiric creature called a sucoyan. Looking like an old woman by day, at night it removes its skin and hides it in the hollow of a tree. Then, it shape-shifts into a CORPSE CANDLE and flies out in search of its prey—a sleeping person that it will drain dry of blood. Like many vampires that have the ability to remove their skin, such as the ASEMA and the LOOGAROO, finding its skin and rubbing it with SALT so that it shrinks will ultimately destroy the sucoyan, as it will die if exposed to direct sunlight.

Source: Allsopp, *Dictionary of Caribbean English Usage*, 161; Beck, *To Windward of the Land*, 209; David, *Folklore of Carriacoum*, 29–30

Sukuyan (Sa-COO-yin)

Variations: Ligaroo, SUCOYAN

A vampiric spirit from Trinidad, the sukuyan appears as a young man or woman. Since it is completely unaffected by sunlight, as well as being one of the very few vampires that actually needs permission to enter into someone's home, the sukuyan begins its hunting during the day. In its shape-shifted form of a handsome young man or attractive young lady, it will knock on doors asking to borrow a cup of flour or a match. If it is given what it asks for, the sukuyan will now be able to enter into the home when it returns at night to begin the process of draining away the blood of the occupants. While it is feeding, the victim suffers from nightmares and sleep paralysis.

To protect one's home from a sukuyan, one must chant, "Thursday, Friday, Saturday, Sunday," three times while making the sign of the cross over every window and doorway, then hang a mirror over them facing outward. When the vampire returns to feed again, it will see itself, assume one of its many animal forms, and flee. Now the animal must be caught and killed by either burning it alive or stoning it to death.

Source: Bisnauth, *History of Religions in the Caribbean*, 96, 154, 174; Rose, *Giants, Monsters and Dragons*, 347; Simpson, *Religious Cults of the Caribbean*, 22, 75

Sundal Bolong (SUN-dil Bal-LONG)

Variations: Sundel Bolong

In Java, there is a vampiric REVENANT known as a sundal bolong ("hollowed bitch"). It is created when a woman commits suicide or when a child who was conceived by rape dies. It appears to its prey, mostly travelers and foreigners, as a beautiful woman with unkempt HAIR wearing its burial shroud. Using its beauty, this vengeful and angry vampire will lure a man to a quiet place with the promise of an indiscretion but instead will turn and attack him, draining him of his blood.

Source: Bunson, *Vampire Encyclopedia*, 250; Geertz, *Religion of Java*, 18; Koentjaraningrat, *Javanese Culture*, 342

Svircolac (SVEER-co-lac)

Variations: Vercolac

In Romania there is a mythological vampiric wolf named Svircolac who has the ability to cause an eclipse. Summoned by a sorcerer to kill for him, Svircolac kills by draining the blood of whomever he is sent after.

Source: Perkowski, *The Darkling*, 40; Summers, *Vampire in Europe;* Taylor, *Buried Soul*, 240

Swawmx

In Burma there is a vampiric deity known as Swawmx.

Source: Bunson, *Encyclopedia of Vampires*, 36; Spence, *Encyclopedia of Occultism*, 135; Wedeck, *Dictionary of Magic*, 83

Talamaur (TALL-ah-mor)

Variation: Talamur, TARUNGA

On the Banks Islands of Australia as well as on the Polynesian Islands there is a type of LIVING VAMPIRE called a talamaur, which can be a force for good or for evil, depending on the person. He is greatly feared by the community he lives in, and the possibility of being banished or even being stoned to death is very real. All talamaur have the ability to astral-project and speak to ghosts. Some have a spirit or a ghost as a familiar (see ASTRAL VAMPIRE).

If the talamaur is an evil and predatory vampire, he will attack people who are dying or the newly dead, feeding off the last bits of their life-energy (see ENERGY VAMPIRE). Should he attack a healthy person, he will do so while the person is asleep, ripping his heart out of his chest and consuming it while it is still beating in order to enslave his soul. The souls of those the talamaur has consumed surround him and are forced to act as a protective shield. This mass of souls is called a TARUNGA, and its specific powers vary depending on the capability of the souls that compose it.

To test if a person is a talamaur, he is held over a pile of burning leaves and forced to breathe in the smoke. If he is a vampire he will confess, giving a full account of all his crimes and naming all of the spirits he controls.

Source: Codrington, The Melanesians, 222; Royal Anthropological Institute, Journal, vol. 10, 285; Summers, Vampire: His Kith and Kin, 227

Tanggal

Variations: ASWANG, Preay ("vampire"), Srei Ap

All throughout Cambodia, Indonesia, Malaysia, Melanesia, and the Trobriand Islands is a vampiric sorcerer known as a tanggal ("comes apart"). By day, it looks like an ordinary woman, but at night it detaches its head from its body and flies off by undulating its intestines and flapping its ears and lungs (see LIVING VAMPIRE). It attacks people for their blood and feces, which it feeds on. The tanggal is easily repelled by GARLIC, SALT, and spices.

Source: Guiley, Complete Vampire Companion, 26; Hastings, Encyclopedia of Religion and Ethics, Part 13, 237; Spence, Encyclopædia of Occultism, 93–94

Tarunga

On the Bank Islands off the coast of Australia lives a large number of people who consider themselves a type of sorcerer called a tarunga (see LIVING VAMPIRE). These individuals claim to have accumulated so much power that they are able to detach their heads from their bodies and shape-shift into invisible vampires. In this form the tarunga are able to drain away the life energy of the recently deceased, a process that takes a few weeks to complete (see ENERGY VAMPIRE). During this time, people in the community will suffer from exceptionally vivid dreams. To prevent a deceased tarunga from feeding, a watch must be maintained at its gravesite as the vampire will not feed if a person is too near.

Source: Codrington, The Melanesians, 249, 254–56; Maberry, Vampire Universe, 275; Sumner, Science of Society, 820

Taxim

A vampiric REVENANT said to exist throughout Eastern Europe, the taxim is a plague-spreading animated corpse fueled only by its desire to enact revenge. The taxim seeks out those who caused it great distress in life, and nothing short of achieving its goal will stop it.

Source: Bunson, Encyclopedia of Vampires, 252

Tenatz (Ten-ANTS)

Variations: Tenac, Tenec

In Bosnia and Montenegro there is a vampiric spirit called a tenatz that possesses a corpse and uses it as its own body. At night, it shape-shifts into a mouse and enters into a person's home. Once inside, it waits for the victim to fall asleep and attacks, draining him of his blood. Simply burning the corpse during the day will destroy the tenatz.

Source: Durham, Some Tribal Origins, 259; Petrovitch, Hero Tales and Legends of the Serbians, 21; Royal Anthropological Institute, Man, 189

Tezcatlipoca (Tehs-cah-TLEE-pooh-cah)

The Aztec people of ancient Mexico had in their pantheon a vampiric god who had domain over material things and of the night called Tezcatlipoca ("Smoking Mirror"). The smoking mirror that he carried in all of his artistic representations allowed him to know the thoughts and deeds of any man. He was a skilled magic user, could shape-shift, and had at his disposal an array of mysterious and unspecified powers.

Tezcatlipoca, when manifesting on earth, could usually be found at the crossroads. There he challenged men to one-on-one combat or tempted them to do evil; should they resist, he rewarded them.

Each year during the fifth month on the Aztec calendar, Toxcatl, a handsome young man was selected to represent the god on earth for the next year. The representative led a lavish life of dancing, feasting, and being worshipped as a god by eight beautiful women chosen to be his companions and four equally beautiful brides. After his year of deification ended, a ritual was performed where he climbed to the top of the temple and broke all of the flutes that he used while he represented Tezcatlipoca. Then, he was sacrificed, his heart ripped from his chest while it was still beating.

Source: Aguilar-Moreno, Handbook to Life in the Aztec World, 76, 145, 146, 207; Lurker, Dictionary of Gods and Goddesses, 342; Payne, History of the New World Called America, 531–37

Thabet Tase (THAB-it SAY)

In Burma there is a type of SUCCUBUS that is called a thabet tase. Created when a woman dies in childbirth, the thabet tase returns to its community and preys on the men there each night.

Source: Hastings, Encyclopedia of Religion and Ethics, 25; Leach, Funk and Wagnalls Standard Dictionary of Folklore, 1104; Scott, Gazetteer of Upper Burma, 28

Thaye Tase (THEY SAY)

In Burma there is a vampiric REVENANT called a thaye tase. It is created when a person has died a violent death. It returns as an ugly giant, causing cholera and smallpox outbreaks wherever it goes. It takes great pleasure in going to the deathbed of those dying and, visible only to them, laughs and revels in their misery.

Source: Bryant, Handbook of Death, 99; Hastings, Encyclopedia of Religion and Ethics, 25; Jobes, Dictionary of Mythology, 1537

Tikoloshe (TIC-ah-la-lish)

Variations: Gilikango, HILI, Thokolosi, Tikaloshe, Tokolosh, Tokoloshe, Tokoloshi

The Xhosa people of Lesotho, Africa, have in their lore a vampiric creature known as a tikoloshe (see AFRICAN VAMPIRE WITCH). It is an excellent familiar for a witch and many do not mind the high price that must be paid for its summoning spell to work—a family member of the witch will die within a year's time of the spell being cast. Accepting this, a tikoloshe is created by removing the eyes and tongue from a corpse, piercing the skull with a red-hot iron poker, and then blowing a magical powder, whose ingredients are a well-guarded secret, into its mouth. The powder will animate and transform the corpse into an obedient and much-prized familiar.

Always male, a tikoloshe is a short, hairy, baboonlike creature with a tall forehead and a receding hairline (see HAIR). It has a single buttock and a penis so long that it keeps it slung over its shoulder. Able to use magic, the tikoloshe will create for itself a magical stone that will allow it to become invisible. It keeps the stone hidden in its mouth at all times. Although it can shapeshift into any form it wishes, there will always be a monkeylike characteristic to it. Should it need to fly, it shape-shifts into the form of a HILI, a type of vampiric bird that is also a part of the Xhosa people's mythology.

In exchange for being the witch's familiar, the tikoloshe will demand a daily supply of cow's milk, food, lodgings, and the right to have sex with the witch whenever it wants (or a woman at his disposal to fulfill his sexual needs should the tikoloshe's witch be a man). In exchange for all of this, the tikoloshe will otherwise be completely at its witch's disposal, day or night.

Very quick and as strong as a man, the tikoloshe's greatest weakness is its voracious sexual appetite that even its witch cannot control. A serial rapist, the tikoloshe will have a collection of women that it will return to assault over and over, traveling hundreds of miles if it must. It feeds off their sexual energy, leaving its victims physically battered and emotionally drained (see ENERGY VAMPIRE). Eventually its repeated assaults will kill the women.

Source: Broster, Amagqirha, 60; Knappert, Bantu Myths and Other Tales, 173–74; Mack, Field Guide to Demons, 35; Scobie, Murder for Magic, 80–82; St. John, Through Malan's Africa, 152–53

Timpanita (Tim-pa-NEAT-na)

Variations: Brucolak, Brukulaco

In the Greek Islands, there is a vampiric REVENANT known as a timpanita. It is created when someone who has been excommunicated from the church dies or when a person of Albanian or Turkish descent dies. Like many GREEK VAMPIRES, its skin is dry and tanned looking, and is pulled tightly over its body. However, this particular species of vampire is noted for its deep and echoing voice.

At night, the timpanita wanders through its former community, using its sonorous voice to call out the names of the people it knew in life. Anyone who responds to its call will either be attacked by the timpanita and have his blood drained from his body or he will die of a mysterious and painful disease. It can also emit an ear-piercing scream and can spread the plague.

To destroy the timpanita it must be decapitated and its head boiled in wine. Then, the entire corpse must be burned to ashes.

Source: Haining, Dictionary of Vampires, 38; Ronay, Truth about Dracula, 22; Volta, The Vampire, 149

Tlaciques (TAL-ah-kays)

Variations: Tlahuelpuchi

The Nahuatl-speaking descendants of the Aztec people of central and southern Mexico have in their culture a living VAMPIRIC WITCH called a tlaciques. There is no way to divine or prevent this witch from being born, and prior to her first menstrual cycle when her blood lust develops, there is no way to predetermine if a young girl is a tlaciques (see LIVING VAMPIRE). The only visual sign that may betray her nature is that as she matures she will develop a limp. Usually when her family discovers that there is a tlaciques amongst them, they will protect her secret out of both fear and a bizarre sense of shame. If anyone in her family kills her, he will carry the curse through his blood and pass it on to his children.

Upwards of four times a month the tlaciques will need to feed and her usual prey are infants, family members who may reveal her secret, or people whom she has quarreled with. First the witch will detach her upper body from her lower so that she can shape-shift into a buzzard, CORPSE CANDLE, cat, dog, flea, or turkey. Her lower body is laid out to form a cross on the ground. While in her CORPSE CANDLE guise, the tlaciques has a hypnotic ability that she can use to cause people to commit suicide. Before she can enter into the home of her intended victim, the tlaciques must have first flown over his home in the form of a buzzard traveling from north to south and then from east to west. Once inside the home, she will glow briefly right before she attacks.

Tlaciques form pacts with one another so as not to infringe on each other's hunting grounds. This is done because the amount of blood that one tlaciques needs to survive is not so great as to be noticed, but should two or more start hunting in the same area their presence would be noted and they all would be at risk of being discovered and killed.

If it is suspected that a tlaciques is in the area, the common repellants of crosses or CRUCIFIXES, GARLIC, holy water, and mirrors will ward it off, as will an onion wrapped in a tortilla.

A tlaciques, should one be discovered for what it is, is usually killed by being clubbed or stoned to death or by any means that does not require touching her while she is in her animal form. Should she be captured in her human form, she is then clubbed or stoned to death followed by removing her sense organs. Her body is then left to rot in an isolated area.

Source: American Folklore Society, *Journal*, vol. 68, 129; Bunson, *Vampire Encyclopedia*, 254; Edmonson, *Nativism and Syncretism*, 161–62; Madsen, *The Virgin's Children*, 167

Toci (Toe-CHI)

Variations: Tlacuantesupe, Tonantzin

The Aztec people of ancient Mexico had in their pantheon a vampiric fertility goddess named Toci. She was particularly attentive to the corn crops. In the eleventh month of the Aztec calendar, Ozomatli, a woman who had been preselected would be ritually sacrificed and skinned. The hide was then donned by the temple priest at the high point of the ceremony. If Toci did not receive her sacrifice, there would be famine.

Source: Aguilar-Moreno, *Handbook to Life in the Aztec World*, 151; Markman, *Flayed God*, 188–90; Ruether, *Goddesses and the Divine Feminine*, 194–95; Salas, *Soldaderas*, 2, 7–8, 24

Tomtin (TOM-tin)

Vampiric fay from the folklore of Germany,

the tomtin are described as small men dressed from head to toe in red. The tomtin were most likely a type of forest spirits that were the servants to the nearly forgotten fertility gods Nacht Ruprecht ("Night Rupert") and Schwartz Peeter ("Black Peter"), who were once worshiped by the ancient Germanic tribes. Sadistic, even for a member of the Unseelie Court, at their master's behest the tomtin would pounce upon travelers and beat them to death with chains or sticks. Then, as the corpses bled out, the tomtin would lap up the blood as it pooled on the ground. When they had finished eating, they would return to their masters carrying with them the hearts and livers of their murder victims.

With the introduction of Christianity to the region, the Church sought to absorb some of the local beliefs into its own to make the transition as easy as possible. Nacht Ruprecht was known to travel the land in winter and visit houses at random, his tomtins in tow. When the forest god came across a worshipper of his, he would reward that person with gifts—all others were left to the tomtins. The Church supplanted Nacht Ruprecht with Germany's own Saint Nicholas. It is suspected that he was chosen because in many regions of Germany the saint was known as Buller Clause, the Belled Nicholas, because he wore both bells and chains upon his person. The tomtin were under Saint Nicholas's command, but they no longer committed murder. Instead, the tomtins would wake sleeping children, pull them from their beds, and quiz them on their catechism. Should they answer incorrectly, the tomtin would whip them with sticks while Saint Nicholas stoned them with lumps of coal. After the beating, the tomtins were allowed to lick the blood from the children. Over the years the story was softened and the tomtins evolved into the happy, toy-making elves who worked for a jolly Old Saint Nic.

Source: Association for Scottish Literary Studies, *Journal*, vol. 12–16, 23; Curran, *Walking with the Green Man*, 42–44, 91

Toyol (Toe-YALL)

A vampiric demon in Malaysian lore, the toyol ("elevated") is created by magic and used by a witch to be her familiar. Taking the body of a deceased baby, the witch performs a ceremony that allows a demonic spirit to possess and animate the corpse, binding it to her to do her bidding. Looking like the GREEN-skinned baby with red eyes that it is, the toyol is usually kept in an earthenware jar called tempayan, which is stored under the witch's home until it is needed, as the toyol is rather mischievous when left to its own devices. It is also something of an accomplished thief, but unless it is told to go and steal something, it only takes half of what is there.

Source: Cremene, *Mythology of the Vampire of Romania*; Fogelson, *Anthropology of Power*, 282; Robbins, *Global Problems*, 62

Triccolitch (Tray-co-LITCH)

Variations: Pricolici, Tricolici

In Romania there is a vampiric were-creature called a triccolitch; it is essentially a variation of the GREEK VAMPIRE VRYKOLAKA and the Serbian vampire VUKODLAK. The triccolitch is able to shape-shift into a dog or a pig.

Source: Cremene, *Mythology of the Vampire of Romania*

Tü

On the Polynesian islands there is a vampiric demon known as a tü ("war" or "to stand"). When a person wants the power to communicate with the dead, he eats a piece of the corpse belonging to the person he wishes to converse with. The spirit, the tü, that once resided in the body will return and appear to the person, seeking to start a friendship with him. As a show of good faith and wanting to make friends, the tü will offer to do favors for the person, such as attacking those who would do its potential new friend harm and drinking their blood.

Source: Carlyon, *Guide to the Gods*, 382; Fornander, *Account of the Polynesian Race*, 170; Handy, *Polynesian Religion*, 265

Uahti (Wah-KE-chee)

In South America, all along the Amazon River and in the nearby jungle there lives a type of vampiric demon called uahti. It is a small and hairy creature with an enlarged penis, large belly, and toeless feet (see HAIR). Following behind a colony of bats, the uahti sexually assaults adolescent girls and adult men, draining away their sexual and life-energy during the assault (see ENERGY VAMPIRE).

Source: Reichel-Dolmatoff, *Shaman and the Jaguar*, 72, 83, 85; Roth, *American Elves*, 106, 107, 108; Wicker, *From the Ground Up*, 33

Uber (Oo-bur)

In Turkey the vampiric REVENANT known as an uber ("overlord," "witch" or "vampire") is created when a person dies through an act of violence or when a foreigner who is not Muslim is buried in Turkish soil.

Source: de Vere, *Dragon Legacy*, 55–56; Jones, *On the Nightmare*, 124; Summers, *Vampire: His Kith and Kin*, 309

Ubour (Oo-bor)

In Bulgaria the ubour ("undead") is a vampiric REVENANT that is created when a person dies a sudden and violent death and the spirit refuses or does not realize it needs to leave its body. After it has been buried for 40 days, the ubour digs itself free from its grave and begins its reign of terror as a vandal, smearing manure on the sides of a person's home and breaking the dishes in his house. It has been speculated that the ubour does this because it is grief stricken and misses being with its family. It looks as it did in life, except that it has one nostril and creates sparks when it moves.

It is active only between noon and midnight and only when all other food sources and options have been exhausted will the ubour seek out a human to attack for his blood. It has a barb on the tip of its tongue that it uses to break a person's skin. However, if the would-be victim has the opportunity, he can offer the ubour something eatable in exchange for his life, an opportunity the vampire will not pass by, no matter what the food may be, even if it is feces.

If an ubour must be destroyed, a trained vampire hunter called a VAMPIRDZHIJA must be employed, as he is able to detect an ubour while it is still unformed and in its grave and knows how to destroy it at each stage of its unlife. The most common method employed is BOTTLING.

Source: Belanger, *Sacred Hunger*, 134; Bunson, *Vampire Encyclopedia*, 259; Maberry, *Vampire Universe*, 240

Udug (Oo-dug)

Variations: Udu, Uttuku, Utuk

In ancient Mesopotamia and Sumer there was a vampiric spirit known as an udug. Created by the ancient gods to be used as a means of punishment against mankind for not properly burying their dead, the udug possessed the corpses and animated them. Once the udug was in the body, the animated corpse began to crave human blood and attacked of its own volition. Originally an udug was seen as neither good nor evil but as a tool that was utilized by the gods. It was later prayed to in the hopes that it would give assistance in the smiting of one's enemies. Eventually, the udug evolved into a demonic being.

The idea of the gods creating a being to be used as a means to punish their people is not uncommon. The gods of ancient Egypt had SEKEHT.

Source: Cunningham, *Deliver Me from Evil*, 34–38, 58–59; Emerton, *Congress Volume: Jerusalem*, 65; Lurker, *Dictionary of Gods and Goddesses*, 356

Umamlambo (Wo-mam-LAMB-oo)

The umamlambo is perhaps the most significant and powerful familiar that an African VAMPIRIC WITCH can hope to have, especially among the Xhosa people who live in southeast Africa (see AFRICAN VAMPIRE WITCH, LIVING VAMPIRE, and TIKOLOSHE). There is a saying among them, "witchcraft goes through the breasts," and in the spirit of this tradition the umamlambo is often passed down through a family line. Fortunately, the umamlambo is considerably adaptable, for if it is passed from a female witch as an inheritance to a male witch, the umamlambo will assume the form of a woman. Then, it will work its way into his life, eventually moving into his home. When they marry, the witch's father will immediately begin to die, but the witch will become wealthier and always have good luck.

The umamlambo, whose natural form is that of a snake, has the ability to shape-shift into any creature it desires. When not in the witch's home, the umamlambo resides in its own underwater home where it is attended to by lizards. Its progeny is called ICHANTI.

Anyone who makes direct eye contact with the umamlambo will die unless he is immediately treated by an herbalist. This happens most often at the water's edge when a person bends down to drink or collect water. To prevent meeting the umamlambo's stare, it is advised to first throw a stone into the water as this will make the umamlambo blink and oftentimes withdraw.

Source: Broster, *Amagqirha*, 60; Hammond-Tooke, *Rituals and Medicines*, 75; Marwick, *Witchcraft and Sorcery*, 371; Royal Anthropological Institute, *Man*, 129

Undeath (Un-DETH)

Variations: Undead, Unlife

Undeath, or *unlife* as it is sometimes referred to, is a word that is used nearly exclusively in regards to vampires and vampiric lore, as it describes a state of being or the existence of an individual that is deceased but still acting in a lifelike manner.

To be undead, a person first has to die. The way in which a person dies is oftentimes a key component in achieving undeath. For instance, numerous cultures believe that if people commit suicide or die while giving birth, they are primed to return to the world of the living as vampiric REVENANTS, beings who exists in a state of undeath. These individuals are clearly deceased, but nevertheless are still active, mobile, and living out an agenda. Depending on the culture, the conditions that can cause a corpse to rise up in a state of undeath varies. The condition of the body and the mindset of the being that has returned varies as well. Most undead beings and creatures are revenants—animated corpses who seek out blood or vital human essences in order to maintain their very existence. Beings who are undead will not die of natural causes and will "live on" until they are destroyed in the very exacting method that their culture or mythology has predetermined.

Source: Adams, *Slayer Slang*, 225; Auerbach, *Our Vampires, Ourselves*, 3–7; Russo, *Vampire Nation*, 14–16

Unholde (Un-hold)

In German vampire lore there is an evil vampiric spirit that acts out against mankind, specifically seeking Christians to be its victims (see GERMAN VAMPIRES). It is called an unholde and its name translates essentially to mean "the one that is not good or beautiful." It abducts its victim, removes his heart, then cooks and consumes it. Then it returns to the corpse and replaces the heart with one it has carved out of wood. The unholde performs a magical ceremony and animates the corpse.

Traditionally, the unholde was considered to be a HEXE, that is, a practitioner of magic. However, it was not until the late seventeenth century that the word *HEXE* came to mean a human practitioner of magic. By the early eighteenth century, it became interchangeable with the word *witch*.

Source: Grimm, *Teutonic Mythology*, 947, 1045, 1061, 1081; Guiley, *Complete Vampire Companion*, 176; Günther, *Tales and Legends of the Tyrol*, 15–16

Upier (Oo-PEER)

Variations: Opyri, Upeer, Uperice, Upi, Upieri, Upierz, Upierzci, Upierzhy, Upior, Upiór, Upiorcsa, Upiroy, Upiry, UPOR, Uppir, Vieszcy, Wampire, WIESZCZY, Wrikodlaki

In Poland, when a male child who was born with teeth dies, he will rise up as a type of vampiric REVENANT known as an upier (upiercsa if female).

Active between noon and midnight, it leaves its grave and seeks out humans to attack, using the barb on the end of its tongue to pierce their skin and drain them of their blood. If it has the opportunity, the upier will remove the person's heart and eat it, as it is especially fond of the taste of that particular organ. When it returns to its grave, it will regurgitate some of the blood it consumed into its COFFIN so that it can submerge itself in it. Like the NACHZEHRER of Germany, the upier will also climb the bell tower and ring the bells, shouting out the names of people in the community. Anyone who hears his name being called while the bells are pealing will die.

In order to kill an upier, it must be burned to ash, but be advised, at some point during the cremation, the vampire will explode into hundreds of small maggots. Each and every single maggot must be found and destroyed, otherwise the upier will rise again, but this time, seeking revenge.

Source: Perkowski, *Vampires of the Slavs*, 163; *Sketches of Imposture*, 208–9; Summers, *Vampire in Lore and Legend*, 158

Upierci (Oo-PEER-see)

Variations: Uppyr

In Russian lore a type of vampiric REVENANT is created when a person commits suicide, dies violently, or practiced witchcraft while he was alive; it is called an upierci. It has the ability to cause a drought so severe that it will even draw moisture out of plants. To destroy an upierci it can either be drowned in a lake or nailed into its grave with an aspen wood stake. However, it must be nailed down in a single blow, otherwise the upierci will revive.

Source: Bryant, *Handbook of Death*, 99; Davison, *Sucking Through the Century*, 354

Upierczi (Oo-PEER-zee)

In Russian lore, there is a type of vampiric REVENANT that is created whenever a witch or a heretic dies. It is called an upierczi. Like the UPIER, it is active between the hours of noon and midnight and also has a stinger under its tongue that it uses to pierce the skin of its human victims in order to drink their blood more easily. It too has the ability to cause severe droughts.

The upierczi must be destroyed in the same fashion as the UPIERCI, that is, by driving an aspen wood stake through its heart in a single blow while it is in its grave. Another method to destroy the upierczi is to burn it to ash, but just like with the upier, the upierczi will at some point explode into maggots, all of which must also be destroyed or else the vampire will return seeking revenge.

Source: Masters, *Natural History of the Vampire*, 101

Upierzyca (Oo-PEER-zee-ca)

The Ruthenian people of eastern Poland have in their lore a vampiric REVENANT called an upierzyca. Always described as a beautiful young woman, on nights of the full moon, the upierzyca hunts for young men. It attacks them and, using the barb on the end of its tongue, will pierce their skin, draining them of their blood.

If a deceased woman is suspected of being an upierzyca, her body must be exhumed. Upon examination the body will not only be undecayed, but the creature's eyes, head, and mouth will still be moving. Its burial shroud may also shows signs of having been partially consumed.

Source: Dundes, *Vampire Casebook*, 8; Haining, *Dictionary of Vampires*, 254; Masters, *Natural History of the Vampire*, 101; Perkowski, *The Darkling*, 113; Volta, *The Vampire*, 143

Upioras (Oo-PORS)

From Polish vampire lore, the upioras is described as looking like a large man. It attacks its victims at night by grabbing them up and smashing their bodies around until their bones are completely pulped. It then sucks out the soup it has made. When it has finished eating, it skins the corpses and wears the skins of its victims. To destroy an upioras, it must be completely soaked in holy water.

Source: Georgieva, *Bulgarian Mythology*; Perkowski, *The Darkling*, 166

Upor

The upor is a Russian vampiric REVENANT that preys on the blood of children. In addition to its ability to shape-shift into chickens, dogs, insects, rats, and small birds, it can also create an empathic and telepathic link with numerous types of animals. Once the empathic link has been established, the upor can use the animal as its familiar as well as use it to spy on potential victims. To destroy an upor, its grave must first be found, and then a successful exorcism must be performed on the corpse.

Source: Indiana University, *Journal*, vol. 14, 255; Maberry, *Vampire Universe*, 285; Perkowski, *The Darkling*, 115

Upyr (Oo-PEER)

Variations: Oupyr, Uppyr

In Russia, there is a vampiric REVENANT called an upyr that is created when a heretic, sorcerer, or witch dies. It can also be created as the child born of the union between a werewolf and a witch. Looking like a normal person, the upyr is active between noon and midnight. It attacks people in their homes, going after the children first and then moving on to the parents. It drains each victim of his blood, and, using its ironlike teeth, gnaws into his chest so that it may consume the heart. In fact, the teeth of the upyr are possibly its greatest assets, as it uses them to chew through the ground that has frozen solid in the winter months so that it can escape its own grave.

To discover where the upyr's grave is, she must, if at all possible, attach a string to a button on its clothing as it flees the scene of one of its attacks. Then, a person can follow the string from the spool of thread back to its grave. Once there, the ground must be completely soaked in holy water and the upyr must be staked through the chest to keep it in its grave, but the stake must be driven through in a single blow or the vampire will rise again. Another method of destruction is to decapitate the vampire and burn its corpse to ashes.

Source: Indiana University, Journal, vol. 14, 255; Oinas, Essays on Russian Folklore, 126–27; Summers, Vampire: His Kith and Kin, 18

Uruku (Or-oo-koo)

Variations: UTUKKU

In ancient Mesopotamia there was a vampiric REVENANT known as an uruku ("vampire which attacks man"). The uruku was created when someone interfered with a person's proper burial rites. It returned as a transparent and ghostlike being, spreading disease and acting as a type of evil muse that inspired criminal behavior.

Source: Konstantinos, Vampires, 19; Rose, Spirits, Fairies, Gnomes, 192; Summers, Vampire: His Kith and Kin, 225

Ustrel (Oo-STRELL)

In Bulgaria when a child who was born on a Saturday dies without having been baptized, then nine days after its burial, it rises from its grave as a type of vampire known as an ustrel ("lost heart"). Almost immediately after it begins its unlife, the ustrel begins to look for cattle upon whose blood it will feed, sometimes up to five a night, and then return to its grave. After ten days of feeding, if it has managed not to get itself killed by a hired VAMPIRDZHIJA, the ustrel will no longer need to return to its grave at night but rather will live, invisibly, in the place between the horns of a cow or ram. This is the perfect place for it to live, as it is hated by wolves that will tear it apart if they can. Roosting atop a cow offers it protection, as humans are likely to prevent wolves from entering into their herds for fear that they are there to hunt and kill their livestock.

Source: Bryant, Handbook of Death, 99; Frazer, Leaves from the Golden Bough, 37; Keyworth, Troublesome Corpses, 68

Ut (Oot)

In India, if a person dies without having a male heir, then they will return as a vampiric REVENANT known as an ut.

Source: Bunson, Vampire Encyclopedia, 106; Daya, Essay on Demonology, 8

Uthikoloshe

Variations: Uhili

The Xhosa people of southeastern South Africa say that the uthikoloshe is one of the most powerful types of familiars that a witch could hope to have. The uthikoloshe is a small and hairy vampiric creature, either male or female, that wears clothes made of sheepskin (see HAIR). It also wears a necklace that has a magical stone charm on it that will allow it to become invisible, as well as being able to send realistic and terrifying dreams to people of themselves being strangled.

The uthikoloshe speaks with a lisp and is fond of playing with children and drinking milk. Normally it is a compassionate creature that keeps to itself and will do no harm to others intentionally, unless it is compelled to do so by its witch. It, like the UMAMLAMBO, lives in a hut under the water where it is attended to by its lizard servants.

SALT is like poison to the uthikoloshe, and poisoned food left for it to find is perhaps the safest way to kill it, if not the surest. The fat from the body of a dead uthikoloshe can be rendered into oil that can be used to kill others of its kind.

Source: Broster, Amagqirha, 58–60; Mayer, Townsmen or Tribesmen, 161, 162; Royal Anthropological Institute, Man, 129

U'tlûñ'tä

Variations: Nûñ'yunu'ï ("Stone Dress")

In the Blue Ridge Mountains of Tennessee, United States, the Cherokee tribe tells of a vampiric creature they call U'tlûñ'tä ("Spear Finger"). A singular entity, it walks along the river looking for children, pretending to be a kindly old woman that they can feel safe with and trust. U'tlûñ'tä has the ability to shape-shift into any animal as well as any specific person it needs to in order to have a successful hunt. After it has gained a child's trust enough for him to let his guard down, U'tlûñ'tä uses its spearlike finger to stab the child through the heart or the back of his neck, killing him. Then it digs through the body for the liver, which it greedily consumes.

Apart from U'tlûñ'tä's amazing shape-shifting abilities, it also has control over stones. It can lift any boulder, no matter its size or weight. U'tlûñ'tä can also fuse two stones into one simply by slamming them together.

Killing U'tlûñ'tä is possible, but not easy. It can only die if stabbed in the heart, which is located in its right hand in the joint where the finger meets the hand. But be advised, this will not be an easy mark to hit as it keeps that hand balled up in a tight fist as often as possible.

U'tlûñ'tä may be something of a nursery bogey, a monster created by concerned parents to teach children not to talk to strangers.

Source: Dale, Tales of the Tepee, 54–57; Mooney, Myths of the Cherokee, 316; Myres, Annual Reports, 316–20

Utukku (Oo-too-coo)

This species of vampire was first mentioned in the Mesopotamian epic, Gilgamesh. The utukku was created when a person died before he could fulfill an obligation, causing his soul to become bound to his corpse, creating a REVENANT. Usually found in deserted places in the desert and mountains and along the ocean's shore, it kills by making direct eye contact with a person, absorbing his life-energy (see ENERGY VAMPIRE). As time passed, this ancient species of vampire became thought of more as a demon.

Source: Rogers, Religion of Babylonia and Assyria, 147–48; Sayce, Religions of Ancient Egypt and Babylonia, 283–87; Thompson, Semitic Magic, 39–40; Wiggermann, Mesopotamian Protective Spirits, 113–14

Vampiir (Vam-PEER)

In northern Europe, in the Republic of Estonia, the concept of a blood-drinking vampire was imported from the neighboring countries of Latvia, Finland, Russia, Sweden, and Ukraine. Calling this vampire a vampiir, it entered silently into a person's home, lay on top of someone, and smothered him to death while he slept. It had the ability to shape-shift into a bat and a wolf; however, a vampiir was only active a few hours each night and was susceptible to sunlight. Like many of the vampires that lived in neighboring countries, the vampiir was killed either by burning it to ash, decapitation, or by hanging.

Source: Bunson, Vampire Encyclopedia, 87; Dundes, Vampire Casebook, 54

Vampijerovic (Vam-pa-DREV-nic)

According to the lore of the Gypsies of the Balkans, a vampijerovic is born the child of a human and a vampire. It looks like a normal person, but it has the ability and drive to hunt down and kill vampires.

Other types of natural-born vampire hunters are the DHAMPIRE, DJADADJII, KRSNIK, LAMPIJEROVIC, and the VAMPIRDZHIJA.

Source: Haining, Dictionary of Vampires, 178; Indiana University, Journal, vol. 14, 266; Masters, Natural History of the Vampire, 143; Perkowski, Vampires of the Slavs, 217

Vampir (Vam-PEER)

Variation: PENANGGLAN, Penangllaen, Penanngallau, Pernanggal, Upeer, VAMPIIR, Vampyras, VRYKOLAKA, Vurkulaka, Wamphyr, Wampire, Wukodalak

In German lore, when a person commits suicide or was a heretic, murder victim, werewolf, or witch in life, he will rise up from the grave as a vampiric REVENANT (see GERMAN VAMPIRES). The vampire has a bloated body, long fingernails, red skin, and blood in and around its mouth. Able to cause drought and illness in cattle, it hunts humans for their blood. Repelled by both GARLIC and silver, it is also mysteriously compelled to count seeds that have been spilled out along the ground.

The vampire can be destroyed by stabbing it through the heart with a wooden stake made of mountain ash, but it must be done with a single blow or the revenant will not die. Another way to destroy the vampire is to behead it, remove its heart, boil it in wine, place it back in the body, and then burn the entire corpse to ash.

Source: Dundes, Vampire Casebook, 73; Indiana University, Journal, vol. 14, 266; Perkowski, The Darkling, 38; Stefoff, Vampires, Zombies, and Shape-Shifters, 17

Vampirdzhii (Vam-per-HEED)

In Bulgaria there is a living, vampiric half-breed called a vampirdzhii, born from the union between a human and a PLATNIK. Blessed by God, this red-eyed being can reveal a vampire for what it is by using holy icons. The vampirdzhii's preferred method of destroying vampires is to prick them with a briar thorn or by boiling the vampire to death in a large cauldron. They are similar to other vampire hunters such as the DHAMPIRE, PLATNIK, and the VAMPIRDZHIJA.

Source: Konstantinos, Occult Truth, 29; Melton, Vampire Book, 367; Perkowski, The Darkling, 82; Ramsland, Science of Vampires, 161

Vampirdzhija (Vam-per-HEED-ah)

From Bulgaria comes another type of vampire hunter known as a vampirdzhija. It specializes in the hunting and destruction of a type of vampire known as an USTREL. Using a highly ritualistic ceremony, on a Saturday morning all the fires in a community with a vampire are extinguished. Then, at the crossroads, the vampirdzhija builds two bonfires that are set aflame with "new fire," that is, fire that is created from the rubbing together of two sticks. Next, all the cattle and sheep are gathered together and herded to pass between the twin bonfires, as the mature USTREL lives in the space in between the animals' horns. The USTREL, rather than being singed, or worse, will leap off the animal and run into the countryside, where wolves will find and devour it. After all of the animals have passed through the bonfires, a fagot of new fire is taken into the community and used to relight all of the fires there.

Source: Melton, *Vampire Book*, 367; Perkowski, *The Darkling*, 82; Ramsland, *Science of Vampires*, 161

Vampirdžia

A type of vampire slayer from the Balkans and western Bulgaria and Macedonia, this quasi-supernatural being has the natural ability to see and detect vampires. This person's circumstances of birth—the son of a vampire—allows him to enjoy an elevated social status as he alone bears the responsibility of being able to purge the community of the vampire that plagues them. He is able to slay vampires by using a gun in addition to the more traditional means. Unlike the SÂBOT-NIK who has the natural ability to see vampires, the vampirdžia must chew upon a magical herb in order to gain this ability. A professional, the vampirdžia is very well paid for his services, either with actual money or with gifts. Women are never born vampirdžia.

Source: McClelland, *Slayers and Their Vampires*, 60

Vampire Chair (Vam-pire Chair)

In Canter County in the mountains of East Tennessee, United States, chair-making brothers Eli and Jacob Odom were famous for their tight-joint, mule-eared, slat-back, hickory-splits, woven seat chairs. Hundreds of their chairs were sold and distributed all over the state between 1806 and the late 1840s, but a pair of the brothers' comfy chairs came into the possession of a woman who was a self-proclaimed vampire. She lived in a cabin in the mountains overlooking the Hiwassee River near Charleston, Tennessee (see LIVING VAMPIRE). Although there are no records of her exploits or of her death, a body alleged to be hers was found in 1917 during the widening of the crossroads near where she was believed to have lived. The body was found buried facedown and fairly well petrified, as there are high levels of minerals in the ground water in that region of the country. Still protruding from her chest was a stake that had been run through her heart. What was most interesting is that the stake was a cradle-lathe support (bottom leg support) for the type of chair that was exclusively made by the much-famed chair-making brothers, Eli and Jacob Odom. It was assumed that the chair that the support came from was looted from the vampire's home after her death, repaired, and re-entered into the community.

After the discovery of the petrified body, the first report of an attack from the vampire chair began to circulate. Whenever someone sat in the chair, he would be held down by an invisible force that made scratches on the person's arms. Eventually, these scratches would well up and bleed, and it was not until a drop of blood hit the floor would the assault end. The vampire chair looks exactly like of one of the several hundred similar chairs in the area, meaning that there is no way to tell at a glance which chair is the vampire chair—until it is too late. The chair is believed to still exist because no one wants to be the one who burns or destroys it for fear of intensifying the curse. Reports have placed it in an antique store and at a garage sale, as well as having been on Tusulum College's campus.

Source: Barnett, *Granny Curse*, 32–34; Burne, *Handbook of Folklore*, 64–65; Masters, *Natural History of the Vampire*, 140

Vampire Dog, Ennerdale

For 65 years there was a vampiric creature, many say it was a dog, that hunted sheep all over England, Ireland, and Scotland from 1810 to 1874 and again briefly from 1905 to 1906. The first report of the animal came in May 1810 in the town of Ennerdale, located near the English and Scottish border. Described as a large dog whose tracks were long and deeply set in the ground, it was reported as killing six or eight sheep a night, ripping holes in their throats and draining all of their blood. None of the carcasses were ever found eaten or even partially consumed. In early September of that same year, a large black dog was spotted in a cornfield and shot. The killings stopped for a brief period of time and resumed again, only this time in Ireland. The idea of a wolf was dismissed as the last one had been spotted back in 1712. The vampire dog was blamed and it was reported to be killing as many as 30 sheep a night by then, its hunger obviously having increased. The sheep were slain as they had been back in England—throats bitten out and drained of blood. The paw prints that were left behind were again described as long with deep and obvious claws. On April 11 the large dog was again shot, this time by an archbishop, only to be sighted again ten days later and a hundred miles away. Again it was shot and again it was sighted, another hundred miles away. All along and throughout, sheep were having their throats ripped out and their blood drained away. In Limerick, Ireland, it bit a man who shortly thereafter went insane and was admitted to Ennis Insane Asylum. On and off the cycle continued. The dog was sighted, the sheep were slaughtered, the dog was shot, and some distance and days later the killings began again. Eventually, in 1874, the dog was shot one final time, and as the people waited for it to reappear, it never did—until nearly 30 years had passed.

The London Mail reported on November 1, 1905, that sheep were found slaughtered in Badminton, their throats ripped out and their blood drained. It was reported as having been shot and killed near Gloucester on November 25 and then again on December 16, in Hinton. On March 19, 1906, 51 sheep were killed in a single night near Guildford. That was the last report of the vampire dog. Throughout its last killing spree, both a hyena and a panther were blamed for the killings, said to have escaped from a menagerie, but no reports of such animals escaping any zoo were ever reported in the papers.

Throughout its career, the Vampire Dog of Ennerdale was credited with killing in all 237,250 sheep, which averages to ten sheep a night. If the numbers are accurate, then the vampire dog consumed 1,594,320 liters of blood, enough to fill two Olympic-sized swimming pools.

Source: Bradley, *The Badminton*, 380–87; Forte, *Lo!*, 150; Hallam, *Ghosts of the North*, 36

Vampire Dog, Shuck

It is possible that reports of vampiric dogs were originally based on sightings of rabid dogs or dogs afflicted with canine leishmania, but the lore of such creatures remains. Described as ferocious and overly aggressive, smelling of death, with glowing red or yellow eyes, vampiric canine REVENANTs such as the AUFHOCKER hunted both animals and humans alike, ripping out their throats and draining the bodies of their blood. The mythology of this creature says that a vampire dog will move into an area and begin killing smaller animals first, like rabbits and cats, before moving on to larger animals such as other dogs and sheep. To destroy this vampire, beheading, shooting, or stabbing will work.

Source: Barber, *Dictionary of Fabulous Beasts*, 134; Porter, *Folklore of East Anglia*, 89–91; Rose, *Giants,*

Monsters, and Dragons, 419; Tongue, *Forgotten Folk Tales*, 70–72

Vampire Horse

On the morning of September 8, 1967, the body of a female Appaloosa pony named Lady was found dead in the San Luis Valley, Colorado, United States. All of the flesh from the shoulders to the tip of its muzzle was missing; the bones of the neck and skull were as white and bleached as bones that had been sitting in the sun for a year. The skull cavity was empty and dry. A strong smell of medicine was in the air and scorch marks were on the ground all around the corpse. Despite the gruesome state of the beloved horse that once belonged to Nellie Lewis, there was not a drop of blood to be found at the scene. Perhaps more interesting is the fact that there was a set of horse hooves all around the body that did not belong to Lady but to another horse, one whose hooves were reported as being 18 inches wide. Lady was the very first of the much-popularized animal mutations that continued uninterrupted for the next 30 years in the San Luis Valley.

A necropsy of the horse's remains showed that it had a badly infected leg at the time of death. A reexamination of the body was made some years later and it was discovered there were two BULLET holes in the animal's pelvic bone.

Source: Keel, *Complete Guide to Mysterious Beings*, 84–85; Murphy, *Mysteries and Legends of Colorado*, 93–99; O'Brien, *Secrets of the Mysterious Valley*, 9–15; Randles, *World's Best "True" UFO Stories*, 83

Vampire Pumpkin

During the 1930s and '40s a researcher named T. P. Vukavonic was studying the Lesani Gypsies of Serbia for a book he went on to write, titled *The Vampire*. Much speculation has always existed around Vukavonic's telling of the Lesani's belief in a vampiric pumpkin, and in truth they may have been teasing the author and made up the story on the spot. No matter if the belief was originally meant to be a joke or the retelling was some bit of old and nearly forgotten lore, the fact remains that the vampire pumpkin has woven itself into the lore of the vampire.

The Lesani Gypsies of Serbia have a belief that by keeping a pumpkin in one's home for more than ten days, by using it as a siphon that has not been opened for three or more years, or by keeping it in the house after Christmas Day will cause this fruit to become a vampire.

The vampiric pumpkin will look much like it did before its spoiling, maintaining its color, shape, and size. Fortunately, the vampire pumpkin does not actually attack anyone in a physical way, making it quite possibly the most harmless of all vampires; however, it does ooze blood and roll around on the floor making an annoying "brr, brr, brr" sound. To destroy the vampire pumpkin, there is a precise process that must be followed. First, the fruit must be boiled in water after which the water is thrown away. Then the vampire is scrubbed with a short whisk broom and the pumpkin is thrown away. Lastly, the broom must be burned.

Source: Gypsy Lore Society, *Journal of the Gypsy Lore Society*, 25–27; Keyworth, *Troublesome Corpses*, 70; Perkowski, *Vampires of the Slavs*, 207; Shashi, *Roma*, 134

Vampiresa (Vam-per-RES-ah)

The word *vampiresa* is used regionally by the Gypsies of southeastern Europe when describing the daughter born of a union between a human and a vampire.

Other such beings born as the result of a vampiric union are the DHAMPIRE, DJADADJII, KRVOIJAC and the LAMPIJEROVIC.

Source: Gypsy Lore Society, *Journal*, 111; Indiana University, *Journal*, vol. 14, 266; Perkowski, *Vampires of the Slavs*, 217

Vampiric Witch (Vam-pie-ric Witch)

A vampiric witch is a living human being who practices some form of magic (not necessarily witchcraft) who also partakes in some sort of vampiric activity such as consuming human flesh, draining life-energy from a living being, or drinking human blood. Sometimes referred to as a sorcerer, a vampiric witch can be of either gender. The act of taking and consuming life is not necessary to sustain the life of a vampiric witch but rather, it very often is a required element in the use of her magic. Very often these witches will have a vampiric familiar assisting them.

A list of vampiric witches and the creatures they use as familiars are ABHARTACH, ASANBONSAM, ASEMA, ASEMANN, ASIMAN, ASRAPA, ASWANG MANNANANGGAL, ASWANG WITCH, AXEMAN, BAISEA, BROXA, BRUJA, CHEVÊCHE, CHORDEVA, DRUDE, DSCHUMA, GAUKEMARES, IARA, ICHANTI, IMPUNDULU, ISITHFUNTELA, JIGAR KHOY, JIGARKHWAR, KARA-KONDJIOLOS, LEYAK, LOOGAROO, RALARATRI, RUVAUSH, SHTRIGA, SOULIS, STREGA, STREGHOI, STRIGA, STRIGES, STRIGOII VII, STRYX, TIKOLOSHE, TLACIQUES, and the UMAMLAMBO.

Source: Ankarloo, *Witchcraft and Magic*, 214–16; Belanger, *Sacred Hunger*, 22; Madsan, *Virgin's Children*, 206; McNally, *In Search of Dracula*, 264

Vampyre (Vam-PIE-er)

Variation: Upior (Polish), Upir (Slownik), Vampyre (Dutch), Wampior (Polish), Wampira (Servian)

In 1734 the word *vampire* was considered to be spelled correctly in the English language as *vampyre*, with its plural form as *vampyres*.

The word was likely created by a French newspaper article that was translated from a German report. Its only connotation then was used to describe an undead creature that preyed upon animals and humans for their blood, and in most cases, spread some sort of illness or disease (see UNDEATH).

The word *vampyre* was still in popular use when John William Polidori published his short story "The Vampyre" in *New Monthly Magazine*'s April 1819 edition. It was about Lord Ruthven and successfully created the archetype of the first aristocratic, heartless, wealthy, world-traveling vampire who would seduce women and lure them into a secluded place to drain them dry of their blood. However, by the time BRAM STOKER'S *DRACULA* was published in 1897, the *y* had already been exchanged for an *i*, as the word we use today, *vampire*, was already in use.

Source: Folklore Forum Society, *Folklore Forum*, vol. 10, 26–28; Hulme, *Myth-land*, 75–76; Polidori, *Vampyre: A Tale*; Senf, *Vampire in Nineteenth-Century English Literature*, 3, 21

Vanpir (Van-PEER)

The word *vanpir* ("werewolf") was said to have been created by an unnamed German officer. In 1726 there were thousands of reports filed that the plague that was running unchecked in the southeast Slavic regions was started by REVENANTs. In life these revenants had been werewolves, but after they died, they had come back as what the locals called *VRYKOLAKA*. The German officer changed the word *vrykolaka* for one he allegedly made up—*vanpir*. No reason has ever been given for his decision to have done this. German newspapers began to pick up on the story and it spread. Eventually it came to France where the odd and obviously foreign word was changed once again, this time to a more familiar and as terror-inspiring word—*VAMPYRE*. Again the story began to spread and managed to make its way over the channel into England. This time the word's spelling was changed to suit its British audience and became *vampire*.

Source: Singh, *The Sun*, 276; Suckling, *Vampires*, 54; White, *Notes and Queries*, vol. 41, 522

Vapir (Va-PEER)

Variations: VEPIR, Vipir

In Bulgaria there is a vampiric REVENANT called a vapir. It is created when a body is not given its proper burial rites, such as being given one final bath, or if a cat, dog, or shadow crosses over the corpse before it can be buried. Drunkards, murderers, thieves, witches, and those who had been excommunicated from the church in life are all likely candidates to rise from the dead as vapirs, either of their own volition or because they had no one to prepare their bodies and give them a proper burial.

The only way to destroy a vapir is to hire a VAMPIRDZHIJA. He will kill the vampire either by using the BOTTLING technique or by staking it with a wooden stake.

Source: Indiana University, *Journal of Slavic Linguistics*, 257–58, 265; MacDermott, *Bulgarian Folk Customs*, 66, 67; Summers, *Werewolf in Lore and Legend*, 15

Varacolaci (Va-ROC-o-loc-ee)

Variations: Murohy, Strigoii, Varacolici, Varcolac, Velkudlaka, Vercolac, Vercolach, Vircolac, Vulcolaca, VUKODLAK, Wercolac

The varacolaci of Romanian vampire lore is created when a baby who was never baptized dies or when a person commits suicide. However, becoming a varacolaci can also be a hereditary condition that can pass down the bloodline for generations.

When the varacolaci rises from its grave as a vampiric REVENANT, it looks as it did in life except that now it is noticeably pale and has dried-out skin.

Although it hunts throughout the year, the varacolaci is particularly active on St. George's Day (April 23) and St. Andrew's Day (November 30), a dangerous prospect indeed as it is quite possibly the strongest of all the vampires. When a varacolaci attacks a person, it drains him of his blood, but its bite does not leave a wound behind. It has the ability to shape-shift into a cat, dog, flea, frog, or spider. The varacolaci can place itself into a deep trance and cause a lunar or solar eclipse to occur. Additionally, it can use its psychic abilities to safely travel anywhere it wishes by a means of astral projection called "midnight spinning." While in this state, its astral form looks like a dragon or some sort of unnamed monster with many mouths. However, if the varacolaci's body is moved while it is in one of its trances, its spirit will not be able to find its way back to its body, causing it to sleep forever.

If a deceased person is suspected of being capable of returning as a varacolaci, his undead resurrection can be prevented if a thorny bush is planted on top of his grave (see UNDEATH). If the person died from an act of suicide, then his body should be thrown into running water as soon as possible.

There is a complex set of rituals that must be properly performed in order to destroy a varacolaci. First, the varacolaci must rise from its grave and be captured. If it is a male, its heart must be removed and cut in half. A nail is to be driven into its forehead and a whole bulb of GARLIC placed into its mouth or, as is done in modern times, filled with quicklime. The body is covered with pig fat taken from a pig that was slaughtered on St. Ignatius Day (July 31). A burial shroud is sprinkled with holy water and wrapped around the body, which is taken to a secluded place and abandoned. If the varacolaci is a female, then iron forks must be driven through its heart and eyes. Then the body is to be buried in a very, very deep grave.

Source: Dundes, *Vampire Casebook*, 25; Mackenzie, *Dracula Country*, 87; McDonald, *Vampire as Numinous Experience*, 124; Taylor, *Buried Soul*, 240

Veles (VEE-la)

Variations: Vile, Vily, Wila

In the vampiric lore of Lithuania there is a type of vampiric fay called a veles that is created when a woman who has been frivolous or idle her whole life finally dies. When it returns, its true form is that of a cloudlike spirit, but it can assume the appearance of a beautiful young woman with long, flowing HAIR and the most beautiful-sounding voice ever heard. Its voice is so alluring and memorable that it causes anyone who has heard it to lose all concerns and thoughts for anything else, including the need to drink, eat, or sleep, for several days. As her prey is typically men, the veles usually appears provocatively dressed or naked.

Veles only ever attack when the mood suits them, using its skill of dance and song to lure a man off into the woods where it will drain his life from him (see ENERGY VAMPIRE). A ring of deep and rich grass is left behind where the veles danced. Walking upon it brings bad luck (see FEAR GORTACH).

Like the SAMODIVA from Bulgarian lore, the veles is a fierce warrior, riding upon deer or a stag, using a bow and arrow when in combat or to hunt. It is so powerful that it shakes the ground when it enters into a physical altercation. In addition to being a warrior and possessing the gift of prophecy, the veles has the ability to magically heal and shape-shift into a falcon, snake, swan, and wolf.

Living in sacred caves, trees, and wells, and receiving offerings of cakes, fresh fruits and vegetables, flowers, and ribbons will keep it happy enough to not want to hunt. From time to time a veles can be persuaded to lend its assistance to a human, but no amount of bribery can convince it—it must be in the mood to be predisposed to helping already. Any vow that is given to a veles must be taken extremely seriously, as the veles will kill anyone who breaks a promise to it.

If a feather can be stolen from the veles while it is in one of its bird forms, it will be greatly weakened, so much so that if it is ever able to regain possession of the feather, it will quickly flee the region. However, if a single HAIR is pulled from its head, the veles will either instantly revert to its true form or die.

Source: Alexander, *Mythology of All Races*, 299; Jakobson, *Selected Writings*, 36–39, 45–46; MacCulloch, *Celtic Mythology*, 300–301; MacDermott, *Bulgarian Folk Customs*, 14, 65, 184

Vepir (Vee-PEER)

Variations: VAPIR, Vipir

In Bulgaria there is a type of vampiric fay called a vepir. It is created in the same fashion as a VAPIR—by its body not receiving proper funerary rites, such as not being given a final bath or if a cat, dog, or shadow crosses over the corpse before it can be buried. Events such as these usually happen to those people in society who do not have anyone to look after their funerary needs, such as those who were drunkards, murderers, thieves, witches, and those who had been excommunicated from the church.

The only way to destroy a vepir is to exhume the body and rebury it facedown. This is done so that it will not be able to dig its way to the surface.

Source: Bryant, *Handbook of Death*, 99; *Journal of Slavic Linguistics*, 265; Perkowski, *The Darkling*, 38; Ronay, *Truth about Dracula*, 22; Summers, *Vampire: His Kith and Kin*, 22

Veshtitsi (Vesh-TITS-ee)

The veshtitsi is a vampiric spirit from the vampire lore of Serbia that feeds off the blood of first-time mothers and their infants.

Source: Georgieva, *Bulgarian Mythology*, 80, 103

Veshtitza (Vesh-TESH-ah)

Variations: Vehtiza, Vjeshtitza, Vjestitza

According to the vampire lore from Montenegro and Serbia, all a woman needs to do to ensure that she returns from the dead as a veshtitza is to practice magic in life. At night, the soul of the witch leaves its body and possesses a black hen or moth to scout out a home that has children in it. This possession lasts until the veshtitza willingly leaves or the sun rises. Then, the soul races back to the body, which then rises up and goes to where the children are. There it uses its powers to cause others to fall into a deep sleep such as a state of sleep paralysis, presumably so as not to wake the parents. It then attacks the children, consuming their hearts and drinking their blood.

Veshtitze, as they are collectively called, are fast even for vampires, but they are not particularly strong. They are susceptible to silver weapons but cannot be killed by one. Only direct exposure to sunlight will kill a veshtitza.

A close-knit breed, they have taken oaths to protect one another. Veshtitza covens gather together, meeting regularly at midnight in the branches of a designated tree. Once gathered, they will share the blood and hearts they took that night among one another.

Source: Folklore Society, *Publications*, 175; Petrovitch, *Hero Tales and Legends*, 20; Radosavljevich, *Who Are the Slavs?*, 17

Vetala (Vee-TA-la)

Variations: BAITAL, Baitala, BETAIL

In India, there is a vampiric spirit that is called a vetala. One is created every time a child dies and does not receive proper funeral rites. When a vetala possesses a corpse it causes a hideous transformation to take place: the feet and hands twist backward; the face twists about until it resembles a fruit bat with slitted eyes; the skin becomes discolored by turning either GREEN, light brown, or white; and the fingernails grow long and carry a poison on them. While the vetala possesses the corpse, it is able to animate it and will use its magic to find human blood to drink, for as long it does so regularly, the body that the vetala is possessing will not decompose. It will call to it a GREEN horse that it will use as its mount.

Using its magic, the vetala will enter into a home by use of an enchanted thread being fed down a chimney. Typically it preys on those who are asleep, using the opportunity to drain them of their blood, but it will also take advantage of a person who has passed out drunk. Women who have gone insane are also fed upon, the idea being no one would believe them if they reported it. But above all, its favorite prey is children. Regardless of whom it attacks, the vetala mostly feeds on intestines and excrement.

Vetalas can cause insanity and miscarriages, and anyone who survives one of its attacks will first suffer through a severe illness before he can begin to recover. However, because of the vetala's ability to see into the past, present, and future, as well as its deep insight into human nature, it is often the goal of a sorcerer to capture one and use it for his own intent.

When not seeking out prey, vetalas are at rest hanging upside down from trees in cemeteries, dark forests, or any deserted place. They may be appeased with offerings of gifts, but should that not work, they can be driven off with the use of magical spells. Should all else fail, the body of the child that caused the creation of the vetala must be found. Then proper funeral rites must be performed over it, essentially destroying the vetala.

Source: Crooke, Introduction to the Popular Religion, 67, 97, 152; Cuevas, Travels in the Netherworld, 95–97; Saletore, Indian Witchcraft, 83

Viechtitsa (Vee-TEATS-ah)

Variations: Vjeshitza, Vjestica

A Slavic species of SUCCUBUS, the viechtitsa preys upon young men who are deeply asleep, causing them to be completely consumed with sexual desire for it (see ENERGY VAMPIRE). Oftentimes this passion and desire is so intense that its human lover dies, which is why its ideal, if not preferred, lover is another type of vampire known as a VOUKODLAKS.

Source: Chaplin, Dictionary of the Occult and Paranormal, 165; Masters, Eros and Evil, 188; Summers, Werewolf in Lore and Legend, 148

Viesczy (VEETS-chee)

Variation: Stryz, Vieszcy, Vieszy, Vjescey, Vjiesce

A vampiric REVENANT from Russia, the viesczy is born either with a caul, with teeth, or as the child of a witch and a werewolf. After it has died, it will rise from its grave as a red-faced vampire seeking out its family or cattle to feed upon. It bites a hole in the chest, just over the heart, using a barb on the bottom of its tongue. It is possible to prevent the vampire from ever leaving its grave by tossing a handful of poppy or carrot seeds into the grave, as the viesczy will be compelled to count them.

Active between noon and midnight, the viesczy spends the rest of its time back in its grave, chewing upon its burial shroud, feet, and hands.

The only way to destroy a viesczy is to burn it to ash. However, care must be taken, because just like with the UPIER and the UPIERCZI, the viesczy's body will explode, but rather than maggots, it will burst out into rats. Each and every one of these animals must be found and killed or else the vampire will return, seeking revenge.

Source: Oinas, Essays on Russian Folklore, 124; Perkowski, Vampires of the Slavs, 162; Ralston, Russian Folk-Tales, 325

Vila (VIL-ah)

Variations: RUSALKA, Samovily, Vily

There is a Slavic myth that when a person is cursed by God or a child dies unbaptized, he will return as a type of vampiric fay known as a vila. When it returns, it will look like a beautiful little girl with long HAIR. Living in clouds, meadows, ponds, and trees, the vila, a very capable combatant, will attack lone travelers. However, like the VELES, offerings of cakes, flowers, fruit, ribbons, and vegetables will prevent its attack. All vile, as they are collectively called, have the ability to control storms and shape-shift into a horse, swan, or wolf.

Source: Auerbach, Our Vampires, Ourselves, 20; Dixon-Kennedy, Encyclopedia of Russian and Slavic Myth, 182; Royal Anthropological Institute, Man, 189

Virika (Vee-RIC-ah)

There is a ghostly flame-red vampiric spirit in India known as a virika ("brave one"). Its teeth have been stained red by the quantity of blood it has consumed. It tends to linger around the home of someone who is dying, gibbering to itself as it is filled with excitement. To prevent it from attacking, a shrine must be built to its honor and filled with food and flowers. If the virika accepts the gifts, it will leave, and the dying will be granted a reprieve, left to depart this life in peace.

Source: Balfour, Cyclopædia of India, 87; Hastings, Encyclopedia of Religion and Ethics, 603; Khanam, Demonology, 23

Vis (VIS)

In Melanesia there is a vampiric being that hunts the Lakalai people of New Britain called a vis. At night the vis flies out in search of prey. When it attacks, it uses its long shiny talons to rip out its victim's eyes before consuming his flesh and drinking his blood.

Source: Moon, Encyclopedia of Archetypal Symbolism, 173; Rose, Giants, Monsters and Dragons, 384

Vjesci (Va-JES-ee) or (VYESKEE)

Variations: Opji, Vjeszczi, Vjeszczi Wupji

In Poland there is the belief that when a person who was born with a caul or teeth is about to die, he will use his last breath to renounce God. The body will retain its heat longer than a corpse should, its limbs will remain limber, the lips stay red, and blood will begin to seep out of its cheeks and fingernails. At midnight on the night of the person's burial, it will rise up as a vjesci from the grave and begin seeking out family members to prey upon. Other than having a ruddy brown complexion and being immensely strong, the vjesci can pass for human.

When a child is born with a caul, it is possible to prevent it from becoming a vjesci at death. The caul must be preserved and on the child's seventh birthday must be ground up and fed to him. Unfortunately, there is no known way to save a child who was born with teeth, but its resurrection can be stopped. To begin, the body will be placed in the COFFIN facedown so should it one day begin to dig its way free, it will be heading in the wrong direction. A CRUCIFIX and a coin must be placed in the corpse's mouth at the time of its burial so that when the vjesci awakens, it will already have something in its mouth to chew upon. A bag of seeds, usually poppy, is also placed in the COFFIN, as the vampire will be compelled to count them all before it will leave its grave; however, it will only count one seed every seven years. Then, a net is wrapped around the COFFIN because if the vjesci should manage to count all the seeds, it will then have to stop and untie all the knots in the net, as that is another irresistible urge it must give in to.

Source: Canadian Centre for Folk Culture Studies, *Paper 1–4*, 8, 21, 23, 25; Lorentz, *Cassubian Civilization*, 70, 132, 133; Perkowski, *Vampires of the Slavs*, 191, 195

Vlkodlak (Va-COD-lic)

Variations: Volkodlak, Volkoslak

A vampiric REVENANT from Serbia, the vlkodlak is created by one of two ways. The first method is when a man under 20 years of age who was a murderer, perjurer, or had sexual intercourse with his mother dies. The other way a young man can become a vlkodlak is if he was killed by a werewolf or ate meat from an animal that was slain by a werewolf. No matter how it is that the vlkodlak came into being, it will rise from its grave as a blood-covered, animated corpse, acting the part of a shameless drunkard. It has the power to cause eclipses.

To prevent a potential corpse from rising as a vlkodlak, its thumbs and toes must be cut off and nail driven into its neck. A vlkodlak, unless it is killed, will wander the earth for exactly seven years. At the end of that time, the vampire dies and its soul is reborn into a human, and the cycle begins again in a different part of the country. To destroy one, the vlkodlak must be stabbed through the stomach with a stake made of HAWTHORN and the HAIR on its body covered with tar. Then the vampire must be set ablaze with a candle that was used during its wake. The fire must be hot enough and burn long enough to render the corpse to ash.

Source: Alexander, *Mythology of All Races*, 299; MacCulloch, *Celtic Mythology*, 229; Mercatante, *Good and Evil*, 98; Turner, *Dictionary of Ancient Deities*, 500

Vodovyj Opyr (Va-DOOLED-de Op-REE)

In Russian folklore there is a vampiric water spirit known as a vodovyj opyr. It lives in lakes, ponds, rivers, and wells, attacking humans and drinking their blood.

Source: Bogatyrëv, *Vampires in the Carpathians*, 171

Vodyanik (Vod-GAN-ic)

According to Slavic lore, there is a vampiric water spirit known as a vodyanik, the male counterpart to the RUSALKA. Its name translates to mean "water grandfather," which is fitting when one considers its appearance. It looks like an old man with a long, GREEN beard and red, round belly and cheeks. Atop its bald head the vodyanik wears a tall and pointed hat it has made of woven reeds and about its waist is a belt made from rushes. All other clothing it may wear is always GREEN.

Vodyanik are, like many fay tend to be, oddly territorial and occasionally unpredictable. For instance, the vodyanik is perfectly fine with people using the water it lives in for bathing, as long as they do not do so during the midnight and noon hours. Should it discover that someone has broken this rule, it will pull him under and drown him, draining the blood from his lifeless corpse. It has been known to help fishermen by assuming the shape of a trout or salmon and driving schools of fish into their nets. Vodyanik will also warn fishermen of approaching storms.

Whenever the mood occurs or the notion strikes, the vodyanik will shape-shift into the form of a handsome young man (who, no matter the circumstance, will be wet all over his left side) in order to attract the attention of a lovely young woman. It may even adopt the guise of someone she knows and trusts in order to trick her. Once it has her near or in the water, it will pull her under and drown her, feeding off her blood as she dies.

As long as the vodyanik remains in the water, it is virtually all-powerful, but as soon as it leaves, its powers and abilities are greatly diminished.

Despite this, the vodyanik can often be found sitting on a river rock, preferably one near a mill, combing out its long, GREEN beard. Every night the vodyanik must leave the river anyway, as it drives its herds of sea-cows and sea-sheep onto land so they may graze.

A vodyanik will take a new bride every so often, choosing its newest mate from those girls who drowned or have in some way been disinherited by their fathers. Whenever one of its wives goes into labor, the vodyanik will leave its home and enter into town seeking the services of a midwife. It will overpay her in gold to see to it that she does a good job. The fairy children that are born are tall with pale skin and have the most beautiful singing voices. They will often sit in the branches of trees and sing.

Source: Alexander, *Mythology of All Races,* 271; Cotterell, *Macmillan Illustrated Encyclopedia,* 247; Mercatante, *Good and Evil,* 96

Volkolak (VOL-co-lac)

Variations: Ukodlak, Vuc, Vuk ("wolf")

In Dalmatia there is a type of vampiric REVENANT that hunts the fields and forests and is known as a volkolak. *Volkolak* means "dead, but alive, resembling an ordinary man," "vampire in 40 days," and "werewolf's son."

Volkolak are created when a man who happens to be a werewolf lives with a woman as her husband but never marries her, gets her pregnant, and then dies before his child is born. The child will, when it eventually dies, rise up 40 days later as this type of vampire. A second way that a volkolak is created happens when a man sells his soul to the devil. When this person dies, he too will become this type of vampire.

Source: Indiana University, *Journal,* vol. 14, 241; Perkowski, *The Darkling,* 53; Summers, *Werewolf in Lore and Legend,* 15

Vompir (VOM-peer)

Variations: KRUVNIK, Vonpir

Throughout Bulgaria and Macedonia there is the prevailing belief in a vampiric spirit known as a vompir, or vompiras if it is a female spirit. The vompir is created when a person is improperly buried or mourned, dies in disgrace, or passes on in some unnatural way, such as in childbirth or by suicide. At night, the vompir enters into the body of a corpse and possesses it. Once in control of the physical body, the vampire animates it and seeks out its prey—a sleeping person. Then it suffocates him and drains the body of blood.

Should a person ever find himself under the assault of a vompir, he must pray to the god of darkness and night, Troyan, or the goddess of beauty and love, Lada, for deliverance.

Apart from its ability to possess and animate corpses, the vompir can also cause nightmares, create droughts, and divert rivers.

A vompir can only be destroyed once it has occupied a corpse. After it has been captured, the vampire must be decapitated followed by the severing of its feet and hands. The body is then to be tied up tightly and either stabbed through the heart with a stake made of aspen wood or have a raven's claw driven into the skull from behind the right ear. Lastly, the body must be buried underneath a huge millstone.

Source: Indiana University, *Journal,* vol. 14, 265; Mayer, *Hungarian,* 174; Perkowski, *The Darkling,* 168

Voukodlaks

Variations: Voukoudlak

A vampiric spirit from Slavic lore, the voukodlaks enters into the body of a sleeping man and possesses him. Once the vampire has control, it will use the body to attack and rape young girls and women until it comes across its ideal mate, another type of vampire known as a VIECHTITSA.

Source: Masters, *Eros and Evil,* 188; Summers, *Werewolf in Lore and Legend,* 148; Wolf, *Dracula: Connoisseur's Guide,* 105–7

Vourdalak (VOUR-da-lacs)

Russian vampiric lore tells of the vourdalak, a particularly evil vampire that resembles a beautiful woman and preys exclusively upon men. It can only be destroyed by decapitating it and burning the body to ashes.

Source: Bunson, *Vampire Encyclopedia*

Vpir (VA-peer)

Variations: Upir

A vampiric spirit from Russian lore, the vpir possesses the corpse of a sorcerer or witch and animates it for its own evil purposes. The vpir attacks nightly those who travel alone, taking great delight in the terror it causes and reveling in the blood it consumes.

Source: Hunter, *Encyclopaedic Dictionary,* 404; Perkowski, *Vampires of the Slavs,* 164; Ralston, *Russian Folk-Tales,* 321

Vrkolak

In Bulgaria, in the Demir-Haskov region, there is a type of vampire known as a vrkolak. Described as looking like a shadow, this vampire is created when the blood from a person who was murdered with a gun or a knife falls to the ground. Fourteen days later, the blood that was spilt will become a vrkolak and immediately set out to spread diseases to the local livestock. The vrkolak can only be slain by a type of vampire seer known as a SÂBOTNIK, who will kill the vampire in the same method that it was created. For example, if the vrkolak was created through a murder committed with a knife, then the SÂBOTNIK must use a knife to slay the vampire. Additionally, a dog that is a SÂBOTNIK can destroy a vrkolak with its bite.

Source: Alexander, *Mythology of All Races*, 229; Baring-Gould, *Book of Were-Wolves*, 64; McClelland, *Slayers and Their Vampires*, 105; Summers, *Werewolf in Lore and Legend*, 16

Vroucolaca

On the Greek island of Myconi was a species of vampire known as a vroucolaca that was immune to the effects of holy water, prayers, religious processions, and being stabbed with swords. The vampire, left unchecked despite the best attempts of the citizens of Myconi to stop it, fed freely and often. Having no other option other than abandoning their island and moving to the nearby islands of Syra or Tinos, one last attempt was made to destroy the vampire. Its body was found and cremated, and as it burned the demon that possessed the corpse fled, never to return.

Source: Aylesworth, *Story of Vampires*, 5

Vrukolak (Vroo-co-lac)

Variations: Ukodlak

A vampiric REVENANT specifically from northern Dalmatia, the vrukolak is created when a person dies the victim of a vrukolak, by being murdered without anyone witnessing the crime, or when a cat or dog is allowed to jump over the body before it can be properly buried. It will first prey on its former family and friends before moving on to other victims. Vrukolak have the ability to create others of its kind and can transfix a person by maintaining continuous eye contact as well as emitting a disturbing shriek.

A vrukolak cannot be destroyed but it can be made incapable of ever rising from its grave and attacking anyone again. The vampire must first have its tendons cut so that it cannot walk. Then it can be nailed into its COFFIN with the last nail being driven through its heart.

Source: Alexander, *Mythology of All Races*, 229; Baring-Gould, *Book of Werewolves*, 64; McClelland, *Slayers and Their Vampires*, 105

Vrukólaka

In the northern regions of Greece there lives a particularly barbaric species of vampire known as a vrukólaka, although the vrukólaka was originally a Slavic vampire. Created when the Devil possesses a corpse, the vrukólaka then rises from its grave and begins to systematically kill first its relatives before moving on to people outside of its family tree. To destroy the vrukólaka, the body must be exhumed and a priest perform an exorcism over the corpse. If this method proves to be unsuccessful, then the body must be cut up into little pieces and burned down to ash.

Source: Leake, *Travels in Northern Greece*, 216; Summers, *Vampire in Europe*, 253; Wright, *Book of Vampires*, 42

Vrykolaka (Vree-COH-la-ka)

Variation: Alastores, Barbalakos, Borbolakas, Bordoukas, Bourbolakas, Bourboulakas, Bourdoulakos, Brykolakas, Kalakhanos, Upirina, Vrukolakes, Vrykolokas, Vurkokalas, Vurvukalas

A vampiric demon from Greek lore, the vrykolaka ("vampire" or "wolf fairy") possess the corpse of a person who died a violent death, was improperly buried, was cursed to UNDEATH by a priest, or was excommunicated by the church (see GREEK VAMPIRES). When it rises from the grave it looks every bit like the bloated, animated corpse that it is. It will go to the homes of the people it knew in life, its former friends and family, and knock upon their doors. Whoever has the misfortune to answer, the vrykolaka, a bloodthirsty and ravenous thing, will ruthlessly attack by day or by night.

Victims who happen to survive the attack of a vrykolaka will become this type of vampire themselves when they die unless they eat some of the dirt from the grave of the body that attacked him.

The vrykolaka can be prevented from attacking if its resting place is found. Then driving a stake through the body it has possessed and into the COFFIN it is resting in will ensure that it will be unable to rise up ever again. However, if someone already knows where the vampire is, killing it would at that point be just as easy as affixing it to the earth. Decapitating the vampire and hiding its head where it cannot be found is used in modern times, but the traditional method of rendering the body to ash is the most certain and effective. The only way to destroy a vrykolaka that was created through excommunication is to have a priest perform a special ceremony over the body followed immediately by either of the methods of destruction previously mentioned.

Originally the vrykolaka was not an evil vampiric being but rather a restless spirit that needed to fulfill a task or see to a need before it could rest in peace. It could be anything from a simple chore to as specifically complex as packing a bag, moving to another part of the country, marring, having children, and living out what would have been the rest of its natural life. It was not until the Greek Orthodox Church became influential enough to sway cultural beliefs that the vrykolaka was considered an implement of the devil. It was deemed that only proper church burial could absolutely prevent the vrykolaka from rising from its grave and doing evil. Being excommunicated from the church absolutely guaranteed that a person would become a vampire.

Source: Aylesworth, *Story of Vampires*, 5; Calmet, *Phantom World*, 113–19; Davenport, *Sketches of Imposture*, 278

Vryolakas (Vree-oh-LAC-az)

In the Republic of Macedonia there is a vampiric REVENANT known as a vryolakas. Like many of the vampiric REVENANTs from that region of the world, Albania, Bulgaria, Greece and Serbia, it is created when an animal such as a cat or dog jumps over the body before it is buried, when a person dies by murder or suicide, if a person eats meat that came from an animal that was killed by a werewolf, or when an evil person who used magic dies.

The vryolakas is active only between the hours of 10 P.M. and the first cock crow of the morning, as it is susceptible to sunlight. It will use that time to seek out unsuspecting people to drain dry of their blood. Vryolakas have a most unusual behavior, even for a vampire, as it has an unexplainable compulsion to pour wine over its face. Some sources claim this is because in life it was a sloppy wine drinker and now in its unlife it is incapable of drinking from a glass. Other sources claim that the vryolakas is created when a person accidentally pours or splashed wine over the face of the deceased which is what causes triggers its vampiric resurrection.

Source: Ronay, *Truth about Dracula*, 22; Stefoff, *Vampires, Zombies, and Shape-Shifters*, 17; Volta, *The Vampire*, 149

Vudkolak (VUD-co-lac)

Variations: VUKODLAK

In southern Slavic regions there is a vampiric REVENANT known as a vudkolak ("wolf's hair"), but this word is also used to refer to a werewolf. When a werewolf dies, on the night of the next full moon it will rise from its grave as this type of vampire. However, if a bird were to fly over the body of an unburied person, he too will also become a vudkolak. To prevent this from happen-

ing, a traditional honor guard made up of family and important people of the community will keep a careful vigil over the body all night long in order to ensure its safety. Should they fail in their task, on the nights of the full moon the vudkolak rises from its grave and shape-shifts into a werewolf in order to hunt humans to feed upon. The grave of a vudkolak can be detected as the grave that crows will not go near.

Source: Guiley, *The Complete Vampire Companion*, 10; Perkowski, *The Darkling*, 38

Vukodlak (VOO-cod-lac)

Variations: Pricolici, TRICCOLITCH, Tricolici, VRUKOLAK, Vukodlack, Vukodlaki, Vukolak, Vukozlak, Vulkodlak, Vulkolak

In Serbia a vampiric REVENANT known as a vukodlak is created whenever a heretic, magic user, or werewolf dies or if a person commits suicide or was murdered. When the vukodlak rises from its grave it looks like a bloated corpse with blood around its mouth, long fingernails, and reddish skin. Its first victims will be its surviving family and friends, and only after they have been killed to the last will it move on to others. Wherever the vukodlak travels it spreads illnesses and carries a plague that affects cattle.

GARLIC and silver will ward off a vukodlak, and throwing a handful of carrot or poppy seeds on the ground will distract it long enough for a victim to easily escape, as it is compelled to pick up and count each seed. The vampire can be destroyed but a specific process that must be adhered to. First it must be stabbed with a stake made of mountain ash. Then the vukodlak is decapitated. Finally, its heart is to be removed from its body and boiled in wine.

Source: Oinas, *Essays on Russian Folklore*, 116; Perkowski, *The Darkling*, 38; Wright, *Book of Vampires*, 90

Vyrkolakas (Vry-COO-low-casz)

Variations: Tympaniaois

The vyrkolakas is a vampiric spirit from Greek lore (see GREEK VAMPIRES). When a werewolf dies, its spirit will return and possess a corpse, which it will animate in order to use as its own. Since the spirit is an entity apart from the body it occupies, it is not considered a REVENANT. Once the body becomes possessed, *timpanios* will occur, meaning its bloated body will become hard, and the skin will become so tight that when it is slapped it will sound like a drum. There is at least one vyrkolakas in every Greek clan.

The vyrkolakas will walk through the community it used to live in, spreading disease and calling out the names of people it once knew. Anyone who happens to see it and look directly at it will die instantly; anyone who should answer its call will die within 24 hours.

Source: Guiley, *Complete Vampire Companion*, 26; Senn, *Were-wolf and Vampire in Romania*, 64; Summers, *Vampire in Lore and Legend*, 258

Vyrkolatios (Vry-COO-low-toes)

The vyrkolatios of Santorini, Greece, is like every other traditional Greek vampire except for one difference—the vyrkolatios keeps its victims alive the entire time it drains them of their blood and consumes their flesh right down to the bone (see GREEK VAMPIRES). Once the unfortunate victim dies, the vyrkolatios stops feeding.

Source: Bunson, *Encyclopedia of Vampires*, 275

Washerwomen of the Night

Variation: Clotha, Kannerez-Noz, Les Lavandieres de la Nuit, Midnight Washerwomen

In England and France there is a type of vampiric ghost that has come to be known as the Washerwomen of the Night. Having been in life women who neglected their religious obligations or were otherwise evil, the washerwomen are always to be found near an isolated source of running water. In England the washerwomen are ghostlike, but in France they have a skeletal appearance; either way, they are considered to be a death omen in both countries.

Very late at night, if a lone traveler comes across them, he must wring out their laundry for them or else the washerwomen will turn and break his arms and legs and throw him in the water. If the washerwomen capture a victim, they will make him wash his own burial cloth. If he does everything they tell him to do, he will survive the experience, otherwise, they will kill him on the spot.

The washerwomen are forever bound to wash the burial shrouds of the unbaptized children unless they can find someone who is willing to take their place.

Source: Curran, *Vampires*, 108–10; *The Gentleman's Magazine*, 150–51; Paulist Fathers, *The Catholic World*, 781; Summers, *Vampire in Lore and Legend*, 2

Werzelya

From Ethiopia comes the tale of a female vampiric demon known as Werzelya. In life Werzelya was the sister of Saint Susenyos, but unlike her sainted brother, she dedicated her life to evil. Werzelya had taken Satan as her lover and through their union, she gave birth to a daugh-

ter. Assuming that the child would have some magical ability since her father was the devil, Werzelya killed the child and drank her blood, gaining the ability to shape-shift into a bird or snake. When Susenyos learned that his sister had relations with the devil, killed her child, and drank her blood, he confronted and killed her. However, Werzelya returned as a vampiric demon and began killing the children of the region, including Susenyos's own newborn son. Susenyos mounted his horse and with spear in his right hand killed her again, as well as her demonic entourage and as many of the evil magicians as he could find. With her dying breath, Werzelya swore that any child who wore Susenyos's medal would be safe from her future assaults should she ever return.

Source: Budge, *Amulets and Superstitions*, 182; Budge, *History of Ethiopia*, 590; Hastings, *Encyclopædia of Religion and Ethics*, 339

White Ladies

Variations: Die Weisse Frau (Germany), Grey Ladies, Ladies in White, Les Dames Blanches (French), Night Ladies, WHITE LADIES OF THE FAU

Throughout the British Isles, England, and France there are a type of vampiric spirits known as the White Ladies. Considered to be a death omen, they are the ghosts of noblewomen who were murdered or otherwise died a tragic death. The White Ladies are described as wearing expensive period clothing and are carrying a ring of keys or chalices that are filled with poison.

When they appear it is always on the nights of the full moon, late into the evening. Although they have been sighted at bridges, cemeteries, and crossroads, most often they are found wandering the halls and grounds of the castles or manor houses where they once lived when alive. They will call out with their hypnotic voices, inviting those who can see them to dance, even though no music can be heard playing. Their touch is icy cold and will drain those they touch of their life-energy (see ENERGY VAMPIRE). Anyone who is unfortunate enough to accept their offer to dance the White Ladies will drain of blood; the bodies of their victims are found lying next to the road.

Some scholars consider the White Ladies to be vampiric fay rather than vampiric spirits since they are susceptible to attacks from weapons made of iron. However, they can also be warded off by brandishing a CRUCIFIX, calling upon God for aid, or having been recently blessed by a priest.

Source: Burne, *Shropshire Folk Lore*, 76–77; Curran, *Vampires*, 72, 184; Holland, *Haunted Wales*, 10, 69; Prince, *Remains of Folklore in Shropshire*, 15

White Ladies of Fau

The White Ladies of Fau, or the Dames Blanche as they are known in their native France, originate from the Juria Lake region. Preying on young men, they lure them off with their extreme physical beauty and magical charms to a secluded area where they turn and attack, draining their victims of their blood.

Of all the White Ladies that have been, the one named Melusian stands out amongst them. She has had numerous pieces of literature, poems, and songs written about her.

Source: Maberry, *Vampire Universe*, 92; Mercier, *Leonarde's Ghost*, 36; Stevens, *Encyclopaedia of Superstitions*, 1417

Wieszczy

Variations: Wieszcy

There is a belief in Poland that a child who is born with a cleft palate and either a caul or teeth will grow up to have a bright red face and suffer from hyperactivity throughout his life. When he eventually dies, he will rise up as a type of barbed-tongue vampiric REVENANT known as a wieszczy. In addition to attacking humans for their blood, the wieszczy will also ring the church bells at midnight and call out the names of people who live in the community. If anyone should hear his own name being called out, he will die.

To prevent a person from rising up as a wieszczy, he must be buried with several crosses made of willow wood, with one placed under each arm, under the chin, and upon the chest. Before the COFFIN is closed a handful of dirt from the deceased's own doorway is to be sprinkled over the body.

Source: Alexander, *Mythology of All Races*, 232; Lorentz, *Cassubian Civilization*, 276; Senn, *Were-wolf and Vampire in Romania*, 66; Taylor, *Death and the Afterlife*, 392

Wili (VE-lee)

Variations: Wiles, Vila, Vile

A vampiric spirit from Poland, a wili is created when a bride dies on her wedding day. Unable to find peace, the wili lingers on, suffering and unable to rest because it was denied the life it should have had. The wili returns looking like a ravishingly beautiful woman wearing a wet, white skirt. At midnight the wili appears on the roadside and will attempt to lure any man it sees into dancing with it. Those who give in to its temptations will become its victim, having their life-energy drained away (see ENERGY VAMPIRE). At dawn, the wili disappears.

Source: Beaumont, *Ballet Called Giselle*, 18–20; Creed, *Monstrous-Feminine*, 59; Perkowski, *Vampires of the Slavs*, 43; Summers, *Vampire in Europe*, 8

De Witte Lever (DE WIT LIV-er)

Variations: Witte Lever ("White Liver")

In the northern regions of the Netherlands there is a type of vampirism that can occur when a person is born with a white liver (see LIVING VAMPIRE). Just like everyone else, the de witte lever ("the white liver") lives a normal life, falls in love, and eventually marries. Sadly for the de witte lever, soon after the wedding day, the spouse becomes sick, begins to waste away, and eventually dies. The de witte lever is a normal human being except for the fact that the white liver is supposedly responsible for the spouse becoming ill and dying (see ENERGY VAMPIRE). Unfortunately, there is no way to test and determine who may have this condition prior to having been married and widowed fairly quickly. After the suspected de witte lever dies, the body can be cut open and examined to verify the condition.

Source: American Folklore Society, *Journal of American Folklore*, vol. 58–59, 323; Barbe, *Vampires, Burial, and Death*, 44; Noyes, *Encyclopedia of the End*, 127

Wukodlak

In the Bulgarian provinces nearest to Albania and Dalmatia the word *wukodlak* ("wolf hair") is used to describe a vampire.

Source: Jones, *Dawn of European Civilization*, 434; Pashley, *Travels in Crete*, 209; Wharton, *North American Review*, 95; Wright, *Book of Vampires*, 105

Wume (WOO-mee)

Near the Bight of Benin along the West African coast in the Gulf of Guinea there is a vampiric being known as a wume. Created when a criminal dies and remains unburied or when a person has been cursed to UNDEATH, the wume is powerful, smart, and notoriously difficult to kill. Usually a band of warriors and a priest, all of whom have been ritualistically cleansed, are sent out to track and destroy one. It is best advised to approach a wume only after it has fed, as it will then drift off into a near comalike sleep. Then the men will be a comparable match for it and will eventually be able to tie its arms down along its body and wrap several layers of rope up and down its body. Once the wume is tightly wrapped, nearly mummylike, the surviving warriors will take the vampire to a secret and isolated location where it is buried in a deep and unmarked grave. Then, the men must never speak of the place or go there again, for the wume will use its ability to compel anyone who walks near its grave to dig it up.

Source: Jones, *Dawn of European Civilization*, 434; Pashley, *Travels in Crete*, 209; Wharton, *North American Review*, 95; Wright, *Book of Vampires*, 105

Wurwolaka (Vour-vah-LA-ka)

In Albania there is a particularly vicious type of vampiric REVENANT known as a wurwolaka. It is one of the few vampires that has the ability to create more of its own kind. The wurwolaka is an ambush predator, and at night it attacks humans, ripping them apart and drinking their blood. Anyone who looks upon it will be stricken with insanity. The only way to destroy this vampire is to burn its body to ashes.

Source: Aylesworth, *The Story of Vampires*, 5; Wright, *The Book of Vampires* 105

Xi Xie Gui

In China there is a vampiric ghost called a xi xie gui. Its name means "suck blood ghost" in Mandarin Chinese. Created when a person's second soul, the P'O, fails to leave the body upon death, the xi xie gui preys upon humans for their blood. Although there is no known way to destroy this vampire, it can be prevented from entering into one's home by placing a length of wood measuring six inches long underneath the house's front door.

Source: Schwarcz, *Place and Memory*, 146

Xiang Shi

A vampiric REVENANT from Chinese lore, the xiang shi is created when a person's second soul, the P'O, fails to leave the body upon death. The xiang shi must consume human blood and flesh; otherwise it will begin to decompose.

Source: Guiley, *The Complete Vampire Companion*, 26

Xipe Totec (SHY-pea TOE-teck)

Xipe Totec ("Our Lord the Flayed One") was one of the vampiric gods of the Aztec people of ancient Mexico. He was described as wearing the skin of the victims who were sacrificed to him, symbolic of the "new skin" that the earth perpetually grows for itself.

The second month of the Aztec calendar was called Tlacaxipehualiztli ("Flaying of Men"). It was during this time when the priests of Xipe Totec would make their human sacrifices, rip-

ping the still-beating hearts out of the bodies and then flaying the skin before discarding the remains. The human hide was dyed yellow and made into a garment called a teocuitlaquemitl ("golden clothes"), which was only worn by Xipe Totec's priests. In the second part of the ceremony, additional sacrifices were tied to a framework and shot with arrows, not necessarily killing them outright. Their blood falling to the ground was symbolic of the spring and its rains, which revitalized the land.

Source: Aguilar-Moreno, *Handbook to Life in the Aztec World*, 151–52, 154; Cramer, *The Devil Within*, 154; Markman, *Flayed God*, 204; Myring, *Vampires, Werewolves and Demons*

Yara-Ma-Yha-Who (YA-rah-MA-YA-WHO)

Australia's premier vampiric creature, the yara-ma-yha-who, looks like a short, red-skinned man with an exceptionally large head and mouth and suckers on its fingers and toes. What is most unusual about this vampire is that it has no teeth whatsoever. It dislikes sunlight and prefers to spend its daylight hours in caves near a water source. An ambush predator, the yara-ma-yha-who hides in the branches of fig trees and attacks anyone who walks underneath it. It grabs him up and, using the suckers on its fingers and toes, drains the blood from its victims. When it is finished, it swallows the body whole. A short while later it will vomit the person back up, whole and alive. A person who is repeatedly attacked by the yara-ma-yha-who will gradually become shorter and shorter until he is the creature's size. Then he will start to grow HAIR all over his body and become a yara-ma-yha-who himself.

The spirit of the fig tree can kill a yara-ma-yha-who by climbing into its ear and making a noise that causes the vampire's own soul to flee its body in the form of tree fungus.

Source: Harrap, *Myths and Legends*, 342; Reed, *Aboriginal Fables*, 142–44; Rose, *Giants, Monsters and Dragons*, 403–44; Smith, *Myths and Legends of the Australian Aboriginals*, 342–44

Yasha (YA-sha)

Variations: Yakkha, Yaksa, Yashi

The yasha is a vampiric creature from Japan. Looking like a vampire bat, it is in fact the reincarnated form of a woman who was filled with anger in her past life.

Source: Bush, *Asian Horror Encyclopedia*, 207; Chopra, *Dictionary of Mythology*, 310; Smith, *Ancient Tales and Folklore*, 217

Yatu Dhana (YA-too DA-han-ah)

Yatu dhana is the name of the vampiric behavior that is displayed by the sorcerers who work in conjunction with the vampiric race of demons known as RAKSHASAS. When these sorcerers consume the flesh of the human remains that the RAKSHASAS leave behind, they are committing yatu dhana.

Source: Bryant, *Handbook of Death*, 99; Macdonell, *Vedic Mythology*, 163; Shendge, *Civilized Demons*, 125

Yezer Ha-Ra (YEEZHR HA-Rah)

A vampiric demon from Hebrew lore, the Yezer Ha-Ra ("the evil inclination in man's nature from birth") only attacks worshippers as they exit the synagogue on Friday nights. It possesses a person's body and drains away his life-energy over a period of some time until the victim dies or the vampire has been successfully exorcised by a rabbi (see ENERGY VAMPIRE). As long as the demon remains in the person's body, it will also be harassing its victim by sending him explicit and intense lustful thoughts.

Source: Curran, *Vampires*, 100; *Ma'aseh Book*, 279–300; Macdonell, *Vedic Reader for Students*, 245

Yuki Ona (OO-key OWN-ah)

Variation: Yuki Onna, Yuki-Onne

In Japanese lore there is a type of vampiric spirit known as a yuki ona ("snow woman"). It levitates rather than walks and appears to its victims as a tall and beautiful woman with impossibly long HAIR and inhumanly pale skin. Sometimes a yuki ona will show itself wearing a pure white kimono, but other times it will appear in the nude. On occasion, it will be holding a child in its arms. A yuki ona is perfectly camouflaged against a snowy backdrop, and combined with its ability to shape-shift into a cloud of mist or falling snow, it can be impossible to find.

The yuki ona is only active in the winter months as its hunting methods require. It will lead travelers astray, assuring they die from exposure or by breathing on them with its icy breath to make sure they meet the same death, but more quickly. It will appear before parents who are looking for their child; the yuki ona will seem to be holding it, beckoning for them to come and claim it. As soon as they do, taking it into their arms, the yuki ona turns them into ice. It has also been known to be aggressive, and although under normal circumstance it must be invited into a home, it will burst into a person's home by sending a gust of icy wind, freezing the occupants, especially the sleeping ones, to death. Not afraid to uses it beauty as a lure, it will tempt men into having sexual intercourse with it, and all the while the yuki ona will drain them of their life-energy, pleasuring them until they die (see ENERGY VAMPIRE). When it wishes it, one look into its eyes will cause a person to go insane. With each death it causes, it absorbs the life-energy of its victims.

It is only on the very rare occasion that a yuki ona will allow a potential victim to live, but he must beg for his life and be so moving and convincing when promising that he will never tell anyone about the encounter that even the icy heart of the yuki ona is moved.

Source: Davis, *Myths and Legends of Japan*, 149–53, 391; Mack, *Field Guide to Demons*, 64; Perez, *Beings*, 35; Smith, *Ancient Tales and Folklore of Japan*, 307–11

Yukshee (YUC-she)

Yukshee is a singular and specific vampiric demon from the Hindu lore of India and she is the most beautiful and sexually insatiable of all the succubi (see SUCCUBUS). If a man has survived an encounter with her, he will be rendered impotent for the rest of his life, as she will have consumed all of his sex drive (see ENERGY VAMPIRE).

Source: Edwardes, *The Jewel in the Lotus*, 108; Riccardo, *Liquid Dreams*, 51; Tyson, *Sexual Alchemy*, 10

Zburator (ZOO-bah-rat-or)

The zburator ("the flying thing") is a vampiric creature from Romanian lore, similar to an INCUBUS. Described as a winged and handsome young man with black eyes and HAIR, it looks like a shooting star as it flies across the sky. At night, the zburator visits young girls and women, has sexual intercourse with them, and drains off some of their life-energy with each visit, leaving them ill, pale, and thin (see ENERGY VAMPIRE). It is easily repelled by leaving a clove of GARLIC on the windowsill.

Source: Lecouteux, *History of Vampires*; Mackenzie, *Dracula Country*, 92; Magyar Tudományos Akadémia, *Acta Ethnographica Hungarica*, 322

Zemu (Zem-oo)

Variations: Zmeu

In the Moldavia region of Romania there is a vampiric spirit similar to an INCUBUS that is known as a zemu. It is the only vampire that does not cast a reflection in a mirror. Similar to the ZBURATOR, the zemu looks like a flame. At night this highly skilled lover visits young girls and widows, shape-shifting into the guise of a handsome young man. It then has sexual intercourse with them, stealing away their life-energy (see ENERGY VAMPIRE). In Transylvanian lore the zemu uses its shape-shifting abilities to change into a lovely young woman in order to seduce shepherds, much like a SUCCUBUS.

Both fast and strong, the zemu has an array of abilities that enables it to be a very successful predator, such as being able to cause hallucinations, desolidification, flight, and shape-shifting into a cloud of dust and mist.

Preventing a zemu from attacking is as simple as hanging a wreath of aconite over the bedroom windows, as this will prevent it from entering. Not particularly given to violence, despite its strength, the zemu can be killed if dealt an otherwise fatal blow with a silver weapon or long-term exposure to direct sunlight.

Source: Dundes, *Vampire Casebook*, 28; Florescu, *Complete Dracula*, 374; Jackson, *Compleat Vampyre;* Riccardo, *Liquid Dreams*, 49

Zméioaca

Zméioaca is a vampiric creature from the lore in southeastern Europe. She is the mother of the ZMEUS, a race of blood-drinking giants.

Source: Bunson, *Encyclopedia of Vampires*

Zmeus (ZEE-muse)

A vampiric race of giants with scaly tails from the lore of southeastern Europe, the Zmeus collect the ears from their victims to eat. Born the children of ZMÉIOACA, the Zmeus have the psychic ability to drain the life-force from their victims at a distance (see ENERGY VAMPIRE).

Source: Bunson, *Encyclopedia of Vampires*, 285; Senn, *Were-wolf and Vampire in Romania*, 41

Bibliography

Abbott, George Frederick. *Macedonian Folklore*. Cambridge, MA: University Press, 1903.

Abrahams, Roger D. *The Man-of-Words in the West Indies: Performance and the Emergence of Creole Culture*. Baltimore: Johns Hopkins University Press, 1983.

Adams, Charles J. *The Encyclopedia of Religion*. New York: Macmillan, 1987.

Adams, Michael. *Slayer Slang: A* Buffy the Vampire Slayer *Lexicon*. Naperville, IL: Sourcebooks, 2004.

Africa and Its Exploration: As Told by Its Explorers Mungo Park, Clapperton, the Landers, Barth, Barkie, Burton, Capello, Stanley, Speke, Schweinfurth, Grant, Nachtigal, Mohr, Iven, Livingstone, Serpa Pinto, Baker, Thomson, Kerr and Emin, with 600 Illustrations and Maps, vol. 2. London: Sampston, Low, Marston and Company, 1890.

Agrawala, Vasudeva Sharana. *India As Known to Pāṇini, a Study of the Cultural Material in the Ashṭādhyāyī*. Lucknow: University of Lucknow, 1953.

Aguilar-Moreno, Manuel. *Handbook to Life in the Aztec World*. New York: Oxford University Press, 2007.

Ahlquist, Diane. *White Light: The Complete Guide to Spells and Rituals for Psychic Protection*. Secaucus, NJ: Citadel Press, 2002.

Alexander, Hartley Burr. *Latin-American Mythology*. Boston: Marshall Jones Company, 1920.

_____, Louis Herbert Gray, John Arnott MacCulloch, and George Foot Moore. *The Mythology of All Races*, vol. 6. Boston: Marshall Jones Company, 1917.

Alip, Eufronio Melo. *Political and Cultural History of the Philippines*. Manila: Alip and Sons, 1954.

Allan, Tony, Michael Kerrigan, and Charles Phillips. *Realm of the Rising Sun: Japanese Myth*. New York: Time-Life Books, 1999.

Allardice, Pamela. *Myths, Gods and Fantasy*. Santa Barbara: ABC-CLIO, 1991.

Allman, Jean Marie, and John Parker. *Tongnaab: The History of a West African God*. Bloomington: Indiana University Press, 2005.

Allsopp, Richard. *Dictionary of Caribbean English Usage*. Kingston, Jamaica: University of the West Indies Press, 2003.

American Anthropological Association, Anthropological Society of Washington. *American Anthropologist*, vol. 69. Berkeley: American Anthropological Association, 1967.

American Anthropological Association. *American Anthropologist*, vol. 100. Berkeley: American Anthropological Association, 1998.

American Association for South Slavic Studies, American Association for Southeast European Studies, South East European Studies Association. *Balkanistica*, vol. 1–3. Bloomington: Slavica Publishers, 2007.

American Folklore Society. *Journal of American Folklore*, vol. 30. Boston: Houghton Mifflin, 1917.

_____. *Journal of American Folklore*, vol. 58–59. Cambridge, MA: American Folklore Society, 1945.

_____. *Journal of American Folklore*, vol. 64. Cambridge, MA: American Folklore Society, 1951.

American Philological Association. *Transactions and Proceedings of the American Philological Association*, vol. 44. Cleveland: Case Western Reserve University, 1913.

Andreescu, Ştefan. *Vlad the Impaler: Dracula*. Bucharest, Romania: The Romanian Cultural Foundation Publishing House, 1999.

Angoff, Allan, and Diana Barth, eds. *Parapsychology and Anthropology: Proceedings of an International Conference held in London, England, August 29–31, 1973; Parapsychology Foundation*. New York: Parapsychology Foundation, 1974.

Anima, Nid. *Witchcraft, Filipino-Style*. Quezon City, Philippines: Omar Publications, 1978.

Ankarloo, Bengt, and Gustav Henningsen. *Early Modern European Witchcraft: Centres and Peripheries*. Oxford: Clarendon Press, 1990.

Ankori, Gannit. *Palestinian Art*. London: Reaktion Books, 2006.

Annandale, Nelson, and Herbert C. Robinson. *Fasciculi Malayenses: Anthropological and Zoological Results of an Expedition to Perak and the Siamese Malay States, 1901–1902*. London: Longmans, Green, 1903.

Anthias, Teukros. *Cyprus Village Tales*. Ann Arbor: MI: University of Michigan Press, 1942.

Appletons' Journal of Literature, Science and Art, no. 118–144. New York: D. Appleton, 1871.

Arbuthnot, F. F. *Early Ideas: A Group of Hindoo Stories*. London: W. H. Allen, 1881.

Arens, William. *The Man-Eating Myth: Anthropology and Anthropophagy*. New York: Oxford University Press, 1980.

Argenti, Philip Pandely, and Herbert Jennings Rose. *The Folk-lore of Chios*. Cambridge: Cambridge University Press, 1949.

Aristotle, Richard Cresswell, and Johann Gottlob Schneider. *Aristotle's History of Animals: In Ten Books*. London: George Bell and Son, 1878.

Ashley, Leonard, R. N. *The Complete Book of Vampires*. New York: Barricade Books, 1998.

Asiatic Society of Calcutta, India, and the Asiatic Society of Bengal. *Bibliotheca Indica*. Calcutta, India: Baptist Mission Press, 1940.

Asiatic Society of Japan. *Transactions of the Asiatic Society of Japan*, vol. 1–50. Yokohama: The Asiatic Society of Japan, 1940.

Ateneo de Davao University, Ateneo de Zamboanga University, and Xavier University. *Kinaadman*, vol. 19–20. Cincinnati: Xavier University, 1997.

Auerbach, Nina. *Our Vampires, Ourselves*. Chicago: University of Chicago Press, 1997.

Aylesworth, Thomas G. *The Story of Vampires*. New York: McGraw-Hill, 1977.

_____. *Vampires and Other Ghosts*. Reading, MA: Addison-Wesley, 1971.

Bailey, Kenneth E. *Jacob and the Prodigal: How Jesus Retold Israel's Story*. Westmont, IL: InterVarsity Press, 2003.

Bakan, Michael B. *Music of Death and New Creation: Experiences in the World of Balinese Gamelan Beleganjur*. Chicago: University of Chicago Press, 1999.

Balfour, Edward. *The Cyclopædia of India and of Eastern and Southern Asia: Commercial, Industrial and Scientific Products of the Mineral, Vegetable, and Animal Kingdoms, Useful Arts and Manufactures*. London: B. Quaritch, 1885.

Bancroft, Hubert Howe. *The Works of Hubert Howe Bancroft*. San Francisco: History Company, 1886.

Barber, Paul. *Vampires, Burial, and Death: Folklore and Reality*. New Haven: Yale University Press, 1988.

Barber, Richard, and Anne Riches. *A Dictionary of Fabulous Beasts*. Sussex: Boydell Press, 2000.

Barfoot, C. C., and Rias van den Doel. *Ritual Remembering: History, Myth and Politics in Anglo-Irish Drama*. New York: Rodopi, 1995.

Barnett, Janet, and Randy Russell. *The Granny Curse, and Other Legends from East Tennessee*. Winston-Salem, NC: John F. Blair, 1999.

Barnhart, Robert K., and Sol Steinmetz. *The Barnhart Dictionary of Etymology*. Bronx, NY: H. W. Wilson, 1988.

Baskin, Wade. *Dictionary of Satanism*. New York: Philosophical Library, 1971.

_____. *The Sorcerer's Handbook*. New York: Philosophical Library, 1974.

Bastian, Adolf. *Indonesien: oder, Die inseln des Malayischen archipel*. Berlin: F. Dümmlers verlagsbuchhandlung, 1884.

_____. *Die Voelker des oestlichen Asien: Studien und Reisen*. Leipzig: Otto Wigand, 1869.

_____, Christian Goodden, and Walter E. J. Tips. *A Journey in Siam (1863)*. Bangkok: White Lotus Press, 2005.

Bathum, Mary Elizabeth. *Ayamara Women Healers: Health and Community*. Madison: University of Wisconsin, 2007.

Battuta, Ibn, and Hamilton Alexander Rosskeen Gibb, trans. *Travels in Asia and Africa, 1325–1354*. London: Routledge, 2004.

Beauchamp, William Martin, and David Cusick. *The Iroquois Trail: Or Foot-Prints of the Six Nations, In Customs, Traditions, and History*. Fayetteville, NY: H. C. Beauchamp Recording Office, 1892.

Beaumont, Cyril W. *A Ballet Called Giselle*. London: Cyril W. Beaumont, 1945.

Beech, Charlotte, Jolyon Attwooll, Jean-Bernard Carillet, and Thomas Kohnstamm. *Chile and Easter Island*. Victoria, Australia: Lonely Planet, 2006.

Belanger, Jeff. *The World's Most Haunted Places: From the Secret Files of ghostvillage.com*. Franklin Lakes, NJ: Career Press, 2004.

Belanger, Michelle A. *The Psychic Vampire Codex: A Manual of Magick and Energy Work*. Boston: Red Wheel, 2004.

_____. *Sacred Hunger, the Vampire in Myth and Reality*. Fort Wayne: Dark Moon Press, 2005.

Bell, Henry Hesketh Joudou. *Obeah: Witchcraft in the West Indies*. London: S. Low, Marston and Company, 1893.

Bell, Michael E. *Food for the Dead—On the Trail of New England's Vampires*. New York: Carroll and Graf, 2002.

Bellezza, John Vincent. *Spirit-Mediums, Sacred Mountains, and Related Bon Textual Traditions in Upper Tibet: Calling Down the Gods*. Boston: Brill, 2005.

Benedict, Laura Watson. *A Study of Bagobo Ceremonial Magic and Myth*. Leyden, MA: E. J. Brill, 1916.

Benjamins, Eso. *The Death of 4 European Gods: Iannus, Jesus, John and Janis*. Victoria, BC, Canada: Trafford, 2006.

Benjamins, Herman Daniël, and Johannes François Snelleman. *Encyclopaedie van Nederlandsch West-Indië*. Dordrecht, Netherlands: M. Nijhoff, 1917.

Benson, Elizabeth P., and Anita Gwynn Cook. *Ritual Sacrifice in Ancient Peru*. Austin: University of Texas Press, 2001.

Berdoe, Edward. *The Origin and Growth of the Healing Art: A Popular History of Medicine in All Ages and Countries*. Whitefish, MT: Kessinger, 2006.

Bernardi, Daniel. *The Persistence of Whiteness: Race and Contemporary Hollywood Cinema*. London: Routledge, 2008.

Beshir, Mohamed Omer. *The Nile Valley Countries, Continuity and Change*. Khartoum, Sudan: University of Khartoum, 1984.

Besson, Gérard A., Stuart Hahn, and Avril Turner. *Folklore and Legends of Trinidad and Tobago*. Paria Bay, Trinidad: Paria, 1989.

Bettany, George Thomas. *Primitive Religions: Being an introduction to the study of religions, with an account of the religious beliefs of uncivilised peoples, Confucianism, Taoism (China), and Shintoism (Japan)*. London: Ward, Lock, Bowden, 1891.

Beyer, Stephan. *The Cult of Tara: Magic and Ritual in Tibet*. Berkeley: University of California Press, 1978.

Bhattacharyya, Bhaskar, Nik Douglas, and Penny Slinger. *The Path of the Mystic Lover: Baul Songs of Passion and Ecstasy*. Rocheste, VT: Inner Traditions/Bear and Company, 1993.

Bilby, Julian W. *Among Unknown Eskimo: An Account of Twelve Years, Intimate Relations with the Primitive Eskimo of Ice-Bound Baffin Land: With a Description of Their Ways of Living, Hunting Customs and Beliefs*. Philadelphia: J. B. Lippincott, 1923.

Billington, Sandra, and Miranda Green. *The Concept of the Goddess*. London: Routledge, 1999.

Bisnauth, Dale. *History of Religions in the Caribbean*. Trenton, NJ: Africa World Press, 1996.

Bitard, Pierre. *Le Monde du Sorcier au Cambodge*. Paris: de Seuil, 1966.

Black, Jeremy A., Graham Cunningham, and Eleanor Robson. *The Literature of Ancient Sumer*. New York: Oxford University Press, 2006.

Blair, Emma Helen, and James Alexander Robertson. *The Philippine Islands 1493–1803*, vol. V. Cleveland: The Arthur H. Clark Company, 1903.

Blanchard, Wendell *Thailand: Its People, Its Society, Its Culture*. New Haven: HRAF Press, 1958.

Blavatsky, Helena Petrovna. *Isis Unveiled: A Master Key to the Mysteries of Ancient and Modern Science and Theology*. Point Loma, CA: The Aryan Theosophical Press, 1919.

_____, and George Robert Stow Mead. *The Theosophical Glossary*. London: Theosophical Publishing Society, 1892.

Bleeck, Arthur Henry, trans. *Avesta: The Religious Books of the Parsees, from Professor Spiegel's German, 3 Volumes in 1*. Hartford, CT: Steven, Austin, 1864.

Blomberg, Catharina. *The Heart of the Warrior: Origins and Religious Background of the Samurai System in Feudal Japan*. London: Routledge, 1994.

Blum, Richard H., and Eva Maria Blum. *The Dangerous Hour: The Lore of Crisis and Mystery in Rural Greece*. London: Chatto and Windus, 1970.

Boatright, Mody Coggin. *The Golden Log*, no. 31. Dallas: Southern Methodist University Press, 1962.

Bogatyrëv, Pëtr. *Vampires in the Carpathians*. Boulder: East European Monographs, 1998.

_____, Bogdan Horbal, Patricia Ann Krafcik, and Stephen Reynolds. *Vampires in the Carpathians: Magical Acts, Rites, and Beliefs in Subcarpathian Rus*. Boulder: East European Monographs, 1998.

Boguet, Henry, and Montague Summers. *An Examen of Witches*. Whitefish, MT: Kessinger, 2003.

Bojtár, Endre. *Foreword to the Past: A Cultural History of the Baltic People*. Budapest: Central European University Press, 1999.

Bolle, Kees W. *The Freedom of Man in Myth*. Nashville: Vanderbilt University Press, 1968.

Bonnefoy, Yves, Wendy Doniger, and Gerald Honigsblum. *American, African, and Old European Mythologies*. Chicago: University of Chicago Press, 1993.

Bonnerjea, Biren. *A Dictionary of Superstitions and Mythology*. Auburn, CA: Singing Tree Press, 1969.

Borges, Jorge Luis, Norman Thomas Di Giovanni, and Margarita Guerrero. *The Book of Imaginary Beings*. New York: Penguin, 1974.

Borlase, William Copeland. *The Dolmens of Ireland: Their Distribution, Structural Characteristics, and Affinities in Other Countries; Together with the Folk-lore Attaching to Them; Supplemented by Considerations on the Anthropology, Ethnology, and Traditions of the Irish People*. London: Chapman and Hall, 1897.

Borrmann, Norbert. *Vampirismus oder die Sehnsucht nach Unsterblichkeit*. München, Germany: Diederichs, 1999.

Botting, Fred, and Dale Townshend. *Gothic: Nineteenth-Century Gothic: At Home with the Vampire*. Oxfordshire: Taylor and Francis, 2004.

Bradley, A. G. "The Wild Dog of Ennerdale." *The Badminton Magazine of Sports and Pastimes*, vol. 13. London: Longmans, Green, 1901.

Branford, Jean. *A Dictionary of South African English*. New York: Oxford University Press, 1992.

Brautigam, Rob. "Asema: The Vampires of Surinam." *International Vampire* 1 (1990): 16–37.

Bremmer, Jan N. *The Early Greek Concept of the Soul*. Princeton, NJ: Princeton University Press, 1987.

Brennan, John T. *Ghosts of Newport: Spirits,*

Scoundrels, Legends and Lore. Gloucestershire: The History Press, 2007.

Breton Legends. *Breton Legends, Translated.* Oxford: Oxford University Press, 1872.

Brewer, Ebenezer Cobham, and Marion Harland. *Character Sketches of Romance, Fiction and the Drama,* vol. 1. New York: Selmar Hess, 1892.

Briggs, Charles Augustus, Samuel Rolles Driver, and Alfred Plummer. *The International Critical Commentary on the Holy Scriptures of the Old and New Testaments: Proverbs, by C. H. Toy.* New York: Scribner, 1899.

Briggs, George Weston. *The Chamars.* Calcutta, India: Association Press, 1920.

Briggs, Katharine Mary. *Encyclopedia of Fairies: Hobgoblins, Brownies, Bogies, and Other Supernatural Creatures.* New York: Pantheon, 1978.

_____. *Nine Lives: The Folklore of Cats.* New York: Pantheon Books, 1980.

Brinton, Daniel Garrison. *Nagualism: A Study in Native American Folk-lore and History.* Philadelphia: MacCalla and Company, 1894.

Broster, Joan A., and Herbert Bourn. *Amaqqirha: Religion, Magic and Medicine in Transkei.* Cape Town, Africa: Via Afrika, 1982.

Brundage, Burr Cartwright. *The Jade Steps: A Ritual Life of the Aztecs.* Salt Lake City: University of Utah Press, 1985.

Bryant, Clifton D. *Handbook of Death and Dying.* Thousand Oaks, CA: Sage, 2003.

Bud-M'Belle, I. *Kafir Scholar's Companion.* Cape Town, Africa: Lovedale Missionary Press, 1903.

Budge, Ernest Alfred Thompson Wallis. *Amulets and Superstitions.* Whitefish, MT: Kessinger, 2003.

_____. *Amulets and Superstitions: The Original Texts with Translations and Descriptions of a Long Series of Egyptian, Sumerian, Assyrian, Hebrew, Christian, Gnostic, and Muslim Amulets and Talismans and Magical Figures, with Chapters on the Evil Eye, the Origin of the Amulet, the Pentagram, and the Swastika.* North Chemsford, MA: Courier Dover, 1978.

_____. *Babylonian Life and History.* New York: Barnes and Noble, 2005.

_____. *A History of Ethiopia, Nubia and Abyssinia: According to the Hieroglyphic Inscriptions of Egypt and Nubia, and the Ethiopian Chronicles.* London: Methuen, 1928.

Buenconsejo, José Semblante. *Songs and Gifts at the Frontier: Person and Exchange in the Agusan Manobo Possession Ritual, Philippines.* London: Routledge, 2002.

Bulfinch, Thomas. *Bulfinch's Greek and Roman Mythology.* Chemsford, MA: Courier Dover, 2000.

Bullough, Vern L., and Bonnie Bullough. *Human Sexuality: An Encyclopedia.* Oxfordshire: Taylor and Francis, 1994.

Bunson, Matthew. *The Vampire Encyclopedia.* New York: Three Rivers Press, 1993.

Burma Research Society. *The Journal of the Burma Research Society,* vol. 46–47. Rangoon: The Burma Research Society, 1963.

Burne, Charlotte Sophia. *Handbook of Folklore.* London: Sedgwick and Jackson, 1914.

_____. *Shropshire Folk Lore, a Sheaf of Gleaning,* vol. 3 (1883). West Yorkshire: E. P. Publishing, 1973.

Burnett, Thom. *Conspiracy Encyclopedia: The Encyclopedia of Conspiracy Theories.* London: Collins and Brown, 2005.

Burns, William E. *Witch Hunts in Europe and America: An Encyclopedia.* Westport, CT: Greenwood, 2003.

Burton, Richard Francis, Isabel Burton, and Ernest Henry Griset. *Vikram and the Vampire: Or, Tales of Hindu Devilry.* London: Tylston and Edwards, 1893.

Bush, Laurence C. *Asian Horror Encyclopedia: Asian Horror Culture in Literature, Manga and Folklore.* San Jose: Writers Club Press, 2001.

Bush, Lewis William. *Japanalia.* New York: D. McKay Company, 1959.

Butts, Robert E., and Graham Solomon. *Witches, Scientists, Philosophers: Essays and Lectures.* New York: Springer, 2000.

Buxton, Richard. *Imaginary Greece: The Contexts of Mythology.* Cambridge: Cambridge University Press, 1994.

Byrne, Sandie. *The Unbearable Saki: The Work of H. H. Munro.* New York: Oxford University Press, 2007.

Calmet, Augustin. *Dissertation sur les apparitions des anges, des démons et des esprits. Et sur les revenans et vampires de Hongrie, de Bohême, de Modavie et de Silésie.* Paris: De Bure, l'aine, 1746.

_____, and Henry Christmas. *The Phantom World: Or, The Philosophy of Spirits, Apparitions, Etc.* London: Richard Bentley, 1850.

_____, _____, and Clive Leatherdale. *Treatise on Vampires and Revenants: The Phantom World: Dissertation on those persons who return to earth bodily, the excommunicated, the oupires or vampires, vroucolacas, etc.* Essex: Desert Island Books, 1993.

Campbell, John Gregorson. *Superstitions of the Highlands and Islands of Scotland: Collected Entirely from Oral Sources.* London: B. Blom, 1900.

Campbell, Joseph. *The Masks of Gods, Volume 1: Primitive Mythology.* New York: Penguin, 1987.

Campion-Vincent, Véronique. *Organ Theft Legends.* Jackson: University Press of Mississippi, 2005.

Canadian Centre for Folk Culture Studies. *Paper: Dossier,* no. 1–4. Ottawa, Canada: National Museums of Canada, 1972.

Candelaria, Cordelia, and Peter J. García. *Encyclopedia of Latino Popular Culture.* Westport, CT: Greenwood, 2004.

Canfield, William Walker, and Cornplanter. *The Legends of the Iroquois.* New York: A. Wessels Company, 1904.

Cannell, Fenella. *Power and Intimacy in the Christian Philippines.* Cambridge: Cambridge University Press, 1999.

Canziani, Estella. *Through the Apennines and the Lands of the Abruzzi: Landscape and Peasant Life.* Boston: Houghton, 1928.

Carle, Rainer, and C. E. Cunningham. *Cultures and Societies of North Sumatra.* Berlin: D. Reimer, 1987.

Carlyon, Richard. *A Guide to the Gods.* London: Heinemann/Quixote, 1981.

Carrasco, David. *The Oxford Encyclopedia of Mesoamerican Cultures: The Civilizations of Mexico and Central America.* New York: Oxford University Press, 2001.

Carter, Margaret Louise. *The Vampire in Literature: A Critical Bibliography.* Ann Arbor: UMI Research Press, 1989.

Cartey, Wilfred G. *The West Indies: Islands in the Sun.* Nashville: Nelson, 1967.

Cassidy, Frederic Gomes, and Joan Houston Hall. *Dictionary of American Regional English: Introduction and A–C.* Cambridge, MA: Harvard University Press, 1985.

Cavendish, Richard. *The Powers of Evil in Western Religion, Magic and Folk Belief.* London: Routledge, 1975.

_____, ed. *Man, Myth and Magic: An Illustrated Encyclopedia of the Supernatural*, vol. 21. Tarrytown, NY: Marshall Cavendish, 1970.

Challice, Annie Emma. *French Authors at Home: Episodes in the Lives and Works of Balzac—Madame de Girardin—George Sand—Lamartine—Léon Gozlan—Lamennais—Victor Hugo, Etc.* London: L. Booth, 1864.

Chambers' Encyclopaedia: A Dictionary of Universal Knowledge for the People, vol. 9. London: W. and R. Chambers, 1874.

Chaplin, James Patrick, and Aline Demers. *Dictionary of the Occult and Paranormal.* New York: Dell, 1976.

Charlesworth, Maxwell John, Diane Bell, Kenneth Maddock, and Howard Morphy. *Religion in Aboriginal Australia: An Anthology.* Brisbane, Australia: University of Queensland Press, 1984.

Chatelain, Héli. *Folk-tales of Angola: Fifty tales, with Ki-mbundu text, literal English translation, introduction, and notes.* Boston: Houghton Mifflin, 1894.

Chiang, Sing-chen Lydia, and Songling Pu. *Collecting the Self: Body and Identity in Strange Tale Collections of Late Imperial China.* Boston: Brill, 2005.

Child, Francis James. *English and Scottish Ballads.* Boston: Little, Brown, 1866.

Chinese Literature, Essays, Articles, Reviews, vol. 24. Colchester: Coda Press, 2002.

Chit, Khin Myo, and Ba Kyi. *Colourful Burma.* Rangoon: Daw Tin Aye, 1988.

Chopra, Ramesh. *Dictionary of Mythology.* New Delhi: Gyan Books, 2005.

Christen, Kimberly A., and Sam D. Gill. *Clowns and Tricksters: An Encyclopedia of Tradition and Culture.* Oxford: ABC-CLIO, 1998.

Christmas, Henry. *The Cradle of the Twin Giants, Science and History.* Cambridge, MA: R. Bentley, 1849.

Clébert, Jean Paul, and Charles Duff. *The Gypsies.* New York: Dutton, 1963.

Clifford, Hugh Charles. *In Court and Kampong: Being Tales and Sketches of Native Life in the Malay Peninsula.* London: Grant Richards, 1897.

_____, and Frank Athelstane Swettenham. *A Dictionary of the Malay Language.* Washington, D.C.: Government Printing Office, 1894.

Clifton, Chas, and Graham Harvey. *The Paganism Reader.* London: Routledge, 2004.

Clothey, Fred W., and A. K. Ramanujan. *The Many Faces of Murukan? The History and Meaning of a South Indian God.* Berlin: Walter de Gruyter, 1978.

Codrington, Robert Henry. *The Melanesians: Studies in Their Anthropology and Folk-lore.* Oxford: Clarendon Press, 1891.

Cohn, Norman Rufus Colin. *Europe's Inner Demons: An Enquiry Inspired by the Great Witch-Hunt.* New York: Basic Books, 1975.

Collin de Plancy, Jacques-Albin-Simon, and Hubert Juin. *Dictionnaire Infernal*, editions 10–18. France, 1992.

Collins, Derek. *Magic in the Ancient Greek World.* Hoboken, NJ: Blackwell, 2008.

Colloquium on Violence and Religion, Colloquium on Violence and Religion at Stanford. *Contagion: Journal of Violence, Mimesis, and Culture*, vol. 5–6. Colloquium on Violence and Religion at Stanford, 1998.

Colman, Penny. *Corpses, Coffins, and Crypts: A History of Burial.* New York: Macmillan, 1997.

Conway, Moncure Daniel. *Demonology and Devil lore.* New York: H. Holt, 1879.

Conybeare, F.C., trans. "The Testament of Solomon." *Jewish Quarterly* xi (Oct. 1898).

Copper, Basil. *The Vampire in Legend, Art and Fact.* Secaucus, NJ: Carol, 1989.

Cordier, Henri, Édouard Chavannes, Paul Demiéville, Jan Julius Lodewijk Duyvendak, Paul Pelliot, and Gustaaf Schlegel. *T'ung pao.* Haiti: E. J. Brill, 1902.

Cork Historical and Archaeological Society. *Journal of the Cork Historical and Archaeological Society.* Cork, Ireland: The Society, 1897.

Coulter, Charles Russell, and Patricia Turner. *Encyclopedia of Ancient Deities.* Jefferson, NC: McFarland, 2000.

Covey, Jacob. *Beasts!* Seattle: Fantagraphics Books, 2007.

Cox, Marian Emily Roalfe. *An Introduction to Folklore.* London: D. Nutt, 1904.

Crabb, George, and J. H. Finley. *Crabb's English Synonymes.* New York: Harper and Brothers, 1917.

Cramer, Marc. *The Devil Within.* London: W. H. Allen, 1979.

Crandon-Malamud, Libbet. *From the Fat of Our Souls: Social Change, Political Process, and Medical Pluralism in Bolivia.* Berkeley: University of California Press, 1993.

Crapanzano, Vincent. *The Hamadsha: A Study in Moroccan Ethnopsychiatry.* Berkeley: University of California Press, 1981.

Crawford, Osbert Guy Stanhope, ed. *Antiquity,* vol. 9. Gloucester: Antiquity Publications, 1935.

Crawley, A. E. *The Idea of the Soul.* Whitefish, MT: Kessinger Publishing, 2006.

Creed, Barbara. *The Monstrous-Feminine: Film, Feminism, Psychoanalysis.* London: Routledge, 1993.

Créméné, Adrien. *Mythologie du Vampire en Roumanie.* France: Rocher, 1981.

_____, Laurence Kersz, and Françoise Zemmal. *La Mythologie du vampire en Roumanie.* Monaco: Rocher, 1981.

Critchfield, Richard. *Villages.* Garden City, NY: Doubleday, 1981.

Cronin, Vincent. *The Last Migration.* London: Hart-Davis, 1957.

Crooke, William. *The Popular Religion and Folklore of Northern India.* London: A. Constable and Company, 1896.

_____, and Reginald Edward Enthoven. *Religion and Folklore of Northern India.* New York: Oxford University Press, 1926.

Cross, Frank Moore, and R. J. Saley. "Phoenician Incantations on a Plaque of the Seventh Century B.C. from Arslan Trash in Upper Syria." *Bulletin of the American Schools of Oriental Research* (1970): 42f.

Crowe, David M. *A History of the Gypsies of Eastern Europe and Russia.* Hampshire: Palgrave Macmillan, 1996.

Crowell, Todd. *Farewell, My Colony: Last Days in the Life of British Hong Kong.* Hong Kong, 2000.

Cuevas, Bryan J. *Travels in the Netherworld: Buddhist Popular Narratives of Death and the Afterlife in Tibet.* New York: Oxford University Press, 2008.

Culebras, Antonio. *Sleep Disorders and Neurologic Diseases.* Danvers, MA: CRC Press, 2007.

Cumont, Franz Valery Marie. *Afterlife in Roman Paganism.* New Haven, CT: Yale University Press, 1922.

Cunningham, Graham. *Deliver Me from Evil: Mesopotamian Incantations, 2500–1500 B.C.* Rome: Pontificium Institutum Biblicum, 1997.

Cunningham, Ian Campbell. *Synagoge.* Berlin: Walter de Gruyter, 2003.

Curl, James Stevens. *The Egyptian Revival: Ancient Egypt as the Inspiration for Design Motifs in the West.* London: Routledge, 2005.

Curran, Bob. *Encyclopedia of the Undead: A Field Guide to the Creatures That Cannot Rest in Peace.* Pompton Plains, NJ: New Page Books, 2006.

_____, and Ian Daniels. *Vampires: A Field Guide to the Creatures That Stalk the Night.* Franklin Lakes, NJ: New Page, 2005.

_____, and _____. *Walking with the Green Man: Father of the Forest, Spirit of Nature.* Franklin Lakes, NJ: Career Press, 2007.

Curtin, Jeremiah. *Hero-Tales of Ireland.* New York: Macmillan, 1894.

Dagyab, Loden Sherap. *Tibetan Religious Art: Texts.* Wiesbaden, Germany: O. Harrassowitz, 1977.

Dale, Edward Everett. *Tales of the Tepee.* Lexington, MA: D. C. Heath, 1920.

Dale-Green, Patricia. *The Archetypal Cat.* Dallas: Spring, 1983.

Dalley, Stephanie. *Myths from Mesopotamia: Creation, the Flood, Gilgamesh, and Others.* New York: Oxford University Press, 1998.

Dana, Charles Anderson. *The American Cyclopaedia.* New York: Appleton, 1878.

Danandjaja, James. *Parallelsacht: Life Cycle Ceremonies in Trunyan, Bali.* Jakarta, Indonesia: Balai Pustaka, 1985.

Daniélou, Alain. *The Myths and Gods of India: The Classic Work on Hindu Polytheism from the Princeton Bollingen Series.* Rocheste, VT: Inner Traditions/Bear and Company, 1991.

Daniels, Cora Linn, and C. M. Stevans. *Encyclopedia of Superstitions, Folklore, and the Occult Sciences of the World*, vol. 2. London: The Minerva Group, 2003.

D'Argent, Jacques. *Voodoo.* Los Angeles: Sherbourne Press, 1970.

Darmesteter, James. *The Zend Avesta.* New York: The Christian Literature Group, 1898.

Darwin, Charles. *A Naturalist's Voyage Round the World.* London: John Murray, 1913.

Davenport, Richard Alfred. *Sketches of Imposture, Deception, and Credulity.* London: T. Tegg and Son, 1837.

David, Christine. *Folklore of Carriacou.* Wildey, Barbados: Coles Printery, 1985.

David-Neel, Alexandra. *Magic and Mystery in Tibet.* New York: Dover, 1971.

_____. *With Mystics and Magicians in Tibet.* New York: Penguin, 1936.

Davidson, Gustav. *A Dictionary of Angels, Including the Fallen Angels.* New York: Free Press, 1967.

Davidson, Hilda Roderick Ellis. *Roles of the Northern Goddess.* London: Routledge, 1998.

Davis, Frederick Hadland. *Myths and Legends of*

Japan. North Chemsford, MA: Courier Dover, 1992.

_____, and Evelyn Paul. *Myths and Legends of Japan.* New York: Farrar and Rinehart, 1932.

Davis, Kenneth C. *Don't Know Much About Mythology: Everything You Need to Know About the Greatest Stories in Human History But Never Learned.* New York: HarperCollins, 2005.

Davis, Mike. *Ecology of Fear: Los Angeles and the Imagination of Disaster.* New York: Vintage Books, 1999.

Davis, Robert Murray. *The Literature of Post-Communist Slovenia, Slovakia, Hungary and Romania: A Study.* Jefferson, NC: McFarland, 2007.

Davis, Wade. *Passage of Darkness: The Ethnobiology of the Haitian Zombie.* Chapel Hill: University of North Carolina Press, 1988.

Davison, Carol Margaret, and Paul Simpson-Housley. *Bram Stoker's Dracula: Sucking Through the Century, 1897–1997.* Toronto: Dundurn Press, 1997.

Day, Peter. *Vampires: Myths and Metaphors of Enduring Evil.* New York: Rodopi, 2006.

Day, William Patrick. *Vampire Legends in Contemporary American Culture: What Becomes a Legend Most.* Lexington: University Press of Kentucky, 2002.

Daya, Dalpatram. *Essay on Demonology of Guzerat.* Bombay, India, 1849.

DeCaroli, Robert. *Haunting the Buddha: Indian Popular Religions and the Formation of Buddhism.* New York: Oxford University Press, 2004.

Dechambre, Amédée. *Dictionnaire encyclopédique des sciences médicales,* vol. 26. Paris: Asselin, 1882.

Dégh, Linda. *Legend and Belief: Dialectics of a Folklore Genre.* Bloomington: Indiana University Press, 2001.

De Gubernatis, Angelo. *Zoological Mythology: Or, The Legends of Animals.* London: Trübner, 1872.

Delcourt, Marie. *Oedipe: ou la légende du conquérant.* Paris: Belles Lettres, 1944.

De Leeuw, Hendrik. *Crossroads of the Caribbean Sea.* New York: J. Messner, 1935.

Delitzsch, Franz, and Matthew George Easton. *Biblical Commentary on the Proverbs of Solomon.* Edinburgh: T. and T. Clark, 1875.

De Magalhães, Basílio. *Folk-lore in Brazil.* Rio de Janeiro, Brazil: Imprensa Nacional, 1945.

Demetrio, Francisco R. *Encyclopedia of Philippine Folk Beliefs and Customs.* Cincinnati: Xavier University, 1991.

_____. *Myths and Symbols of the Philippines.* Manila, Philippines: National Book Store, 1981.

de Molina, Christoval, Francisco de Avila, Polo de Ondegardo, Juan de Santa Cruz, Clements Robert Markham, Pachacuti Yamqui Salcamay-hua. *Narratives of the Rites and Laws of the Yncas.* London: The Hakluyt Society, 1873.

de Nebesky-Wojkowitz, René. *Oracles and Demons of Tibet: The Cult and Iconography of the Tibetan Protective Deities.* Kathmandu: Tiwari's Pilgrims, 1993.

Denning, Melita, and Osborne Phillips. *Practical Guide to Psychic Self-Defense: Strengthen Your Aura.* Woodbury, MN: Llewellyn Worldwide, 2001.

Dennis, Geoffrey W. *The Encyclopedia of Jewish Myth, Magic and Mysticism.* Woodbury, MN: Llewellyn, 2007.

Dennys, Nicholas Belfield. *A Descriptive Dictionary of British Malaya.* London: London and China Telegraph Office, 1894.

de Plancy, Jacques-Albin-Simon Collin, and Wade Baskin. *Dictionary of Demonology.* New York: Philosophical Library, 1965.

De Quincey, Thomas. *Confessions of an English Opium-Eater: And, Suspiria de Profundis.* Boston: Ticknor and Fields, 1864.

Deren, Maya. *Divine Horsemen: The Living Gods of Haiti.* Kingston, NY: McPherson, 1983.

Desmangles, Leslie Gérald. *The Faces of the Gods: Vodou and Roman Catholicism in Haiti.* Chapel Hill: The University of North Carolina Press, 1992.

de Vere, Nicholas Tracy Twyman. *The Dragon Legacy: The Secret History of an Ancient Bloodline.* San Diego: Book Tree, 2004.

DiAntonio, Robert E. *Brazilian Fiction: Aspects and Evolution of the Contemporary Narrative.* Fayetteville: University of Arkansas Press, 1989.

Dickens, Charles, ed. *All The Year Round: A Weekly Journal.* London: F. M. Evans and Company, 1871.

Dickinson, Joy. *Haunted City: An Unauthorized Guide to the Magical, Magnificent New Orleans of Anne Rice.* Secaucus, NJ: Carol, 1995.

Dillon, Arthur Edmund Denis Lee-Dillon. *Winter in Iceland and Lapland: By the Hon. Arthur Dillon.* 2 vols. London: Henry Colburn, 1840.

Diószegi, Vilmos, and Mihály Hoppál. *Shamanism: Selected Writings of Vilmos Diószegi.* Budapest: Akadémiai Kiadó, 1998.

Dixon-Kennedy, Mike. *Encyclopedia of Russian and Slavic Myth and Legend.* Oxford: ABC-CLIO, 1998.

Dominicis, María Canteli, and John J. Reynolds. *Repase y escriba: curso avanzado de gramática y composición.* Hoboken, NJ: John Wiley and Sons, 2002.

Dömötör, Tekla. *Hungarian Folk Beliefs.* Bloomington: Indiana University Press, 1982.

Doniger, Wendy. *Britannica Encyclopedia of World Religions.* Encyclopaedia Britannica, 2006.

Donner, H., and W. Rollig: *Kanaanaische und aramaische Inchrifien* [Wiesbaden, Ger.] (1966): 44.

Dorson, Richard Mercer. *The British Folklorists: A History.* Oxfordshire: Taylor and Francis, 1999.

_____. *Folk Legends of Japan.* North Clarendon, VT: Tuttle Pub, 1962.

Dowson, John. *Classical Dictionary of Hindu Mythology and Religion, Geography, History, and Literature.* London: Trübner and Company, 1870.

Doyle, John Robert. *Francis Carey Slater.* New York: Twayne, 1971.

Drakakis, John, and Dale Townshend. *Gothic Shakespeares.* Oxfordshire: Taylor and Francis, 2009.

Drizari, Nelo. *Albanian-English and English-Albanian Dictionary.* New York: Ungar, 1957.

Drury, Nevill. *The Dictionary of the Esoteric: 3000 Entries on the Mystical and Occult Traditions.* New Delhi, India: Motilal Banarsidass, 2004.

Dube, Saurabh. *Untouchable Pasts: Religion, Identity, and Power Among a Central Indian Community, 1780–1950.* Albany: SUNY Press, 1998.

Du Chaillu, Paul Belloni, and Victor Semon Pérard. *King Mombo.* New York: C. Scribner's Sons, 1902.

Dumont, Jean-Paul. *Visayan Vignettes: Ethnographic Traces of a Philippine Island.* Chicago: University of Chicago Press, 1992.

Dundes, Alan. *The Vampire: A Casebook.* Madison: University of Wisconsin Press, 1998.

Durham, Mary Edith. *Some Tribal Origins, Laws and Customs of the Balkans.* London: George Allen and Unwin, 1928.

Durrant, Jonathan Bryan. *Witchcraft, Gender, and Society in Early Modern Germany.* Boston: Brill, 2007.

Durrell, Lawrence. *The Greek Islands.* New York: Viking Press, 1978.

Dyer, T. H. Thiselton. "The Will-o'-the-Wisp and Its Folklore." *The Popular Science Monthly* 19. New York: D. Appleton, 1881.

Eason, Cassandra. *Fabulous Creatures, Mythical Monsters, and Animal Power Symbols: A Handbook.* Westport, CT: Greenwood, 2007.

Ēchīasuksā, Čhulālongkōnmahāwitthayālai Sathāban. *Asian Review,* vol. 2. Bangkok: Institute of Asian Studies, Chulalongkorn University, 2003.

Edmonson, Munro S. *Nativism and Syncretism,* vol. 19. New Orleans: Tulane University Press, 1960.

Edwardes, Allen, and D. A. Kinsley. *The Jewel in the Lotus: A Historical Survey of the Sexual Culture of the East.* New York: Julian Press, 1959.

Edwards, Agustín. *My Native Land: Panorama, Reminiscences, Writers and Folklore.* London: E. Benn, 1928.

Eighteen-Bisang, Robert, Robert Michael Barsanti, Elizabeth Miller, and Bram Stoker. *Bram Stoker's Notes for Dracula: A Facsimile Edition.* Jefferson, NC: McFarland, 2008.

Einarsson, Bjarni, and Kungliga Biblioteket, Sweden. *The Saga of Gunnlaug Serpent-Tongue and Three Other Sagas: Perg. 4:0, NR 18 in the Royal Library, Stockholm.* Hellerup, Denmark: Rosenkilde and Bagger, 1986.

Eliade, Mircea, and Charles J. Adams. *The Encyclopedia of Religion.* New York: Macmillan, 1987.

Ellis, Peter Berresford. *A Dictionary of Irish Mythology.* Oxford: ABC-CLIO, 1987.

Ellis, Stewart M. *Mainly Victorian.* Hialeah, FL: Thompson Press, 2007.

Elsie, Robert. *A Dictionary of Albanian Religion, Mythology, and Folk Culture.* New York: New York University Press, 2001.

Emerton, John Adney. *Congress Volume: Jerusalem, 1986.* Boston: Brill, 1988.

Encyclopedia Americana: A Library of Universal Knowledge, vol. 3. New York: Encyclopedia Americana, 1918.

Encyclopedia Americana or "Conversations Lexicon," being a general dictionary of Arts, Sciences, Literature, Biography, History, Ethics, and Political Economy, vol. 6. Glasgow, Scotland: Blackie and Son, 1832.

Endicott, Kirk Michael. *An Analysis of Malay Magic.* Oxford: Clarendon Press, 1970.

Ennemoser, Joseph. *The History of Magic, translated from German by William Howitt, to which is added an appendix of the most remarkable and best authenticated stories of apparitions, dreams, second sight, somnambulism, predictions, divinations, witchcraft, vampires, fairies, table-turning, and spirit-rapping selected by Mary Howitt, in two volumes.* London: Henery G. Bohn, 1854.

Enriquez, Colin Metcalfe. *A Burmese Enchantment.* Calcutta: Thacker, Spink and Company, 1916.

Espinosa, José Manuel, and the American Folklore Society. *Spanish Folk-Tales from New Mexico,* no. 30. Millwood, NY: Kraus Reprint, 1969.

Espiritu, Precy. *Intermediate Ilokano: An Integrated Language and Culture Reading Text.* Honolulu: University of Hawaii Press, 2004.

Evans, Tammy. *Porphyria: The Woman Who Has "the Vampire Disease."* Far Hills, NJ: New Horizon Press, 1997.

Evans-Wentz, Walter Yeeling. *The Fairy-Faith in Celtic Countries.* London: Oxford University Press, 1911.

Evelyn-White, Hugh G., trans. *Hesiod, the Homeric Hymns, and Homerica.* Charleston, SC: BiblioBazaar, 2007.

Eyrbyggja Saga. New York: Penguin Classics, 1989.

Fanthorpe, R. Lionel, and Patricia Fanthorpe. *The World's Most Mysterious Places.* Toronto: Dundurn Press, 1999.

Farrar, Frederic William. *Life of Christ.* New York: Dutton, 1877.

Farson, Daniel. *The Man Who Wrote Dracula: A Biography of Bram Stoker.* New York: St. Martin's Press, 1975.

Fauth, W. "*S-s-m bn P-d-r-s-a.*" *ZDGM* CXX [Wiesbaden, Ger.] (1971): 299f.

Field, Margaret Joyce. *Religion and Medicine of the Gā People.* Accra, Ghana: Presbyterian Book Depot, 1961.

_____. *Search for Security: An Ethno-psychiatric Study of Rural Ghana.* Evanston, IL: Northwestern University Press, 1962.

Fielding, Xan. *The Stronghold: An Account of the Four Seasons in the White Mountains of Crete.* London: Secker and Warburg, 1953.

Fiérobe, Claude, ed. *Dracula: Mythe et Metamorphoses.* Paris: Presses Univ. Septentrion, 2005.

Fjelstad, Karen, and Thị Hiền Nguyễn. *Possessed by the Spirits: Mediumship in Contemporary Vietnamese Communities.* DeKalb, IL: Southeast Asia Program Publications, 2006.

Fleming, Maurice, and Alan McGowan. *Not of This World: Creatures of the Supernatural in Scotland.* Edinburgh: Mercat, 2002.

Flint, Valerie Irene Jane, Bengt Ankarloo, and Stuart Clark. *Witchcraft and Magic in Europe: Ancient Greece and Rome.* London: Continuum International, 1999.

Florescu, Radu, and Raymond T. McNally. *The Complete Dracula.* Acton, MA: Napc/Copley Custom Textbooks, 1992.

_____, and _____. *Dracula: A Biography of Vlad the Impaler, 1431–1476.* New York: Hawthorn Books, 1973.

Flynn, John L. *Cinematic Vampires: The Living Dead on Film and Television, from The Devil's Castle (1896) to Bram Stoker's Dracula (1992).* Jefferson, NC: McFarland, 1992.

Fogelson, Raymond D., and Richard Newbold Adams. *The Anthropology of Power: Ethnographic Studies from Asia, Oceania, and the New World.* New York: Academic Press, 1977.

Folkard, Richard, and the Francis Bacon Library. *Plant Lore, Legends and Lyrics: Embracing the Myths, Traditions, Superstitions, and Folk-lore of the Plant Kingdom.* London: S. Low, Marston, Searle, and Rivington, 1884.

Folklore Society of Great Britain. *Folklore,* vol. 1. Folk-lore Society, 1890.

_____. *Folklore,* vol. 13. Folk-lore Society, 1902.

_____. *The Folk-lore Record,* vol. 3. Folk-lore Society, 1880.

_____. *The Folk-Lore Record,* vol. 4. Folk-lore Society, 1893.

_____. *The Folk-Lore Record,* vol. 6. Folk-lore Society, 1895.

_____. *The Folk-lore Record,* vol. 61. Folk-lore Society, 1907.

_____. *The Folk-lore Record,* vol. 79–80. Folk-lore Society, 1919.

_____. *The Folk-lore Record,* vol. 87–88. Folk-lore Society, 1927.

Fontenrose, Joseph Eddy. *Python.* New York: Biblo and Tannen, 1974.

Forbes, Duncan. *The Baital Pachchise: Or The Twenty-Five Tales of a Sprite.* Whitefish, MT: Kessinger, 2000.

Ford, Michael W. *Book of the Witch Moon, Choronzon Edition.* Charlotte, NC: Lulu.com, 2006.

Forlong, James George Roche. *Faiths of Man: Encyclopedia of Religions,* vol. 3. New Hyde Park: University Books, 1964.

Fornander, Abraham. *An Account of the Polynesian Race: Its Origins and Migrations, and the Ancient History of the Hawaiian People to the Times of Kamehameha I.* Rutland, VT: Charles E. Tuttle, 1969.

Forte, Charles. *Lo!* New York: Claude Kendall, 1931.

Foundation for the Promotion of the Translation of Dutch Literary Works. *Writing in Holland and Flanders.* Amsterdam: Foundation for the Promotion of the Translation of Dutch Literary Works, 1960.

Fradenburgh, Jason Nelson. *Fire from Strange Altars.* Cincinnati: Cranston and Stowe, 1991.

Fraenkel, Ernst. *Die baltischen Sprachen: Ihre Beziehungen zu einander und zu den indogermanischen Schwesteridiomen als Einfuhrung in die Baltische Sprachwissenschaft.* Heidelberg, Germany: C. Winter, 1950.

Franklin, Rosalind. *Baby Lore: Superstitions and Old Wives Tales from the World Over Related to Pregnancy, Birth and Babycare.* Cornwall: Diggory Press, 2005.

Franklyn, Julian. *Dictionary of the Occult.* Whitefish, MT: Kessinger, 2003.

Frazer, James George. *The Belief in Immortality and the Worship of the Dead: The Belief Among the Aborigines of Australia, the Torres Straits Islands, New Guinea and Melanesia.* London: Dawsons, 1968.

_____. *The Fear of the Dead in Primitive Religion.* New York: Macmillan, 1936.

Frazer, James George, and George W. Stocking. *The Golden Bough: A Study in Magic and Religion.* New York: Penguin Classics, 1996.

Frazer, James George, and Lilly Grove Frazer. *Leaves from the Golden Bough.* New York: Macmillan, 1924.

Frédéric, Louis, and Käthe Roth. *Japan Encyclopedia.* Cambridge, MA: Harvard University Press, 2005.

Freedman, David Noel, Astrid B. Beck, and Allen C. Myers. *Eerdmans Dictionary of the Bible.* Grand Rapids: William. B. Eerdmans, 2000.

Friend, Hilderic. *Flowers and Flower Lore,* vol.1. London: W. S. Sonnenschein and Company, 1884.

Furuto, Sharlene Maeda, and Sharlene B. C. L. Furuto. *Culturally Competent Practice: Skills, Interventions, and Evaluations.* Boston: Allyn and Bacon, 2001.

Gadsby, Meredith. *Sucking Salt: Caribbean Women Writers, Migration, and Survival.* Columbia: University of Missouri Press, 2006.

Gaelic Society of Inverness. *Transactions of the Gaelic Society of Inverness,* vol. 14. Edinburgh: Gaelic Society of Inverness, 1889.

Gallop, Rodney. *Portugal, A Book of Folk-Ways.* Cambridge: Cambridge University Press, 1936.

Gandhi, Maneka. *The Penguin Book of Hindu Names.* New York: Penguin Books, 1993.

Garcia, J. Neil C. *Philippine Gay Culture: The Last Thirty Years: Binabae to Bakla, Silahis to MSM.* Diliman, Philippines: University of the Philippines Press, 1996.

Gardner, Fletcher. *Philippine Folklore.* San Antonio: Palm Tree Press, 1941.

Gardner, Gerald Brosseau. *The Meaning of Witchcraft.* Opa Locka, FL: The Aquarian Press, 1959.

Gardner, Vivien, and Susan Rutherford. *The New Woman and Her Sisters: Feminism and Theatre, 1850–1914.* New York: Harvester Wheatsheaf, 1992.

Garg, Gangā Rām. *Encyclopaedia of the Hindu World.* New Delhi, India: Concept, 1992.

Garnett, Lucy Mary Jane, and John S. Stuart-Glennie. *The Women of Turkey and Their Folklore.* London: D. Nutt, 1890.

Gaster, Moses. *Ma'aseh Book: Book of Jewish Tales and Legends.* Philadelphia: The Jewish Publication Society of America, 1934.

Gazetteer of Bombay State, vol. 20. Bombay, India: Government Central Press, 1954.

Geertz, Clifford. *The Religion of Java.* Chicago: University of Chicago Press, 1976.

The Gentleman's Magazine and Historical Review xvi (Jan.–June). London: Grant and Company, 1876.

Georgieva, Ivanichka. *Bulgarian Mythology.* Sofia, Bulgaria: Syvat Publishers, 1985.

Gerard, Emily. *The Land Beyond the Forest: Facts, Figures, and Fancies from Transylvania.* Brooklyn: AMS Press Inc., 2005.

Gerrits, André, and Nanci Adler. *Vampires Unstaked: National Images, Stereotypes and Myths in East Central Europe.* Amsterdam, 1995.

Gettings, Fred. *Dictionary of Demons: A Guide to Demons and Demonologists in Occult Lore.* North Pomfret, VT: Trafalgar Square, 1988.

Gibb, Hamilton Alexander Rosskeen, Koninklijke Nederlandse Akademie van Wetenschappen, and Johannes Hendrik Kramers. *Shorter Encyclopaedia of Islam.* Ithaca: Cornell University Press, 1953.

Gill, Sam D., and Irene F. Sullivan. *Dictionary of Native American Mythology.* New York: Oxford University Press, 1994.

Gimbutas, Marija Alseikaite, and Joan Marler. *From the Realm of the Ancestors: An Anthology in Honor of Marija Gimbutas.* Manchester, CT: Knowledge, Ideas and Trends, 1997.

Gimlette, John Desmond. *Malay Poisons and Charm Cures.* New York: Oxford University Press, 1971.

Ginzberg, Louis, and Boaz Cohen. *The Legends of the Jews: From Joshua to Esther,* vol. 4. Philadelphia: The Jewish Publication Society of America, 1913.

Ginzburg, Carlo, and Raymond Rosenthal. *Ecstasies: Deciphering the Witches' Sabbath.* Chicago: University of Chicago Press, 2004.

Glut, Donald F. *The Dracula Book.* Lanham, MD: Scarecrow Press, 1975.

Golan, Ariel. *Prehistoric Religion: Mythology, Symbolism.* Jerusalem: A. Golan, 2003.

Goonatilleka, M. H. *Masks and Mask Systems of Sri Lanka.* London: Tamarind Books, 1978.

Gordon, Joan, and Veronica Hollinger. *Blood Read: The Vampire as Metaphor in Contemporary Culture.* Philadelphia: University of Pennsylvania Press, 1997.

Gow, Peter. *An Amazonian Myth and Its History.* New York: Oxford University Press, 2001.

Graham, Walter Armstrong. *Siam: A Handbook of Practical, Commercial, and Political Information.* Chicago: F. G. Browne, 1913.

Grand, John. *Exploring Proverbs: An Expository Commentary.* Grand Rapids: Kregel, 2002.

Grauer, Armgard, and John Kennedy. "The Dogri: Evil Beings of the Nile." In *Nubian Ceremonial Life,* edited by John Kennedy, 114–124. Berkeley: University of California Press, 1978.

Graves, Robert. *The White Goddess: A Historical Grammar of Poetic Myth.* New York: Octagon Books, 1978.

Gray, Louis Herbert, Stephen Herbert Langdon, John Arnott MacCulloch, George Foot Moore, and Alice Werner. *The Mythology of All Races.* Boston: Marshall Jones Company, 1931.

Greene, Richard Gleason. *The International Cyclopedia: A Compendium of Human Knowledge,* vol. 14. New York: Dodd and Mead, 1890.

Gregg, Gary S. *Culture and Identity in a Muslim Society.* New York: Oxford University Press, 2007.

Gregory, Constantine, and Craig Glenday. *Vampire Watcher's Handbook: A Guide for Slayers.* New York: Macmillan, 2003.

Greiger, Wilhelm. *Civilization of the Eastern Iranians in Ancient Times—With an Introduction to the Avesta Religion.* London: Henery Frowed Amen Corner, 1886.

Griffith, Ralph Thomas Hotchkin, and Jagdish Lal Shastri. *The Hymns of the Rigveda.* New Delhi, India: Motilal Banarsidass, 1973.

Grimassi, Raven. *Italian Witchcraft: The Old Religion of Southern Europe.* Woodbury, MN: Llewellyn Worldwide, 2000.

Grimm, Jacob, and James Steven Stallybrass. *Teutonic Mythology.* London: G. Bell and Sons, 1883.

Grimm, Wilhelm, and Donald Ward. *The German Legends of the Brothers Grimm.* Philadelphia: Institute for the Study of Human Issues, 1981.

Grimstad, Kaaren, and Kongelige Bibliotek, Denmark. *Volsunga saga.* Dudweiler, Germany: AQ-Verlag, 2000.

Groot, Jan Jakob Maria. *The Religion of the Chinese.* New York: Macmillan, 1912.

Guerrero, Amadís María. *A Stun of Islands.* Published by the author, 2003.

Guiley, Rosemary, and J. B. Macabre. *The Complete Vampire Companion.* New York: Macmillan, 1994.

Guirand, Félix. *Larousse Encyclopedia of Mythology.* Lancaster: Prometheus Press, 1959.

Gulick, John. *The Middle East: An Anthropological Perspective.* Lanham, MD: University Press of America, 1983.

Günther, Marie Alker. *Tales and Legends of the Tyrol.* London: Chapman and Hall, 1874.

Gustafson, Axel Carl Johan, and Kirk Collection at Brown University. *The Foundation of Death: A Study of the Drink-Question.* New York: Funk and Wagnalls, 1887.

Gypsy Lore Society. *Journal of the Gypsy Lore Society.* Edinburgh: The Society, 1939.

_____. *Journal of the Gypsy Lore Society.* Edinburgh: The Society, 1958.

_____. *Journal of the Gypsy Lore Society.* Edinburgh: The Society, 1964.

Haase, Donald. *The Greenwood Encyclopedia of Folktales and Fairy Tales.* Westport, CT: Greenwood, 2008.

Haining, Peter. *A Dictionary of Vampires.* London: Robert Hale, 2001.

Hallam, Jack. *Ghosts of the North.* Devon: David and Charles, 1976.

Hammond-Tooke, W. D. *Bhaca Society: A People of the Transkeian Uplands, South Africa.* New York: Oxford University Press, 1962.

Handy, Edward Smith Craighill. *Polynesian Religion.* Honolulu: The Museum, 1927.

Hanson, Kenneth. *Secrets from the Lost Bible.* Tulsa: Council Oak Books, 2004.

Hardin, Terri. *Supernatural Tales from Around the World.* New York: Barnes and Noble, 1995.

Harris, Jason Marc. *Folklore and the Fantastic in Nineteenth-Century British Fiction.* Surrey: Ashgate, 2008.

Harris, Rivkah. *Gender and Aging in Mesopotamia: The Gilgamesh Epic and Other Ancient Literature.* Norman: University of Oklahoma Press, 2003.

Hartnup, Karen. *On the Beliefs of the Greeks: Leo Allatios and Popular Orthodoxy.* Boston: Brill Academic, 2004.

Hartshorne, Charles Henry. *A Guide to Alnwick Castle.* London: Longmans, Green, Reader, and Dyer, 1865.

Hasluck, Frederick William, Richard McGillivray Dawkins, and Margaret Masson Hardie Hasluck. *Letters on Religion and Folklore.* London: Luzac and Company, 1926.

Hasluck, Margaret Masson Hardie. *The Unwritten Law in Albania.* New York: Cambridge University Press, 1954.

Hastings, James. *Encyclopedia of Religion and Ethics, Part 8.* Whitefish, MT: Kessinger, 2003.

_____, Louis Herbert Gray, and John Alexander Selbie. *Encyclopaedia of Religion and Ethics,* vol. 3. Edinburgh: T. and T. Clark, 1908.

_____, _____, and _____. *Encyclopaedia of Religion and Ethics,* vol. 4. Edinburgh: T. and T. Clark, 1914.

_____, _____, and _____. *Encyclopaedia of Religion and Ethics,* vol. 12. Edinburgh: T. and T. Clark, 1922.

Hauck, Dennis William. *The International Directory of Haunted Places: Ghostly Abodes, Sacred Sites, and Other Supernatural Locations.* New York: Penguin, 2000.

Hayes, Bill. *Five Quarts: A Personal and Natural History of Blood.* New York: Random House, 2005.

Hayward, Richard, and Humbert Craig. *In Praise of Ulster.* Belfast, Ireland: W. Mullan, 1946.

Hearn, Lafcadio, and Genjiro Yeto. *Kotto: Being Japanese Curios, with Sundry Cobwebs.* New York: Macmillan, 1910.

Hearn, Lafcadio, and Keichu Takénouche. *Kwaidan: Stories and Studies of Strange Things.* Boston: Houghton Mifflin, 1904.

Heinze, Ruth-Inge. *Proceedings of the Fifth International Conference on the Study of Shamanism and Alternate Modes of Healing: Held at the St. Sabina Center, San Rafael, California, September 3 to September 5, 1988.* Berkeley: Independent Scholars of Asia, 1989.

_____. *Tham Khwan: How to Contain the Essence of Life: A Socio-psychological Comparison of a Thai Custom.* Singapore: Singapore University Press, 1982.

Heldreth, Leonard G., and Mary Pharr. *The Blood Is the Life: Vampires in Literature.* Madison: Popular Press, 1999.

Henderson, George. *The Norse Influence on Celtic Scotland.* Glasgow, Scotland: J. Maclehose, 1910.

Herskovits, Melville Jean. *Life in a Haitian Valley.* Garden City, NY: Anchor Books, 1971.

_____, and Frances Shapiro Herskovits, Mieczyslaw Kolinski. *Suriname Folk-lore.* New York: Columbia University Press, 1936.

Hertz, Wilhelm. *Der Werwolf: Beitrag zur Sagengeschichte.* Stuttgart, Germany: Verlag A. Kröner, 1862.

Hickey, Eric W. *Sex Crimes and Paraphilia*. Upper Saddle River, NJ: Prentice Hall, 2005.

Hicks, Jim, ed. *Transformations*. New York: Time-Life Books, 1989.

Hikosaka, Shu, and G. John Samuel. *Encyclopaedia of Tamil Literature: Introductory Articles*. Madras, India: Institute of Asian Studies, 1990.

Hill, Polly. *Rural Hausa: A Village and a Setting*. Cambridge: Cambridge University Press, 1972.

Hitchcock, Ethan Allen. *A Traveler in Indian Territory: The Journal of Ethan Allen Hitchcock, Late Major-General in the United States Army*. Norman: University of Oklahoma Press, 1996.

Ho, Hg. *Abracadaver: Cross-Cultural Influences in Hong Kong's Vampire Movies*. Hong Kong: Urban Council, 1989.

Hobart, Angela, Albert Leemann, and Urs Ramseyer. *The People of Bali*. New York: Wiley-Blackwell, 2001.

Hodgson, Janet. *The God of the Xhosa: A Study of the Origins and Development of the Traditional Concepts of the Supreme Being*. New York: Oxford University Press, 1982.

Hodivala, Shahpurshah Hormasji. *Studies in Indo-Muslim History: A Critical Commentary on Elliot and Dowson's History of India as Told by Its Own Historians, with a Foreword by Sir Richard Burn: Supplement*. Bombay, India: Islamic Book Service, 1979.

Hodous, Lewis. *Folkways in China*. London: Arthur Probsthain, 1929.

Hoiberg, Dale, and Indu Ramchandani. *Students' Britannica India*. Maharashtra, India: Popular Prakashan, 2000.

Holland, Richard. *Haunted Wales: A Survey of Welsh Ghostlore*. Atlanta: Landmark, 2005.

Holloway, Joseph E. *Africanisms in American Culture*. Bloomington: Indiana University Press, 2005.

Holyfield, Dana. *Encounters with the Honey Island Swamp Monster*. Pearl River, LA: Honey Island Swamp Books, 1999.

Hoops, Johannes. *Kommentar zum Beowulf*. Heidelberg, Germany: Carl Winter, 1932.

Hopkins, E. Washburn. *Epic Mythology*. New York: Motilal Banarasidass, 1969.

Hoppál, Mihály, and Eszter Csonka-Takács. *Eros in Folklore*. Budapest: Akadémiai Kiadó, 2002.

Horowitz, Wayne. *Mesopotamian Cosmic Geography*. Winona Lake, IN: Eisenbrauns, 1998.

Hort, Barbara E. *Unholy Hungers: Encountering the Psychic Vampire in Ourselves and Others*. Boston: Shambhala, 1996.

Houran, James. *From Shaman to Scientist: Essays on Humanity's Search for Spirits*. Lanham, MD: Scarecrow Press, 2004.

Howard, James H., and Willie Lena. *Oklahoma Seminoles Medicines, Magic and Religion*. Norman: University of Oklahoma Press, 1990.

Howe, Leo. "Gods, People, Spirits and Witches: The Balinese System of Person-Definition." *Bijdragen tot de Taal, Landen Volkenkunde* (1984): 193–222.

Howell, Signe. *Society and Cosmos: Chewong of Peninsular Malaysia*. New York: Oxford University Press, 1984.

Howey, M. Oldfield. *The Cat in Magic and Myth*. North Chemsford, MA: Courier Dover Publications, 2003.

Howitt, Alfred William. *The Native Tribes of South-East Australia*. New York: Macmillan, 1904.

Hubbs, Joanna. *Mother Russia: The Feminine Myth in Russian Culture*. Bloomington: Indiana University Press, 1993.

Hufford, David J. *The Terror That Comes in the Night: An Experience-Centered Study of Supernatural Assault Traditions*. Philadelphia: University of Pennsylvania Press, 1989.

Hughes, Jon G. *Celtic Plant Magic: A Workbook for Alchemical Sex Rituals*. Rochester, VT: Inner Traditions/Bear and Company, 2003.

Hulme, Frederick Edward. *Myth-land*. London: S. Low, Marston, Searle and Rivington, 1886.

Hurwitz, Siegmund. *Lilith, the First Eve: Historical and Psychological Aspects of the Dark Feminine*. Einsiedeln, Switzerland: Daimon, 1992.

Hurwood, Bernhardt J. *Passport to the Supernatural: An Occult Compendium from All Ages and Many Lands*. New York: Taplinger, 1972.

_____. *Vampires, Werewolves and Ghouls*. New York: Ace, 1973.

Huss, Roy, and Theodore J. Ross. *Focus on the Horror Film*. Upper Saddle River, NJ: Prentice-Hall, 1972.

Huxley, Francis. *The Invisibles*. London: Hart-Davis, 1966.

Icon Group International, Inc. *Folklore: Webster's Quotations, Facts and Phrases*. San Diego: ICON Group International, Inc., 2008.

_____. *Foresters: Webster's Quotations, Facts and Phrases*. San Diego: ICON Group International, Inc., 2008.

_____. *Hanging: Webster's Quotations, Facts and Phrases*. San Diego: ICON Group International, Inc., 2008.

_____. *Sacrificing: Webster's Quotations, Facts and Phrases*. San Diego: ICON Group International, Inc., 2008.

_____. *Victims: Webster's Quotations, Facts and Phrases*. San Diego: ICON Group International, Inc., 2008.

Iinkai, Nihon Yunesuko Kokunai. *Japan: Its Land, People and Culture*. Tokyo: Bureau, Ministry of Finance, 1958.

Indian Psychoanalytical Society. *Samīkṣa*, vol. 1–14. Bombay: Indian Psychoanalytical Society, 1947.

Indiana University Linguistics Club. *Journal of*

Slavic Linguistics, vol. 14. Bloomington: Indiana University Linguistics Club, 2007.

Institut za balkanistika. *Études balkaniques*. Sofia, Bulgaria: Édition de lA'cadémie bulgare des sciences, 1994.

International African Institute. *Ethnographic Survey of Africa*. Oxford: International African Institute, 1950.

Ivanits, Linda J. *Russian Folk Belief*. Armonk, NY: M.E. Sharpe, 1992.

Jackson, Nigel Aldcroft. *The Compleat Vampyre: The Vampire Shaman, Werewolves, Witchery and the Dark Mythology of the Undead*. Somerset: Capall Bann, 1995.

Jackson-Laufer, Guida Myrl, and Guida M. Jackson. *Encyclopedia of Traditional Epics*. Oxford: ABC-CLIO, 1994.

Jacobs, David Michael. *UFO and Abductions: Challenging the Borders of Knowledge*. Lawrence: University of Kansas Press, 2000.

Jacobs, Joseph. *Celtic Fairy Tales*. London: David Nut, 1892.

_____, William Crooke, Alfred Trübner Nutt, Arthur Robinson Wright, Folklore Society (Great Britain), MetaPress, JSTOR (Organization). *Folklore*, vol. 11. London: Folklore Society, 1900.

Jacobs, Joseph, John Dickson Batten, and Donald Haase. *English Fairy Tales, Folklore and Legends*. Oxford. ABC-CLIO, 2002

Jahoda, Gustav. *The Psychology of Superstition*. New York: Penguin, 1970.

Jakobson, Roman. *Selected Writings: On Verse, Its Masters and Explorers*. Berlin: Walter de Gruyter, 1962.

Japan Society of London. *Bulletin no. 50–62—The Japan Society of London*. London: Japan Society of London, 1966.

_____. *Transactions and Proceedings of the Japan Society, London*, vol. 9. London: Kegan Paul, Trench, Trübner, 1912.

Jastrow, Morris. *The Religion of Babylonia and Assyria*. Oxford: Ginn and Company, 1898.

Jayatilaka, Don Baron, Wilhelm Geiger, and Helmer Smith. *A Dictionary of the Sinhalese Language*. Ceylon, Sri Lanka: The Royal Asiatic Society, 1935.

Jennaway, Megan. *Sisters and Lovers: Women and Desire in Bali*. Lanham, MD: Rowman and Littlefield, 2002.

Jennings, Gary. *Black Magic, White Magic*. New York: Dial Press, 1964.

Jensen, Gordon D., and Luh Ketut Suryani. *The Balinese People: A Reinvestigation of Character*. New York: Oxford University Press, 1992.

Jobes, Gertrude. *Dictionary of Mythology, Folklore and Symbols*. Lanham, MD: Scarecrow Press, 1961.

Jocano, F. Landa. *Folk Medicine: In a Philippine Municipality*. Manila, Philippines: National Museum Publication, 1973.

Jockin-La Bastide, J. A. G. van Kooten, and Jacob Kramers. *Cassell's English-Dutch, Dutch-English Dictionary*. London: Cassell, 1981.

Johnston, Sarah Iles. *Restless Dead: Encounters Between the Living and the Dead in Ancient Greece*. Berkeley: University of California Press, 1999.

Jones, David E. *Evil in Our Midst: A Chilling Glimpse of Our Most Feared and Frightening Demons*. New York: Square One, 2001.

Jones, Ernest. *On the Nightmare*. London: Hogarth Press, 1949.

Jones, Griffith Hartwell. *The Dawn of European Civilization*. London: Kegan Paul, Trench, Trübner, 1903.

Jones, Stephen. *The Essential Monster Movie Guide, a Century of Creature Features on Film, TV and Video*. New York: Watson-Guptill, 2000.

_____, and Forrest Ackerman. *The Essential Monster Movie Guide: A Century of Creature Features on Film, TV and Video*. New York: Billboard Books, 1990.

Jones, Steven Swann. *The New Comparative Method: Structural and Symbolic Analysis of the Allomotifs of "Snow White."* Helsinki, Finland: Suomalainen Tiedeakatemia, 1990.

Jordan, Michael. *Encyclopedia of Gods: Over 2,500 Deities of the World*. Darby, PA: Diane Books, 1998.

Just, Peter. "Conflict Resolution and Moral Community Among the Dou Donggo." In *Conflict Resolution: Cross-Cultural Perspectives*, edited by K. Avruch, P. W. Black, and J. A. Scimecca, 107–143. Westport, CT: Greenwood, 1991.

Kadir, Abdullah bin Adbul, and Abdullah A. H. Hill. *The Hikayat Abdullah*. New York: Oxford University Press, 1970.

Kane, Alice, and Sean Kane. *The Dreamer Awakes*. Orchard Park, NY: Broadview Press, 1995.

Kanellos, Nicolás, Claudio Esteva Fabregat, Alfredo Jiménez, Francisco A. Lomelí, Alfredo Jiménez Núñez, Félix Padilla, and Thomas Weaver. *Handbook of Hispanic Cultures in the United States: Literature and Art*. Houston: Arte Publico Press, 1993.

Kang, Xiaofei. *The Cult of the Fox: Power, Gender, and Popular Religion in Late Imperial and Modern China*. New York: Columbia University Press, 2006.

Kapferer, Bruce. *A Celebration of Demons: Exorcism and the Aesthetics of Healing In Sri Lanka*. Oxford: Berg, 1991.

Keating, Geoffrey. *The History of Ireland* (Seathrun Ceitinn, *Foras Feasa na Eireann*). 1634.

Keegan, John, and John O'Hanlon. *Legends and*

Poems: Now First Collected. Dublin: Sealy, Bryers and Walker, 1907.

Keel, John A. *The Complete Guide to Mysterious Beings.* New York: Macmillan, 2002.

Keightley, Thomas. *The Fairy Mythology: Illustrative of the Romance and Superstition of Various Countries.* London: G. Bell and Sons, 1850.

Keith, Arthur Berriedale. *The Religion and Philosophy of the Veda and Upanishads.* Cambridge, MA: Harvard University Press, 1925.

_____. *The Sanskrit Drama in Its Origin, Development, Theory and Practice.* New Delhi: Motilal Banarsidass, 1992.

Kelly, John, J. T. Clarke, Archibald Cregeen, William Gill, and John Ivon Mosley. *Fockleyr Manninagh as Baarlagh.* Douglas, Isle of Man: The Manx Society, 1866.

Kent, Raymond K. *Early Kingdoms in Madagascar, 1500–1700.* Austin: Holt, Rinehart and Winston, 1970.

Kenyon, Theda. *Witches Still Live.* Whitefish, MT: Kessinger, 2003.

Keown, Damien. *Buddhism and Abortion.* Honolulu: University of Hawaii Press, 1998.

Kessler, Joan C. *Demons of the Night: Tales of the Fantastic, Madness, and the Supernatural from Nineteenth-Century France.* Chicago: University of Chicago Press, 1995.

Keyworth, David. *Troublesome Corpses: Vampires and Revenants, from Antiquity to the Present.* Essex: Desert Island Books, 2007.

Khanam, R. *Demonology: Socio-religious Belief of Witchcraft.* New Delhi, India: Global Vision, 2003.

Kiberd, Declan. *Irish Classics.* Cambridge, MA: Harvard University Press, 2001.

Kiev, Ari. *Magic, Faith, and Healing: Studies in Primitive Psychiatry Today.* New York: Free Press of Glencoe, 1964.

Kihara, Hitoshi, ed. *Scientific Results of the Japanese Expeditions to Nepal Himalaya, 1952–1953: Peoples of Nepal Himalaya.* Kyoto, Japan: Fauna and Flora Research Society, 1955.

Kinahan, Frank. *Yeats, Folklore, and Occultism: Contexts of the Early Work and Thought.* London: Unwin Hyman, 1988.

Kirk, Geoffrey Stephen. *Myth: Its Meaning and Functions in Ancient and Other Cultures.* Berkeley: University of California Press, 1973.

Klein, Barbro Sklute. *Legends and Folk Beliefs in a Swedish American Community.* Salem, N.H.: Ayer, 1980.

Klinger, Leslie S., Neil Gaiman, and Bram Stoker. *The New Annotated Dracula.* New York: W. W. Norton, 2008.

Klostermaier, Klaus K. *A Concise Encyclopedia of Hinduism.* Oxford: Oneworld, 1998.

Knapp, Bettina Liebowitz. *Machine, Metaphor, and the Writer: A Jungian View.* University Park: Penn State Press, 1989.

_____. *Women, Myth, and the Feminine Principle.* Albany: SUNY Press, 1997.

Knappert, Jan. *The Aquarian Guide to African Mythology.* Wellingborough: Aquarian, 1990.

_____. *Bantu Myths and Other Tales.* Boston: Brill Archive, 1977.

_____. *The Encyclopaedia of Middle Eastern Mythology and Religion.* Boston: H. Holt, 1879.

_____. *Myths and Legends of the Congo.* London: Heinemann Educational Books, 1971.

Koch, Kurt E. *Occult ABC.* Grand Rapids: Kregel, 1981.

Koén-Sarano, Matilda, and Reginetta Haboucha. *King Solomon and the Golden Fish: Tales from the Sephardic Tradition.* Detroit: Wayne State University Press, 2004.

Koentjaraningrat and Southeast Asian Studies Program. *Javanese Culture.* New York: Oxford University Press, 1985.

Kolata, Alan L. *Valley of the Spirits: A Journey into the Lost Realm of the Aymara.* Hoboken, NJ: John Wiley and Sons, 1996.

Koltuv, Barbara Black. *The Book of Lilith.* York Beach, ME: Nicolas-Hays, 1986.

Konrad, Alexander N. *Old Russia and Byzantium: The Byzantine and Oriental Origins of Russian Culture.* Vienna, Austria: W. Braumüller, 1972.

Konstantinos. *Vampires: The Occult Truth.* Woodbury, MN: Llewellyn Worldwide, 1996.

Kosambi, D. D. *An Introduction to the Study of Indian History.* Maharashtra, India: Popular Prakashan, 1996.

Kramer, Heinrich, and Jacob Sprenger. *Malleus Maleficarum.* Mineola, NY: Dover, 1971.

Krappe, Alexander Haggerty. *Balor with the Evil Eye: Studies in Celtic and French Literature.* Whitefish, MT: Kessinger, 2006.

Krech, Shepard. *Spirits of the Air: Birds and American Indians in the South.* Athens: University of Georgia Press, 2009.

Krevter, Peter Mario. *Der Vampirglaube in Sudosteurope: Studien zur Genese, Bedeutung und Funkton.* Berlin: Weidler, 2001.

Kroeber, A. L. *Peoples of the Philippines.* New York: American Museum Press, 1919.

Kubiiovych, Volodymyr, and Naukove Tovarystvo im. Shevchenka. *Ukraine: A Concise Encyclopaedia,* vol. 1. Toronto: University of Toronto Press, 1963.

Kuhn, Philip A. *Soulstealers: The Chinese Sorcery Scare of 1768.* Cambridge, MA: Harvard University Press, 1990.

Laderman, Carol. *Wives and Midwives: Childbirth and Nutrition in Rural Malaysia.* Berkeley: University of California Press, 1987.

Laderman, Gary, and Luis D. León. *Religion and*

American Cultures: An Encyclopedia of Traditions, Diversity, and Popular Expressions. Oxford: ABC-CLIO, 2003.

Laguerre, Michel S. *Voodoo Heritage.* Thousand Oaks, CA: Sage, 1980.

Landman, Isaac. *The Universal Jewish Encyclopedia: An Authoritative and Popular Presentation of Jews and Judaism Since the Earliest Times.* New York: The Universal Jewish Encyclopedia, Inc., 1943.

Lane, Edward William, ed. *Selections from the Kurán, commonly known in England as the Koran, with an interwoven commentary translated from the Arabic, methodically arranged and illustrated with notes chiefly from Sale's edition: to which is prefixed an introduction, taken from Sale's preliminary discourse, with corrections and additions: by Edward William Lane.* London: James Madden and Company, 1843.

Lang, Andrew. *The Lilac Fairy Book.* Fairfield, IA: First World, 2005.

_____, and Ben Kutcher. *The Blue Fairy Book.* London: Longmans, Green, 1901.

Langton, Edward. *Essentials of Demonology.* New York: AMS Press, 1981.

Latourette, Kenneth Scott. *The Chinese.* New York: Macmillan, 1934.

Laubscher, Barend Jacob Frederick. *The Pagan Soul.* Cape Town, Africa: H. Timmins, 1975.

Lawson, John Cuthbert. *Modern Greek Folklore and Ancient Greek Folklore.* Cambridge: Cambridge University Press, 1910.

Le Roy, Alexander. *The Religion of the Primitives.* New York: Macmillan, 1922.

Leach, Maria, and Jerome Fried. *Funk and Wagnalls Standard Dictionary of Folklore, Mythology, and Legend.* New York: Funk and Wagnalls, 1949.

_____. *Funk and Wagnalls Standard Dictionary of Folklore, Mythology, and Legend.* New York: Funk and Wagnalls, 1972.

_____. *Funk and Wagnalls Standard Dictionary of Folklore, Mythology, and Legend.* San Francisco: Harper San Francisco, 1984.

Leake, William Martin. *Travels in Northern Greece.* London: J. Rodwell, 1835.

Leary, James P. *Wisconsin Folklore.* Madison: University of Wisconsin Press, 1999.

Leatherdale, Clive. *Dracula: The Novel and the Legend: A Study of Bram Stoker's Gothic Masterpiece.* Essex: Desert Island Books, 1993.

Lecouteux, Claude. *The History of the Vampire.* Paris: Éditions Imago, 1999.

Lee, Kit Antares, and Charles Spaegel. *Tanah Tujuh: Close Encounters with the Temuan Mythos.* Kuala Lumpur, Malaysia: Silverfish Books, 2007.

Leeming, David Adams, and Jake Page. *Goddess: Myths of the Female Divine.* New York: Oxford University Press, 1996.

Leeuw, Hendrik De. *Crossroads of the Caribbean Sea.* New York: Garden City, 1968.

Leland, Charles Godfrey. *Etruscan Roman Remains in Popular Tradition.* London: T. F. Unwin, 1892.

_____, and Elizabeth Robins Pennell. *Gypsy Sorcery and Fortune Telling: Illustrated by Numerous Incantations, Specimens of Medical Magic, Anecdotes and Tales.* London: T. Fisher Unwin, 1891.

Leonard, George. *The Asian Pacific American Heritage: A Companion to Literature and Arts.* Oxfordshire: Taylor and Francis, 1999.

Levack, Brian P. *The Witchcraft Sourcebook.* London: Routledge, 2004.

_____. *The Witch-Hunt in Early Modern Europe.* Essex: Pearson Longman, 2006.

Lewis, James R. *Satanism Today: An Encyclopedia of Religion, Folklore, and Popular Culture.* Oxford: ABC-CLIO, 2001.

Lewis, Paul White, and Elaine Lewis. *Peoples of the Golden Triangle: Six Tribes in Thailand.* Bangkok: River Books, 1998.

Leyden, John, and Walter Scott. *Poems and Ballads: With a Memoir by Sir W. Scott, and Suppl. by R. White.* Kelso: J. and J. H. Rutherfurd, 1875.

Lincoln, Bruce. *Myth, Cosmos, and Society: Indo-European Themes of Creation and Destruction.* Cambridge, MA: Harvard University Press, 1986.

Lindahl, Carl, John Lindow, and John McNamara. *Medieval Folklore: An Encyclopedia of Myths, Legends, Tales, Beliefs, and Customs.* Oxford: ABC-CLIO, 2000.

Liverpool, Hollis. *Rituals of Power and Rebellion: The Carnival Tradition in Trinidad and Tobago, 1763–1962.* Chicago: Research Associates School Times, 2001.

The Living Age, vol. 4. Boston: Littell, Son and Company, 1845.

Llosa, Mario Vargas, and Edith Grossman. *Death in the Andes.* New York: Macmillan, 2007.

Lockyer, Norman. *Nature,* vol. 113. New York: Macmillan Journals, 1924.

Lodge, Olive. *Peasant Life in Yugoslavia.* New York: AMS Press, 1981.

Loewenthal, Kate Miriam. *Religion, Culture and Mental Health.* Cambridge: Cambridge University Press, 2007.

Lopatin, Ivan Alexis. *The Cult of the Dead Among the Natives of the Amur Basin.* Paris: Mouton, 1960.

Lopez, Mellie Leandicho. *A Handbook of Philippine Festivals.* Honolulu: University of Hawaii Press, 2003.

Lorentz, Friedrich, Adam Fischer, and Tadeusz Lehr-Spławiński. *The Cassubian Civilization.* London: Faber and Faber, Limited, 1935.

Louis-Frédéric, Käthe Roth. *Japan Encyclopedia.* Cambridge, MA: Harvard University Press, 2005.

Lurker, Manfred. *Dictionary of Gods and Goddesses, Devils and Demons*. London: Routledge Kegan and Paul, 1987.

Luther, Martin, Henry Eyster Jacobs, and Adolph Spaeth. *Works of Martin Luther: With Introductions and Notes*. Philadelphia: A. J. Holman Company, 1931.

Lysaght, Patricia. *The Banshee: The Irish Death Messenger*. Darby, PA: Diane, 1996.

Maberry, Jonathan. *Vampire Universe: The Dark World of Supernatural Beings That Haunt Us, Hunt Us, and Hunger for Us*. Secaucus, NJ: Citadel Press, 1996.

Macafee, Caroline. *A Concise Ulster Dictionary*. New York: Oxford University Press, 1996.

Maccoby, Hyam. *A Pariah People: The Anthropology of Anti-Semitism*. London: Constable, 1996.

MacCulloch, John Arnott. *The Celtic and Scandinavian Religions*. New York: Cosimo, Inc., 2005.

_____, Louis Herbert Gray, and Frantisek Krupicka. *Celtic Mythology*. Boston: Marshall Jones Company, 1918.

MacDermott, Mercia. *Bulgarian Folk Customs*. London: Jessica Kingsley, 1998.

MacDonald, Margaret Read. *The Storyteller's Sourcebook: A Subject, Title, and Motif Index to Folklore Collections for Children*. New York: Neal-Schuman, 1982.

Macdonell, Arthur Anthony. *Vedic Mythology*. Whitefish, MT: Kessinger, 2007.

_____. *A Vedic Reader for Students: Containing Thirty Hymns of the Rigveda in the Original Samhita and Pada Texts*. Oxford: Clarendon Press, 1917.

MacGillivray, Royce. "*Dracula*: Bram Stoker's Spoiled Masterpiece." *Queens Quarterly* 79 (1972): 518–527.

Mack, Carol K., and Dinah Mack. *A Field Guide to Demons, Fairies, Fallen Angels and Other Subversive Spirits*. New York: Arcade, 1998.

Mackay, Charles. *The Gaelic Etymology of the Languages of Western Europe: And More Especially of the English and Lowland Scotch, and Their Slang, Cant, and Colloquial Dialects*. London: Trübner and Company, 1877.

Mackenzie, Andrew. *Dracula Country: Travels and Folk Beliefs in Romania*. London: Barker, 1977.

Mackenzie, Donald A. *Myths of Babylonia and Assyria*. Whitefish, MT: Kessinger Publishing, 2004.

MacKillop, James. *Dictionary of Celtic Mythology*. New York: Oxford University Press, 1998.

Maclean, Calum I. *The Highlands*. London: B. T. Batsford, 1959.

MacPherson, Malcolm. *The Blood of His Servants*. New York: Times Books, 1984.

Madan, T. N. *Non-renunciation: Themes and Interpretations of Hindu Culture*. New York: Oxford University Press, 1987.

Madsen, William. *The Virgin's Children: Life in an Aztec Village Today*. Westport, CT: Greenwood, 1969.

Magyar Tudományos Akadémia. *Acta ethnographica hungarica*, vol. 37. Budapest: Akadémiai Kiadó, 1991.

Mahaffy, John Pentland, and Archibald Henry Sayce. *A History of Classical Greek Literature*. London: Longmans, Green, 1883.

Making of America Project. *The Atlantic Monthly*, vol. 49. Boston: Atlantic Monthly Company, 1882.

_____. *Harper's Magazine*, vol. 10. New York: Harper's Magazine Company, 1855.

Malbrough, Ray T. *Hoodoo Mysteries: Folk Magic, Mysticism and Rituals*. Woodbury, MN: Llewellyn Worldwide, 2003.

Manguel, Alberto, Eric Beddows, James Cook, Graham Greenfield, and Gianni Guadalupi. *The Dictionary of Imaginary Places*. Boston: Houghton Mifflin Harcourt, 2000.

Manoukian, Madeline. *Akan and Ga-Adangme Peoples of the Gold Coast*. New York: Oxford University Press, 1950.

Markale, Jean, and Annie Mygind. *Women of the Celts*. London: G. Cremonesi, 1975.

Markman, Peter T. *The Flayed God: The Mesoamerican Mythological Tradition—Sacred Texts and Images from Pre-Columbian Mexico and Central America*. San Francisco: Harper, 1992.

Marra, Michael F. *Japanese Hermeneutics: Current Debates on Aesthetics and Interpretation*. Honolulu: University of Hawaii Press, 2002.

Martin, Joel W. *Sacred Revolt: The Muskogees' Struggle for a New World*. Boston: Beacon Press, 1993.

Marwick, Ernest Walker. *The Folklore of Orkney and Shetland*. Lanham, MD: Rowman and Littlefield, 1975.

_____, and J. D. M. Robertson. *An Orkney Anthology: The Selected Works of Ernest Walker Marwick*. Edinburgh: Scottish Academic Press, 1991.

Marwick, Max. *Witchcraft and Sorcery: Selected Readings*. New York: Penguin Books, 1982.

Massé, Henri. *Persian Beliefs and Customs*. New Haven: Human Relations Area Files, 1954.

Massola, Aldo. *Bunjil's Cave: Myths, Legends and Superstitions of the Aborigines of South-East Australia*. Melbourne, Australia: Lansdowne Press, 1968.

Masson, Hervé. *Le diable et la possession démoniaque: exorcismes et exorcistes: Possession et possédés dans le monde contemporain*. Paris: P. Belfond, 1975.

Masters, Anthony. *The Natural History of the Vampire*. London: Hart-Davis, 1972.

Masters, R. E. L. *Eros and Evil: The Sexual Psychopathology of Witchcraft, Contains the Complete*

Text of Sinistrari's Demoniality. New York: Viking Press, 1974.

Mayer, Philip. *Townsmen or Tribesmen: Conservatism and the Process of Urbanization in a South African City.* New York: Oxford University Press, 1971.

McAndrew, John P. *People of Power: A Philippine Worldview of Spirit Encounters.* Quezon City, Philippines: Ateneo de Manila University Press, 2001.

McClelland, Bruce. *Slayers and Their Vampires: A Cultural History of Killing the Dead.* Ann Arbor: University of Michigan Press, 2006.

McCormack, Anthony M. *The Earldom of Desmond 1463–1583: The Decline and Crisis of a Feudal Lordship.* Dublin, Ireland: Four Courts Press, 2005.

McDonald, Beth E. *The Vampire as Numinous Experience: Spiritual Journeys with the Undead in British and American Literature.* Jefferson, NC: McFarland, 2004.

McHugh, James Noel. *Hantu Hantu: An Account of Ghost Belief in Modern Malaya.* Singapore: D. Moore for Eastern Universities Press, 1959.

McKinnell, John, Klaus Düwel, and Rudolf Simek. *Runes, Magic and Religion: A Sourcebook.* Vienna, Austria: Fassbaender, 2004.

McKinnell, John, and Rudolf Simek with Klaus Düwel. *Runes, Magic and Religion: A Sourcebook.* Vienna, Austria: Fassbaender, 2004.

McLean, Stuart John. *The Event and Its Terrors: Ireland, Famine, Modernity.* Stanford: Stanford University Press, 2004.

McLeish, Kenneth. *Myth: Myths and Legends of the World Explored.* New York: Facts on File, 1996.

McNally, Raymond T. *A Clutch of Vampires: These Being Among the Best from History and Literature.* New York: New York Graphic Society, 1974.

_____, and Radu Florescu. *In Search of Dracula, the History of Dracula and Vampires.* Boston: Mariner Books, 1994.

M'Dowall, William. *Among the Old Scotch Minstrels: Studying Their Ballads of War, Love, Social Life, Folk-lore and Fairyland.* Edinburgh: D. Douglas, 1888.

Mead, Margaret, and Nicolas Calas. *Primitive Heritage: An Anthropological Anthology.* New York: Random House, 1953.

The Melbourne Review 10, no. 37–40. Melbourne, Australia: George, Robertson and Company, 1882.

Melland, Frank Hulme. *In Witch-Bound Africa: An Account of the Primitive Kaonde Tribe and Their Beliefs.* London: Seeley, Service and Company, Limited, 1923.

Melton, J. Gordon. *The Vampire Book: The Encyclopedia of the Undead.* Canton, MI: Visible Ink Press, 1999.

Mercatante, Anthony S. *Good and Evil: Mythology and Folklore.* New York: Harper and Row, 1978.

Mercier, Christophe, Kathryn A. Edwards, and Susie Speakman Sutch. *Leonarde's Ghost: Popular Piety and "The Appearance of a Spirit" in 1628.* Kirksville, MO: Truman State University, 2008.

Mercier, Vivian. *The Irish Comic Tradition.* Oxford: Clarendon Press, 1962.

Merrett, Robert James. *Man and Nature: Proceedings of the Canadian Society for Eighteenth-Century Studies.* Kelowna, Canada: Academic Printing and Publishing, 1984.

Messadié, Gérald, and Marc Romano. *A History of the Devil.* Bunkyo, Japan: Kodansha International, 1996.

Metcalf, Peter, and Richard Huntington. *Celebrations of Death: The Anthropology of Mortuary Ritual.* Cambridge: Cambridge University Press, 1991.

Métraux, Alfred. *Voodoo in Haiti.* New York: Oxford University Press, 1959.

Mew, James. *Traditional Aspects of Hell: Ancient and Modern.* London: S. Sonnenschein, 1903.

Meyer, Elard Hugo. *Mythologie der Germanen.* Strazburg, Germany: Karl J. Trübner, 1903.

Meyer, Johann Jakob. *Sexual Life in Ancient India: A Study in the Comparative History of Indian Culture.* New Delhi, India: Motilal Banarsidass, 1989.

Meyerson, Julia. *Tambo: Life in an Andean Village.* Austin: University of Texas Press, 1990.

Michael, Carroll. *From a Persian Tea House: Travels in Old Iran.* London: Tauris Parke Paperbacks, 2007.

Minnis, Natalie. *Chile.* New York: Langenscheidt, 2002.

Mladen, Davidovic. *Dutch-English, English-Dutch Dictionary: With a Brief Introduction to Dutch Grammar.* New York: Hippocrene Books, 1990.

Modern Asian Studies, vol. 19. Cambridge: Cambridge University Press, 1985.

Moeljo, Djoko. *Bali, the World's Belonging.* Semarang, Indonesia: Dahara Prize, 1993.

Moffat, James Clement. *A Comparative History of Religions.* New York: Dodd and Mead, 1889.

Moilanen, Irene. *Last of the Great Masters? Woodcarving Traditions in Myanmar—Past and Present.* Jyväskylä, Finland: University of Jyväskylä, 1995.

Monaghan, Patricia. *Women in Myth and Legend.* London: Junction Books, 1981.

Moon, Beverly. *An Encyclopedia of Archetypal Symbolism,* vol. 1. Boston: Shambhala, 1997.

Mooney, James. *Myths of the Cherokee and Sacred Formulas of the Cherokees.* Fairview, NC: Bright Mountain Books, 1992.

Moorey, Teresa. *The Fairy Bible.* New York: Sterling, 2008.

Morgenstern, Julian, and Paul Tice. *The Doctrine of Sin in the Babylonian Religion.* San Diego: Book Tree, 2002.

Morris, Katherine. *Sorceress or Witch? The Image of Gender in Medieval Iceland and Northern Europe.* Lanham, MD: University Press of America, 1991.

Motley, James. Tales of the Cymry: with Notes, Illustrative and Explanatory. London: Longmans and Paternostersro, 1848.

Muchembled, Robert, and Jean Birrell. *A History of the Devil: From the Middle Ages to the Present.* New York: Wiley-Blackwell, 2003.

Muir, Henry Dupee. *Songs and Other Fancies.* Chicago: Henry Dupee Muir, 1901.

Muller, "Among Caribbean Devils and Duppies." *The Century Illustrated Monthly Magazine* LXXXVIII (May 1914–Oct. 1914). New York: The Century Company, 1914.

Murphy, Jan. *Mysteries and Legends of Colorado: True Stories of the Unsolved and Unexplained.* Guilford, CT: Globe Pequot, 2007.

Muss-Arnolt, William. *A Concise Dictionary of the Assyrian Language.* Berlin: Reuther and Reichard, 1905.

Myres, John Linton, Aylward Manley Blackman, John Percival Droop, Percy Edward Newberry, and Thomas Eric Peet. *Annals of Archaeology and Anthropology*, vol. 2. Liverpool: University Press of Liverpool, 1909.

Myring, Lynn. *Vampires, Werewolves and Demons.* London: Usborne, 1979.

Nan Nü. Men, Women, and Gender in Early and Imperial China. Boston: Brill, 1999.

Nansen, Fridtjof. *Eskimo Life.* London: Longmans, Green, 1894.

National Psychological Association for Psychoanalysis of the United States. *The Psychoanalytic Review*, vol. 4. New York: W. A. White and S. E. Jelliffe, 1917.

Neale, John Mason. *A History of the Holy Eastern Church*, vol. 2. London: J. Masters, 1850.

Needham, Joseph, Francesca Bray, Christian Daniels, Peter J. Golas, Christoph Harbsmeier, H. T. Huang, Dieter Kuhn, Nicholas K. Menzies, Tsuen-Hsuin Tsien, and Ling Wang. *Science and Civilisation in China.* Cambridge: Cambridge University Press, 2000.

Nemet-Nejat, Karen Rhea. *Daily Life in Ancient Mesopotamia.* Westport, CT: Greenwood Publishing Group, 1998.

New York Folklore Society. *New York Folklore Quarterly*, vol. 29–30. Ithaca: Cornell Univ. Press, 1973.

Nguyen, Trieu Dan. *A Vietnamese Family Chronicle: Twelve Generations on the Banks of the Hat River.* Jefferson, NC: McFarland, 1991.

Nicholson, Irene, and Cottie Arthur Burland. *Mexican and Central American Mythology.* London: Newnes, 1983.

Nickell, Joe. *The Mystery Chronicles: More Real-Life X-Files.* Lexington: University Press of Kentucky, 2004.

The Nineteenth Century and After: A Monthly Review 63 (Jan.–June 1908). London: Spottiswoode and Company, 1908.

Noyes, Deborah. *Encyclopedia of the End: Mysterious Death in Fact, Fancy, Folklore, and More.* Boston: Houghton Mifflin, 2008.

Núñez, Benjamín. *Dictionary of Afro-Latin American Civilization.* Westport, CT: Greenwood, 1980.

Nuzum, Eric. *The Dead Travel Fast: Stalking Vampires from Nosferatu to Count Chocula.* New York: Macmillan, 2007.

Nyarlathotep and Jesse Lindsay. *Ardeth—The Made Vampire.* Raleigh, NC: Lulu.com, 2006.

O'Brien, Christopher. *Secrets of the Mysterious Valley.* Kempton, IL: Adventures Unlimited Press, 2007.

O'Connor, Frank. *A Book of Ireland.* Glasgow, Scotland: Collins, 1960.

O'Donnell, Elliott. *Confessions of a Ghost Hunter.* Whitefish, MT: Kessinger, 2003.

O'Driscoll, Dennis. *Hidden Extras.* London: Anvil Press Poetry, 1988.

Oeconomides, D. B. "Yello danes les Traditions des peoples Hellenique et Roumain." *International Congress for Folk Narrative Research in Athens* [Athens] (1965): 328–334.

Oesterley, W. O. E. *Immortality and the Unseen World: A Study in Old Testament Religion 1921.* Whitefish, MT: Kessinger, 2004.

Ogilvie, John, and Charles Annandale. *The Imperial Dictionary of the English Language.* Glasgow, Scotland: Blackie and Son, 1883.

Oinas, Felix J. *Essays on Russian Folklore and Mythology.* Bloomington: Slavica Publishers, 1985.

Olsen, Karin E., and L. A. J. R. Houwen. *Monsters and the Monstrous in Medieval Northwest Europe.* Wilsele, Belgium: Peeters, 2001.

Oosthuizen, Gerhardus Cornelis. *Afro-Christian Religion and Healing in Southern Africa.* Lewiston, NY: E. Mellen Press, 1989.

Ouellette, Jennifer. *The Physics of the Buffyverse.* New York: Penguin, 2006.

Owusu, Heike. *Voodoo Rituals: A User's Guide.* New York: Sterling, 2002.

Paglia, C. *Sexual Personae: Art and Decadence from Nefertiti to Emily Dickinson.* New York: Penguin 1992.

Pakistan Historical Society. *Journal of the Pakistan Historical Society*, vol. 26. Karachi, Pakistan: Pakistan Historical Society, 1978.

Palgrave, Francis, Geoffrey Palgrave Barker, and Robert Harry Inglis Palgrave. *The Collected Historical Works of Sir Francis Palgrave, in 10 volumes*, vol. 7. London: Cambridge University Press, 1921.

Pálsson, Hermann, and Paul Geoffrey Edwards. *Eyrbyggja Saga.* New York: Penguin Classics, 1989.

Pandolfo, Stefania. *Impasse of the Angels: Scenes from a Moroccan Space of Memory*. Chicago: University of Chicago Press, 1997.

Paraiso, Salvador, and Jose Juan Paraiso. *The Balete Book: A Collection of Demons, Monsters, Elves and Dwarfs from the Philippine Lower Mythology*. Quezon City, Philippines: Giraffe Books, 2003.

Pareto, Vilfredo. *The Mind and Society: A Treatise on General Sociology*. Mineola, NY: Dover, 1935.

Parsons, Elsie Worthington Clews. *Folk-lore of the Antilles, French and English*. Austin: The American Folk-lore Society, 1943.

Pashley, Robert. *Travels in Crete*. London: John Murray, 1837.

Paulist Fathers. *The Catholic World, a Monthly Magazine of Literature and Science* 21 (April–Sept. 1875). New York: The Catholic Publication Society, 1875.

Paxson, Margaret. *Solovyovo: The Story of Memory in a Russian Village*. Bloomington: Indiana University Press, 2005.

Payne, Edward John. *History of the New World Called America*. Oxford: Clarendon Press, 1892.

Peabody, Selim Hobart, and Charles Francis Richardson. *The International Cyclopedia: A Compendium of Human Knowledge, rev. with large additions*. New York: Dodd and Mead, 1898.

Pearson, Karl. *The Chances of Death, and Other Studies in Evolution: Woman as witch. Ashiepattle. Kindred group-marriage. The German passion-play. Appendix: And Other Studies in Evolution*. London: E. Arnold, 1897.

Pearson, Raymond. *National Minorities in Eastern Europe, 1848–1945*. Hampshire: Palgrave Macmillan, 1983.

Peek, Philip M., and Kwesi Yankah. *African Folklore: An Encyclopedia*. Oxfordshire: Taylor and Francis, 2004.

Perez, Tony, and Cecille Legazpi. *Beings: Encounters of the Spirit Questors with Non-Human Entities*. Wrentham, MA: Anvil, 1999.

Perkowski, Jan Louis. *The Darkling: A Treatise on Slavic Vampirism*. Columbus, OH: Slavica Publishers, 1989.

_____. *Vampires of the Slavs*. Columbus, OH: Slavica Publishers, 1976.

Perrot, Georges, Walter Armstrong, and Charles Chipiez. *A History of Art in Chaldæa and Assyria*. London: Chapman and Hall, 1884.

Perusse, Roland I. *Historical Dictionary of Haiti*. Lanham, MD: Scarecrow Press, 1977.

Petrinovich, Lewis F. *The Cannibal Within*. New Brunswick, NJ: Aldine Transaction, 2000.

Petrovich, Woislav M. *Hero Tales and Legends of the Serbs*. London: G. Harrap, 1914, 1915, 1923.

Petzoldt, Ruth, and Paul Neubauer. *Demons: Mediators Between This World and the Other—Essays on Demonic Beings from the Middle Ages to the Present*. New York: Peter Lang, 1998.

Phillips, Charles, and Michael Kerrigan. *Forests of the Vampire: Slavic Myth*. Amsterdam: Time-Life Books BV, 1999.

Phillpotts, Eden. *Loup-Garou!* London: Sands and Company, 1899.

Philp, Howard Littleton, and Carl Gustav Jung. *Jung and the Problem of Evil*. London: Rockliff, 1958.

Philpott, Stuart B. *West Indian Migration: The Montserrat Case*. London: Athlone Press, 1973.

Phongphit, Seri, and Kevin Hewison. *Thai Village Life: Culture and Transition in the Northeast*. Bangkok: Munnithi Muban, 1990.

Pliny, John Bostock, and Henry Thomas Riley. *The Natural History of Pliny*. London: H. G. Bohn, 1857.

Plutarch, and John Langhorne, trans. *Lives, Translated from the Original Greek: With Notes, Critical and Historical; and a Life of Plutarch*. New York: Harper and Brothers, 1860.

Pócs, Éva. *Between the Living and the Dead: A Perspective on Witches and Seers in the Early Modern Age*. Budapest: Central European University Press, 1999.

_____. *Fairies and Witches at the Boundary of South-Eastern and Central Europe*. Helsinki, Finland: Suomalainen Tiedeakatemia, 1989.

Point Park College, Pennsylvania Folklore Society. *Keystone Folklore Quarterly* 1–17. Pittsburgh: Point Park College, 1956.

Polidori, John William. *The Vampyre: A Tale*. London: Sherwood, Neely, and Jones, 1819.

Pollack, David. *Reading Against Culture: Ideology and Narrative in the Japanese Novel*. Ithaca: Cornell University Press, 1992.

Polomé, Edgar C., and Roger Pearson. *Perspectives on Indo-European Language, Culture and Religion: Studies in Honor of Edgar C. Polomé*, vol. 2. Washington, D.C.: Institute for the Study of Man, 1992.

Pomfret, John. *Chinese Lessons: Five Classmates and the Story of the New China*. New York: Macmillan, 2006.

Porter, Enid. *The Folklore of East Anglia*. Lanham, MD: Rowman and Littlefield, 1974.

Pottier, Edmond. *Catalogue des antiquités assyriennes*. Paris: Musées Nationaux, 1924.

Poulton, M. Cody. *Spirits of Another Sort: The Plays of Izumi Kyoka*. Ann Arbor: The University of Michigan, 2001.

Prahlad, Anand. *The Greenwood Encyclopedia of African American Folklore: A–F*. Westport, CT: Greenwood, 2006.

Pranandu, Mihindukulasurya Ar. Pi. Susanta. *Rit-*

uals, *Folk Beliefs, and Magical Arts of Sri Lanka*. Sri Lanka, India: S. Godage and Brothers, 2000.

Preece, Warren E., ed. *The New Encyclopaedia Britannica*, vol. 30. Chicago: Encyclopaedia Britannica, 1974.

Price, Ardin C., and Trishina Leszczyc. *The Dracula Cookbook of Blood*. Alabama: Mugwort Soup Publications, 1993.

Prince, Albertine. *The Remains of Folklore in Shropshire*. Madison: University of Wisconsin, 1915.

Proceedings—Pacific Northwest Conference on Foreign Languages, vol. 15. Eugene, OR: Pacific Northwest Conference on Foreign Languages, 1964.

Pughe, William Owen. *A Dictionary of the Welsh Language, explained in English: with numerous illustrations, from the literary remains and from the living speech of the Cymmry. To which is prefixed, a Welsh grammar*. London: Thomas Gee, 1832.

Radford, Edwin. *Encyclopedia of Superstitions 1949*. Whitefish, MT: Kessinger, 2004.

Radosavljevich, Paul Rankov. *Who Are the Slavs? A Contribution to Race Psychology*. Boston: R. G. Badger, 1919.

Rae, Simon. *Breath Becomes the Wind: Old and New in Karo Religion*. Dunedin, New Zealand: University of Otago Press, 1994.

Rafinesque, Constantine Samuel. *Genius and Spirit of the Hebrew Bible: Including the Biblic Philosophy of Celestial Wisdom, Religion and Theology, Astronomy and Realization, Ontology and Mythology, Chronometry and Mathematics. Being the First Series of Biblic Truths, Ascertained and Explained by the True Restored Names*. Philadelphia: The Eleutherium of Knowledge, 1838.

Ralston, William R. Sheddon. *Russian Folktales*. London: Smith, Elder, and Company, 1873.

Ramos, Maximo D. *The Aswang Syncrasy in Philippine Folklore: with illustrative accounts in vernacular texts and translations*. Quezon City, Philippines: Philippine Folklore Society, 1971.

_____. *The Creatures of Midnight: Faded Deities of Luzon, the Visayas and Mindanao*. Quezon City, Philippines: Island Publishers, 1967.

_____. *Creatures of Philippine Lower Mythology*. Diliman, Philippines: University of the Philippines Press, 1971.

Ramsland, Katherine M. *The Science of Vampires*. New York: Berkley Books, 2002.

Randles, Jenny, Peter A. Hough, and Jason Hurst. *World's Best "True" UFO Stories*. New York: Sterling, 1995.

Rappoport, Angelo Solomon, and J. H. Amshewisz. *Myth and Legend of Ancient Israel*. London: Gresham, 1928.

Rattray, Robert Sutherland, and Johann Gottlieb Christaller. *Ashanti Proverbs: The Primitive Ethics of a Savage People*. Oxford: Clarendon Press, 1916.

Reader's Digest, eds. *Strange Stories, Amazing Facts: Stories That Are Bizarre, Unusual, Odd, Astonishing, and Often Incredible*. New York: Reader's Digest Association, Inc., 1976.

Reddall, Henry Frederic. *Fact, Fancy, and Fable: A New Handbook for Ready Reference on Subjects Commonly Omitted from Cyclopaedias; Comprising Personal Sobriquets, Familiar Phrases, Popular Appellations, Geographical Nicknames, Literary Pseudonyms, Mythological Characters, Red-Letter Days, Political Slang, Contractions*. Chicago: A. C. McClurg, 1892.

Redfern, Nicholas, and Andy Roberts. *Strange Secrets: Real Government Files on the Unknown*. New York: Simon and Schuster, 2003.

Reed, A.W. *Aboriginal Fables and Legendary Tales*. Chatswood, Australia: New Holland Publishing, 2006.

Reichel-Dolmatoff, Gerardo. *The Shaman and the Jaguar: A Study of Narcotic Drugs Among the Indians of Colombia*. Philadelphia: Temple University Press, 1975.

Reventlow, Ernst. *The Vampire of the Continent*. Bellevue, IA: The Jackson Press, 1916.

Reyes, Soledad S. *Tellers of Tales, Singers of Songs: Selected Critical Essays*. Malate, Manila: De La Salle University Press, 2001.

Reynolds, Barrie. *Magic, Divination, and Witchcraft Among the Barotse of Northern Rhodesia*. Berkeley: University of California Press, 1963.

Rhys, John. *Celtic Folklore, Welsh and Manx*. Oxford: Clarendon Press, 1901.

Riccardo, Martin V. *Liquid Dreams of Vampires*. Woodbury, MN: Llewellyn Publications, 1996.

_____. *Vampires Unearthed: The Complete Multimedia Vampire and Dracula Bibliography*. New York: Garland, 1983.

Richardson, J. Michael, and J. Douglas Rabb. *The Existential Joss Whedon: Evil and Human Freedom in* Buffy the Vampire Slayer, Angel, Firefly *and* Serenity. Jefferson, NC: McFarland, 2006.

Richardson, Maurice. "The Psychoanalysis of Ghost Stories." *The Twentieth Century* 166 (1959): 419–431.

Rickels, Laurence A. *The Vampire Lectures*. Minneapolis: University of Minnesota Press, 1999.

Ridpath, John Clark, ed. *The Standard American Encyclopedia of Arts, Sciences, History, Biography, Geography, Statistics, and General Knowledge*, vol. 7. New York: The Encyclopedia Publishing Company, 1899.

Rigaud, Milo, Robert B. Cross, and Odette Mennesson-Rigaud. *Secrets of Voodoo*. Sylva, NC: City Lights Books, 1969.

Rink, Henry. *Tales and Traditions of the Eskimo: with a sketch of their habits, religion, language and other peculiarities.* London: William Blackwood and Sons, 1875.

Ripley, George, and Charles Anderson Dana. *The New American Cyclopædia: A Popular Dictionary of General Knowledge.* New York: Appleton, 1869.

Ritson, Joseph: *Ancient Engleish Metrical Romances.* London: W. Bulmer and Company, 1802.

Rivière, Jean M., and H. E. Kennedy. *Tantrik Yoga: Hindu and Tibetan.* Newburyport, MA: S. Weiser, 1970.

Robbins, Richard Howard. *Global Problems and the Culture of Capitalism.* Boston: Allyn and Bacon, 1998.

Robbins, Rossell Hope. *The Encyclopedia of Witchcraft and Demonology.* New York: Crown, 1959.

Robinson, Fred C. *The Tomb of Beowulf and Other Essays on Old English.* Cambridge, MA: Blackwell, 1993.

Robinson, Herbert Spencer, and Knox Wilson. *Myths and Legends of All Nations.* New York: Garden City, 1950.

Roces, Alfredo, and Grace Roces. *Culture Shock! Philippines.* New York: Times Books International, 1986.

Rodd, Rennell, James Rennell, and Tristan James Ellis. *The Customs and Lore of Modern Greece.* London: D. Stott, 1892.

Rodell, Paul A. *Culture and Customs of the Philippines.* Westport, CT: Greenwood, 2002.

Rodrigues, Etienne Alexander. *The Complete Hindoo Pantheon, Comprising the Principal Deities Worshipped by the Natives of British India Throughout Hindoostan: Being a Collection of the Gods and Goddesses Accompanied by a Succinct History and Descriptive of the Idols.* Vepery Madres, India: Oriental Lithograph Press, 1842.

Rogers, Robert William. *The Religion of Babylonia and Assyria, Especially in Its Relations to Israel: Five Lectures Delivered at Harvard University.* New York: Eaton and Mains, 1908.

Róheim, Géza, and Alan Dundes. *Fire in the Dragon and Other Psychoanalytic Essays on Folklore.* Princeton, NJ: Princeton University Press, 1992.

Róheim, Géza, and Roger Ernle Money-Kyrle. *The Riddle of the Sphinx: Or, Human Origins.* London: Hogarth Press, 1934.

Roma, vol. 3. Lancashire: Roma Publications, 1977.

Ronay, Gabriel. *The Dracula Myth.* London: W. H. Allen, 1972.

_____. *The Truth About Dracula.* New York: Stein and Day, 1972.

Roraff, Susan, and Laura Comacho. *Chile.* Portland, OR: Publisher Graphic Arts Center, 2001.

Roscher, Wilhelm Heinrich, and Hillman, James. *Pan and the nightmare, being the only translation (from the German by A. V. O'Brien) of Ephialtes: a pathological-mythological treatise on the nightmare in classical antiquity, together with an essay on Pan, serving as a psychological introduction to Roscher's Ephialtes by James Hillman.* New York: Spring Publications, 1972.

Rose, Carol. *Giants, Monsters, and Dragons: An Encyclopedia of Folklore, Legend, and Myth.* New York: W. W. Norton, 2001.

_____. *Spirits, Fairies, Gnomes, and Goblins: An Encyclopedia of the Little People.* Oxford: ABC-CLIO, 1996.

Rose, Herbert Jennings. *A Handbook of Greek Mythology.* New York: E. P. Dutton, 1959.

Roth, Henry Ling, Andrew Lang, and Hugh Brooke Low. *The Natives of Sarawak and British North Borneo: Based Chiefly on the Mss. of the Late H. B. Low, Sarawak Government Service.* London: Truslove and Hanson, 1896.

Roth, John E. *American Elves: An Encyclopedia of Little People from the Lore of 380 Ethnic Groups of the Western Hemisphere.* Jefferson, NC: McFarland, 1997.

Roucek, Joseph Slabey. *Slavonic Encyclopaedia.* New York: Philosophical Library, 1949.

Rowthorn, Chris, John Ashburne, David Atkinson, Andrew Bender, and Craig McLachlan. *Japan.* Victoria, Australia: Lonely Planet, 2003.

Roy, Brajdeo Prasad. *The Later Vedic Economy.* Patna, India: Janaki Prakashan, 1984.

Royal Anthropological Institute of Great Britain and Ireland. *Indian Antiquary.* Delhi, India: Swati Publications, 1897.

_____. *Indian Antiquary*, vol. 58. Delhi, India: Swati Publications, 1929.

_____. *Journal of the Royal Anthropological Institute of Great Britain and Ireland*, vol. 10. London: Royal Anthropological Institute, 1881.

_____. *Man*, vol. 23–25. London: Royal Anthropological Institute, 1888.

Royal Society of Antiquaries of Ireland. *Journal of the Royal Society of Antiquaries of Ireland*, vol. 72–73. Dublin, Ireland: The Society, 1942.

Rubin, Miri. *Corpus Christi: The Eucharist in Late Medieval Culture.* Cambridge: Cambridge University Press, 1992.

Ruether, Rosemary Radford. *Goddesses and the Divine Feminine: A Western Religious History.* Berkeley: University of California Press, 2006.

Rulandus, Martinus. *Lexicon of Alchemy.* Whitefish, MT: Kessinger, 1992.

Russell, Alexander David. *Legends of the Bocas, Trinidad.* London: C. Palmer, 1922.

Russell, Jeffrey Burton. *Witchcraft in the Middle Ages.* Ithaca: Cornell University Press, 1972.

Russo, Arlene. *Vampire Nation*. Woodbury, MN: Llewellyn Worldwide, 2008.

Ryan, William Francis. *The Bathhouse at Midnight: An Historical Survey of Magic and Divination in Russia*. University Park: Penn State Press, 1999.

_____. *Russian Magic at the British Library: Books, Manuscripts, Scholars, Travelers*. London: British Library, 2006.

St. Clair, Sheila. *Mysterious Ireland*. Kent: Robert Hale Ltd., 1994.

St. John, Robert. *Through Malan's Africa*. Garden City, NY: Doubleday, 1954.

Salas, Elizabeth. *Soldaderas in the Mexican Military: Myth and History*. Austin: University of Texas Press, 1990.

Saletore, Rajaram Narayan. *Indian Witchcraft*. New Delhi, India: Abhinav Publications, 1981.

Santiago, Fundación, Guadalupe Forés-Ganzon, and Luis Mañeru. *La Solidaridad*. Pasig City, Philippines: Fundación Santiago, 1996.

Sarkar, Benoy Kumar. *The Folk Element in Hindu Culture: A Contribution to Socio Religious Studies in Hindu Folk Institutions*. Whitefish, MT: Kessinger, 2004.

Saunders, G. E. *Borneo Folktales and Legends*. Kuching: Borneo Literature Bureau, 1976.

Saxo, Oliver Elton and Frederick York Powell, eds. *The First Nine Books of the Danish History of Saxo Grammaticus*. Madison, AL: Norrœna Society, 1906.

Sayce, Archibald Henry. *The Religions of Ancient Egypt and Babylonia: The Gifford Lectures on the Ancient Egyptian and Babylonian Conception of the Divine Delivered in Aberdeen*. New York: T. and T. Clark, 1903.

Scarborough, Dorothy. *The Supernatural in Modern English Fiction*. New York: G. P. Putnam's Sons, 1917.

Schapera, Isaac. *The Bantu-Speaking Peoples of Southern Africa: An Ethnographical Survey*. London: Routledge and K. Paul, 1937.

Schiefner, Anton, William Ralston, and Shedden Ralston. *Tibetan Tales, Derived from Indian Sources*. Boston: James R. Osgood, 1882.

Schmalstieg, William R. *An Introduction to Old Church Slavic*. Bloomington: Slavica Publishers, 1983.

Schwarcz, Vera. *Place and Memory in the Singing Crane Garden*. Philadelphia: University of Pennsylvania Press, 2008.

Schwartz, Howard. *Reimagining the Bible: The Storytelling of the Rabbis*. New York: Oxford University Press, 1998.

_____, and Caren Loebel-Fried. *Tree of Souls*. New York: Oxford University Press, 2004.

Scobie, Alastair. *Murder for Magic: Witchcraft in Africa*. London: Cassell, 1965.

Scott, James George, and John Percy Hardiman.

Gazetteer of Upper Burma and the Shan States. New York: AMS Press, 1900.

Sebald, Hans. *Witchcraft: The Heritage of a Heresy*. St. Louis: Elsevier, 1978.

Seekins, Donald M. *Historical Dictionary of Burma (Myanmar)*. Lanham, MD: Rowman and Littlefield, 2006.

Selby, Martha Ann, and Indira Viswanathan Peterson. *Tamil Geographies: Cultural Constructions of Space and Place in South India*. Albany: SUNY Press, 2008.

Seler, Eduard, Augustus Henry Keane, and Joseph Florimond Loubat. *Codex Fejérváry-Mayer: An Old Mexican Picture Manuscript in the Liverpool Free Public Museums*. London: T. and A. Constable, 1902.

Senf, Carol A. *Science and Social Science in Bram Stoker's Fiction*. Westport, CT: Greenwood, 2002.

_____. *The Vampire in Nineteenth-Century English Literature*. Bowling Green, OH: Bowling Green State University Popular Press, 1988.

Senn, Harry A. *Were-wolf and Vampire in Romania*. Boulder: East European Monographs, 1982.

Serag, Sebastian Sta. Cruz. *The Remnants of the Great Ilonggo Nation*. Quezon City, Philippines: Rex Bookstore, Inc., 1997.

Sha, Sirdar Ikbal Ali. *Occultism, Its Theory and Practice*. Whitefish, MT: Kessinger, 2003.

Shashi, Shyam Singh. *Encyclopedia Indica*. New Delhi, India: Anmol, 1996.

_____. *Roma, the Gypsy World*. New Delhi, India: Sundeep Prakashan, 1990.

Shastri, Jagdish Lal. *Ancient Indian Tradition and Mythology*. India: Delhi Varanasi Patna Motilal Banarsidass, 1969.

Shendge, Malati J. *The Civilized Demons: The Harappans in Rigveda*. New Delhi, India: Abhinav Publications, 2003.

Shepard, Leslie, Nandor Fodor, and Lewis Spence. *Encyclopedia of Occultism and Parapsychology*. Detroit: Gale, 1985.

Shipley, Joseph Twadell. *Dictionary of Early English*. New York: Philosophical Library, 1955.

Shirane, Haruo, and Sonja Arntzen. *Traditional Japanese Literature: An Anthology, Beginnings to 1600*. New York: Columbia University Press, 2007.

Shoumatoff, Alex. *Legends of the American Desert: Sojourns in the Greater Southwest*. New York: Alfred A. Knopf, 1997.

Shuker, Karl. *The Beasts That Hide from Man: Seeking the World's Last Undiscovered Animals*. New York: Cosimo, Inc., 2003.

Silver, Alain, and James Ursini. *The Vampire Film: From Nosferatu to Interview with the Vampire*. Pompton Plains, NJ: Limelight Editions, 1997.

Silver, Carole G., and Calvert Watkins. *Strange and Secret Peoples: Fairies and Victorian Consciousness.* New York: Oxford University Press, 2000.

Simpson, George Eaton. *Religious Cults of the Caribbean: Trinidad, Jamaica, and Haiti.* Río Piedras, Puerto Rico: University of Puerto Rico, 1970.

Singh, Madanjeet. *The Sun: Symbol of Power and Life.* New York: H. N. Abrams, 1993.

Singh, Nagendra Kr. *Vedic Mythology.* New Delhi, India: APH Publishing, 1997.

Sinha, Abdhesh Prasad. *Religious Life in Tribal India: A Case-Study of Dudh Kharia.* New Delhi, India: Classical Publishing Company, 1989.

Skal, David J. *Hollywood Gothic: The Tangled Web of Dracula from Novel to Stage to Screen.* New York: Macmillan, 2004.

Skeat, Walter William. *Malay Magic.* New York: Macmillan, 1900.

_____, and Charles Otto Blagden. *Pagan Races of the Malay Peninsula.* New York: Macmillan, 1906.

Slate, Joe H. *Psychic Vampires: Protection from Energy Predators and Parasites.* Woodbury, MN: Llewellyn Worldwide, 2002.

Slater, Candace. *Dance of the Dolphin: Transformation and Disenchantment in the Amazonian Imagination.* Chicago: University of Chicago Press, 1994.

Sluijter, Paula Catharina Maria. *Ijslands volksgeloof.* Haarlem, Netherlands: H. D. Tjeenk Willink and Zoon n.v., 1936.

Smedley, Edward, Elihu Rich, William Cooke Taylor, and Henry Thompson. *The Occult Sciences: Sketches of the Traditions and Superstitions of Past Times, and the Marvels of the Present Day.* Boston: Adamant Media Corporation, 2001.

Smith, Frederick M. *The Self Possessed: Deity and Spirit Possession in South Asian Literature and Civilization.* New York: Columbia University Press, 2006.

Smith, George, Archibald Henry Sayce, Society for Promoting Christian Knowledge of Great Britain. *Assyria from the Earliest Times to the Fall of Nineveh.* London: Society for Promoting Christian Knowledge, 1897.

Smith, Michael Llewellyn. *The Great Island: A Study of Crete.* Essex: Longmans, 1965.

Smith, Richard Gordon, and Mo-No-Yuk. *Ancient Tales and Folklore of Japan: By Richard Gordon Smith.* London: A. and C. Black, 1908.

Smith, Robert John. *Ancestor Worship in Contemporary Japan.* Stanford: Stanford University Press, 1974.

Smith, William Ramsay. *Myths and Legends of the Australian Aboriginals.* London: George G. Harrap, 1930.

Sofer, Andrew. *The Stage Life of Props.* Ann Arbor: University of Michigan Press, 2003.

Somany, Ganga. *Shiva and Shakti: Mythology and Art.* Jaipur, India: Bookwise, 2002.

Sotesiri, Roj. *The Study of Puan Community, Pho Si Village, Tambon Bang Pla Ma, Suphan Buri.* Bangkok: Office of the National Culture Commission, Ministry of Education, 1982.

Soustelle, Jacques. *Daily Life of the Aztecs, on the Eve of the Spanish Conquest, Jacques Soustelle.* Stanford: Stanford University Press, 1970.

South, Malcolm. *Mythical and Fabulous Creatures: A Source Book and Research Guide.* Westport, CT: Greenwood, 1987.

Southern Illinois University at Carbondale. *Southeast Asia.* Carbondale: Center for Vietnamese Studies, Southern Illinois University at Carbondale, 1971.

Southey, Robert. *Thalaba the Destroyer.* London: Longman, Hurst, Rees, Orme, and Brown, 1814.

Spaulding, A. Timothy. *Re-forming the Past: History, the Fantastic, and the Postmodern Slave Narrative.* Columbus: Ohio State University Press, 2005.

Spence, Lewis. *An Encyclopædia of Occultism: A Compendium of Information on the Occult Sciences, Occult Personalities, Psychic Science, Magic, Demonology, Spiritism and Mysticism.* New York: Dodd, Mead, 1920.

_____. *Magic and Mysteries of Mexico.* Whitefish, MT: Kessinger, 2003.

_____. *The Magic Arts in Celtic Britain.* New York: Dover, 1999.

_____. *The Minor Traditions of British Mythology.* London: Rider and Company, 1948.

_____. *Mysteries of Celtic Britain.* Whitefish, MT: Kessinger, 2004.

_____. *Myths of Mexico and Peru.* London: George Harrap, 1913.

_____, and Marian Edwardes. *A Dictionary of Non-classical Mythology.* New York: E. P. Dutton, 1915.

Spiro, Melford E. *Burmese Supernaturalism.* Philadelphia: Institute for the Study of Human Issues, 1978.

Stanojević, Stanoje. *Narodna enciklopedija srpsko-hrvatsko-slovenačka,* vol. 3. Zagreb, Croatia: Bibliografski zavod d.d., 1925.

Stefan, Hock. *Die Vampyrsagen und ihre Verwertung in der deutschen Litteratur.* Berlin: A. Duncker, 1900.

Stefoff, Rebecca. *Vampires, Zombies, and Shape-Shifters.* New York: Benchmark Books, 2007.

Stein, Gordon. *The Encyclopedia of the Paranormal.* New York: Prometheus Books, 1996.

Stein, Rolf Alfred, and Phyllis Brooks. *The World in Miniature: Container Gardens and Dwellings in Far Eastern Religious Thought.* Chicago: Stanford University Press, 1990.

Stephens, Walter. *Demon Lovers: Witchcraft, Sex, and the Crisis of Belief.* Chicago: University of Chicago Press, 2002.

Stephenson, Marcia. *Gender and Modernity in Andean Bolivia.* Austin: University of Texas Press, 1999.

Stetkevych, Suzanne Pinckney. *The Mute Immortals Speak: Pre-Islamic Poetry and the Poetics of Ritual.* Ithaca: Cornell University Press, 1993.

Steuding, Hermann, Karl Pomeroy Harrington, and Herbert Cushing Tolman. *Greek and Roman Mythology.* New York: Leach, Shewell, and Sanborn, 1897.

Stevens, Charles McClellan. *Encyclopaedia of Superstitions, Folklore, and the Occult Sciences of the World: A Comprehensive Library of Human Belief and Practice in the Mysteries of Life.* Milwaukee: J. H. Yewdale and Sons, 1903.

Stevenson, Jay. *The Complete Idiot's Guide to Vampires.* New York: Alpha Books, 2001.

Stewart, Hugh Fraser, and Arthur Augustus Tilley. *The Romantic Movement in French Literature Traced by a Series of Texts.* New York: Oxford University Press, 1921.

Stewart, Pamela J., and Andrew Strathern. *Witchcraft, Sorcery, Rumors, and Gossip.* Cambridge: Cambridge University Press, 2004.

Stoddart, John. *Encyclopædia Metropolitana: Or, System of Universal Knowledge.* London: Richard Griffin and Company, 1855.

Stoker, Bram. *Dracula.* New York: Signet Classics, 1997.

Stoneman, Richard. *Greek Mythology: An Encyclopedia of Myth and Legend.* Northamptonshire: Aquarian Press, 1991.

Stookey, Lorena Laura. *Thematic Guide to World Mythology.* Westport, CT: Greenwood, 2004.

Strassberg, Richard E. *A Chinese Bestiary: Strange Creatures from the Guideways through Mountains and Sea.* Berkeley: University of California Press, 2002.

Stratilesco, Tereza. *From Carpathian to Pindus: Pictures of Roumanian Country Life.* Boston: John W. Luce, 1907.

Strickmann, Michel, and Bernard Faure. *Chinese Magical Medicine.* Stanford: Stanford University Press, 2002.

Stuart, Roxana. *Stage Blood: Vampires of the 19th Century Stage.* Madison: Popular Press, 1994.

Suckling, Nigel. *Vampires.* London: Aappl, 2006.

Sue, Eugène. *The Mysteries of Paris.* London: Chapman and Hall, Limited, 1845.

Sugden, Chris, and Vinay Samuel. *The Gospel Among Our Hindu Neighbours.* Bangalore, India: Partnership in Missions-Asia, 1983.

Summers, Montague. *Geography of Witchcraft.* Whitefish, MT: Kessinger, 2003.

_____. *The Vampire in Europe.* Whitefish, MT: Kessinger, 2003.

_____. *The Vampire in Lore and Legend.* New York: Dover, 2001.

_____. *Vampire: His Kith and Kin.* Whitefish, MT: Kessinger, 2003.

_____. *Werewolf.* Whitefish, MT: Kessinger, 2003.

Sumner, William Graham, Maurice Rea Davie, and Albert Galloway Keller. *The Science of Society,* vol. 2. New Haven: Yale University Press, 1927.

Sundararajan, K. R., and Bithika Mukerji. *Hindu Spirituality.* New Delhi, India: Motilal Banarsidass, 2003.

"Superstition and Knowledge." *The Quarterly Review* 29 (1823): 440–475. London: John Murray.

Suter, Ann. *Lament: Studies in the Ancient Mediterranean and Beyond.* New York: Oxford University Press, 2008.

Sylva, Carmen, and Alma Strettell. *Legends from River and Mountain.* London: G. Allen, 1896.

Symonds, John Addington. *Renaissance in Italy: Italian Literature.* London: Smith, Elder, 1881.

Szasz, Ferenc Morton. *Larger Than Life: New Mexico in the Twentieth Century.* Albuquerque: University of New Mexico Press, 2006.

Szigethy, Anna, and Anne Graves. *Vampires: From Vlad Drakul to the Vampire Lestat.* Toronto: Key Porter Books, 2001.

Taberner, Stuart, and Paul Cooke. *German Culture, Politics, and Literature into the Twenty-First Century: Beyond Normalization.* Rochester: Boydell and Brewer, 2006.

Takenobu, Yoshitaro. *Kenkyusha's New Japanese-English Dictionary.* Tokyo: Kenkyusha, 1940.

Tanaka, Stefan. *New Times in Modern Japan.* Princeton, NJ: Princeton University Press, 2004.

Tannahill, Reay, *Flesh and Blood: A History of the Cannibal Complex.* New York: Stein and Day, 1975.

Tate, Peter. *Flights of Fancy: Birds in Myth, Legend and Superstition.* New York: Random House, 2008.

Taylor, Edward B. *Primitive Culture: Researches into the Development of Mythology, Philosophy, Religion, Language, Art and Custom.* Whitefish, MT: Kessinger, 2007.

Taylor, Richard P. *Death and the Afterlife: A Cultural Encyclopedia.* Oxford: ABC-CLIO, 2000.

Taylor, Timothy. *The Buried Soul: How Humans Invented Death.* Boston: Beacon Press, 2004.

Terras, Victor Amy, Mandelker, and Roberta Reeder. *The Supernatural in Slavic and Baltic Literature: Essays in Honor of Victor Terras.* Bloomington: Slavica Publishers, 1988.

Theal, Georg Mc Call. *Faffir (Xhosa) Folk-lore: A Selection from the Traditional Tales.* Charleston, SC: Forgotten Books, 2007.

Theodore, Herzl Gaster. *Myth, Legend and Custom in the Old Testament.* New York: HarperCollins, 1970.

_____. *Thespis: Ritual, Myth, and Drama in the Ancient Near East.* Garden City, NY: Doubleday, 1961.

_____, and James George Frazer. *Myth, Legend, and Custom in the Old Testament: A Comparative Study with Chapters from Sir James G. Frazer's Folklore in the Old Testament.* New York: Harper and Row, 1975.

Theosophical Society. *The Theosophist,* vol. 36. Madras, India: Theosophical Society, 1915.

Thigpen, Kenneth A. *Folklore and the Ethnicity Factor in the Lives of Romanian-Americans.* Bloomington: Indiana University, 1973.

Thomas, Robert Murray. *Folk Psychologies Across Cultures.* Thousand Oaks, CA: Sage, 2001.

Thomas, William Isaac, and Florian Znaniecki. *The Polish Peasant in Europe and America: Monograph of an Immigrant Group.* Boston: Richard G. Badger Gorman Press, 1918.

Thompson, Laurence G. *Studies of Chinese Religion: A Comprehensive and Classified Bibliography of Publications in English, French, and German through 1970.* Encino, CA: Dickenson, 1976.

Thompson, Reginald Campbell. *The Devils and Evil Spirits of Babylonia, Being Babylonian and Assyrian Incantations Against the Demons, Ghouls, Vampires, Hobgoblins, Ghosts, and Kindred Evil Spirits, which Attack Mankind.* London: Luzac, 1903–1904.

_____. *Semitic Magic, Its Origins and Development.* London: Luzac, 1908.

Thorndike, Lynn. *History of Magic and Experimental Science.* New York: Columbia University Press, 1941.

Thorpe, Benjamin. *Northern Mythology: Scandinavian Popular Traditions and Superstitions.* London: E. Lumley, 1851.

Thurston, Edgar. *Omens and Superstitions of Southern India.* New York: McBride, Nast and Company, 1912.

Tierney, Patrick. *Highest Altar: Unveiling the Mystery of Human Sacrifice.* New York: Penguin, 1990.

Toki, Zenmaro. *Japanese No Plays.* Tokyo: Japan Travel Bureau, 1954.

Tolkien, John Ronald Reuel. *Beowulf: The Monster and the Critics.* New York: HarperCollins, 1997.

Tondriau, Julien L. *A Dictionary of Devils and Demons.* New York: Pyramid, 1972.

Tongue, Ruth L. *Forgotten Folk Tales of the English Counties.* London: Routledge and K. Paul, 1970.

Tozer, Henry Fanshawe. *Researches in the Highlands of Turkey: Including Visits to Mounts Ida, Athos, Olympus, and Pelion, to the Mirdite Albanians, and Other Remote Tribes: with Notes on the Ballads, Tales, and Classical Superstitions of the Modern Greeks.* London: J. Murray, 1869.

Trachtenberg, Joshua. *Jewish Magic and Superstition.* Charleston, SC: Forgotten Books, 1961.

Tramp, George Dewey. *Waray-English Dictionary.* Springfield, VA: Dunwoody Press, 1985.

Tremearne, Arthur John Newman. *The Ban of the Bori: Demons and Demon-Dancing in West and North Africa.* London: Heath, Cranton and Ouseley Ltd., 1914.

_____. *The Tailed Head-Hunters of Nigeria: An Account of an Official's Seven Years' Experience in the Northern Nigerian Pagan Belt, and a Description of the Manners, Habits, and Customs of the Native Tribes.* Philadelphia: J. B. Lippincott, 1912.

Tresidder, Jack. *The Complete Dictionary of Symbols.* San Francisco: Chronicle Books, 2005.

Trevelyan, Marie. *Folk-lore and Folk-stories of Wales.* Whitefish, MT: Kessinger, 1973.

Triefeldt, Laurie. *People and Places.* Sanger, CA: Quill Driver Books, 2007.

Trumbull, Henry Clay. *The Blood Covenant: A Primitive Rite and Its Bearings on Scripture.* Philadelphia: J. D. Wattles, 1893.

Tuke, Daniel Hack. *A Dictionary of Psychological Medicine: Giving the Definition, Etymology and Synonyms of the Terms Used in Medical Psychology, with the Symptoms, Treatment, and Pathology of Insanity and the Law of Lunacy in Great Britain and Ireland.* London: P. Blakiston, 1892.

Tuke, James H. *A Visit to Connaught in the Autumn of 1847* [London] (1848): 18–19.

Turner, Patricia, and Charles Russell Coulter. *Dictionary of Ancient Deities.* New York: Oxford University Press, 2001.

Twitchell, James B. *The Living Dead: A Study of the Vampire in Romantic Literature.* Durham: Duke University Press, 1987.

Tyson, Donald. *Sexual Alchemy: Magical Intercourse with Spirits.* Woodbury, MN: Llewellyn, 2000.

University College of the West Indies. *Caribbean Quarterly,* vol. 45. Mona, Jamaica: University College of the West Indies, 1999.

University of Missouri. *The University of Missouri Studies,* vol. 10. Columbia: University of Missouri Press, 1935.

University of Puerto Rico. *Atenea,* vol. 13–17. Facultad de Artes y Ciencias, Universidad de Puerto Rico, 1993.

University of San Carlos. *Philippine Quarterly of Culture and Society,* vol. 10–11. Cebu City: University of San Carlos, 1981.

University of the Philippines. *Asian Studies,* vol. 8–9. Quezon City, Philippines: Philippine Center for Advanced Studies, 1970.

University of the Philippines College of Liberal Arts. *The Diliman Review,* vol. 16–17. Manila, Philippines: University of the Philippines, 1968.

University of the Witwatersrand Department of Bantu Studies. *African Studies,* vol. 14–15. Johannesburg, South Africa: Witwatersrand University Press, 1955.

Vaillant, George Clapp, and C. A. Burland. *The Aztecs of Mexico: Origin, Rise and Fall of the Aztec Nation*. New York: Penguin, 1950.

Vajda Talasi, I. and L. Vajda Talasi. "Hexe, Hexendruck." *Acta Ethnographica* 4 (1950): 129–69. Budapest: Akademiai Kiado, 1950.

van der Toorn, Karel, Bob Becking, Pieter Willem van der Horst. *Dictionary of Deities and Demons in the Bible*. Grand Rapids: William. B. Eerdmans, 1999.

Van Scott, Miriam. *The Encyclopedia of Hell*. New York: Macmillan, 1999.

Van Vleet, Krista E. *Performing Kinship: Narrative, Gender, and the Intimacies of Power in the Andes*. Austin: University of Texas Press, 2008.

Vangh, Aba. *Magie Tibetaine*. Brussels, Belgium: Savoir pour Etre, 1993.

Varner, Gary R. *Creatures in the Mist: Little People, Wild Men and Spirit Beings Around the World: A Study in Comparative Mythology*. New York: Algora, 2007.

Varrin, Claudia. *A Guide to New York's Fetish Underground*. Secaucus, NJ: Citadel Press, 2002.

Verma, Dinesh Chandra. *Social, Economic, and Cultural History of Bijapur*. Delhi, India: Idarah-i Adabiyat-i Delli, 1990.

Vicary, John Fulford. *An American in Norway*. London: W. H. Allen, 1885.

Vijayalakshmy, Ca. Vē Cuppiramaniyan, R. *Philosophical Heritage of the Tamils*. Chennai, India: International Institute of Tamil Studies, 1983.

Villeneuve, Roland, and Jean-Louis Degaudenzi. *Le Musée des Vampires*. Paris: Henri Veyrier, 1976.

Voigt, Vilmos. *Folk Narrative and Cultural Identity: 9th Congress of the International Society for Folk-Narrative Research*, vol. 1. Budapest: Loránd Eötvös University, Dept. of Folklore, 1995.

Volta, Ornella. *The Vampire*. London: Tandem Books, 1963.

Voltaire. *A Philosophical Dictionary: From the French*. London: W. Dugdale, 1843.

Wachtel, Nathan, and Carol Volk. *Gods and Vampires: Return to Chipaya*. Chicago: University of Chicago Press, 1994.

Waghorne, Joanne Punzo, Norman Cutler, and Vasudha Narayanan. *Gods of Flesh, Gods of Stone: The Embodiment of Divinity in India*. New York: Columbia University Press, 1996.

Wagner, Philip L., ed. *Aspects of Contemporary Ukraine*. New Haven, CT: Human Relations Area Files, 1955.

Waringhien, Edward Langton, G. *La démonologie: étude de la doctrine juive et chrétienne, son origine et son développement*. France: Payot, 1951.

Warner, Elizabeth. *Russian Myths*. Austin: University of Texas Press, 2002.

Watson, James L., Evelyn Sakakida Rawski, and the U.S. Joint Committee on Chinese Studies. *Death Ritual in Late Imperial and Modern China*. Berkeley: University of California Press, 1990.

Watson, Malcolm. *Rural Sanitation in the Tropics: Being Notes and Observations in the Malay Archipelago, Panama and Other Lands*. London: John Murray, 1915.

Wedeck, Harry Ezekiel. *Dictionary of Spiritualism*. New York: Philosophical Library, 1971.

_____. *Treasury of Witchcraft*. New York: Philosophical Library, 1994.

Weismantel, Mary. *Cholas and Pishtacos: Stories of Race and Sex in the Andes* (Women in Culture and Society Series). Chicago: The University of Chicago Press, 2001.

Welland, Michael. *Sand: The Never-Ending Story*. Berkeley: University of California Press, 2009.

Werne, Edward Theodore Chalmers. *China of the Chinese*. London: Sir Issaic Pitman and Sons, 1920.

Werner, Alice. *Myths and Legends of the Bantu*. London: George G. Harrap, 1933.

Westermarck, Edward. *Pagan Survivals in Mohammedan Civilization*. New York: Macmillan, 1933.

Wharton, Edith, Edward Everett, Henry Cabot Lodge, James Russell Lowell, and Jared Sparks. *The North American Review*. Boston: O. Everett, 1836.

White, Luise. *Speaking with Vampires: Rumor and History in Colonial Africa*. Berkeley: University of California Press, 2000.

Whitelaw, Alexander, ed. *The Popular Encyclopedia: Or, "Conversations Lexicon."* London: Blackie and Son, 1846.

Whitney, William Dwight, and Benjamin Eli Smith. *The Century Dictionary and Cyclopedia: A Work of Universal Reference in All Departments of Knowledge with a New Atlas of the World*. New York: The Century Company, 1911.

Wicker, Nancy L., and Bettina Arnold. *From the Ground Up: Beyond Gender Theory in Archaeology—Proceedings of the Fifth Gender and Archaeology Conference, University of Wisconsin-Milwaukee, October 1998*. Oxford: Archaeopress, 1999.

Widengren, Geo, and C. Jouco Bleeker. *Historia Religionum: Handbook for the History of Religions*. Leiden, Netherlands: E. J. Brill, 1969.

Wiggermann, F. A. M. *Mesopotamian Protective Spirits: The Ritual Texts*. Boston: Brill, 1992.

Wigoder, Geoffrey. *Encyclopaedic Dictionary of Judaica*. New York: Leon Amiel, 1974.

Wilde, Jane Francesca Elgee. *Ancient Legends, Mystic Charms, and Superstitions of Ireland: With Sketches of the Irish Past. To which is appended a chapter on "The ancient race of Ireland."* Boston: Ticknor and Company, 1888.

Wilgowicz, Pérel. *Le vampirisme, de la dame blanche au golem: Essai sur la pulsion de mort et sur l'irreprésentable (Collection Psychanalyse)*. France: Césura Lyon édition, 1991.

Williams, Gerhild Scholz. *Ways of Knowing in Early Modern Germany: Johannes Praetorius as a Witness to His Time*. Surrey: Ashgate Publishing, Ltd., 2006.

Williams, Henry Smith. *The Historians' History of the World: A Comprehensive Narrative of the Rise and Development of Nations as Recorded by Over Two Thousand of the Great Writers of All Ages*. London: Hooper and Jackson, 1909.

Williams, Joseph J. *Psychic Phenomena of Jamaica*. New York: Dial Press, 1934.

_____. *Voodoos and Obeahs: Phases of West India Witchcraft*. Whitefish, MT: Kessinger, 2003.

Willis, Roy G. *World Mythology*. New York: Macmillan, 1993.

Wilson, Colin. *The Occult: A History*. New York: Vintage Books, 1971.

Wilson, Monica Hunter. *Reaction to Conquest: Effects of Contact with Europeans on the Pondo of South Africa*. London: David Philip, 1979.

Winn, Chris. *I Never Knew That About Ireland*. New York: Macmillan, 2007.

Winstedt, Richard. *The Malay Magician: Being Shaman, Saiva and Sufi*. Oxfordshire: Taylor and Francis, 1982.

Wolf, Leonard. *Dracula: The Connoisseur's Guide*. Portland, OR: Broadway Books, 1997.

Wonderley, Anthony Wayne, and Hope Emily Allen. *Oneida Iroquois Folklore, Myth, and History: New York Oral Narrative from the Notes of H. E. Allen and Others*. Syracuse: Syracuse University Press, 2004.

Wood, John George. *The Natural History of Man: Being an Account of the Manners and Customs of the Uncivilized Races of Men*, vol. 1. London: G. Routledge, 1874.

_____. *The Uncivilized Races of Men in All Countries of the World*. San Francisco: J. A. Brainerd, 1882.

Woods, Damon L. *The Philippines: A Global Studies Handbook*. Oxford: ABC-CLIO, 2006.

Woodward, Ian. *The Werewolf Delusion*. New York: Paddington Press, 1979.

Wright, Dudley. *The Book of Vampires*. Detroit: Omnigraphics, 1989.

_____. *Vampires and Vampirism*. London: W. Rider and Son, 1914.

Wurmser, Léon, and Heidrun Jarass. *Jealousy and Envy: New Views About Two Powerful Emotions*. Mahwah, NJ: Lawrence Erlbaum, 2007.

Yashinsky, Dan. *Tales for an Unknown City*. Kingston, Ontario: McGill-Queen's Press, 1992.

Yeats, William Butler. *Fairy and Folk Tales of the Irish Peasantry*. North Chemsford, MA: Courier Dover Publications, 1991.

Young, Kenneth. *The Greek Passion: A Study in People and Politics*. London: Dent, 1969.

Zell-Ravenheart, Oberon, and Ash Dekirk. *A Wizard's Bestiary: A Menagerie of Myth, Magic, and Mystery*. Franklin Lakes, NJ: New Page Books, 2007.

Znamenski, Andrei A. *Shamanism in Siberia: Russian Records of Indigenous Spirituality*. Dordrecht, Netherlands: Kluwer Academic, 2003.

Index